Preventive Care Sourcebook 1997–1998

ASPEN REFERENCE GROUP

Betty Ankrapp
Editor

Sandra Bloom Painter
Senior Editor

Sara Nell Di Lima
Managing Editor

AN ASPEN PUBLICATION®
Aspen Publishers, Inc.
Gaithersburg, Maryland
1997

Orders: (800) 638-8437
Customer Service: (800) 234-1660

About Aspen Publishers • For more than 35 years, Aspen has been a leading professional publisher in a variety of disciplines. Aspen's vast information resources are available in both print and electronic formats. We are committed to providing the highest quality information available in the most appropriate format for our customers. Visit Aspen's Internet site for more information resources, directories, articles, and a searchable version of Aspen's full catalog, including the most recent publications: **http://www.aspenpub.com**

Aspen Publishers, Inc. • The hallmark of quality in publishing
Member of the worldwide Wolters Kluwer group.

ISBN: 0-8342-0880-6

Printed in the United States of America

1 2 3 4 5

Table of Contents

Advisory Board iv

Introduction v

Health and Wellness Promotion 1
- Design, Evaluation, and Implementation 3
  - Community/Public Health Programs 5
  - Corporate/Health Care Programs 8
- General Health Promotion Materials 23
- Health Assessments 33
- Mental Health and Mental Disorders 43
  - Mental Health and Mental Illness 45
  - Eating Disorders 50
  - Stress Management 51
- Nutrition and Weight Management 57
- Physical Activity and Fitness 63
- Substance Abuse 73
  - All Substances 75
  - Alcohol and Other Drugs 80
  - Tobacco 82
- Wellness Professional Resources 89

Health and Injury Protection 101
- Environmental Health 103
- Food and Drug Safety 111
- Occupational Safety and Health 117
- Oral Health 125
- Unintentional Injuries 129
- Violence-related Injuries 137

Disease Management and Prevention 149
- Asthma 151
- Cancer 155
- Diabetes 163
- Eye Disease 167
- Heart Disease and Stroke 171
- Other Chronic Conditions and Diseases 177
- Immunizations and Infectious Diseases 189
- Sexually Transmitted Diseases, HIV Infection, and AIDS 197

Special Needs and Populations 209
- Family Planning and Sex Education 211
- Maternal/Child and Women's Health 217
- Older Adults 235
- People with Disabilities 241

Federal Agencies and Offices 247

State Health Promotion and Prevention Offices 255

Hotlines and Toll-free Information Lines 261

Resources for Racial and Ethnic Populations 267

Organization Index 269

Subject Index 279

Advisory Board

Introduction

Preventive care and wellness promotion is leading today's health care agenda. Improving the health of all Americans through prevention is a national initiative of the U.S. Department of Health and Human Services. Managed care and capitation are focusing unprecedented attention on preventive care as an effective strategy for containing health care costs and improving outcomes. Increasingly, clinicians, educators, and administrators in varied settings are charged with incorporating preventive care goals into daily tasks as well as long-term plans. Providers, payers, businesses, and organizations are forming coalitions to more effectively maximize health and wellness within their communities. To address these demands, we developed the *Preventive Care Sourcebook.* The *Sourcebook* provides instant reference to a growing range of practical and innovative resources for planning, implementing, and evaluating preventive care activities and programs.

The *Sourcebook* is divided into four major sections corresponding to key components of preventive care: Health and Wellness Promotion; Health and Injury Protection; Disease Management and Prevention; and Special Needs and Populations. Chapters within each section distinguish between specific health risks and types of programming. Each chapter begins with an at-a-glance chart to help you quickly locate those organizations that can provide the type of resource you need. After each chart, organization listings appear alphabetically. Each listing provides complete contact information and descriptions of the following products and services available:

- Web site
- Hotline or Toll-free Information Line (including automated and operator-assisted lines; crisis or emergency service; referral service; answers to questions or requests for materials)
- Clearinghouse or Resource Center (offering an extensive collection of materials available to order; references; bibliographic searches)
- Electronic Information Resources (e.g., fax-on-demand, online or bulletin board services)
- Database or Statistical Information (in print or electronic medium)
- Special Campaigns, Events, or Programs (sponsored promotions and initiatives)
- Consumer or Patient Education Materials (features up to three sample titles; prices and availability are subject to change)
- Publications for Health Professionals (features up to three specific titles; prices and availability are subject to change)
- Classes or Conferences (for both health professionals and consumer/patient; includes presentations, courses, seminars, workshops, educational sessions)
- Technical Assistance (e.g., consulting services; special task groups; referrals)
- Other Products and Services (e.g., incentive programs, software programs; telephone advice lines)
- Grants, Funding, or Awards

Additional resources and Federal agencies are listed at the end of each chapter. There are four appendixes:

- Federal government resources
- State government resources
- Hotlines and toll-free information numbers
- Resources for racial and ethnic populations

Two indexes provide alphabetical listings by organization name and subject matter.

We hope you will find that the *Preventive Care Sourcebook* is an indispensable tool for achieving preventive care success. An expanded and completely updated edition will be published each year. Your suggestions for improving the usefulness of the *Sourcebook* are always welcome.

Health and Wellness Promotion

Design, Evaluation, and Implementation 3
  Community/Public Health Programs 5
  Corporate/Health Care Programs 8
General Health Promotion Materials 23
Health Assessments 33
Mental Health and Mental Disorders 43
  Mental Health and Mental Illness 45
  Eating Disorders 50
  Stress Management 51
Nutrition and Weight Management 57
Physical Activity and Fitness 63
Substance Abuse 73
  All Substances 75
  Alcohol and Other Drugs 80
  Tobacco 82
Wellness Professional Resources 89

Design, Evaluation, and Implementation

Products/Services Offered

Organization	web site	hotline/toll-free information line	clearinghouse/resource center	electronic information resources	database/statistical information	special campaigns/events/programs	consumer/patient education materials	publications for health professionals	classes/conferences	technical assistance	other products/services	grants/funding/awards	Page No.
Community/Public Health Programs													
The Advertising Council Inc	■							■				■	**5**
American Hospital Association	■							■					**5**
American Public Health Association	■							■					**5**
Aspen Publishers Inc	■							■					**5**
CD Publications								■					**5**
The Commonwealth Fund	■		■							■		■	**6**
Felix, Burdine and Associates Inc	■				■					■			**6**
Dr. Trevor Hancock										■			**6**
Health Education Services	■							■					**6**
National Center for Health Education	■					■				■			**6**
National Council of La Raza Center for Health Promotion	■		■				■	■	■	■			**7**
Novela Health Education	■									■			**7**
Public Health Foundation	■							■					**7**
Research Grant Guides Inc								■					**8**
Stanford Center for Research in Disease Prevention	■							■		■			**8**
Tyler Norris Associates								■	■	■			**8**
Corporate/Health Care Programs													
Access Health Inc	■										■		**8**
American Heart Association	■									■			**9**
American Institute for Preventive Medicine	■					■				■	■		**9**

Products/Services Offered

Organization	web site	hotline/toll-free information line	clearinghouse/resource center	electronic information resources	database/statistical information	special campaigns/events/programs	consumer/patient education materials	publications for health professionals	classes/conferences	technical assistance	other products/services	grants/funding/awards	Page No.
Ashby*Montrose & Company									■	■			9
Corporate Fitness Midwest Inc									■	■			9
EMC^2	■						■				■		10
Fitcorp											■		10
Greenstone Healthcare Solutions	■			■						■	■		10
Health Decisions International LLC											■		10
Health Evaluation Systems Inc									■				11
Health First Consulting Corporation										■			11
Healthier People Software										■			11
HealthStyle	■										■		11
Healthy Achievers							■			■			11
Human Resources Institute Inc	■						■	■	■				11
Informed Access Systems Inc							■				■		12
International Parish Nurse Resource Center	■							■	■	■			12
Stasica Associates										■			12
StayWell Health Management Systems Inc											■		12
Strategic Marketing Group Inc									■	■			13
Summex Corporation	■							■		■			13
TriHealth Preventive Health Systems										■	■		13
Wellness Councils of America (WELCOA)				■				■	■	■			13
Wellness Quest	■						■		■		■		14
Wellsource Inc	■									■	■		14

Additional Resources 14

Federal Agencies 19

COMMUNITY/PUBLIC HEALTH PROGRAMS

■ The Advertising Council Inc

261 Madison Ave
New York, NY 10016-2303
212-922-1500
Fax: 212-922-1676
E-mail: adcouncil@prodigy.com
Web site: http://www.adcouncil.org

National nonprofit private organization whose mission is to identify a select number of significant public issues and stimulate action on those issues through communications programs that make a measurable difference in our society and the source of public service advertising.

Publications for Health Professionals

Public Service Advertising Bulletin, bimonthly, current PSA info for media decision makers; How to Create Effective Public Service Advertising, 90 min videotape and workbook, available for rental or purchase. Please contact Paula Veale, VP-Public Affairs.

Grants, Funding, or Awards

Campaign assistance for major national campaigns and endorsed campaigns; available only to qualified sponsors (nonprofit 501(c)(3) organizations, private foundations, government agencies, or coalitions of such agencies and organizations); applications must be made in writing. Contact Luana Lewis, Director-Proposals, for information and application questionnaires.

■ American Hospital Association

One North Franklin
Chicago, IL 60606
Contact: Publications, 800-242-2626
312-422-3000
Web site: http://www.amhpi.com

National membership organization of individuals and health care institutions dedicated to promoting the welfare of the public through its leadership and assistance to its members in the provision of better health services for all people.

Publications for Health Professionals

An Agenda for Action: Community Health Improvement Through 2000, 15 pp pamphlet, $25; Background and Resources for a Community Health Status Focus, 44 pp book, $40. Please contact for complete publications list.

■ American Public Health Association

1015 15th St NW
Washington, DC 20005
Contact: Publication Sales, 301-893-1894, PO Box 753, Waldorf, MD 20604-0753
202-789-5600
TDD: 202-789-6573
Web site: http://www.apha.org

National nonprofit multi-disciplinary association of professionals in public health and related fields that works to protect and promote personal and environmental health. Develops standards, promulgates recommended rules, and publishes pamphlets, books, model codes, and educational materials.

Publications for Health Professionals

Healthy Communities 2000: Model Standards, 3rd edition, 470 pp manual, provides guidelines for community attainment of Year 2000 objectives, $35. Please contact for complete publications list.

■ Aspen Publishers Inc

7201 McKinney Circle
PO Box 990
Frederick, MD 21704
800-638-8437 (Order Dept)
Fax: 301-695-7931
Web site: http://www.aspenpub.com

Publisher of books, manuals, journals, newsletters, and electronic products for professionals in the fields of health administration, nursing, allied health, and education.

Publications for Health Professionals

Inside Preventive Care, monthly newsletter, proven strategies for improving community health and managing patient demand, $179/yr; Community Health Education and Promotion Manual, guide to implementing effective community health programs, $149/yr; Managing Health Promotion Programs: Leadership Skills for the 21st Century, book, administrative guide, $49/yr. Please contact for complete publications list.

■ CD Publications

8204 Fenton St
Silver Spring, MD 20910-4571
800-666-6380
301-588-6380
Fax: 301-588-6385
E-mail: cdpubs@clark.net

Publisher of newsletters, reports, and resource guides that identify funding sources, provide fundraising advice, and keep readers updated on budget proposals affecting public policy in health, education, and social services.

Publications for Health Professionals
Community Health Funding Report, semi-monthly newsletter, funding and news for agencies and hospitals, $269/yr; Grant Tips, 64 pp report, advice from grant officials for proposal writers, $25; Government Assistance Almanac, 889 pp book, resource guide of assistance programs available, $145. Please contact for complete publications list.

■ The Commonwealth Fund

One E 75th St
New York, NY 10021-2692
Contact: Communications Dept, 212-606-3506
212-606-3842
Fax: 212-606-3500
E-mail: cmwf@cmwf.org
Web site: http://www.cmwf.org

Nonprofit New York City-based national foundation that undertakes independent research on health and social issues. Its mission is to enhance the common good by looking for new opportunities to help Americans live healthy and productive lives, and to assist specific groups with serious and neglected problems. Engages in independent research in health and social policy issues.

Clearinghouse or Resource Center
The Commonwealth Fund Resource Center: 212-606-3506; Published Fund-supported work, single copy free; other books and articles, must contact publisher directly. Please contact for a complete publications list.

Technical Assistance
Current four national program areas are: Improving Health Care Services; Bettering the Health of Minority Americans; Advancing the Well-Being of Elderly People; and Developing the Capacities of Children and Young People.

Grants, Funding, or Awards
Grants for health and social issues related projects.

■ Felix, Burdine and Associates Inc

5100 Tilghman St, Ste 215
Allentown, PA 18104-9102
Contact: Yvette Musselman, Office Manager
610-366-1310
Fax: 610-366-1322
Web site: http://felixburdine.com

National for-profit community health development company dedicated to teaching communities how to plan, develop, and implement community health status improvement interventions. Utilizes the techniques of community organization, health status assessment, and is founded on community health development principles.

Database or Statistical Information
The National Health Survey©, report and data that detail the results of survey of a national sample of U.S. adults in the areas of functional status, access to care, preventive service utilization, and community issues. $295.

Technical Assistance
Consulting services in the area of community partnership development, community health status assessment, health status improvement initiatives, and strategic planning.

■ Dr. Trevor Hancock

28 Napier St
Kleinburg, Ontario, Canada, L0J 1C0
905-893-2808
Fax: 905-893-2107
E-mail: thancock@orion.yorku.ca

International consultant on healthy cities, healthy communities, health promotion, and health futurism from local communities to the World Health Organization. Focus is on the environmental, social, and economic determinants of health at the community level.

Technical Assistance
Consulting services. Please contact for further information.

■ Health Education Services

PO Box 7126
Albany, NY 12224
518-439-7286
Fax: 518-439-7286 *51
Web site: http://www.hes.org

Nonprofit distributor of current health education, promotional publications, posters, and videos, most of which have been produced by the New York State Department of Health or the New York State Department of Environmental Conservation. (Health Education Services is a Division of Health Research Inc.)

Publications for Health Professionals
Community In Action, brochure, 5 steps for planning program, $12 for 100 copies; Writing Public Service Announcements, $15 for 100; other guides for health education and community outreach planning. Please contact for complete publications list.

■ National Center for Health Education

72 Spring St, Ste 208
New York, NY 10012-4019

Contact: Urvi R Dalal, 212-334-9470 x25
212-334-9470
Fax: 212-334-9845
Web site: http://www.nche.org

Nonprofit organization dedicated to leading the nation in the implementation of life-long comprehensive health education. Designs and disseminates Growing Healthy®, a comprehensive school health education curriculum for students in grades K–6, which teaches students skills that will enable them to adopt healthy attitudes and behaviors. Call WRS Group Inc at 800-551-3488 for Growing Healthy and National Health Education Week materials.

Special Campaigns, Events, or Programs
National Health Education Week, in October, curriculum for designated topic and related materials.
Technical Assistance
Technical assistance available for comprehensive school health education, teacher training, and Growing Healthy.

■ National Council of La Raza Center for Health Promotion

1111 19th St NW, Ste 1000
Washington, DC 20036
Contact: Lupe Lemus, 202-785-1670
202-785-1670
Fax: 202-776-1792
E-mail: hpacheco@nclr.org
Web site: http://www.nclr.org

Private, nonprofit, nonpartisan organization that serves as an advocate for Hispanic Americans on health and other public policy issues. The NCLR's Center for Health Promotion works to increase the access of Hispanics to health care and to provide public health materials and capacity-building assistance to Hispanic community-based organizations. The Center has three major programs: Maternal and Child Health Program; HST Prevention Project, and Hispanic Health Liaison Project.

Clearinghouse or Resource Center
NCLR Distribution Center: 301-604-7983; PO Box 291, Annapolis Junction, MD 20701; Health, immigration, poverty, and general public information available. Cost of materials $5 to $15.
Consumer or Patient Education Materials
Center for Health Promotion, fact sheet, provides Hispanic data on health issues, free. Please contact for complete catalog.
Publications for Health Professionals
Healthy Horizons, guide, designed to assist Hispanic CBO in health education, $15; The State of Hispanic Health, report, presents most up-to-date data on Hispanic Health, $15. Please contact for complete publications list.
Classes and Conferences
Annual conference, 5 days, 2- to 3-hr health-related seminars. Contact Lizette P Rosales.
Technical Assistance
Hispanic Health Liaison Project works to improve health status by providing information on critical diseases (diabetes, breast and cervical cancer, cardiovascular diseases, asthma); technical assistance, trainings, educational information to community-based organizations.

■ Novela Health Education

1001 Broadway, Ste 100
Seattle, WA 98122
800-677-4799
Fax: 206-720-4382
E-mail: novela@u.washington.edu
Web site: http://weber.u.washington.edu/~novela

National nonprofit publisher and distributor of multicultural health education materials including videos, fotonovelas, comic books, games, and manuals, of which many are available in Spanish. Maintains a mail order catalog of materials on topics including HIV/AIDS; STDs; alcohol and other drugs; prenatal and child health; sexual abstinence; aging; diabetes; motor vehicle and pesticide safety. Also custom produces media under contract.

Technical Assistance
Consultation on development of health education and outreach campaigns; develops videos and fotonovelas under contract for other agencies.

■ Public Health Foundation

1220 L St NW, Ste 350
Washington, DC 20005
Contact: Rita Kelliher, Sarah Pfau, Mike Barry, 202-898-5600 x3015
202-898-5600
Fax: 202-898-5609
Web site: http://www.phf.org

National nonprofit organization whose mission is to assist the Association of State and Territorial Health Officers and the National Association of County and City Health Officials in supporting official state and local public health agencies' efforts to achieve healthy people and healthy communities within their jurisdictions. Develops and maintains partnerships with the academic community and other public and private organizations engaged in public health related activities.

Publications for Health Professionals

Measuring Expenditures For Essential Health Services, report, free; Program planning and monitoring self-instructional manuals, set of four includes: Assessment of Health Status Problems, Health Services Needs Assessment, Setting Objectives, and Evaluation: Monitoring Progress Towards Achievement of Objectives.

■ Research Grant Guides Inc

PO Box 1214
Loxahatchee, FL 33470-1214
407-795-6129
Fax: 407-795-7794 (for orders)

Publisher of directory guides listing foundation profiles and information on grant funding.

Publications for Health Professionals

Directory of Operating Grants, Second Edition, 670 foundation profiles with 3,000 grant entries, $58.50; Directory of Health Grants, First Edition, 750 foundation profiles with 3,200 grant entries, $59.50. Order must be mailed or faxed.

■ Stanford Center for Research in Disease Prevention

Health Promotion Resource Center
1000 Welch Rd
Palo Alto, CA 94304-1885
Contact: SCRDP Distribution Center
415-723-0003
Fax: 415-725-6906
E-mail: distribution@scrdp.stanford.edu
Web site: http://www-med.Stanford.EDU:8/MedCenter/SCRDP/

Nonprofit educational resource center that produces and disseminates print and video materials on cardiovascular disease risk factors, injury prevention, and community health promotion.

Publications for Health Professionals

Health Promotion in Diverse Cultural Communities, manual, guidebook for developing culturally-sensitive programs, $14; Public Health Advocacy, manual, discusses what agencies & communities can do to advocate for a health issue, $24; How-to Guides for Community Health Promotion, set, covers 23 different aspects of the health promotion process, $54.75. Please contact for complete publications list.

Technical Assistance

Consulting on choosing or implementing promotion programs, call 415-725-4406.

■ Tyler Norris Associates

2119 Mapleton Ave
Boulder, CO 80304
303-444-3366
Fax: 303-444-1001
E-mail: tnorris@ncl.org

Consulting firm that provides consultation to communities and organizations to improve community health and long-term sustainability.

Publications for Health Professionals

Healthy Community Handbook, book, resource to community catalysts.

Classes and Conferences

Healthy Communities. Please contact for complete information.

Technical Assistance

Community health planning; community partnerships.

CORPORATE/HEALTH CARE PROGRAMS

■ Access Health Inc

11020 White Rock Rd
Rancho Cordova, CA 95670
Contact: Lori Delappe, 916-851-4103 or Kim Brimmer, 916-851-4248
800-762-6500
916-851-4000
Fax: 916-852-3890
Web site: http://www.access-health.com

For-profit company that develops and operates membership-based health care information products and services that enable its clients—managed care organizations, self-insured employers, and integrated health care delivery networks—to provide a broad range of information services to help consumers with every aspect of managing their own health care. Services are delivered through access to registered nurses via the telephone, workplace kiosks, online services, print communications, and consumer videos.

Other Products and Services

Toll-free telephone service to registered nurses; AudioHealth Library; provider referral; counseling services; online services; print communications. Please contact for complete information.

■ American Heart Association

7272 Greenville Ave
Dallas, TX 75231-4596
Contact: Fulfillment Center, 800-611-6083
800-AHA-USA1 (800-242-8721)
214-373-6300
Web site: http://www.amhrt.org

National nonprofit voluntary organization of 56 affiliated state and metropolitan organizations with 2,000 local offices. Funds and supports basic biomedical research, public policy advocacy, and educational programs for the public, business and industry, and health professionals.

Technical Assistance

Heart At Work, worksite health promotion program, contact Corporate Programs and Promotions at 214-706-1936; Heart Power!, contact Youth Team Group at 214-706-1327; Hoops for Heart and Jump Rope for Heart, contact 214-706-1239.

■ American Institute for Preventive Medicine

30445 Northwestern Hwy, Ste 350
Farmington Hills, MI 48334-3102
Contact: Order Dept, 810-539-1800 x239
800-345-2476
810-539-1800
Fax: 810-539-1808
E-mail: aipm@healthy.net
Web site: http://aipm.healthy.net

International for-profit developer and provider of health promotion programs, self-help kits, and self-care publications. Works with over 5,000 corporations, HMOs, and hospitals to reduce health care costs, lower absenteeism, and improve morale. Services include those for self-care, smoking cessation, weight control, stress management, self-esteem enhancement, prenatal education, fitness center management, nutrition, and EAP education.

Special Campaigns, Events, or Programs

National Wise Health Care Consumer Month, February, Event ideas for corporations, hospitals, and managed care organizations, booklet titled Being a Wise Health Care Consumer, information on medical self-care. Contact Elaine Frank.

Technical Assistance

Consultation on the design, implementation, marketing, and evaluation of health promotion programs in both corporate and health care settings available.

Other Products and Services

Nurse advice line, audio library, prenatal education, wellness libraries, self-care workshops, self-care promotional materials, and self-care software.

■ Ashby*Montrose & Company

1777 S Harrison St, Ste 505
Denver, CO 80210
Contact: Gary Montrose
303-753-0708
Fax: 303-753-0112

National consulting firm with two decades of experience with consumer-focused demand management, including strategic planning, business development, program planning, evaluation, provider training, integration with other services and systems. Experience includes health promotion and disease prevention, consumer empowerment, multi-media, telecommunications and Internet strategies; organization development toward building demand management as a core competency; strategic alliance building.

Classes and Conferences

Programs available for 1 hr, ½ day, or 1 day on following topics: Demand management, industry trends—today and tomorrow; Cost benefit studies, what works . . . evaluation and industry experience; Information technology, new opportunities, new alliances. Please contact for complete information.

Technical Assistance

Consulting, organizational development, program evaluation, program design, cost benefit modeling, strategy and implementation planning for demand management services affecting consumers and providers.

■ Corporate Fitness Midwest Inc

11469 Olive Blvd, Ste 251
St Louis, MO 63141-7108
Contact: Harold Denlow
800-645-2535
314-994-7323
Fax: 314-994-1545
E-mail: cfm@welltech.com

For-profit full-service health promotion company with expertise in providing multi-level prevention and intervention programs for all types of fitness/wellness centers. Offers creative programs and services to build healthier people and organizations through healthier lifestyles.

Classes and Conferences
Various health, fitness, wellness topics including smoking cessation. Please contact for pricing and complete information.
Technical Assistance
Consultation on design, planning, and management of fitness/wellness centers; health promotion specialist available to plan and administer wellness programs.

■ EMC² (Employee Managed Care Corporation)

701 Fifth Ave, Ste 2600
Seattle, WA 98104-7015
Contact: Sales Dept, 800-927-9225
800-755-2136
206-749-1100
Fax: 206-749-1125
E-mail: emc2@emcsquared.com
Web site: http://www.emcsquared.com

For-profit company offering a full range of cost saving solutions for health care benefit providers. Programs educate, motivate, and empower members to make better use of the health care system from prenatal care to chronic disease management.

Consumer or Patient Education Materials
The CareWise Guide: Self-care from Head to Toe, book, covers almost 200 medical concerns and prevention; CareWise for Older Adults: Self-care for Lifelong Health, book, covers more than 300 medical concerns; CareWise NEWS, quarterly newsletter, empowering and educating members. Can be customized. Please contact for pricing and complete information.
Other Products and Services
CareWise®, comprehensive health information program; BabyWise™, perinatal risk assessment and decision-counseling program; LivingWise®, lifestyle risk assessment and behavior modification program; CareSupport™, disease management program; Nurse On Call, telephone triage and decision support system; audiolibrary. Please contact for pricing and complete information.

■ Fitcorp

Prudential Center, Ste 200
800 Boylston St
Boston, MA 02199-8007
Contact: Laurie Selvaggio, 617-375-5600 x185
617-375-5600
Fax: 617-375-5649

For-profit company providing health promotion and fitness services delivered through network of public fitness centers or at private on-site centers.

Other Products and Services
The Fitcorp Wellness Benefit, state-of-the art fitness services and worksite health promotion planning, including: individual health profiles, health screenings, healthy lifestyle seminars, lifestyle management programs, health fairs. Can also help develop and manage private fitness centers.

■ Greenstone Healthcare Solutions

7000 Portage Rd
Kalamazoo, MI 49001
Contact: Cindy Casserly
800-947-3367
616-833-1221
Fax: 616-833-0371
E-mail: cindycasserly@am.pnu.com
Web site: http://www.ghsnet.com/

Comprehensive disease management consulting company that works with managed care organizations, providers, and employers to identify and target clinical process or evidence-based outcome improvement project and provide systematic solutions.

Electronic Information Resources
Disease Management Forum web site: http://www.sapien.net/dm/, offers discussion groups and news related to disease management.
Technical Assistance
Disease management consulting to identify risks in a population and develop services to modify risks and improve outcomes.
Other Products and Services
Personal empowerment programs, cost varies upon volume; other customized services available.

■ Health Decisions International LLC

1667 Cole Blvd, 3rd Fl
Golden, CO 80401
Contact: Dana Brandorff, 303-384-1634
800-403-0099
303-278-1700
Fax: 301-278-4860

For-profit company providing Demand Management® and medical management products, services, and information enabling individuals to make better health decisions, practice better health behaviors, and use medical care appropriately.

Other Products and Services

Informed Choice, a non-directive, non-prescriptive, 24-hr telephone-based nurse counseling service, with following products: Triage, Shared Decisions, Disease Management, Lifestyle Management, Prenatal Plus; also includes an audio library of prerecorded medical topics.

■ Health Evaluation Systems Inc

2620 Thousand Oaks Blvd, Ste 2300
Memphis, TN 38118
Contact: Ross Ose
800-318-0429
Fax: 901-368-4333

For-profit company that offers preventive services including drug and alcohol testing, health risks appraisals, behavior modification programs, physical examinations, and medical surveillance.

Classes and Conferences

Behavior modification programs.

■ Health First Consulting Corporation

4040 Vincennes Cir, Ste 600
Indianapolis, IN 46268
Contact: Monica Earlywine
317-879-4188
Fax: 317-879-4049

National consulting company that specializes in comprehensive worksite health promotion programs.

Technical Assistance

Consulting services for planning and implementing worksite health promotion programs including health risk assessments, on-site seminars, customized newsletters.

■ Healthier People Software

2161 Spring Meade Cove
Germantown, TN 38139
Mailing Address:
PO Box 38623
Memphis, TN 38183-0623
Contact: Joe Hogan
800-256-1953
901-751-4136
404-872-2100
Fax: 901-751-3107

For-profit company providing health risk assessments and nutrition assessments to hospitals, universities, employers, and public health agencies. Provides support services for implementation, including program design, evaluation, and customization.

Technical Assistance

Actuarial consultation available for managed care organizations and employers; program evaluation, risk analysis, claims experience.

■ HealthStyle

11469 Olive Blvd, Ste 251
St Louis, MO 63141-7108
Contact: Lisa McKee
800-645-2535
314-994-7323
Fax: 314-994-1545
E-mail: healthstyle@welltech.com
Web site: http://www.welltech.com/healthstyle

National for-profit company that develops and distributes unique health and fitness incentive programs and products.

Other Products and Services

Connecting Healthy Lifestyles™, wellness incentive program, $99; can also design customized incentive programs and products.

■ Healthy Achievers

22 Hayes Rd
Madbury, NH 03820-9511
603-743-3838
Fax: 603-749-7310
E-mail: ohshealthy@aol.com

Consulting firm specializing in worksite health promotion and occupational safety programs and materials.

Consumer or Patient Education Materials

Complete education program kits with video and reproducible materials, 18 topic areas available including: Achieving Well-Being; Achieving an Active Lifestyle; Men's Health, $95. Please contact for complete catalog.

Technical Assistance

Consulting for corporate wellness programs and fitness center management and design.

■ Human Resources Institute Inc

115 Dunder Rd
Burlington, VT 05401
Contact: Judd Allen
800-800-3004
802-862-8855
Fax: 802-862-6389
E-mail: allenjudd@aol.com
Web site: http://members.aol.com/allenjudd/webpage.htm

Consulting firm that works to empower individuals, groups, and organizations, to take charge of their cultures. Provides the tools to create supportive cultural environments.

Consumer or Patient Education Materials
With a Little Help from My Friends, video & user's guide, peer support video for healthier lifestyles, $89. Please contact for complete catalog.
Publications for Health Professionals
The Organizational Unconscious: How to Create the Corporate Culture You Want and Need, book. Please contact for complete publications list.
Classes and Conferences
Wellness Mentor Training, 1-day seminar for up to 20 participants, provides information and skills needed to effectively support family, friends, and coworkers making health behavior changes, $1,980. Please contact for complete list and schedule.

■ Informed Access Systems Inc
310 Interlocken Pkwy, Ste A
Broomfield, CO 80021
Contact: Sales Dept, 303-404-1865
800-829-2550
303-443-4600
Fax: 303-443-3909
E-mail: info@iasi.com

For-profit company that offers a patient assessment service for providers.

Consumer or Patient Education Materials
FirstHelp™, book, self-care guide.
Other Products and Services
FirstHelp™, patient assessment service, encompassing 24-hr telephone nurse advice and information for triage, pre-authorization and disease management; audio library.

■ International Parish Nurse Resource Center
205 W Touhy Ave, Ste 104
Park Ridge, IL 60068
Contact: Rusty McDermott, 847-698-4759
800-556-5368
847-698-4755
Fax: 847-692-5109
E-mail: parish.nurse.resource.center@worldnet.att.net
Web site: http://www.advocatehealth.com

Nonprofit resource center whose mission is to promote the development of quality parish nurse programs through research, education, and consultation.

Publications for Health Professionals
Reaching Out: Parish Nursing Services: An Institutional/Congregational Partnership, manual, for implementing parish nurse programs, $29; Congregational Health Services, handbook, for offering a health promotion program, $24; Perspectives in Parish Nursing Practice, semi-annual newsletter, free. Please contact for complete publications list.
Classes and Conferences
Annual Westberg Symposium, 2½ days, for interested nurses, clergy, hospital administrators, nursing educators, $200; Introduction Courses, 2½ days, to concept of parish nursing, $200; Advanced seminars. Please contact for complete list and schedule.
Technical Assistance
Consultation services and initial information packets on the concept of parish nursing and/or the start-up of parish nurse programs in the various models are available to various groups.

■ Stasica Associates
1505 E Central Rd
Arlington Heights, IL 60005
Contact: Edward R Stasica
847-640-8308

Consulting firm and speaker in the areas of wellness program planning, design, and evaluation; health consumerism education; and health benefit cost management.

Technical Assistance
Consulting services for wellness program planning, design, and evaluation; health consumerism education; health benefit cost management.

■ StayWell Health Management Systems Inc
1340 Mendota Heights Rd
St Paul, MN 55120-1128
Contact: Lynn Henry
800-373-3577
612-454-3577
Fax: 612-454-4062

National for-profit provider of employee assistance and wellness programs to corporations, helping employers encourage healthier, more productive employees while controlling the costs of health care.

Other Products and Services
Employee assistance and wellness programs including health advice telephone helpline.

■ Strategic Marketing Group Inc

3801 E Florida Ave, Ste 400
Denver, CO 80210
Contact: David C Franzblau
800-733-1530
303-759-1610
Fax: 303-759-2010
E-mail: 76530.1417@compuserve.com

Consulting firm that provides health care organizations with market analysis, marketing, and strategic planning services. Offers computerized data mapping for health-related problem analysis and community needs analyses as special areas of expertise.

Classes and Conferences
Customized workshops, lectures, and executive planning retreats. Contact for complete information.

Technical Assistance
Consulting services spanning the full range of market analysis, new service planning, and program development. Experts in ambulatory care, emergency health services, and geographic data analysis.

■ Summex Corporation

1099 N Meridian St, Ste 920
Indianapolis, IN 46204
Contact: Lisa A Zigler
800-884-5044
317-630-3456
Fax: 317-630-3450
E-mail: summex@summex.com
Web site: http://www.in.net/summex

Consulting firm whose mission is to be the nation's premier provider of integrated demand management products and services that maximize each individual's personal health management knowledge, skills, and motivation.

Publications for Health Professionals
Wellness manuals include: Planning Wellness, sound advice for developing worksite wellness program; Using Wellness Incentives, positive tools for healthy lifestyles; Key Documents, useful forms for your wellness program, $34.95 ea. Please contact for complete publications list.

Technical Assistance
Consulting services; Comprevent, non-worksite based health management system combines HRA, serial feedback, medical self-care book, monthly newsletter, and at risk health counseling; Comincents, turnkey, comprehensive incentive system; Comscript, integrated health management system and comprehensive worksite-based employee health management.

■ TriHealth Preventive Health Systems

8044 Montgomery Rd, Ste 525
Cincinnati, OH 45236
Contact: Pamela J Clark
518-891-1622
Fax: 518-891-7286

International nonprofit consulting firm whose purpose is to optimize the health status of the individuals, organizations, and populations it serves with an emphasis on prevention, education, and positive lifestyle interventions.

Technical Assistance
Consulting services including claims analysis, strategic planning, identification of risks, and program planning and implementation.

Other Products and Services
Lifestyle Management, a telephonic health education and lifestyle management program that assists and motivates individuals through personalized education and coaching.

■ Wellness Councils of America (WELCOA)

Community Health Plaza
7101 Newport Ave, Ste 311
Omaha, NE 68152-2100
402-572-3590
Fax: 402-572-3594
E-mail: welcoa@neonramp.com

National nonprofit membership organization dedicated to promoting healthier lifestyles for all Americans, especially through health promotion activities at the workplace, has a nationwide network of locally affiliated Wellness Councils and direct network members serving corporate members and their employees. Acts as a national clearinghouse and information center on corporate health promotion for companies everywhere.

Electronic Information Resources
Fax-on-Demand: 402-498-9805 code 100 (must call from your fax machine phone), Cost-benefits summary of corporate health promotion programs (document #101); list of America's healthiest companies (document #102).

Publications for Health Professionals
How-to-Guide books for health planners include: Healthy, Wealthy & Wise, $95; Health Fairs, $30; HealthTrip incentive campaign, $89. Please contact for complete publications list.

Classes and Conferences
Fundamentals of Workplace Health Promotion, 1–2 days, covers basics; other seminars and workshops; fee varies. Please contact for complete list and schedule.
Technical Assistance
Technical assistance available and included with membership.

■ Wellness Quest

1541 7 1/2 Ave NE
Rochester, MN 55906
Contact: Jeff Haebig
507-281-3143
Fax: 507-287-0259
E-mail: wellness@infonet.isl.net
Web site: http://www.wellnessquest.coml

National for-profit company that offers highly spirited worksite incentive programs, motivational workshops, and fun inspirational books and calendars.

Consumer or Patient Education Materials
Care-toons Calendar, desktop, cartooned multi-year calendar, $9.95; Care-toons Journal, spiral book, cartooned health info and journal, $9.95; Toon Ups, book, health challenges and cartoons, $9.95. Discounts available for quantity orders. Materials can be customized; Please contact for complete catalog.
Classes and Conferences
Wellness Education Jubilation, audience-action wellness funshops, humor and healing workshops, 45 mins to 3 hours, $500 to $1,500. Please contact for complete list and schedule.
Other Products and Services
Quick Quest Incentive Programs, 2- to 4-week incentive programs; motivational keynotes; audience-active assembly programs for school and community health fairs, hearty parties.

■ Wellsource Inc

15431 SE 82nd Dr, Ste D
PO Box 569
Clackamas, OR 97015
Contact: Area sales representative
800-533-9355
503-656-7446
Fax: 503-650-0880
E-mail: well@wellsource-in.com
Web site: http://www.wellsource-inc.com

International consulting firm that develops software systems, health risk appraisals (HRA); offers training and support for managing risk factors, tracking health outcomes; and serves health promotion professionals.

Technical Assistance
Research and consulting services for evaluating health behavior and health outcomes.
Other Products and Services
Software systems, including Managed Prevention System.

ADDITIONAL RESOURCES

■ Alexander & Alexander Consulting Group

First Market Tower
525 Market St, Ste 700
San Francisco, CA 94105-2715
Contact: Tracy Byars, Director of Marketing
415-222-7200
Fax: 415-222-7014
Web site: http://www.alexalex.com

■ American Association for Health Plans

1129 20th St NW, Ste 600
Washington, DC 20036
Contact: Publications Distribution Center,
800-631-2750 (credit card orders only)
202-778-3200
Fax: 202-331-7487
Web site: http://www.aahp.org/

■ American Association of School Administrators

1801 N Moore St
Arlington, VA 22209
Contact: Publications, 301-617-7802
703-528-0700
Web site: http://www.aasa.org

■ American College of Epidemiology

401 E Jefferson St, Ste 205
Rockville, MD 20850
Mailing Address:
PO Box 10639
Rockville, MD 20849
Contact: Mary Cassidy
301-251-0594
Fax: 301-279-6749
E-mail: epiinfo@amcollepi.org

■ American Health Planning Association

1000 16th St NW, Ste 604
Washington, DC 20036
202-371-1515
703-573-3100
Fax: 703-573-1276

■ **American School Health Association**
PO Box 708
7263 State Rt 43
Kent, OH 44240
330-678-1603
Fax: 330-678-4526

■ **Asian and Pacific Islanders American Health Forum Inc**
116 New Montgomery St, Ste 531
San Francisco, CA 94105
415-541-0866
Fax: 415-512-3881

■ **Association of Asian Pacific Community Health Organizations**
1440 Broadway, Ste 510
Oakland, CA 94612
510-272-9536
Fax: 510-272-0817

■ **Catholic Health Association**
1875 Eye St NW
Washington, DC 20006
202-296-3993
Fax: 202-296-3997

■ **The Center for Studying Health System Change**
600 Maryland Ave SW, Ste 550
Washington, DC 20024
202-484-5261
Fax: 202-484-9258
E-mail: center@hschange.com

■ **Center for the Advancement of Health**
2000 Florida Ave NW, Ste 210
Washington, DC 20009-1231
202-387-2829
Fax: 202-387-2857
E-mail: cfah@cfah.org
Web site: http://www.cfah.org

■ **Circle Solutions Inc**
2070 Chain Bridge Rd, Ste 450
Vienna, VA 22182-2536
Contact: Karen Stiansen, Office Manager
703-821-8955
Fax: 703-821-2098
E-mail: info@circsol.com

■ **The Conference Board Inc**
845 Third Ave
New York, NY 10022
212-759-0900
E-mail: info@conf-board.org

■ **Corporate Fitness Works**
18558 Office Park Dr
Gaithersburg, MD 20879
301-417-9697
Fax: 301-417-0651

■ **Council of State and Territorial Epidemiologists**
2872 Woodcock Blvd, #303
Atlanta, GA 30341-4015
770-458-3811
Fax: 770-458-8516

■ **Council on Foundations**
1828 L St NW
Washington, DC 20036
202-466-6512
Fax: 202-785-3926
Web site: http://www.cof.org

■ **Education Development Center Inc**
55 Chapel St
Newton, MA 02158-1060
617-969-7100
Fax: 617-969-5979
Web site: http://www.edc.org

■ **Employee Assistance Program Association**
2101 Wilson Blvd, Ste 500
Arlington, VA 22201
703-522-6272
Fax: 703-522-4585
E-mail: eapamain@aol.com

■ **Fitness Systems**
3500 W 80th St, Ste 130
Minneapolis, MN 55431
Contact: Jim Narum, President
612-893-5537
Fax: 612-831-7264

■ **The Foundation Center**
79 Fifth Ave
New York, NY 10003-3076
800-424-9836 (Order Dept)
212-620-4230
Fax: 212-807-3677 (Orders)
Web site: http://fdncenter.org

■ The Grantsmanship Center
1125 W Sixth St, 5th Fl
PO Box 17220
Los Angeles, CA 90017
213-482-9860
Fax: 213-482-9863
Web site: http://www.tgci.com

■ Greater Talent Network Inc
150 Fifth Ave
New York, NY 10011
800-326-4211
212-645-4200
Fax: 212-627-1471
Web site: http://www.greatertalent.com

■ Health Awareness Inc
53526 Hunters Crossing
Utica, MI 48315
Contact: Worksite Wellness Programs
810-677-1130
Fax: 810-677-1131

■ Health Education Foundation
2600 Virginia Ave NW, Ste 502
Washington, DC 20037
202-338-3501
Fax: 202-965-6520

■ Health Enhancement Systems Inc
2805 Ashman St
Midland, MI 48640
Mailing Address:
PO Box 1335
Midland, MI 48641-1335
800-326-2317
517-839-0852
Fax: 517-839-0025

■ Health Insurance Association of America
555 13th St NW, Ste 600E
Washington, DC 20004-1109
202-824-1600
Web site: http://www.hiaa.org

■ Health Management Corporation
PO Box 26016
Richmond, VA 23260
800-523-9279
804-289-5022
Fax: 804-289-5047
E-mail: hmcorp@mindspring.com

■ The Health Project
1166 Avenue of the Americas, 43rd Fl
New York, NY 10036
212-345-7336
Fax: 212-345-5999
Web site: http://healthproject.stanford.edu/

■ Health Resources Publishing
Brinley Professional Bldg
3100 Hwy 138
Wall Township, NJ 07719-1442
800-516-4343
Fax: 908-681-0490
E-mail: mcic@monmouth.com
Web site: http://www.themcic.com

■ HealthDesk Corporation
2560 Ninth St, Ste 220
Berkeley, CA 94710
Contact: Peter O'Donnell, President
510-883-2190
E-mail: PeterO@HealthDesk.com

■ HealthMatters
33 Edgell Rd
Framingham, MA 01701
Contact: Gerald L Evans, MD, Director
508-626-0000

■ Institute for Alternative Futures
100 N Pitt St, Ste 235
Alexandria, VA 22314
Contact: Kathy Scott, Marketing Coordinator
703-684-5880
Fax: 703-684-0640
E-mail: futures@altfutures.com
Web site: http://www.altfutures.com

■ The Institute for Educational Leadership
1001 Connecticut Ave NW, Ste 310
Washington, DC 20036
202-822-8405
Fax: 202-872-4050
E-mail: iel@iel.org
Web site: http://www.iel.org

■ Institute of Medicine
National Academy of Sciences
2101 Constitution Ave NW
Washington, DC 20418
Contact: Publications, 800-624-6242
202-334-2169 (Public Inquiries)
202-334-2383 (Health Promotion and Disease Division)
Web site: http://www.nas.edu

- **Johnson and Johnson Health Care Systems Inc**
425 Hoes Ln
Piscataway, NJ 08855
Contact: Health Management Division, 800-443-3682
908-562-3000
Fax: 908-562-3092

- **Joint Commission on Accreditaton of Healthcare Organizations (JCAHO)**
One Renaissance Blvd
Oakbrook Terrace, IL 60181
Contact: Customer Service: 630-792-5800, Division of Research & Evaluation: 630-792-5894
630-792-5000
Fax: 630-792-5644
Web site: http://www.jcaho.org

- **The Lewin Group**
9302 Lee Hwy, Ste 500
Fairfax, VA 22031-1214
Contact: Lucia Davidson, 703-218-5526
703-218-5500
Fax: 703-218-5501
Web site: http://www.lewin.com

- **National Academy Press**
2101 Constitution Ave NW
Washington, DC 20418
800-624-6242
202-334-3313
Fax: 202-334-2451
Web site: http://www.nap.edu

- **National Assembly of National Voluntary Health and Social Welfare Organizations**
1319 F St, Ste 601
Washington, DC 20004
202-347-2080
Fax: 202-939-4517
E-mail: nassembly@aol.com
Web site: http://www.nassembly.org

- **National Association of Community Action Agencies**
1100 17th St NW, Ste 500
Washington, DC 20036
202-265-7546
Fax: 202-265-8850
E-mail: info@nacaa.org
Web site: http://www.nacaa.org

- **National Association of Community Health Centers Inc**
1330 New Hampshire Ave NW, Ste 122
Washington, DC 20036
202-659-8008
Fax: 202-659-8519

- **National Association of County & City Health Officials (NACCHO)**
440 First St NW, Ste 500
Washington, DC 20001
202-783-5550
Fax: 202-783-1583
Web site: http://www.naccho.org

- **National Association of State Boards of Education**
1012 Cameron St
Alexandria, VA 22314
703-684-4000
Fax: 703-836-2313
Web site: http://www.nasbe.org

- **The National Center for Health Promotion**
PO Box 524
Saline, MI 48034-2292
800-250-5105
313-429-3065
Fax: 800-250-4560
E-mail: nchp2@ix.netcom.com
Web site: http://www.welltech.com/nchp/

- **National Civic League**
1445 Market St, Ste 300
Denver, CO 80202-1728
800-223-6004
303-571-4343
Fax: 303-571-4404
E-mail: ncl@csn.net
Web site: http://www.ncl.org/ncl

- **National Committee for Quality Assurance**
2000 L St NW, Ste 500
Washington, DC 20036
800-839-6487 (Publication Center)
202-955-3500
Fax: 202-955-3599
Web site: http://www.ncqa.org

■ **National Institute for Health Care Management**
1818 N St NW, Ste 300
Washington, DC 20036
202-296-4426
Fax: 202-296-4319

■ **National League of Cities**
1301 Pennsylvania Ave NW
Washington, DC 20004
Contact: Publications Center, 301-725-4299
202-626-3000
Fax: 202-626-3043
E-mail: pa@nlc.org
Web site: http://www.cais.com/nlc

■ **The National PTA**
330 N Wabash Ave, Ste 2100
Chicago, IL 60611-3690
312-670-6782
Fax: 312-670-6783
Web site: http://www.pta.org

■ **The National Public Health and Hospital Institute**
1212 New York Ave NW, Ste 800
Washington, DC 20005
202-408-0229
Fax: 202-408-0235
E-mail: naph@naph.org
Web site: http://www.naph.org/NPHHI.html

■ **National Rural Health Association**
One W Armour Blvd, Ste 301
Kansas City, MO 64111
816-756-3140
Fax: 816-756-3144
E-mail: mail@nrharural.org
Web site: http://www.NRHArural.org

■ **National Urban League**
500 E 62nd St
New York, NY 10021
Contact: Rose Jefferson, Communications Dept
212-310-9000
Fax: 212-755-2026
E-mail: info@nul.org
Web site: http://www.nul.org

■ **National Wellness Speakers Bureau**
3722 W 50th St, #110
Minneapolis, MN 55410
Contact: Robin J Ogden, Marketing Director
612-925-4090
Fax: 612-925-2125
E-mail: wellspeak@aol.com

■ **New York Business Group on Health Inc**
386 Park Ave S, Ste 508
New York, NY 10016-8804
212-252-7440
Fax: 212-252-7448
E-mail: NYBGH@ix.netcom.com

■ **NOVA HealthCare Group**
1106 Jeff Ryan Dr
Herndon, VA 22070
Contact: Ira D Singer, President
703-709-7830
Fax: 703-709-9657
E-mail: idsinger@gslink.com

■ **Points of Light Foundation**
1737 H St NW
Washington, DC 20006
Mailing Address:
PO Box 665434
Washington, DC 20035
Contact: Catalog Services, 800-272-8306
202-223-9186
Fax: 202-223-9526

■ **Public Relations Society of America**
33 Irving Pl, 3rd Fl
New York, NY 10003-2376
212-995-2230
Fax: 212-995-0757
E-mail: hdq@prsa.org
Web site: http://www.prsa.org

■ **Robert Wood Johnson Foundation**
Route 1 and College Rd E
PO Box 2316
Princeton, NJ 08543-2316
Contact: Barbara Sherwood, Communications Dept
609-452-8701
E-mail: mail@rwjf.org
Web site: http://www.rwjf.org

■ **The Taft Group**
835 Penobscot Bldg
Detroit, MI 48226
800-877-8238
Fax: 313-961-6083
Web site: http://www.gale.com

■ **The United Way of America**
701 N Fairfax St
Alexandria, VA 22314-2045
Contact: Curt Johnson, Community Building Program, 703-683-7835
800-892-2757
703-683-7100
Fax: 703-683-7840
Web site: http://www.unitedway.org

■ **VHA Inc**
Community Health Improvement
220 East Las Colinas Blvd
Irving, TX 75039-5500
Mailing Address:
PO Box 140909
Irving, TX 75014-0909
Contact: Deborah A Stewart, Program Manager
800-468-6842
972-830-0077
Fax: 972-830-0332
Web site: http://www.vha.com

■ **W K Kellogg Foundation**
One Michigan Avenue E
Battlecreek, MI 49017-4058
616-968-1611
Fax: 616-968-0413
Web site: http://www.wkkf.org

■ **Washington Business Group on Health**
777 N Capitol St NE, Ste 800
Washington, DC 20002
202-408-9320
Fax: 202-408-9332
E-mail: wbgh@wbgh.com
Web site: http://www.wbgh.com/~signe/

FEDERAL AGENCIES

■ **Agency for Health Care Policy and Research (AHCPR)**
Office of Public Health and Science
U.S. Dept of Health & Human Services
2101 E Jefferson St
Rockville, MD 20852
301-594-1433
Fax: 301-594-3212

Publications Clearinghouse
PO Box 8547
Silver Spring, MD 20907-8547
800-358-9295
(410-381-3150 callers outside the U.S. only)
AHCPR InstantFAX: 301-594-2800
Web site: http://www.ahcpr.gov/

Primary source of Federal support for research on medical treatment effectiveness and health care cost, quality, and access. Sponsors the development of clinical practice guidelines; evaluates health care technologies; works to increase the quantity and quality of data for research purposes; and analyzes data on health care use and expenditures, health insurance, long-term care, hospital performance, and other policy-relevant issues. Also publishes consumer information on medical problems and their treatment. Research Activities is a free monthly periodical summarizing published findings, grants, and contract awards. Publications catalog available from AHCPR Publications Clearinghouse; some publications must be ordered from the National Technical Information Service or the Government Printing Office.

■ **Bureau of Primary Health Care (BPHC)**
Health Resources and Services Administration
4350 East West Hwy
Bethesda, MD 20814
Program for Special Populations Division: 301-594-4420
Office of Minority and Women's Health: 301-594-4490

Mission is to increase access to comprehensive primary and preventive health care and to improve the health status of underserved and vulnerable populations, such as the homeless and people with or at risk for HIV infection. Materials are available from the National Clearinghouse for Primary Care Information: 800-400-2742.

■ Centers for Disease Control and Prevention (CDC)

Office of Public Health and Science
U.S. Dept of Health & Human Services
1600 Clifton Rd NE, M/S D-25
Atlanta, GA 30333
Public Inquiries: 404-639-3286; Fax: 404-639-1537
Publications: 404-639-3534
CDC Voice Information System: 404-332-4555 (M–F 8AM–4:30PM ET)
CDC Wonder web site: http://wonder.cdc.gov/ (to locate reports, guidelines, or data)
Web site: http://www.cdc.gov

Federal health agency whose mission is to promote health and quality of life by preventing and controlling disease, injury, and disability. It works with partners throughout the nation and the world to monitor health, detect and investigate health problems, conduct research to enhance prevention, develop and advocate sound public health policies, implement prevention strategies, promote healthy behaviors, foster safe and healthful environments, and provide leadership and training.

■ Epidemiology Program Office (EPO)

Centers for Disease Control and Prevention
1600 Clifton Rd NE, M/S C-08
Atlanta, GA 30333
Morbidity and Mortality Weekly Report (MMWR): 404-639-2104
MMWR web site: http://www.cdc.gov/epo/mmwr/mmwr.html
Web site: http://www.cdc.gov/epo/

Mission is to strengthen the public health system by coordinating public health surveillance at CDC and providing domestic and international support through scientific communications, statistical and epidemiologic consultation, and training of experts in surveillance, epidemiology, applied public health, and prevention effectiveness.

■ Health Care Financing Administration (HCFA)

U.S. Dept of Health & Human Services
Baltimore, MD 21244
General Information: 410-786-3000
Bureau of Data Management and Strategy: 410-786-1800
Office of National Health Statistics: 410-786-7933
Medicare Statistical Hotline: 410-786-3689
Web site: http://www.hcfa.gov

Federal agency that administers Medicare, Medicaid, related quality assurance programs; also demonstration projects to test cost and effectiveness of preventive services.

■ Health Resources and Services Administration (HRSA)

Office of Public Health and Science
U.S. Dept of Health & Human Services
5600 Fishers Ln, Rm 14-45
Rockville, MD 20857
Communications Office: 301-443-3376
Fax: 301-443-1989
Web site: http://www.hrsa.dhhs.gov/

Agency whose mission is to improve America's health care system and the health of the American people. Administers programs related to access, quality, equity, and cost of health care. Supports state and community efforts to deliver care to underserved areas and to groups with special health needs.

■ National Center for Chronic Disease Prevention & Health Promotion (NCCDPHP)

Centers for Disease Control and Prevention
4770 Buford Hwy NE
Atlanta, GA 30341-3724
Technical Information Services Branch: 770-488-5080
Chronic Disease Notes & Reports: 770-488-5050; Fax: 770-488-5095
Web site: http://www.cdc.gov/nccdphp/nccdhome.html

Plans, directs, and coordinates a national program for the prevention of premature mortality, morbidity, and disability due to chronic illnesses and conditions and promotes the overall health of the population.

■ National Clearinghouse for Primary Care Information

2070 Chain Bridge Rd, Ste 450
Vienna, VA 22182-2536
800-400-2742
703-902-1248

Clearinghouse that provides information services and distributes publications focusing on ambulatory care, financial management, primary health care, and health services administration of special interest to professionals working in primary care centers. Also for the planning, development, and delivery of ambulatory health care to urban and rural areas that have shortages of medical personnel and service. Bilingual medical phrase books, a directory of federally funded health centers, and an annotated bibliography also available. Sponsored by the Bureau of Primary Health Care, Health Resources and Services Administration.

■ National Health Information Center (NHIC)

Office of Disease Prevention and Health Promotion (ODPHP)
Office of Public Health and Science (OPHS)
PO Box 1133
Washington, DC 20013-1133
800-336-4797
301-565-4167
Fax: 301-984-4256
E-mail: nhicinfo@health.org
Web site: http://nhic-nt.health.org

A health information referral service of the ODPHP, OPHS, U.S. Dept of Health and Human Services. Links health professionals and consumers who have health questions to organizations best able to provide answers. Provides a variety of health information resource materials, a toll-free telephone service, and a database of health-related organizations. Produces directories, resource guides, bibliographies on various health topics in print and electronic form; disseminates other publications of ODPHP and OPHS agencies.

■ National Institutes of Health (NIH)

Office of Public Health and Science
U.S. Dept of Health & Human Services
Bldg 1, Rm 344
9000 Rockville Pike
Bethesda, MD 20892
Division of Public Information: 301-496-5787
Web site: http://www.nih.gov

Responds to requests for information from the general public and professional public, and directs requests to the proper NIH source. Produces a variety of materials relating to NIH as a whole including a consumer health service, a science news service, a monthly press calendar, and the NIH information index. Materials produced by various NIH institutes and divisions, as found in the NIH Publications List, should be requested directly from the appropriate unit.

■ National Library of Medicine (NLM)

National Institutes of Health
Bldg 38, Rm 2S10
8600 Rockville Pike
Bethesda, MD 20894
800-272-4787
301-496-6308
NLM Reference Desk: 301-496-6095 (for medical questions)
MEDLARS Management Service Desk: 800-638-8480 or 301-496-6193
Web site: http://www.nlm.nih.gov

NLM's mission is to collect, preserve, and disseminate biomedical information, and has assembled the largest collection of biomedical literature in the world. Services of NLM include computer-based literature retrieval services, interlibrary loan services, programs of grant support for medical libraries, communications research and training, toxicology information services, and publications. NLM has 40 specialized databases composing the Medical Literature Analysis and Retrieval System (MEDLARS) available through a nationwide network. Individuals with microcomputers and modems can have direct access through the software GRATEFUL MED.

■ National Technical Information Service (NTIS)

5285 Port Royal Rd
Springfield, VA 22161
703-487-4650
Fax: 703-321-8547
Fax Direct® Title List Service: 703-487-4099
Fax Direct® Product Information Service: 703-487-4140
NTIS Product Announcements Fax: 800-758-5804 ext. 104707
FedWorld® Help Desk: 703-487-4223
E-mail: orders@ntis.fedworld.gov
Web site: http://www.prnewswire.com

Self-supporting agency offering extensive collection of scientific, technical, engineering, and business-related data available on a wide range of subjects with special emphasis on the best selling categories of business, health and the environment. Catalogs are available at no cost.

■ Office of Disease Prevention and Health Promotion (ODPHP)

Office of Public Health and Science
U.S. Dept of Health & Human Services
200 Independence Ave SW, Rm 738G
Washington, DC 20201
202-401-6295
Fax: 202-205-9778
Health Communications Dept: 202-205-5968

Healthy People 2000 Management Team: 202-205-8583
National Coordinating Committee on Worksite Health Promotion: 202-205-9007
Web site: http://odphp.oash.dhhs.gov/

Provides leadership in stimulating, coordinating, and unifying national disease prevention and health promotion strategies among federal, state, and local agencies and major private and voluntary organizations. Initiatives include Healthy People 2000, Put Prevention into Practice, and the Guide to Clinical Preventive Services. Offers publications in the area of federal programs and policy, community and school health promotion programs, health promotion at the worksite, nutrition, and health communication that are available from the National Health Information Center (NHIC) or the Government Printing Office.

■ U.S. Government Printing Office (GPO)

Washington, DC 20402-9325
202-512-1800
Fax: 202-512-2250
Web site: http://www.access.gpo.gov
Superintendents of Documents
PO Box 371954
Pittsburgh, PA 15250-7954
Web site: http://www.access.gpo.gov/su_docs/

General Health Promotion Materials

Organization	web site	hotline/toll-free information line	clearinghouse/resource center	electronic information resources	database/statistical information	special campaigns/events/programs	consumer/patient education materials	publications for health professionals	classes/conferences	technical assistance	other products/services	grants/funding/awards	**Page No.**
American Institute for Preventive Medicine	■					■	■	■	■	■	■		**25**
Center for Medical Consumers								■					**25**
Channing L Bete Co Inc							■						**25**
Clinical Reference Systems Ltd	■										■		**25**
Coffey Communications Inc	■						■						**26**
Dreyfuss Hunt Inc							■						**26**
Films for the Humanities & Sciences							■						**26**
Hall-Foushee Communications Inc										■			**26**
Harvard Medical School Health Publications Group	■						■						**26**
Health Information Resource Center	■					■		■			■	■	**27**
Health Letter Associates							■						**27**
Healthwise Incorporated	■						■			■	■		**27**
Homeopathic Educational Services	■						■	■					**27**
Hope Publications							■						**27**
Info Vision							■				■		**28**
Lange Productions										■			**28**
Longe Life Libraries	■		■				■	■	■	■	■		**28**
Mayo Clinic Health Information				■			■						**28**
Medical Data Source	■										■		**29**
Park Nicollet HealthSource							■						**29**
Performance Resource Press Inc							■						**29**

Products/Services Offered

Organization	web site	hotline/toll-free information line	clearinghouse/resource center	electronic information resources	database/statistical information	special campaigns/events/programs	consumer/patient education materials	publications for health professionals	classes/conferences	technical assistance	other products/services	grants/funding/awards	Page No.
Planetree Health Library							■						29
Princeton Health Systems Inc							■	■		■	■		29
Pritchett & Hull Associates Inc	■						■	■					30
Rutherford Publishing Inc	■						■						30
Scott Publishing Inc (Personal Best)	■						■						30
Vitality Inc	■			■			■	■					30
Your HealthStyle	■						■						31

Additional Resources 31

Federal Agencies 32

■ American Institute for Preventive Medicine

30445 Northwestern Hwy, Ste 350
Farmington Hills, MI 48334-3102
Contact: Order Dept, 810-539-1800 x239
800-345-2476
810-539-1800
Fax: 810-539-1808
E-mail: aipm@healthy.net
Web site: http://aipm.healthy.net

International for-profit developer and provider of health promotion programs, self-help kits, and self-care publications. Works with over 5,000 corporations, HMOs, and hospitals to reduce health care costs, lower absenteeism, and improve morale. Services include those for self-care, smoking cessation, weight control, stress management, self-esteem enhancement, prenatal education, fitness center management, nutrition, and EAP education.

Special Campaigns, Events, or Programs

National Wise Health Care Consumer Month, February, Event ideas for corporations, hospitals, and managed care organizations, booklet titled Being a Wise Health Care Consumer, information on medical self-care. Contact Elaine Frank.

Consumer or Patient Education Materials

HealthyLife Self-Care Guides, booklets address 10 to 27 topics, book addresses 130 topics; EAP brochures, posters and booklets, 14 topics; Pricing varies upon quantity ordered. Materials can be customized; Please contact for complete catalog.

Publications for Health Professionals

Health at Home, paperback, teaches consumers to make better health care decisions, $17.95; A Year of Health Hints, hardcover, provides 365 one-page tips on wellness, $23.95. Please contact for complete publications list.

Classes and Conferences

Smoking Cessation, Weight Control, and Stress Management programs available. Please contact for pricing and complete list.

Technical Assistance

Consultation on the design, implementation, marketing, and evaluation of health promotion programs in both corporate and health care settings available.

Other Products and Services

Nurse advice line, audio library, prenatal education, wellness libraries, self-care workshops, self-care promotional materials, and self-care software.

■ Center for Medical Consumers

237 Thompson St
New York, NY 10012
Contact: Kristin Kalajainen
212-674-7105
Fax: 212-674-7100

Nonprofit organization offering a medical library designed specifically for the lay public. Contains extensive subject files with the latest information on current medical treatments and over 1,500 books and periodicals. Has substantial information on both mainstream and alternative treatments, such as acupuncture, herbalism, and nutrition.

Publications for Health Professionals

HealthFacts, monthly newsletter, review of recent health information, $25/yr.

■ Channing L Bete Co Inc

200 State Rd
S Deerfield, MA 01373-0200
800-628-7733 (Sales and Customer Service)
413-665-7611
Fax: 800-499-6464

Publisher of informational and educational booklets, videos, posters, calendars, books, and display racks. Booklets use a distinctive, condensed format—called scriptography—which combines key words and graphics to explain a variety of subjects and is appropriate for different age groups and reading levels.

Consumer or Patient Education Materials

Self-care information center display can be filled with booklets covering a range of topics. Booklets and videos. Topics include: Drug-Free Workplace Act, Employee Assistance Programs. Please contact for pricing and ask for the Staff Development catalog.

■ Clinical Reference Systems Ltd

7100 E Belleview Ave, Ste 208
Greenwood Village, CO 80111-1635
Contact: Ellen Graves, Marketing Coordinator
800-237-8401
303-220-1661
Fax: 303-220-1685
E-mail: crs-info@cliniref.com
Web site: http://www.patienteducation.com

Publisher of patient education and clinical reference software for the international healthcare community. Committed to development of computer-based health information to enhance communication between provider and patient. More than 30,000 programs are now at work in physician offices, clinics, hospitals, medical school residency programs, occupational clinics, medical and consumer libraries.

Other Products and Services

Health & Drug Information Library, CD-ROM, database of health care information covering a broad range of topics. Please contact for pricing and complete information.

■ Coffey Communications Inc

1505 Business One Cir
Walla Walla, WA 99362-9421
Contact: Kip Kelly
800-253-2030 (Order Dept)
509-525-0101
Fax: 509-525-0281
E-mail: coffey@coffeycomm.com
Web site: http://www.coffeycomm.com

Publisher of custom and syndicated publications in a variety of styles and formats for the hospital and managed care industries nationwide.

Consumer or Patient Education Materials

Health Scene, newsletter, consumer-oriented health care information; Keeping Well, newsletter, preventive health care information; Life and Health booklets, comprehensive information on a single health topic. Materials can be customized; Please contact for complete catalog.

■ Dreyfuss Hunt Inc

443 Western Ave
PO Box 35280
Boston, MA 02135
Contact: Customer Service
800-871-9525
617-254-5000
Fax: 617-254-5099

Publisher of health, wellness, safety, prevention, and financial/money-management materials.

Consumer or Patient Education Materials

Brochures on wide range of health topics; TopHealth, health promotion and wellness newsletter. Pricing varies upon quantity ordered; Materials can be customized; Low literacy; Spanish languages available. Please contact for complete catalog.

■ Films for the Humanities & Sciences

12 Perrine Rd
Monmouth Junction, NJ 08852-2728
Mailing Address:
PO Box 2053
Princeton, NJ 08543-2053
800-257-5126 (Order Dept)
609-275-1400
Fax: 609-275-3767
E-mail: custserv@films.com

Leading distributor of educational health videos, videodisc, and CD-ROM programs to hospitals, health departments, and other health agencies. Many topics covered including aging, AIDS, cancer, mental health, safety, substance abuse, and domestic violence.

Consumer or Patient Education Materials

More than 600 health-related programs including The New Living Body, videotape, 10-part series covering entire human body, $949; Wellness in the Workplace, videotape, includes easy-to-institute plans, $89.95. Please contact for complete catalog.

■ Hall-Foushee Communications Inc

1313 Fifth St SE, Ste 214B
Minneapolis, MN 55414
Contact: Nancy Hall
800-478-3829
612-379-3829
Fax: 612-379-3829
E-mail: 76633.3416@compuserve.com

For-profit company specializing in health communications planning and production of audiovisual and print materials. Focus on disease prevention and health promotion campaigns and materials.

Technical Assistance

Consulting services available for special projects.

■ Harvard Medical School Health Publications Group

164 Longwood Ave
Boston, MA 02115
617-432-1485
Fax: 617-432-1802
Web site: http://www.med.harvard.edu/publications/health_publications/.index.html

Nonprofit educational institution's publishing group of monthly consumer health newsletters.

Consumer or Patient Education Materials

Monthly newsletters: Harvard Health Letter, Harvard Heart Letter, Harvard Women's Health Watch, Harvard Mental Health Letter, $32/yr ea; Special reports on specific health issues, call 617-432-3939 for order information.

■ Health Information Resource Center

621 E Park Ave
Libertyville, IL 60048
Contact: Carole Klein-Alexander, 847-816-8660
800-828-8225
847-816-8660
Fax: 847-816-8662
E-mail: hlthinfo@aol.com
Web site: http://www.acpinc.com/healthinfo.html

National for-profit private clearinghouse of consumer health information and membership organization sponsoring many different programs and activities.

Special Campaigns, Events, or Programs
National Family Health and Fitness Day USA, last Sunday in September, Contact Carole Klein-Alexander, 847-816-8660.

Publications for Health Professionals
Health Events Calendar, yearly, $19.95; Consumer Health Online, updated yearly, $29.95; Health and Medical Media, yearly, media contacts for health care professionals, $199. Please contact for complete publications list.

Other Products and Services
Contact for information regarding membership.

Grants, Funding, or Awards
National Health Information Awards, program to recognize excellence in consumer health information. Contact Carole Klein-Alexander, 847-816-8660.

■ Health Letter Associates

632 Broadway
New York, NY 10012
Contact: Lisa Natoli
212-505-2255
Fax: 212-505-5462

Publisher of consumer medical and health information.

Consumer or Patient Education Materials
University of California at Berkeley Wellness Letter, monthly newsletter, $39/yr; The Johns Hopkins Medical Letter Health After 50, monthly newsletter, $39/yr.

■ Healthwise Incorporated

373 W Fort St
PO Box 1989
Boise, ID 83701
Contact: Regional Manager (for applicable state)
208-345-1161
Fax: 208-345-1897
Web site: http://www.healthwise.org

Nonprofit organization developing health promotion and medical self-care educational programs and publications. Mission is to help people do a better job of staying healthy and taking care of their health problems.

Consumer or Patient Education Materials
Healthwise Handbook, self-care manual, $16.95; Healthwise for Life: Medical Self-Care for Healthy Aging, self-care manual for older adults, $18.95. Discounts available for quantity orders. Low literacy; Spanish and German languages available. Please contact for complete catalog.

Technical Assistance
Consultation, Train-the-Trainer, and keynote addresses available.

Other Products and Services
Healthwise Knowledgebase™, Windows-based information system that helps consumers prepare for medical decisions with their doctors.

■ Homeopathic Educational Services

2124 Kittredge St
Berkeley, CA 94704
Contact: Dana Ullman MPH
510-649-0294
Fax: 510-649-1955
E-mail: mail@homeopathic.com
Web site: http://www.homeopathic.com

Publisher and leading resource center for homeopathic books, tapes, medicines, software, research, and general information. Directory of homeopathic practitioners in the U.S. is also available.

Consumer or Patient Education Materials
Various publications available; some low literacy. Please contact for complete catalog.

Publications for Health Professionals
Various publications available. Please contact for complete publications list.

■ Hope Publications

350 E Michigan Ave, Ste 301
Kalamazoo, MI 49007-3851
Contact: Customer Service
800-334-4094
616-343-0770
Fax: 616-343-6260
E-mail: 70603.2451@compuserve.com

Publisher that provides health publications to the managed care industry with a fully integrated line of newsletters, booklets, brochures, self-health kits, calendars, videos, and posters covering many issues and topics. Also offers a custom publishing department that can create publications to meet precise needs.

Consumer or Patient Education Materials

Brochures; booklets; Hope Health Calendar; videos; posters; newsletters include: Hope Health Letter, written in a down-to-earth style; Healthy Bites, a tightly-written business-letter format; Looking Forward, written for older audience. Pricing varies upon quantity ordered. Materials can be customized; Low literacy; Spanish languages available. Please contact for complete catalog.

■ Info Vision

13425 A St
Omaha, NE 68144
Contact: Ken King
800-237-1808
402-330-3335
Fax: 402-330-9544
E-mail: video@info-vision.com

For-profit company selling health and wellness videos by catalog.

Consumer or Patient Education Materials

Covert Bailey's Fit or Fat, 13-tape series as seen on PBS, $39 ea or $450/complete set; other videos for topics including: asthma, breast cancer, cholesterol, diabetes, headaches, $25–$39. Please contact for complete catalog.

Other Products and Services

Lending Library Software, windows-based, for inventory record keeping and management, $250.

■ Lange Productions

7661 Curson Ter
Los Angeles, CA 90046
213-874-4730
213-874-0132
Fax: 213-874-3318
E-mail: langevideo@aol.com

For-profit creator, producer, and distributor of videotape and CD-ROM products on health care topics for hospitals, managed care companies, and pharmaceutical companies.

Technical Assistance

Consultation on development and production of video and CD-ROM products.

■ Longe Life Libraries

730 Waukegan Rd, Ste 110
Deerfield, IL 60015
Contact: Michelle Morrissey
847-948-9279
Fax: 847-948-9280
E-mail: longelife@aol.com
Web site: http://www.longelife.com

For-profit company whose purpose is to provide reliable health and lifestyle information for consumers. Two objectives of the company are: to review and track all print, audiovisual, and electronic media; and to establish resource centers that offer easy and appropriate access to credible consumer health information. These resource centers are in every state located in health care organizations, businesses, churches, drugstores, and schools.

Clearinghouse or Resource Center

Longe Life Libraries Health Resource Center: 847-948-9279; database of more than 15,000 reviewed and annotated health items on wellness, disease management, prevention, lifestyle; all available for purchase.

Consumer or Patient Education Materials

Core Collections™ Libraries, comprehensive focused collection of resources includes: Core Reference Collection, Core Wellness Collection, Cancer Collection, Mature Health Collection, Core Woman Collections, $495. Materials can be customized; Low literacy; Please contact for complete catalog.

Publications for Health Professionals

Longe Life Latest, quarterly newsletter, listings of new materials, $29/yr. Please contact for complete publications list.

Classes and Conferences

Designing a Resource Center, 2 hrs, 4 hrs, or full day, provides overview or complete explanation of setting up and managing a resource center; Among the Stacks, 1 or 2 hrs, to motivate consumers to take charge of their health. Please contact for complete list and schedule.

Technical Assistance

Consultation on design of fully functioning resource centers; service in all aspects of operations, acquisition of media, management, maintenance, marketing of consumer-oriented resource center.

Other Products and Services

KeepTrack™ Library Management Software, designed especially for program managers or volunteers, $149; Space Saver Portable Resource Center, 4-panel 6-ft long, 44-in high table-top display, $3,295, materials sold separately.

■ Mayo Clinic Health Information

200 First St SW
Rochester, MN 55905

Contact: Mike Casey or Dan Newton
800-430-9699
Fax: 507-284-5410

Division of the Mayo Clinic that produces consumer health publications including newsletters, booklets, books, and CD-ROMs, providing people with timely, reliable, and easy-to-understand health, wellness, and self-care information. Materials appropriate for health promotion initiatives.

Electronic Information Resources
Mayo Health Oasis online health information web site, http://www.mayo.ivi.com

Consumer or Patient Education Materials
Mayo Clinic Family Health Book, 1,300 pp book, comprehensive guide, $40; Mayo Clinic Health Letter, monthly newsletter, $24/yr; Mayo Clinic Health Letter Booklets, practical information in important health areas. Please contact for volume discounts and complete catalog.

■ Medical Data Source

5959 W Century Blvd, Ste 1000
Los Angeles, CA 90045
Contact: Scott Dustin
800-998-4637
310-641-3111
Fax: 310-641-0335
E-mail: mds@mdsdata.com
Web site: http://www.mdsdata.com

For-profit organization that provides printed health and medical information to health care consumers. Patient education programs are tailored to fit the needs of managed care organizations, corporations, or individuals. Information is available on everything from the common cold to a rare disease.

Other Products and Services
Individual or corporate membership allows access to Health and Medical Information Database containing 750 diagnostic-specific overviews; prescription drug information; comprehensive reports; self-care handbook; and monthly newsletter. Please contact for complete information.

■ Park Nicollet HealthSource

3800 Park Nicollet Blvd
Minneapolis, MN 55416
Contact: Scott Laurent, Sales
800-372-7776
Fax: 612-993-1840

Nonprofit organization, a part of the Institute for Education and Research HealthSystem Minnesota, that develops and produces health promotion publications in self-care, health care consumerism, chronic conditions, and lifestyle education.

Consumer or Patient Education Materials
Well Advised, book, covers adult and child self-care for over 80 conditions; and coordinated brochures, video and instructor guide; A Primer for Prevention, book; WellTimes, quarterly newsmagazine. Pricing varies upon quantity ordered. Materials can be customized; Please contact for complete catalog.

■ Performance Resource Press Inc

1270 Rankin St, Ste F
Troy, MI 48083
Contact: Nancy Rodgers
800-453-7733
800-499-5718 (toll-free fax) (in-state)
810-588-7733
Fax: 810-588-6633

Behavioral health care publishing and communications company dedicated to improving human performance and health; provides prevention materials for safe schools, communities, and workplace programs.

Consumer or Patient Education Materials
Employee assistance posters; Helping Hand pamphlets on 40 different behavioral health topics; Health Sentry, quarterly employee/patient newsletter. Materials can be customized; Please contact for complete catalog.

■ Planetree Health Library

2040 Webster St
San Francisco, CA 94115
415-923-3680

Nonprofit consumer-oriented resource that houses a medical library open to the public. Provides information on all health topics including self-care, complementary, and alternative approaches to healing.

Consumer or Patient Education Materials
Personalized packets of information available for a fee. Please contact for pricing and complete information.

■ Princeton Health Systems Inc

9 Mercer St
Princeton, NJ 08540
Contact: Beth Young
800-437-6668
609-924-7799
Fax: 609-497-0739
E-mail: byoung23@aol.com

Consulting firm that offers a single source for multiple health promotion and disease prevention materials and services nationwide.

Consumer or Patient Education Materials
Various materials available from many vendors; prices same as or up to 5% below list price from vendor. Materials can be customized; Low literacy; Spanish languages available. Please contact for complete catalog.
Publications for Health Professionals
Various materials available from many vendors; prices same as or up to 5% below list price from vendor. Please contact for complete publications list.
Technical Assistance
Consultation for health promotion design.
Other Products and Services
Health risk intervention programs; health screening services, flu shots.

■ Pritchett & Hull Associates Inc

3440 Oakcliff Rd NE, Ste 110
Atlanta, GA 30340-3079
800-241-4925 (Order Dept)
770-451-0602
Fax: 770-454-7130
Web site: http://www.p-h.com/

Publisher and producer of unique patient education materials that are known for clear, simple illustrations, easy reading level, humor, and "down-home" warmth and support. Materials include pamphlets, books, slides, and newsletter.

Consumer or Patient Education Materials
Various materials including books: Ready to Quit, tips on becoming a nonsmoker, $3.15; Wake Up Call, reducing risks for a heart attack, $2; Take Charge of Your Health, prevention tool for women, $1.95. Materials can be customized; Low literacy; Please contact for complete catalog.
Publications for Health Professionals
The PEN, quarterly newsletter, current issues in patient education for patient educators, $28. Please contact for complete publications list.

■ Rutherford Publishing Inc

4567 Lakeshore Dr
PO Box 8853
Waco, TX 76714
Contact: Ronnie Marroquin
800-815-2323
817-751-1194
Fax: 817-751-7698
E-mail: rpublish@rpublish.com
Web site: http://www.rpublish.com

Publisher of monthly newsletter, Total Wellness®, which encourages individuals to set goals and take action in key areas of life, including family, physical, mental, financial, ethical, and social.

Consumer or Patient Education Materials
Total Wellness®, monthly newsletter, $25/yr. Materials can be customized.

■ Scott Publishing Inc (Personal Best)

420 Fifth Ave S, Ste D
Edmonds, WA 98020-3464
Contact: Julie Downs
800-888-7853
206-775-8777
Fax: 206-775-8250
E-mail: info@personalbest.com
Web site: http://www.personalbest.com

Publisher of newsletters who creates original articles and illustrations designed to motivate healthy lifestyle changes and reduce inappropriate use of the health care system.

Consumer or Patient Education Materials
Personal Best, 8 pp monthly, for general audience; Well & Wise, 8 pp monthly, for seniors/retirees; Live It Up!, 4 pp quarterly, low-literacy version; Viva Bien, quarterly, in Spanish; all newsletters covering varied topics. Pricing varies upon quantity ordered and all can be customized. Please contact for complete information.

■ Vitality Inc

8080 N Central Exwy, Ste 1510
Dallas, TX 75206
Contact: Steve Schaul
800-554-0015
214-573-6500
Fax: 214-573-6510
Web site: http://www.vitality.com

Publisher specializing in tools and services designed to promote better health and productivity.

Electronic Information Resources
Vitality-on-Demand: 800-863-7736, free service to subscribers to order documents by fax.
Consumer or Patient Education Materials
Vitality Magazine, monthly, health and wellness information; Book of Vitality, manual, self-care reference guide; Vitality brochures on 16 topics.

Materials can be customized; Low literacy; Please contact for pricing and complete information.

Publications for Health Professionals

Workplace Vitality, 10 times/yr newsletter, for human resource professionals, $59/yr.

■ Your HealthStyle

5009 N Pennsylvania, Ste 114
Oklahoma City, OK 73112
Contact: Cindy Sheffield
800-214-1156
405-843-4310
Fax: 405-843-1265
E-mail: yhs@oklahoma.net
Web site: http://www.oklahoma.net/~yhs

Publisher of Your HealthStyle health awareness newsletter—an effective tool for communicating health and wellness information through corporate, hospital, or community wellness programs.

Consumer or Patient Education Materials

Your HealthStyle, monthly newsletter, includes health, safety and wellness information; Senior version available quarterly; both can be customized. Pricing varies upon quantity ordered. Please contact for complete information.

ADDITIONAL RESOURCES

■ Avery Publishing Group

120 Old Broadway
Garden City Park, NY 11040
800-548-5757
516-741-2155
Fax: 516-742-1892

■ Chiltern Hills Wellness

2930 Anthony Ln
PO Box 18067
Minneapolis, MN 55418
Contact: Kurt Swanson
612-789-7861
Fax: 612-781-3525
E-mail: 102234,1735@compuserve.com

■ Courier Communications

1260 Winchester Park, Ste 122
Smyrna, GA 30080-6546
800-222-1849 (Order Dept)
Fax: 770-801-9831 (Orders)

■ Education Programs Associates

Bldg D, Rm 40
One W Campbell Ave
Campbell, CA 95008
408-374-3720
Fax: 408-374-7385

■ First Marketing Company

3300 Gateway Dr
Pompano Beach, FL 33069
Contact: Mark A Boline, Director, Health Care Publications
800-641-9251
954-979-0700
Fax: 954-971-4707
E-mail: MBoline@First-Marketing.com

■ Health Edco

A Division of WRS Group Inc
PO Box 21207
Waco, TX 76702-1207
800-299-3366 x295
Fax: 817-751-0221
E-mail: sales@wrsgroup.com
Web site: http://www.wrsgroup.com

■ Krames Communications

1100 Grundy Ln
San Bruno, CA 94066-3030
800-333-3032 (Order Dept)
415-742-0400
Fax: 415-244-4512

■ Milner-Fenwick Inc

2125 Greenspring Dr
Timonium, MD 21093
800-432-8433
301-252-1700
Fax: 301-252-6316

■ Mosby Consumer Health Division

8910 SW Gemini Dr
Beaverton, OR 97008
Contact: Tom Hatcher, Product Manager, 503-520-2160
800-729-5285 (Order Dept)
503-520-9550
Fax: 503-520-0985
E-mail: tom.hatcher@mosby.com
Web site: http://www.mosby.com

■ **National Health Enhancement Systems**
3200 N Central Ave, #1700
Phoenix, AZ 85012-2437
Contact: Marketing Dept
800-345-3342
602-230-7575
Fax: 602-274-6158

■ **National Institute for Healthcare Research**
6110 Executive Blvd, Ste 908
Rockville, MD 20852
301-984-7162
Fax: 301-984-8143

■ **Nidus Information Services**
175 Fifth Ave, Ste 2338
New York, NY 10010
899-334-WELL (899-334-9355)
212-260-4268
Fax: 212-529-2349
E-mail: Nidus@aol.com

■ **Parlay International**
5900 Hollis St, Ste Q
PO Box 8871
Emeryville, CA 94662-0817
800-457-2752
510-601-1000
Fax: 510-601-1008

■ **Positive Promotions**
40-01 168th St
Flushing, NY 11358
800-635-2666
718-858-4199
Fax: 800-635-2329

■ **Wellness Associates**
21489 Orr Springs Rd
Ukiah, CA 95482
Mailing Address:
Box 5433
Mill Valley, CA 94942
415-383-3806
E-mail: wa@thewellspring.org
Web site: http://www.thewellspring.org

■ **Whole Person Associates**
210 West Michigan
Duluth, MN 55802-1908
800-247-6789
Fax: 218-727-0505
E-mail: books@wholeperson.com
Web site: http://www.wholeperson.com

FEDERAL AGENCIES

■ **Consumer Information Center (CIC)**
18th and F Streets NW, Rm G142
Washington, DC 20405
202-501-1794
Fax: 202-501-4281

Distributes publications on topics such as prenatal care, parenting, nutrition, exercise, weight control, and child safety. Offers the Consumer Information Catalog and a list of Federal Information Centers. Publications are available at the center or from Consumer Information Catalog, Pueblo, CO 81009, 719-948-4000.

■ **Office of Alternative Medicine (OAM)**
National Institutes of Health (NIH)
Bldg 31, Rm 5B-38
9000 Rockville Pike
Bethesda, MD 20892
301-402-2466
Fax: 301-402-4741

Office of Alternative Medicine's Clearinghouse
PO Box 8218
Silver Spring, MD 20907-8218
888-644-6226; Fax: 301-495-4957

Established to support research to evaluate alternative medical practices and to determine their effectiveness, and to help integrate effective treatments into mainstream medical practice. It does not provide referrals and cannot advise patients about specific alternative therapies. The Clearinghouse serves as an information resource for alternative and conventional practitioners and members of the public seeking further information.

Health Assessments

Organization	web site	hotline/toll-free information line	clearinghouse/resource center	electronic information resources	database/statistical information	special campaigns/events/programs	consumer/patient education materials	publications for health professionals	classes/conferences	technical assistance	other products/services	grants/funding/awards	Page No.
American Hospital Association	■							■					35
Check Up Centers of America	■									■	■		35
Computerized Health Systems Inc											■		35
EMC^2	■									■			35
Felix, Burdine and Associates Inc	■				■					■			35
Greenstone Healthcare Solutions	■									■			36
Health Evaluation Systems Inc										■			36
Health Examinetics Inc										■			36
Health First Consulting Corporation										■			36
Healthier People Network Inc									■	■			36
Healthier People Software							■			■	■		36
Human Resources Institute Inc	■									■			37
Johnson Institute	■									■			37
MicroFit	■										■		37
National Association of School Nurses	■							■					37
National Wellness Institute Inc	■									■			38
Network Health Systems™										■	■		38
Princeton Health Systems Inc										■			38
Society for Healthcare Strategy and Market Development								■					38
StayWell Health Management Systems Inc										■			38
Strategic Marketing Group Inc										■			39

Products/Services Offered

Organization	web site	hotline/toll-free information line	clearinghouse/resource center	electronic information resources	database/statistical information	special campaigns/events/programs	consumer/patient education materials	publications for health professionals	classes/conferences	technical assistance	other products/services	grants/funding/awards	Page No.
Summex Corporation	■									■			39
TriHealth Preventive Health Systems										■			39
Tyler Norris Associates								■	■	■			39
Wellsource Inc	■									■			39

Additional Resources 40

Federal Agencies 41

■ American Hospital Association

One North Franklin
Chicago, IL 60606
Contact: Publications, 800-242-2626
312-422-3000
Web site: http://www.amhpi.com

National membership organization of individuals and health care institutions dedicated to promoting the welfare of the public through its leadership and assistance to its members in the provision of better health services for all people.

Publications for Health Professionals

Community Health Assessment: A New Generation, report, provides new strategies, $110; Community Assessment: A Model "How-To" Based on Two Communities' Experience, 6 pp booklet, $15. Please contact for complete publications list.

■ Check Up Centers of America

26565 W Agoura Rd, Ste 300
Calabasas, CA 91302-1984
Contact: Patricia Johnson
800-894-2426
818-878-2330
Fax: 818-880-8045
Web site: http://www.lifelines.com

National for-profit organization offering employers and insurers a basic health assessment and screening capability to increase awareness of health status and promote healthy habits. Screenings can be conducted in community or worksites; attendees receive a 6-page report from a computerized health risk appraisal summarizing their health status and biometrics information.

Technical Assistance

Design and develop relevant health assessment programs that meet requirements of the payer for organizations of 500 or more. Please contact for complete information.

Other Products and Services

Interface with nurse call lines regarding output of reports taken at health screenings available; Global fee for all services combined can be quoted. Please contact for complete information.

■ Computerized Health Systems Inc

4775 Tait Rd
Dayton, OH 45429
Contact: Richard L Miller MD, President
937-298-8641
Fax: 937-298-8641
E-mail: drrmilr@aol.com

Small healthware vendor of medical information software.

Other Products and Services

MedWare™ Windows-based software program allowing limitless analysis and classification; contains modules for health risk analysis, personal medical history, interval medical history, breast cancer occurrence risk.

■ EMC² (Employee Managed Care Corporation)

701 Fifth Ave, Ste 2600
Seattle, WA 98104-7015
Contact: Sales Dept, 800-927-9225
800-755-2136
206-749-1100
Fax: 206-749-1125
E-mail: emc2@emcsquared.com
Web site: http://www.emcsquared.com

For-profit company offering a full range of cost saving solutions for health care benefit providers. Programs educate, motivate, and empower members to make better use of the health care system from prenatal care to chronic disease management.

Technical Assistance

LivingWise™, lifestyle risk assessment and behavior modification program.

■ Felix, Burdine and Associates Inc

5100 Tilghman St, Ste 215
Allentown, PA 18104-9102
Contact: Yvette Musselman, Office Manager
610-366-1310
Fax: 610-366-1322
Web site: http://felixburdine.com

National for-profit community health development company dedicated to teaching communities how to plan, develop, and implement community health status improvement interventions. Utilizes the techniques of community organization, health status assessment, and is founded on community health development principles.

Database or Statistical Information

The National Health Survey©, report and data that detail the results of survey of a national sample of U.S. adults in the areas of functional status, access to care, preventive service utilization, and community issues. $295.

Technical Assistance

Consulting services in the area of community partnership development, community health status assessment, health status improvement initiatives, and strategic planning.

■ Greenstone Healthcare Solutions

7000 Portage Rd
Kalamazoo, MI 49001
Contact: Cindy Casserly
800-947-3367
616-833-1221
Fax: 616-833-0371
E-mail: cindycasserly@am.pnu.com
Web site: http://www.ghsnet.com/

Comprehensive disease management consulting company that works with managed care organizations, providers, and employers to identify and target clinical process or evidence-based outcome improvement project and provide systematic solutions.

Technical Assistance

You First™, health risk assessment, cost varies upon volume.

■ Health Evaluation Systems Inc

2620 Thousand Oaks Blvd, Ste 2300
Memphis, TN 38118
Contact: Ross Ose
800-318-0429
Fax: 901-368-4333

For-profit company that offers preventive services including drug and alcohol testing, health risks appraisals, behavior modification programs, physical examinations, and medical surveillance.

Technical Assistance

Health risk assessments available.

■ Health Examinetics Inc

10920 Via Frontera
San Diego, CA 92127-1704
Contact: Bruce H Meyer, 800-232-2332 x312
800-232-2332
619-485-0933
Fax: 619-485-8133
E-mail: lowercosts@healthex.com

For-profit company providing health services nationwide. Programs are designed to assist corporations, labor, governmental agencies, school districts, and associations in controlling health care costs.

Technical Assistance

Consulting; risk rating programs; health risk assessments.

■ Health First Consulting Corporation

4040 Vincennes Cir, Ste 600
Indianapolis, IN 46268
Contact: Monica Earlywine
317-879-4188
Fax: 317-879-4049

National consulting company that specializes in comprehensive worksite health promotion programs.

Technical Assistance

Consulting services for planning and implementing worksite health promotion programs including health risk assessments, on-site seminars, customized newsletters.

■ Healthier People Network Inc

1549 Clairmont Rd, Ste 205
Decatur, GA 30033-4636
Contact: Dr. Edwin B Hutchins
404-636-3127
Fax: 404-636-0105

Nonprofit organization committed to empowering individuals to take responsibility for their own health and well-being by using a computerized instrument known as the Health Risk Appraisal. The organization continues the work that Dr. Hutchins directed for the Centers for Disease Control Health Risk Appraisal update.

Classes and Conferences

Co-sponsor of Society of Prospective Medicine annual meeting, held in conjunction with meetings of the American College of Preventive Medicine and the Association of Teachers of Preventive Medicine.

Technical Assistance

Healthier People Network Health Risk Appraisal, includes computer software, supporting book and manual, and supplementary materials, $195 initial membership. Training workshops, support service for implementation, customization of software, and presentations to groups also available.

■ Healthier People Software

2161 Spring Meade Cove
Germantown, TN 38139

Mailing Address:
PO Box 38623
Memphis, TN 38183-0623
Contact: Joe Hogan
800-256-1953
901-751-4136
404-872-2100
Fax: 901-751-3107

For-profit company providing health risk assessments and nutrition assessments to hospitals, universities, employers, and public health agencies. Provides support services for implementation, including program design, evaluation, and customization.

Consumer or Patient Education Materials
QuickQuest brochures and pamphlets on a selection of wellness topics. Materials can be customized; Please contact for complete catalog.

Technical Assistance
Consulting provided for program customization.

Other Products and Services
Health Risk Appraisal, software to produce health risk appraisals, $295. Nutritional Health Assessment reports, $10 each for processing.

■ Human Resources Institute Inc

115 Dunder Rd
Burlington, VT 05401
Contact: Judd Allen
800-800-3004
802-862-8855
Fax: 802-862-6389
E-mail: allenjudd@aol.com
Web site: http://members.aol.com/allenjudd/webpage.htm

Consulting firm that works to empower individuals, groups, and organizations, to take charge of their cultures. Provides the tools to create supportive cultural environments.

Technical Assistance
Lifegain Health Culture Audit, survey designed to assess how supportive a culture is of healthy lifestyle choices.

■ Johnson Institute

7205 Ohms Ln
Minneapolis, MN 55439-2159
Contact: Dee Stuart
800-231-5165
612-831-1630
Fax: 612-831-1631
E-mail: info@johnsoninstitute.com
Web site: http://www.johnsoninstitute.com

For-profit organization that provides products and services to schools, families, organizations, and communities to prevent and intervene with problems such as alcohol and drug abuse, violence, suicide, and emotional stress.

Technical Assistance
Behavioral health survey measuring organizational risk for 24 factors; Student survey measuring school's risk for alcohol, drugs, violence, and other factors.

■ MicroFit

1077B Independence Ave
Mountain View, CA 94043
Contact: Dave Finsthwait
800-822-0405
415-969-7296
Fax: 415-969-2067
E-mail: wavy@microfit.com
Web site: http://www.microfit.com

Manufacturer of an interactive, online fitness assessment system featuring real-time super VGA graphic displays, Polar heart-rate monitor, and simplified menu-driven operation.

Other Products and Services
Completely self-contained system that evaluates body fat, strength, flexibility, heart rate, blood pressure, and cardiovascular condition. Supplemental software programs include: client contact and database management; group reports; wellness assessments; exercise plans; and nutritional assessments. Please contact for complete information and pricing.

■ National Association of School Nurses

PO Box 1300
Scarborough, ME 04070-1300
Contact: Judy Barker
207-883-2117
Fax: 207-883-2683
E-mail: nasn@aol.com
Web site: http://www.vrmedia.com/nurses/

Nonprofit organization whose mission is to advance the practice of school nursing and provide leadership in the delivery of quality health programs to the school community.

Publications for Health Professionals
Quality Nursing Intervention in the School Setting, 600 pp manual, includes physical assessment criteria, $95; Vision Screening Guidelines, Hearing Screening Guidelines, and Postural Screening Guildelines, $11 each.

■ National Wellness Institute Inc

1045 Clark St, Ste 210
PO Box 827
Stevens Point, WI 54481-0827
Contact: Krista Wittkopf
800-243-8694
715-342-2969
Fax: 715-342-2979
E-mail: nwi@wellnessnwi.org
Web site: http://www.wellnessnwi.org/

Nonprofit organization whose mission is to help individuals lead better lives by serving a worldwide network of health promotion and wellness professionals and organizations by providing professional education; furnishing information and resources; developing and distributing wellness-related products and services, research, and national and international leadership. The National Wellness Association is the membership division of the Institute.

Technical Assistance

TestWell®: Health Risk Appraisal and LifeStyle Assessment, software programs; TestWell®: Wellness Inventory, self-scoring assessment tool.

■ Network Health Systems™

89 Centennial Trail
Bozeman, MT 59715
Contact: James P Bangs
800-942-8391
406-587-7740
Fax: 406-587-7740
E-mail: nhsjim@aol.com

National for-profit consulting firm that provides health risk assessments and other services to individuals, organizations, providers, and risk bearers.

Technical Assistance

Health risk assessments covering illness and premature death caused by 52 diseases or conditions; predictions based on 44 risks (stressors) and analyzed; consultation to plan interventions and follow-up to high risk individuals.

Other Products and Services

Health fairs; education materials; program provider screening for intervention; coordinating blood tests and education programs for employee groups. Costs vary depending on services requested. Contact for complete information.

■ Princeton Health Systems Inc

9 Mercer St
Princeton, NJ 08540
Contact: Beth Young
800-437-6668
609-924-7799
Fax: 609-497-0739
E-mail: byoung23@aol.com

Consulting firm that offers a single source for multiple health promotion and disease prevention materials and services nationwide.

Technical Assistance

Offers a wide range of health risk questionnaires and software products available from many vendors; consultation to compare and select the best options and pilot program allowing test runs; generally, discounts offered on software, processing, and paper products.

■ Society for Healthcare Strategy and Market Development

One North Franklin
Chicago, IL 60606
Contact: Publications, 800-242-2626
312-422-3738
Fax: 312-422-4577

Personal membership group of the American Hospital Association and is the largest health care strategic planning, marketing, communications, and business development organization of its kind in the nation. Committed to helping members and their organizations work to improve the health status and quality of life in their communities.

Publications for Health Professionals

Community Health Assessment: A New Generation, report, $110; Background and Resources for a Community Health Status Focus, book, $40, Community Assessment: A "How-To" Based on Two Communities' Experience, booklet, $15. Please contact for complete publications list.

■ StayWell Health Management Systems Inc

1340 Mendota Heights Rd
St Paul, MN 55120-1128
Contact: Lynn Henry
800-373-3577
612-454-3577
Fax: 612-454-4062

National for-profit provider of employee assistance and wellness programs to corporations, helping employers encourage healthier, more productive employees while controlling the costs of health care.

Technical Assistance
Health risk assessments include Health Path, lifestyle assessment; Health Step, instant lifestyle assessment; Health Share, chronic disease and lifestyle assessment for managed care.

■ Strategic Marketing Group Inc
3801 E Florida Ave, Ste 400
Denver, CO 80210
Contact: David C Franzblau
800-733-1530
303-759-1610
Fax: 303-759-2010
E-mail: 76530.1417@compuserve.com

Consulting firm that provides health care organizations with market analysis, marketing, and strategic planning services. Offers computerized data mapping for health-related problem analysis and community needs analyses as special areas of expertise.

Technical Assistance
Consulting services spanning the full range of market analysis, new service planning, and program development. Experts in ambulatory care, emergency health services, and geographic data analysis.

■ Summex Corporation
1099 N Meridian St, Ste 920
Indianapolis, IN 46204
Contact: Lisa A Zigler
800-884-5044
317-630-3456
Fax: 317-630-3450
E-mail: summex@summex.com
Web site: http://www.in.net/summex

Consulting firm whose mission is to be the nation's premier provider of integrated demand management products and services that maximize each individual's personal health management knowledge, skills, and motivation.

Technical Assistance
Consulting services; Comprevent, non-worksite based health management system combines HRA, serial feedback, medical self-care book, monthly newsletter, and at risk health counseling; Summex Health Monitor and Health Monitor Checkup, morbidity-based HRA available in several versions, including Spanish and Senior, and serial feedback tool.

■ TriHealth Preventive Health Systems
8044 Montgomery Rd, Ste 525
Cincinnati, OH 45236
Contact: Pamela J Clark
518-891-1622
Fax: 518-891-7286

International nonprofit consulting firm whose purpose is to optimize the health status of the individuals, organizations, and populations it serves with an emphasis on prevention, education, and positive lifestyle interventions.

Technical Assistance
Consulting services including identification of risks.

■ Tyler Norris Associates
2119 Mapleton Ave
Boulder, CO 80304
303-444-3366
Fax: 303-444-1001
E-mail: tnorris@ncl.org

Consulting firm that provides consultation to communities and organizations to improve community health and long term sustainability.

Publications for Health Professionals
Healthy Community Handbook, book, resource to community catalysts; You Get What You Measure, book, measuring community health.
Classes and Conferences
Healthy Communities; Health Indicators. Please contact for complete information.
Technical Assistance
Community indicators and benchmarking.

■ Wellsource Inc
15431 SE 82nd Dr, Ste D
PO Box 569
Clackamas, OR 97015
Contact: Area sales representative
800-533-9355
503-656-7446
Fax: 503-650-0880
E-mail: well@wellsource-in.com
Web site: http://www.wellsource-inc.com

International consulting firm that develops software systems, health risk appraisals (HRA); offers training and support for managing risk factors, tracking health outcomes; and serves health promotion professionals.

Technical Assistance

The Personal Wellness Profile, comprehensive health risk assessment and information management system; many other HRAs available; consulting services and software customization services.

ADDITIONAL RESOURCES

■ Eris Survey Systems Inc
6363 Hollister Dr
Indianapolis, IN 46224
Contact: Bruce Sturgill, Director of Marketing
317-290-8322
Fax: 317-290-8333
E-mail: erismail@erisinfo.com
Web site: http://www.erisinfo.com

■ HCIA—Response
1485 S County Trail
East Greenwich, RI 02818
Contact: Sales Dept
800-522-1440
401-885-6900
Fax: 401-885-6905
E-mail: info@hcia.com
Web site: http://www.hcia.com

■ Health Management Research Center
University of Michigan
401 Washtenaw Ave
Ann Arbor, MI 48109-2214
313-763-2462
Fax: 313-763-2206
Web site: http://www.umich.edu/~hmrc/

■ Health Management Resources
59 Temple Pl, Ste 704
Boston, MA 02111-9980
Contact: Corporate Health Services
800-977-9876
617-357-9876
Fax: 617-357-9690

■ Information Transfer Systems Inc
209 E Washington, Ste 200
Ann Arbor, MI 48104
Contact: Bruce M Brock PhD
313-994-0003
Fax: 313-994-1128

■ Institute for Alternative Futures
100 N Pitt St, Ste 235
Alexandria, VA 22314
Contact: Kathy Scott, Marketing Coordinator
703-684-5880
Fax: 703-684-0640
E-mail: futures@altfutures.com
Web site: http://www.altfutures.com

■ Johnson and Johnson Health Care Systems Inc
425 Hoes Ln
Piscataway, NJ 08855
Contact: Health Management Division, 800-443-3682
908-562-3000
Fax: 908-562-3092

■ Premier
PO Box 668800
Charlotte, NC 28266-8800
Contact: Laura Yandell, Corporate Communications
704-529-3300
Fax: 704-527-3654

■ Prospective Medicine Center
6220 Lawrence Dr
Indianapolis, IN 46226
Contact: Pamela Hall
800-418-9482
317-549-3600
Fax: 317-549-3670

■ U.S. Conference of Local Health Officers
1620 Eye St, Ste 400
Washington, DC 20006
202-293-7330
Fax: 202-293-2352
Web site: http://www.usmayors.org/uscm

■ VHA Inc
Community Health Improvement
220 East Las Colinas Blvd
Irving, TX 75039-5500
Mailing Address:
PO Box 140909
Irving, TX 75014-0909
Contact: Deborah A Stewart, Program Manager
800-468-6842
972-830-0077
Fax: 972-830-0332
Web site: http://www.vha.com

FEDERAL AGENCIES

■ **National Center for Health Statistics (NCHS)**
Centers for Disease Control and Prevention
6525 Belcrest Rd, Rm 1064
Hyattsville, MD 20782
301-436-8500
E-mail: nchsquery@nch20a.em.cdc.gov
Web site: http://www.cdc.gov/nchswww/nchshome.htm

Collects, analyzes, and disseminates data on health in the U.S. to guide actions and policies to improve the health of Americans. Findings from surveys conducted are released in the Vital and Health Statistics series and the Advanced Data series. Much of the data collected and compiled is indexed in the National Technical Information Service database, available online through DIALOG and BRS. Publications are available in electronic format from the NCHS homepage, the Government Printing Office, and/or the National Technical Information Service.

Mental Health and Mental Disorders

Products/Services Offered

Organization	web site	hotline/toll-free information line	clearinghouse/resource center	electronic information resources	database/statistical information	special campaigns/events/programs	consumer/patient education materials	publications for health professionals	classes/conferences	technical assistance	other products/services	grants/funding/awards	**Page No.**
Mental Health and Mental Illness													
American Association of Suicidology	■						■	■	■				**45**
American Institute for Preventive Medicine	■						■						**45**
American Mental Health Counselors Association	■					■	■	■	■	■			**45**
American Self-Help Clearinghouse	■			■			■	■		■			**46**
American Suicide Foundation		■					■	■				■	**46**
Channing L Bete Co Inc							■						**46**
Clinical Reference Systems Ltd	■										■		**46**
Depression After Delivery Inc (DAD)							■	■					**47**
Geriatric Psychiatry Alliance	■	■					■	■		■			**47**
Health Professions Press								■					**47**
Journeyworks Publishing							■						**47**
Mental Health Materials Center									■	■			**47**
National Community Mental Healthcare Council						■		■		■			**48**
National Depressive and Manic-Depressive Association							■	■		■			**48**
National Foundation for Depressive Illness	■	■					■			■			**48**
National Mental Health Association	■	■	■		■		■	■	■	■			**48**
National Mental Health Consumers' Self-Help Clearinghouse		■					■	■	■	■			**49**
National Mental Health Services Knowledge Exchange Network	■	■		■		■	■	■					**49**

Organization	web site	hotline/toll-free information line	clearinghouse/resource center	electronic information resources	database/statistical information	special campaigns/events/programs	consumer/patient education materials	publications for health professionals	classes/conferences	technical assistance	other products/services	grants/funding/awards	Page No.
Eating Disorders													
Anorexia Nervosa and Related Eating Disorders Inc	■						■		■				**50**
Eating Disorders Awareness and Prevention (EDAP)	■					■	■	■	■				**50**
Gürze Books	■						■						**50**
National Center for Overcoming Overeating							■		■	■			**50**
National Eating Disorders Organization	■						■	■					**51**
Overeaters Anonymous							■	■					**51**
Stress Management													
American Institute for Preventive Medicine	■								■				**51**
The American Institute of Stress	■		■					■	■				**52**
Association for Applied Psychophysiology and Biofeedback	■						■		■	■			**52**
Audio Vision							■	■					**52**
Award-Winning Presentations							■	■	■				**52**
Channing L Bete Co Inc							■						**53**
Human Dynamics Inc									■	■			**53**
National Health Video Inc							■						**53**
Organizational Designs in Communication Inc	■						■		■	■			**53**
PATH Associates									■				**53**
Professional Psychology Services									■				**54**
Additional Resources													**54**
Federal Agencies													**55**

MENTAL HEALTH AND MENTAL ILLNESS

■ American Association of Suicidology

4201 Connecticut Ave NW, Ste 310
Washington, DC 20008
Contact: Amy McDonough
202-237-2280
Fax: 202-237-2282
E-mail: mcdo117w@wonder.em.cdc.gov
Web site: http://www.cyberpsych.org

National nonprofit organization whose goal is to understand and prevent suicide. Serves as a clearinghouse for information and referrals on suicide-related issues.

Consumer or Patient Education Materials
Surviving Suicide, quarterly newsletter, for survivors, support group leaders, and those who have lost a loved one to suicide, $20/yr; Suicide in Youth and What You Can Do About It—A Guide for Students, pamphlet, $7.50/pkg of 25; Suicide of Older Men and Women, pamphlet, first one free, $2/pkg of 10. Please contact for complete catalog.

Publications for Health Professionals
Suicide Prevention/Crisis Intervention Directory, updated every fall, lists more than 600 crisis agencies in U.S. and Canada, $15; Directory of Survivor Support Groups, updated every fall, lists survivor support groups in U.S. and Canada, $7. Please contact for complete publications list.

Classes and Conferences
Annual conference, 4 days, interventions, prevention programs, and research in suicides, $260.

■ American Institute for Preventive Medicine

30445 Northwestern Hwy, Ste 350
Farmington Hills, MI 48334-3102
Contact: Order Dept, 810-539-1800 x239
800-345-2476
810-539-1800
Fax: 810-539-1808
E-mail: aipm@healthy.net
Web site: http://aipm.healthy.net

International for-profit developer and provider of health promotion programs, self-help kits, and self-care publications. Works with over 5,000 corporations, HMOs, and hospitals to reduce health care costs, lower absenteeism, and improve morale. Services include those for self-care, smoking cessation, weight control, stress management, self-esteem enhancement, prenatal education, fitness center management, nutrition, and EAP education.

Consumer or Patient Education Materials
HealthyLife Mental Fitness Guide, 96 pp, self-care guide includes 25 mental health conditions to review; Minding Your Mental Health: A Consumer's Guide, 20 pp booklet, offers answers and helpful information for treatment; Pricing varies upon quantity ordered; Please contact for complete catalog.

■ American Mental Health Counselors Association

801 N Fairfax St, Ste 304
Alexandria, VA 22314
Contact: Lee Davis
800-326-2642
703-548-6002
Fax: 703-548-4775
E-mail: amhcahq@pie.org
Web site: http://pie.org/amhca

Nonprofit professional association for masters and doctoral-level mental health counselors whose purpose is to maintain mental health counseling as a distinct and viable profession within the health care domain. Focuses on state and federal mental health policy; managed care; public awareness; and professional development.

Special Campaigns, Events, or Programs
National Mental Health Counseling Week, 1st week of May, press releases, PSAs, articles, interviews, speakers, posters. Contact PAS Committee Staff.

Consumer or Patient Education Materials
Mental Health Brights, brochures, topics include: eating disorders, conflict resolution, free single copy, $7.50/25. Low literacy; Please contact for complete catalog.

Publications for Health Professionals
AMHCA Advocate, newsletter 8–10 times/yr, free with membership, $25; Journal of Mental Health Counseling, quarterly, free with membership, $61–$119/yr. Please contact for complete publications list.

Classes and Conferences
Call for referral to state chapter for complete information on classes and seminars.

Technical Assistance
Managed care consulting; position papers.

■ American Self-Help Clearinghouse

Northwest Covenant Medical Center
25 Pocono Rd
Denville, NJ 07834-2995
800-367-6274 (in-state)
201-625-7101
201-625-9565
Fax: 201-625-8848
TDD: 201-625-9053
E-mail: ashc@bc.cybernex.net
Web site: http://www.cmhc.com/selfhelp/

National nonprofit organization providing information on national self-help groups dealing with addictions, bereavement, disabilities, health, mental health, parenting, rare disorders, and other issues. Also information on local and state self-help clearinghouses.

Electronic Information Resources
Sourcebook Online, Check web site for lists of toll-free specialty numbers; information on national, state and local self-help groups.

Consumer or Patient Education Materials
Ideas and Considerations, sheet, how-to on starting a self-help group; Self-Help Clearinghouses, sheet, list of local & state clearinghouses; both free with SASE.

Publications for Health Professionals
Self-Help Sourcebook, bi-yearly book, information and contacts on groups, how-to material, $10.

Technical Assistance
If no group or support network exists anywhere for your problem, can provide assistance to help you start one.

■ American Suicide Foundation

120 Wall St, 22nd Fl
New York, NY 10005
Contact: Matthew Nock
800-ASF-4042 (800-273-4042)
212-410-1111
Fax: 212-269-7259

National nonprofit foundation whose purpose is the prevention of suicide through research and education.

Hotline or Toll-free Information Line
American Suicide Foundation Information Line: 800-ASF-4042 (800-273-4042) (M–F 9AM–5PM ET) Operator assisted, referral service, requests for materials.

Consumer or Patient Education Materials
What To Do If You Suspect A Loved One May Be Contemplating Suicide, pamphlet, single copy free.

Publications for Health Professionals
Lifesavers, quarterly, newsletter, free with membership; ASF National Directory of Survivor Support Groups, $23. Please contact for complete publications list.

Grants, Funding, or Awards
Funds for research in area of suicide and related topics. Contact by mail or phone for application and guidelines.

■ Channing L Bete Co Inc

200 State Rd
S Deerfield, MA 01373-0200
800-628-7733 (Sales and Customer Service)
413-665-7611
Fax: 800-499-6464

Publisher of informational and educational booklets, videos, posters, calendars, books, and display racks. Booklets use a distinctive, condensed format—called scriptography—which combines key words and graphics to explain a variety of subjects and is appropriate for different age groups and reading levels.

Consumer or Patient Education Materials
Booklets and videos. Topics include: anger, anorexia nervosa, bulimia, depression, suicide. Some Spanish language available. Please contact for pricing and ask for the Patient Education catalog.

■ Clinical Reference Systems Ltd

7100 E Belleview Ave, Ste 208
Greenwood Village, CO 80111-1635
Contact: Ellen Graves, Marketing Coordinator
800-237-8401
303-220-1661
Fax: 303-220-1685
E-mail: crs-info@cliniref.com
Web site: http://www.patienteducation.com

Publisher of patient education and clinical reference software for the international healthcare community. Committed to development of computer-based health information to enhance communication between provider and patient. More than 30,000 programs are now at work in physician offices, clinics, hospitals, medical school residency programs, occupational clinics, medical and consumer libraries.

Other Products and Services
Behavioral Health Advisor software program, customized patient information handouts covering adult mental illness, disorders, and behavioral problems. Please contact for pricing and complete information.

■ Depression After Delivery Inc (DAD)

PO Box 1282
Morrisville, PA 19067
800-944-4PPD (800-944-4773)
215-295-3994

National nonprofit organization provides support, education, and referral for women and families coping with mood disorders associated with childbearing.

Consumer or Patient Education Materials
Information packet contains information on pregnancy and postpartum disorders, professional referral list, list of volunteer telephone contacts and support groups.
Publications for Health Professionals
Heart Strings, quarterly newsletter, $30.

■ Geriatric Psychiatry Alliance

1201 Connecticut Ave, #300
Washington, DC 20036
888-463-6472
301-654-7850
Fax: 202-835-8891
E-mail: aagpgpa@aol.com
Web site: http://www.aagpgpa.org

Nonprofit educational program of the American Association of Geriatric Psychiatry whose mission is to raise awareness of psychiatric disorders affecting the elderly by educating primary care physicians, other providers of health care services, policy makers, and consumers.

Hotline or Toll-free Information Line
Geriatric Psychiatry Alliance Information Line: 888-INFO-GPA (888-463-6472) (M–F 8AM–10PM ET) Operator assisted, referral service, requests for information.
Consumer or Patient Education Materials
Depression in Late Life: Not a Natural Part of Aging, brochure, comprehensive consumer education information, free. Please contact for complete catalog.
Publications for Health Professionals
Diagnosis and Treatment of Late-Life Depression: Making a Difference, 23 pp monograph, designed primarily for primary care physicians, free. Please contact for complete publications list.
Technical Assistance
Speakers bureau.

■ Health Professions Press

409 Washington Ave, Ste 500
Baltimore, MD 21204
Mailing Address:
PO Box 10624
Baltimore, MD 21285
410-337-9585
Fax: 410-337-8539
E-mail: hpp@pbrookes.com

Publisher of professional references and textbooks on long-term care, gerontology, and health adminstration, plus practical resources for nursing home staff, caregivers, and other service providers.

Publications for Health Professionals
Developing Support Groups for Individuals with Early-Stage Alzheimer's Disease: Planning, Implementation, and Evaluation, book, $27. Please contact for complete publications list.

■ Journeyworks Publishing

736 Chestnut St
Santa Cruz, CA 95060
Mailing Address:
PO Box 8466
Santa Cruz, CA 95061-8466
800-775-1998
408-423-1400
Fax: 408-423-8102

Publisher of health promotion materials for clinics, hospitals, schools, and health departments covering a variety of topics including fitness, women's health, sexual abstinence, teen pregnancy prevention, STDs and HIV, mental wellness, tobacco use prevention, and smoking cessation.

Consumer or Patient Education Materials
Dealing with Depression; Asking For Help; When You Feel Lonely; pamphlets, free review sample, pricing varies upon quantity ordered. Materials can be customized; Please contact for complete catalog.

■ Mental Health Materials Center

PO Box 304
Bronxville, NY 10708
Contact: Alex Sareyan, 914-337-6596
914-337-6596

Nonprofit organization dedicated to facilitating the effective dissemination and utilization of the best available health and mental health education aids, and provides publishing and marketing assistance to nonprofit or governmental agencies.

Classes and Conferences
Stigma and Mental Illness seminars, 2½ days conducted regionally, skills enhancement for persons responsible for mental health information and education. Please contact for complete list and schedule.
Technical Assistance
Consultation services to agencies in developing and marketing educational resources, particularly publications.

■ National Community Mental Healthcare Council

12300 Twinbrook Pkwy, Ste 320
Rockville, MD 20852
301-984-6200
E-mail: ncmhchq@pie.org

Nonprofit organization representing direct care providers, state associations, public authorities, integrated service networks and associations. Provides public policy information, legislative advocacy, managed care technical assistance, and training products and services to assist and equip members for health care reform.

Special Campaigns, Events, or Programs
Mental Health Month, May, promotional kit includes background information, press releases, fact sheets, PSAs.
Publications for Health Professionals
National Council News, 11 times yearly, newsletter, current information, $40/yr. Please contact for complete publications list.
Technical Assistance
Managed care consulting service available.

■ National Depressive and Manic-Depressive Association

700 N Franklin St, Ste 501
Chicago, IL 60610
Contact: Kim Fadim
800-826-3632
312-642-0049
Fax: 312-642-7243

Nonprofit organization whose mission is to educate patients, families, professionals, and the public concerning the nature of depressive and manic-depressive illness as a medical disease; to foster self-help for patients and families; to eliminate discrimination and stigma; to improve the availability and quality of help and support, and to advocate for research toward the elimination of these illnesses.

Consumer or Patient Education Materials
Depression Illness: A Guide for Patient and Family, book, introduction to illness, $3; Diagnosis, Treatment and Support, booklet, free; How to Cope with Depression, booklet, $5.40.
Publications for Health Professionals
The Depression Workbook, book, step-by-step guidance to taking responsibility, $12; Your Brother's Keeper, book, social support for recovery from depression, $20.75. Please contact for complete publications list.
Technical Assistance
Referral to local chapters and support groups throughout the U.S.

■ National Foundation for Depressive Illness

PO Box 2257
New York, NY 10116
800-248-4344
Web site: http://www.depression.org

Nonprofit foundation that distributes information on the incidence, symptoms, and treatments for depression and manic depression.

Hotline or Toll-free Information Line
National Foundation for Depressive Illness Information Line: 800-248-4344 24-hr automated, pre-recorded information.
Consumer or Patient Education Materials
Information packet sent upon receipt of written request and SASE as instructed per information line. Donation requested but not required.
Technical Assistance
Doctor and support group referrals.

■ National Mental Health Association

1021 Prince St
Alexandria, VA 22314-2971
Contact: Tonya A McCreary
800-969-NMHA (800-969-6642)
703-684-7722
Fax: 703-684-5968
Web site: http://www.worldcorp.com/dc-online/nmha

Nonprofit voluntary health organization with over 300 affiliates in 35 states addressing all issues related to mental health and mental illness. Focus areas include advocacy; prevention; public education; information and referral at the national and local level.

Hotline or Toll-free Information Line
National Mental Health Information Center Inquiry Line: 800-969-NMHA (800-969-6642) 24-hr operator assisted, referral service, answers questions, requests for materials.

Clearinghouse or Resource Center

National Mental Health Information Center: 800-969-NMHA (800-969-6642); information and referral database of local and national mental health organizations; pamphlets, fact sheets, other education materials, single copy free.

Database or Statistical Information

National Mental Health Association Prevention Clearinghouse, computerized database providing prevention-related services including access to a Prevention Program Database, a Prevention Network, and a Resource Database of over 4,000 prevention advocates and professionals. Free. Contact Sandy McElhaney, Director of Prevention, 703-838-7506.

Consumer or Patient Education Materials

Various materials available including books, 40 pamphlets, and over 100 fact sheets on variety of mental health topics. Some discounts available for quantity orders. Please contact for complete catalog.

Publications for Health Professionals

The Bell, quarterly, $18/yr; Prevention Update, quarterly, $85/yr; Getting Started in Prevention Series, 2 vol includes The Guide to Establishing Community-Based Prevention Programs and Directory of Model Programs to Prevent Mental Disorders and Promote Mental Health, $37.90. Please contact for complete publications list.

Classes and Conferences

Workshops and seminars; annual National Mental Health Conference, 3–4 days. Please contact for complete list and schedule.

Technical Assistance

Technical assistance; speakers' bureau; national programs include: National Public Education Campaign on Clinical Depression, National Head Start Association Partnership; Model Prevention Programs.

■ National Mental Health Consumers' Self-Help Clearinghouse

1211 Chestnut St, Ste 1000
Philadelphia, PA 19107
800-553-4539
215-751-1810
Fax: 215-636-6310
E-mail: thekey@delphi.com

Nonprofit clearinghouse that handles thousands of inquiries concerning the needs of the consumer/survivor movement and offers a consumer library.

Hotline or Toll-free Information Line

National Mental Health Consumers' Self-Help Clearinghouse Information Line: 800-553-4539 (M–F 9AM–5PM ET) Automated, referral service, answers questions, requests for materials.

Consumer or Patient Education Materials

Various brochures and pamphlets available at average cost of $2 ea. Please contact for complete catalog.

Publications for Health Professionals

The Key, quarterly newsletter, $15. Please contact for complete publications list.

Classes and Conferences

Several conferences held annually. Please contact for complete list and schedule.

Technical Assistance

Consultation available for self-help groups.

■ National Mental Health Services Knowledge Exchange Network

11426 Rockville Pike, #405
Rockville, MD 20852
Mailing Address:
PO Box 42490
Washington DC, DC 20015
800-789-2647
301-984-6283
Fax: 301-984-8796
TDD: 301-443-9006
E-mail: ken@mentalhealth.org
Web site: http://www.mentalhealth.org/

Federally supported program that serves as the clearinghouse for the Substance Abuse and Mental Health Services Administration's Center for Mental Health Services. A one-stop source of information and resources on prevention, treatment, and rehabilitation services for mental illness. Developed for users of mental health services and their families; the general public; policy makers; the media; and those who design, finance, and provide mental health services.

Hotline or Toll-free Information Line

National Mental Health Services Knowledge Exchange Network Telephone Service: 800-789-2647 (8:30AM–5PM ET) Operator assisted, referral service, answers questions, requests for materials.

Electronic Information Resources

KEN electronic bulletin board system: 800-790-2647, allows users to join various newsgroups to exchange ideas and information.

Special Campaigns, Events, or Programs

Caring for Every Child's Mental Health: Communities Together Campaign, 1996–approx 1999, brochures, fact sheets, and radio PSAs.

Consumer or Patient Education Materials

Consumers Guide to Mental Health Services, brochure, Q&A's about mental health; Children's and

Adolescents' Mental Health, brochure, info for families on child mental health; free. Please contact for complete catalog.

Publications for Health Professionals

Mental Health Directory 1995, book updated every 5 yrs, national listing of mental health centers; Mental Health, United States, 1994, book, updated every 2 yrs, national statistics; free. Please contact for complete publications list.

EATING DISORDERS

■ Anorexia Nervosa and Related Eating Disorders Inc

PO Box 5102
Eugene, OR 97405
Contact: Dr J Bradley Rubel
541-344-1144
Web site: http://www.anred.com

National nonprofit organization that provides free and low-cost information about anorexia nervosa, bulimia, binge eating disorder, and compulsive exercising.

Consumer or Patient Education Materials

ANRED Alert, newsletter, 10 issues/yr, $15; Eating and Exercise Disorders, 14 pp booklet, overview and self-help tips, $1; Eating and Exercise Disorders brochure, summary of info in booklet, $7.50 for 25.

Classes and Conferences

Seminars include: Inservice for professionals, 2–8 hrs; Dying to Be Thin, length varies. Please contact for complete information.

■ Eating Disorders Awareness and Prevention (EDAP)

603 Stewart St, Ste 803
Seattle, WA 98101
Contact: Robin Griffith
206-382-3587
Fax: 202-292-9890
Web site: http://members.aol.com/edapinc

National nonprofit organization dedicated to increasing the awareness and prevention of eating disorders through education. Provides educational information to health care professionals, educators, community organizations, families and the public; and sponsors National Eating Disorders Awareness Week.

Special Campaigns, Events, or Programs

National Eating Disorders Awareness Week, 1st full week in February, brochures, posters, buttons, educational information packets, videos.

Consumer or Patient Education Materials

Videos; booklets; buttons; posters; brochures include: Eating Disorders Information; Eating Disorders Prevention. Some materials free. Please contact for pricing and complete catalog.

Publications for Health Professionals

Quarterly Newsletter, networking resource for educational outreach professionals and current news, $35; General Prevention and Awareness Materials for Educators of Grades K–12; collection of articles, handouts, other info, $5; Early Childhood Prevention Packet for Elementary School Educators, set of presentation guidelines, $5. Please contact for complete publications list.

Classes and Conferences

Classes available vary by local chapters. Please contact for complete list and schedule.

■ Gürze Books

3420 Woodland Way
Carlsbad, CA 92008
Mailing Address:
PO Box 2238
Carlsbad, CA 92018
800-756-7533
619-434-7533
Fax: 619-434-5476
E-mail: gurze@aol.com
Web site: http://www.gurze.com

Publisher and distributor of quality information on eating disorders recovery, research, education, advocacy, and prevention. Catalog contains selected books and tapes on food problems of all kinds, and is widely circulated to individuals who are suffering, their loved ones, the health care professionals who treat them, and educators who are working towards prevention.

Consumer or Patient Education Materials

Bulimia: A Guide to Recovery, book; many other titles and materials available. Please contact for complete catalog.

■ National Center for Overcoming Overeating

315 W 86th St, Ste 17B
New York, NY 10024
212-875-0442
Fax: 212-874-6596

Nonprofit organization committed to ending body hatred and dieting whose philosophy is based on the books, When Women Stop Hating Their Bodies and Overcoming Overeating, written by Jane Hirschmann and Carol Munter.

Consumer or Patient Education Materials

Overcoming Overeating, audiotape, intro to anti-diet approach to curing compulsive eating, $35; When Women Stop Hating Their Bodies, audiotape, advanced material for curing body hatred and eating problems, $35; Preventing Childhood Eating Problems, book available in Spanish, Dutch, Portuguese, German, and Finnish, $10. Contact Tree Farm Communications, 800-468-0464 to order.

Classes and Conferences

Workshops, 1-day, weekends, or full week. Please contact for complete list and schedule.

Technical Assistance

Consultation; Centers available in various parts of the country with trained professionals who run groups and see individuals seeking to cure compulsive eating.

■ National Eating Disorders Organization

6655 S Yale Ave
Tulsa, OK 74136
Contact: Barbara Fleming, Coordinator
918-481-4044
Fax: 918-481-4076
Web site: http://www.laureate.com

Nonprofit organization whose mission is to increase understanding and contribute toward the prevention of all forms of eating disorders and obesity. Provides education, consultation, and treatment referral services nationally and internationally.

Consumer or Patient Education Materials

Skin Deep, video, eating disorders prevention video developed and produced by Disney Educational Productions, $199; Eating Disorders Support Group Information Packet, how to develop a group, $5. Please contact for complete catalog.

Publications for Health Professionals

Eating Disorders Information Packet, includes overview, warning signs, guidelines to approach person with disorder, reading and resource list, $10; 5 Day Lesson Plan on Eating Disorders, $65; International Treatment Referral Directory and Support Group Registry. Please contact for complete publications list.

■ Overeaters Anonymous

6075 Zenith Ct NE
Rio Rancho, NM 87124
Mailing Address:
PO Box 44020
Rio Rancho, NM 87174-4020
Contact: Virginia Jensen, Public Information
505-891-2664
Fax: 505-891-4320

Nonprofit fellowship of individuals who, through shared experience, strength, and hope, are recovering from compulsive overeating. Welcomes everyone who wants to stop eating compulsively. No dues or fees for members.

Consumer or Patient Education Materials

A Program of Recovery, pamphlet, how to tell if compulsive overeater, $.20; Fifteen Questions, questionnaire to determine if compulsive overeater, 20/$1. Some Spanish languages available. Please contact for complete catalog.

Publications for Health Professionals

Introducing OA to Health Care Professionals, pamphlet, 10/$1; Treatment and Beyond, pamphlet, explains transition from treatment to OA, $.40; Courier, newsletter, news and information for professional community, free. Please contact for complete publications list.

STRESS MANAGEMENT

■ American Institute for Preventive Medicine

30445 Northwestern Hwy, Ste 350
Farmington Hills, MI 48334-3102
Contact: Order Dept, 810-539-1800 x239
800-345-2476
810-539-1800
Fax: 810-539-1808
E-mail: aipm@healthy.net
Web site: http://aipm.healthy.net

International for-profit developer and provider of health promotion programs, self-help kits, and self-care publications. Works with over 5,000 corporations, HMOs, and hospitals to reduce health care costs, lower absenteeism, and improve morale. Services include those for self-care, smoking cessation, weight control, stress management, self-esteem enhancement, prenatal education, fitness center management, nutrition, and EAP education.

Classes and Conferences
Systematic Stress Management, 7 topics available, each can be presented as a one-hour workshop; Group Program and Guided Self-Help Kit also available. Please contact for pricing and complete list.

■ The American Institute of Stress

124 Park Ave
Yonkers, NY 10703
Contact: JoAnn Ogawa
800-24-RELAX (800-247-3529)
914-963-1200
Fax: 914-965-6267
E-mail: stress124@earthlink.net
Web site: http://www.stress.org

Nonprofit organization that serves as a clearinghouse for information on all stress related matters. Concerned with all aspects of stress, ranging from its role in physical and mental health, to occupational and other psychosocial sources of stress, and stress reduction strategies.

Clearinghouse or Resource Center
American Institute of Stress Clearinghouse: 914-963-1200; constantly updated extensive library of reprints from both scientific and lay literature. Informational packets available, avg 15–20 pp, $35 minimum charge, letter of request must be submitted by mail, fax, or e-mail.
Publications for Health Professionals
Health and Stress, monthly newsletter, reports on latest advances in stress research and related health topics, included with membership.
Classes and Conferences
Annual International Congress on Stress, 1 week in Switzerland, plenary session on stress related subjects. Please contact for complete list and schedule.

■ Association for Applied Psychophysiology and Biofeedback

10200 W 44th Ave, Ste 304
Wheat Ridge, CO 80033-2840
Contact: Kathleen Schaefer
303-422-8436
303-422-8892
Fax: 303-422-8894
E-mail: aapb@resourcenter.com
Web site: http://www.aapb.org

International nonprofit association for the study of applied psychophysiology and biofeedback, dedicated to advancing the field through support of research and expansions of clinical and educational applications of biofeedback; promotion of high standards of professional practice, ethics and education, and dissemination of information to the public.

Consumer or Patient Education Materials
Client Info Paper, booklet; What is Biofeedback, flyer; both describe biofeedback, free.
Classes and Conferences
Annual meeting, 4–5 days, scientific presentations, educational sessions, cost varies; Fall Workshop, 2–6 days, subject and cost varies.
Technical Assistance
Referrals to practitioners.

■ Audio Vision

3 Morningside Pl
Norwalk, CT 06854
Contact: James E Porter
800-367-1604
203-838-9225
Fax: 203-866-3421

For-profit organization specializing in stress management training products for hospitals and corporations.

Consumer or Patient Education Materials
A Day Away from Stress, video, for relaxation with or without narration, $195; Short Circuiting Stress, 17 min video, focuses on cognitive techniques for reducing stress, $195; Just Relax, audiotape, with or without narration, $10.95. Please contact for complete catalog.
Publications for Health Professionals
Stress Profiler, 8 pp booklet, helps access stresses and strengths, $5.95; Keeping Your Stress in Balance, 11 pp booklet, reproducible articles on stress, $19.95; 7 Steps to Stress Management, complete kit of text and tape, to conduct 4 1-hr stress management seminars, $299. Please contact for complete publications list.

■ Award-Winning Presentations

1034 Page St
San Francisco, CA 94117-2219
Contact: Allen Klein
415-431-1913
Fax: 415-431-8600
E-mail: allenklein@aol.com

Speaker and author.

Consumer or Patient Education Materials
Whole Mirth Catalog, catalog of humor books and tapes, $1. Please contact for complete catalog.
Publications for Health Professionals
Healing Power of Humor, book, how to lighten-up not-so-funny stuff, $9.95; Quotations To Cheer You Up,

resource quote book, $9.95. Please contact for complete publications list.

Classes and Conferences

Presentations available: Bye-Bye Burnout, humor in everyday situations; Lighter Side of Change, humor in the workplace; The Courage To Laugh, humor in death and dying situations; Length varies from ½ hour to all day. Please contact by phone or fax for fee.

■ Channing L Bete Co Inc

200 State Rd
S Deerfield, MA 01373-0200
800-628-7733 (Sales and Customer Service)
413-665-7611
Fax: 800-499-6464

Publisher of informational and educational booklets, videos, posters, calendars, books, and display racks. Booklets use a distinctive, condensed format—called scriptography—which combines key words and graphics to explain a variety of subjects and is appropriate for different age groups and reading levels.

Consumer or Patient Education Materials

Booklets and videos about different kinds of stress and stress management. Some Spanish language available. Please contact for pricing and ask for the Patient Education catalog.

■ Human Dynamics Inc

216-2 Swing Road Office Park
Greensboro, NC 27409
Contact: Dr Raymond Cienik
800-258-1170
910-854-0120
Fax: 910-854-9232
E-mail: hdynamics@aol.com

Consulting firm specializing in human resources strategic planning; program and project management; team building; executive coaching; and executive training for government, health care, research, educational, and service related organizations. Specialized programs available in the areas of avoiding professional burnout for executives, time management, and stress management.

Classes and Conferences

Avoiding Professional Burnout, 1 day, customized executive seminar, $2,595; Program/Project Management, 3 days, targeted to health care executives, $7,595; Stress Management, 1 day, customized to client personnel, $2,395.

Technical Assistance

Customized manpower studies; employee/client attitudinal surveys; strategic planning consultation; team building programs; program planning management assistance. Specialized training services on nursing leadership development and non-profit board management available.

■ National Health Video Inc

12021 Wilshire Blvd, Ste 550
Los Angeles, CA 90025
Contact: Ed Weinstock, 310-268-2812
800-543-6803
Fax: 310-477-8198
E-mail: healthvid@aol.com

For-profit producer and distributor of patient education videotapes for use in education and counseling.

Consumer or Patient Education Materials

Stress Management, videotape, describes cognitive methods, $79.95; Behavior Modification, videotape, $79.95.

■ Organizational Designs in Communication Inc

7240 Davenport Rd, Ste 203
Goleta, CA 93117
Mailing Address:
PO Box 60609
Santa Barbara, CA 93160-0609
Contact: Dr Frederick Elias
800-551-2800
805-968-1666
Fax: 805-968-1666
E-mail: odc@west.net
Web site: http://www.west.net/~odc

Consulting firm providing individuals and organizations with training and support of quality improvement programs; including communication and conflict resolution.

Consumer or Patient Education Materials

I Can I Will, self-help book or tape, $12.95 and $6.95.

Classes and Conferences

Stress Management, 1 or 2 days, master your life and create peak performance, $250/person; Conflict Resolution, 1 or 2 days, $250/person; Communication Mastery, 1 day, $250/person. Please contact for complete list and schedule.

Technical Assistance

Consulting services on stress management, conflict resolution, team building, and communication skills.

■ PATH Associates

8 Barranco Ct
Towson, MD 21204-4202

Contact: Bob Younglove
410-821-0538
Fax: 410-821-0538

Consulting firm that coaches and teaches individuals with health problems how to change their habits, attitudes, and behaviors to become healthier, happier, and more successful in achieving their goals.

Classes and Conferences

Preventing Stress, 1 day, changing self to be less stressed, $1,400. Please contact for complete list and schedule.

■ **Professional Psychology Services**
One Rittenhouse Sq, Ste 701
Philadelphia, PA 19103
Contact: Dr Marion Frank, 215-567-1306
215-567-1306
Fax: 215-567-1113

For-profit organization specializing in mental health services offering assessments, consultations, referrals, and counseling for organizations onsite or in offices located in Philadelphia and Southern New Jersey.

Classes and Conferences

Seminars available include: Critical Incident Debriefings, Stress Management, and Diversity Training. Please contact for complete list and schedule.

ADDITIONAL RESOURCES

■ **American Anorexia/Bulimia Association**
293 Central Park West, Ste 1R
New York, NY 10024
212-501-8351
Fax: 212-501-0342
Web site: http://members.aol.com/amanbu

■ **American Psychiatric Association**
1400 K St NW, Ste 1050
Washington, DC 20005
Contact: Division of Public Affairs
202-682-6220
E-mail: pubafrs@psych.org
Web site: http://www.psych.org

■ **American Psychological Association**
750 First St NE
Washington, DC 20002-4242
202-336-5500
Web site: http://www.apa.org

■ **The Carter Center**
453 Freedom Pkwy
Atlanta, GA 30307
Contact: Office of Public Information, 404-331-3900
404-420-5165
E-mail: carterweb@emory.edu
Web site: http://www.emory.edu/CARTER_CENTER

■ **Healthworks**
2501 SE Madison
Portland, OR 97214
503-232-3522

■ **Institute for Mental Health Initiatives**
4545 42nd St NW, Ste 311
Washington, DC 20016
202-364-7111
Fax: 202-363-3891
E-mail: instmhi@aol.com
Web site: http://www.imhi.org/imhi

■ **KidsPeace**
The National Center for Kids in Crisis
National Campaign Headquarters
575 Madison Ave, Ste 1006
New York, NY 10022
212-605-0153
Fax: 212-605-0509
Web site: http://www.kidspeace.org

■ **National Alliance for the Mentally Ill**
200 N Glebe Rd, Ste 1015
Arlington, VA 22203-3754
800-950-NAMI (800-950-6264)
703-524-7600
Fax: 703-524-9094

■ **National Association of Anorexia Nervosa and Associated Disorders**
P O Box 7
Highland Park, IL 60035
847-831-3438
Fax: 847-433-4632
Web site: http://www.healthtouch.com

■ **The National Center for Health Promotion**
PO Box 524
Saline, MI 48034-2292
800-250-5105
313-429-3065
Fax: 800-250-4560
E-mail: nchp2@ix.netcom.com
Web site: http://www.welltech.com/nchp/

■ **National Mental Illness Screening Project**
One Washington St, Ste 304
Wellesley, MA 02181-1706
Contact: Douglas G Jacobs, Executive Director
617-239-0071
Fax: 617-431-7447

■ **National Resource Center on Homelessness and Mental Illness**
262 Delaware Ave
Delmar, NY 12054
800-444-7415
518-439-7415
Fax: 518-439-7612
E-mail: nrc@prainc.com

■ **TMI North America Inc**
181 Carlos Dr, Ste 102
San Rafael, CA 94903
800-541-3800
415-957-1133
Fax: 415-882-4960
E-mail: tmiusa@aol.com

■ **World Federation for Mental Health**
1021 Prince St
Alexandria, VA 22314
703-838-7543
Fax: 703-519-7648
E-mail: wfmh@erols.com
Web site: http://www.ab.umd.edu/wfmh.html

FEDERAL AGENCIES

■ **Center for Mental Health Services (CMHS)**
Substance Abuse and Mental Health Services Administration
Parklawn Bldg, Rm 13-103
5600 Fishers Ln
Rockville, MD 20857
External Liaison Office: 301-443-2792
Web site: http://www.samhsa.gov/cmhs/cmhs.htm

Heads efforts to speed the application of mental treatments for patients with mental illness. In partnership with states, leads national efforts to demonstrate, evaluate, and disseminate service delivery models to treat mental illness, promote mental health, and prevent the development or worsening of mental illness when possible. Current information is made available through the National Mental Health Services Knowledge Exchange Network (KEN): 800-789-2647.

■ **National Institute of Mental Health (NIMH)**
National Institutes of Health
5600 Fishers Ln, Rm 7C-02
Rockville, MD 20857
Information Branch: 301-443-4513
Fax: 301-443-4279
D/ART (Depression Awareness, Recognition & Treatment) Education Program: 800-421-4211
Panic and Other Anxiety Disorders Education Program: 800-64-PANIC (800-647-2642) (Spanish-speaking operators available)
888-8-ANXIETY (888-826-9438)
Fax-on-Demand: 301-443-5158
E-mail: nimhinfo@nih.gov
Web site: http://www.nimh.nih.gov

Conducts and supports research that seeks to understand, treat, and prevent mental illness. Printed materials on basic behavioral research, neuroscience of mental health, rural mental health, children's mental disorders, schizophrenia, paranoia, depression, bipolar disorder, seasonal affective disorder, learning disabilities, Alzheimer's disease, and panic, obsessive compulsive, and other anxiety disorders are available from the Information Branch. Information is also available from three toll-free numbers and a fax-on-demand number.

■ **Substance Abuse and Mental Health Services Administration (SAMHSA)**
Office of Public Health and Science
U.S. Dept of Health & Human Services
Parklawn Bldg, Rm 13C-05
5600 Fishers Ln
Rockville, MD 20857
Public Affairs: 301-443-8956
Information Line: 301-443-3783
Funding Opportunities: Bulletin Board Service: 800-424-2294 (9600,N,8,1)
Web site: http://www.samhsa.gov

Agency whose mission is to assure that quality substance abuse and mental health services are available to the people who need them and to ensure that prevention and treatment knowledge is used more effectively in the general health care system. Is composed of three centers: Center for Mental Health Services, Center for Substance Abuse Prevention, and Center for Substance Abuse Treatment.

Nutrition and Weight Management

Products/Services Offered

Organization	web site	hotline/toll-free information line	clearinghouse/resource center	electronic information resources	database/statistical information	special campaigns/events/programs	consumer/patient education materials	publications for health professionals	classes/conferences	technical assistance	other products/services	grants/funding/awards	Page No.
American Dietetic Association	■	■	■			■	■	■					58
American Institute for Cancer Research	■	■					■					■	58
American Institute for Preventive Medicine	■								■				58
Anatomical Chart Company							■						58
Balboa Publishing							■	■	■	■	■		59
Channing L Bete Co Inc							■						59
Choice Diets Inc	■						■	■					59
DINE Systems Inc	■										■		59
Health Education Services	■						■						60
Lowfat Lifeline							■	■					60
Mayo Clinic Health Information				■			■						60
NASCO	■						■						60
National Association of State Units on Aging			■										60
Price-Pottenger Nutrition Foundation	■						■	■		■			61

Additional Resources 61

Federal Agencies 62

American Dietetic Association

216 W Jackson Blvd, Ste 800
Chicago, IL 60606-6995
Contact: Customer Service, 312-899-0040 x5000
312-899-0040
Fax: 312-899-1757
Web site: http://www.eatright.org

Nonprofit organization of food and nutrition professionals in the U.S. whose mission is to serve the public through the promotion of optimal nutrition, health, and well-being. Members include clinical and community dietetics professionals, food service managers, educators, researchers, dietetic technicians, and students. Covers a wide range of practice areas and special interests, including diet counseling for weight control, cholesterol reduction, diabetes, renal, and other health concerns.

Hotline or Toll-free Information Line

Consumer Nutrition Hotline: 800-366-1655 (M–F 8AM–8PM CT) Automated line, referral service, answers questions.

Clearinghouse or Resource Center

National Center for Nutrition and Dietetics: 312-899-0040 x4653; Public education center that operates consumer nutrition hotline and resource library providing access to many databases; sponsors National Nutrition Month and promotes Project LEAN public awareness campaign.

Special Campaigns, Events, or Programs

National Nutrition Month, March, promotional materials include: posters, fitness, personal, and culinary items. Contact Customer Service, 312-899-0040 x5000.

Consumer or Patient Education Materials

Healthy Start brochures, promotion for young children ages 2 to 6, 4 topics, $6.26 for 25; Nutrition fact sheets, reproducible on 23 topics, includes resources and references, $28.75; various education pamphlets. Low literacy; Please contact for complete catalog.

Publications for Health Professionals

Journal of the American Dietetic Association, monthly journal, $98/yr; Worksite Nutrition: A Guide to Planning, Implementation, and Evaluation, $12; Learning the New Food Labels: An Educator's Slide Kit, 52 slides and 14 reproducible handout sheets, $90. Please contact for complete publications list.

American Institute for Cancer Research

1759 R St NW
Washington, DC 20009
800-843-8114
202-328-7744
Fax: 202-328-7226
Web site: http://www.aicr.org

National nonprofit cancer charity organization focusing on cancer prevention through diet and nutrition. Also funds grants in the study of the link between diet and cancer.

Hotline or Toll-free Information Line

AICR Nutrition Hotline: 800-843-8114 (M–F 9AM–5PM ET); answers questions and requests for materials. Registered dietitians will research questions and return calls; no charge for service.

Consumer or Patient Education Materials

Brochures include: Hints for a Healthy Weight; Diet & Cancer: What's the Link?; Taking a Closer Look at Phytochemicals; free single copy, discounts available for quantity orders. Please contact for complete catalog.

Grants, Funding, or Awards

Grants available for research on the role of diet and nutrition in cancer prevention. Contact Research Dept.

American Institute for Preventive Medicine

30445 Northwestern Hwy, Ste 350
Farmington Hills, MI 48334-3102
Contact: Order Dept, 810-539-1800 x239
800-345-2476
810-539-1800
Fax: 810-539-1808
E-mail: aipm@healthy.net
Web site: http://aipm.healthy.net

International for-profit developer and provider of health promotion programs, self-help kits, and self-care publications. Works with over 5,000 corporations, HMOs, and hospitals to reduce health care costs, lower absenteeism, and improve morale. Services include those for self-care, smoking cessation, weight control, stress management, self-esteem enhancement, prenatal education, fitness center management, nutrition, and EAP education.

Classes and Conferences

HealthyLife Weigh, 24 weekly sessions, teaches weight control and how to lower cholesterol; Weight No More, total lifestyle approach to weight control; Group Program and Guided Self-Help Kit also available. Please contact for pricing and complete list.

Anatomical Chart Company

8221 N Kimball
Skokie, IL 60076-2956
800-621-7500 (Order Dept)
847-679-4700
Fax: 847-674-0211

Mail order company catering to the professional or student in need of biological or scientific charts and models of the human anatomy.

Consumer or Patient Education Materials
One-Pound Glob of Fat Model, dramatic, innovative tool for motivating weight control, $21; Nutrition information posters and charts including: Keys to Healthy Eating and Sodium Content of Foods, $1.95–$36.95. Please contact for complete catalog.

■ Balboa Publishing

11 Library Pl
San Anselmo, CA 94960
Contact: Bob Mellin
415-453-8886
Fax: 415-453-8888
E-mail: balboa pub@aol.com

Publisher and distributor of pediatric and adult obesity training and patient materials for health professionals.

Consumer or Patient Education Materials
SHAPEDOWN, pediatric obesity program, $18.95; The Solution, adult obesity program, $25. Materials can be customized; Low literacy; Please contact for complete catalog.

Publications for Health Professionals
SHAPEDOWN, license package, pediatric obesity program, $475; The Solution, license package, adult obesity program, $475. Please contact for complete publications list.

Classes and Conferences
SHAPEDOWN, 40 hr class, pediatric obesity program, $200; The Solution, 20 hr class, adult obesity program, $100. Please contact for complete list and schedule.

Technical Assistance
Computerized biopsychosocial assessment for adolescents. 900-number for adult consulting.

Other Products and Services
Triage call center (900-number) and patient referral service.

■ Channing L Bete Co Inc

200 State Rd
S Deerfield, MA 01373-0200
800-628-7733 (Sales and Customer Service)
413-665-7611
Fax: 800-499-6464

Publisher of informational and educational booklets, videos, posters, calendars, books, and display racks. Booklets use a distinctive, condensed format—called scriptography—which combines key words and graphics to explain a variety of subjects and is appropriate for different age groups and reading levels.

Consumer or Patient Education Materials
Booklets and videos about good nutrition; sodium, fiber, and fat in diets. Some Spanish language available. Please contact for pricing and ask for the Patient Education catalog.

■ Choice Diets Inc

9301 Cedarcrest Dr
Bethesda, MD 20814
Mailing Address:
PO Box 2053
Rockville, MD 20847-2053
Contact: Ron Goor, PhD
301-897-9360
Fax: 301-530-5835
E-mail: ctl@choicediets.com
Web site: http://www.choicediets.com

For-profit company offers complete ready-to-deliver weight loss/healthy eating programs.

Consumer or Patient Education Materials
Choose to Lose Weight Loss Program Participant Kit, includes 2 books, workbook, food diary, audiotape, and handouts, $42 ea; Eater's Choice Cholesterol-Lowering Program Participant Kit, includes 1 book, workbook, food diary, audiotape, and handouts, $32 ea.

Publications for Health Professionals
Choose to Lose Weight Loss Program Professional Kit, includes leader's guide, videotape, marketing materials, and participant materials, $175; Eater's Choice Cholesterol-Lowering Program Professional Kit, includes leader's guide, marketing materials, and participant materials, $150. Please contact for complete publications list.

■ DINE Systems Inc

586 N French Rd, Ste 2
Amherst, NY 14228
716-688-2400
Fax: 716-688-2505
E-mail: dine@aol.com
Web site: http://www.dinesystems.com

For-profit company that develops and markets nutrition education and analysis software to assist professionals with helping patients improve their health.

Other Products and Services
DINE® Healthy software program, nutrient analysis and education, $129; Pyramid Challenge software program, nutrition education using the Food Guide Pyramid, $99.

■ Health Education Services

PO Box 7126
Albany, NY 12224
518-439-7286
Fax: 518-439-7286 *51
Web site: http://www.hes.org

Nonprofit distributor of current health education, promotional publications, posters, and videos, most of which have been produced by the New York State Department of Health or the New York State Department of Environmental Conservation. (Health Education Services is a Division of Health Research Inc.)

Consumer or Patient Education Materials

Nutrition instruction program guides appropriate for levels kindergarten through grade 12, $6–$25. Please contact for complete catalog.

■ Lowfat Lifeline

234 Cass St
PO Box 1889
Port Townsend, WA 98368-0060
Contact: Valerie Parker, MS
800-294-9801 (Order Dept)
360-379-9724
Fax: 360-385-6835
E-mail: lowfat@olympus.net

Distributor of health education resources to support company, community, and hospital wellness programs. Materials available cover topics including: nutrition, fitness, substance abuse, stress management, and worksite wellness.

Consumer or Patient Education Materials

Copier ready handouts, slides, videos, reference books, and cookbooks. Please contact for complete catalog.

Publications for Health Professionals

Instructor's kits available for diabetes education, heart health, general nutrition, label reading, and weight control; materials vary; price range $30–$60. Please contact for a complete catalog.

■ Mayo Clinic Health Information

200 First St SW
Rochester, MN 55905
Contact: Mike Casey or Dan Newton
800-430-9699
Fax: 507-284-5410

Division of the Mayo Clinic that produces consumer health publications including newsletters, booklets, books, and CD-ROMs, providing people with timely, reliable, and easy-to-understand health, wellness, and self-care information. Materials appropriate for health promotion initiatives.

Electronic Information Resources

Mayo Health Oasis online health information web site, http://www.mayo.ivi.com

Consumer or Patient Education Materials

Healthy Weight Plan, 96 pp book, practical plan for safe weight loss, $12.95; Mayo Clinic Health Letter, monthly newsletter, $24/yr; Mayo Clinic Sports Health & Fitness CD-ROM, $49.95. Please contact for volume discounts and complete catalog.

■ NASCO

901 Janesville Ave
Ft Atkinson, WI 53538-0901
Contact: Dan Christianson, Health Care Dept,
414-563-2446 x237
800-558-9595
414-563-2446
Fax: 414-563-8296
E-mail: lifeform@nascofa.com
Web site: http://www.nascofa.com

For-profit developer, producer, and distributor of health education products worldwide.

Consumer or Patient Education Materials

Videos, charts, posters, folding displays, models, games, and stickers covering nutrition pyramid, healthy eating, and eating disorders; also body fat and muscle replicas. $5–$259. Discounts available for quantity orders. Please contact for complete catalog.

■ National Association of State Units on Aging

1225 I St NW, Ste 725
Washington, DC 20005
Contact: Cindy Wellons
202-898-2578
Fax: 202-898-2583
E-mail: staff@nasua.org

Nonprofit public interest organization that provides information, technical assistance, and professional development support to its members—the 57 state and territorial government agencies on aging. Works to promote social policy at the federal and state levels responsive to the needs of older Americans.

Clearinghouse or Resource Center

National Resource Center on Nutrition and Aging: 202-898-2578; 1225 I St NW, Ste 725, Washington, DC 20005; Conducts biennial conferences to disseminate cutting edge nutrition research to practitioners; publications related to operation of senior nutrition programs. (Operated in collaboration with National Association of Nutrition and Aging Services Programs.)

■ Price-Pottenger Nutrition Foundation

2667 Camino del Rio S, Ste 109
San Diego, CA 92108-3767
Mailing Address:
PO Box 2614
La Mesa, CA 91943-2614
Contact: Order Line, 800-366-3748
619-574-7763
619-574-7765
Fax: 619-574-1314
E-mail: ppnf@aol.com
Web site: http://www.healthy.net/ppnf

International nonprofit educational organization serving as a clearinghouse of information on nutrition, alternative health management, preventive medicine, ecology, and organic gardening. Library collection houses over 10,000 books, tapes, and reprints.

Consumer or Patient Education Materials
Various materials available including booklets, books, bibliographies, videos, $2.50–$100. Please contact for complete catalog.

Publications for Health Professionals
Price-Pottenger Nutrition Foundation Health Journal, quarterly journal, free with membership.

Technical Assistance
Health care professional referral service.

ADDITIONAL RESOURCES

■ American School Food Service Association

1600 Duke St, 7th Fl
Alexandria, VA 22314
703-739-3900
Fax: 703-739-3915

■ Dairy Management Inc

O'Hare International Center
10255 W Higgins Rd, Ste 900
Rosemont, IL 60018-5616
Contact: Diana Broj, Program Marketing Director
800-426-8271
847-803-2000
Fax: 847-803-2077

■ Dump Your Plump

PO Box 30
South Haven, MI 49090
800-67-PLUMP (800-677-5867)
616-639-1592
Fax: 616-637-2268
Web site: http://www.qtm.net/dump_your_plump/

■ Food and Nutrition Board

Institute of Medicine, National Academy of Sciences
2101 Constitution Ave NW
Washington, DC 20418
Contact: Publications, 800-624-6242
202-334-1732
Fax: 202-334-2316
Web site: http://www.nas.edu

■ The National Center for Health Promotion

PO Box 524
Saline, MI 48034-2292
800-250-5105
313-429-3065
Fax: 800-250-4560
E-mail: nchp2@ix.netcom.com
Web site: http://www.welltech.com/nchp/

■ Nutrition Screening Initiative

1010 Wisconsin Ave NW, Ste 800
Washington, DC 20007
Contact: Sarah Williams
202-625-1662
Fax: 202-338-2334

■ Produce for Better Health Foundation

1500 Casho Mill Rd
PO Box 6035
Newark, DE 19714-6035
302-738-7100
Fax: 302-738-4825
Web site: http://www.dcpc.nci.nih.gov/5aday

■ Society for Nutrition Education

2850 Metro Dr, Ste 416
Minneapolis, MN 55425-1412
612-854-0035
Fax: 612-854-7869
E-mail: lansi001@gold.pc.umn.edu

■ Weight Watchers International

175 Crossways Park W
Woodbury, NY 11797
Contact: Consumer Affairs Dept
516-390-1400

■ **Wheat Foods Council**
5500 S Quebec, Ste 111
Englewood, CO 80111
303-694-5828
Fax: 303-694-5807
E-mail: wfc@wheatfoods.org
Web site: http://www.wheatfoods.org

FEDERAL AGENCIES

■ **Center for Food Safety and Applied Nutrition (CFSAN)**
U.S. Food and Drug Administration
200 C St SW, M/S HFS-55
Washington, DC 20204
Consumer Education Staff: 202-205-5004
General Inquiries and Seafood Hotline: 800-FDA-4010 (800-332-4010)
Office of Food Labeling (Div of Technical Evaluation): 202-205-5483
Web site: http://vm.cfsan.fda.gov/list.html

Regulates all food and cosmetic products other than meat and poultry. Responsible for food safety, nutrition, food labeling, and economic fraud.

■ **Division of Nutrition and Physical Activity**
National Center for Chronic Disease Prevention & Health Promotion (NCCDPHP)
Centers for Disease Control and Prevention
4770 Buford Hwy NE, M/S K-46
Atlanta, GA 30341-3724
770-488-4721
Fax: 770-488-5473
Nutrition and Physical Activity Information Line: 888-232-4674

Provides leadership in promoting healthy dietary practices and moderate physical activity through epidemiology and behavioral research, health communications, surveillance, training, international assistance and policy development. Published the Physical Activity and Health: A Report of the Surgeon General.

■ **Food and Nutrition Information Center (FNIC)**
National Agricultural Library
Argricultural Research Service, U.S. Department of Agriculture
10301 Baltimore Blvd, Rm 304
Beltsville, MD 20705-2351
301-504-5719
Fax: 301-504-6409
TDD: 301-504-6856
E-mail: fnic@nal.usda.gov
Web site: http://www.nal.usda.gov/fnic/

Established to serve the information needs of persons interested in human nutrition, food service management, and food technology. Provides print and audiovisual materials for consumers and bibliographies and resource guides for professionals on topics in human nutrition.

■ **National Diabetes Information Clearinghouse (NDIC)**
One Information Way
Bethesda, MD 20892-3560
301-654-3327
Fax: 301-907-8906
E-mail: ndic@aerie.com

An information and referral service of the National Institute of Diabetes and Digestive and Kidney Disease (NIDDK); responds to written inquiries, develops and distributes publications about diabetes, and provides referrals to diabetes organizations, including support groups. Consumer materials available on diabetes management, foot care, nutrition, dental care, insulin, self-blood glucose monitoring, diabetes in older Americans, diabetes in young people, and eye care. Professional materials available about all aspects of diabetes and its management, including pregnancy, exercise, nutrition, diabetic retinopathy, and resources for patient education materials. Maintains a database of these materials from which literature searches are generated.

■ **Weight Control Information Network (WIN)**
1 WIN Way
Bethesda, MD 20892-3665
800-946-8098
301-570-2177
Fax: 301-570-2186

An information and referral service of the National Institute of Diabetes and Digestive and Kidney Disease (NIDDK). Develops and disseminates the latest information about obesity and weight control to the public. Information is available about obesity, childhood obesity, prescription medicines to control obesity, physical activity and its role in weight control, and dietary guidelines for good health.

Physical Activity and Fitness

Products/Services Offered

Organization	web site	hotline/toll-free information line	clearinghouse/resource center	electronic information resources	database/statistical information	special campaigns/events/programs	consumer/patient education materials	publications for health professionals	classes/conferences	technical assistance	other products/services	grants/funding/awards	Page No.
ACA Council on Sports Injuries and Physical Fitness								■					64
Aerobics and Fitness Association of America	■	■					■	■	■	■			64
American College of Sports Medicine	■						■	■					64
American Medical Athletic Association	■							■	■				64
American Running and Fitness Association	■					■	■	■		■			65
BioFitness Systems Inc	■			■						■			65
Corporate Fitness Midwest Inc										■			65
Fitcorp											■		65
Fitness Finders Inc					■		■	■	■	■	■		66
Health Education Services	■							■					66
HealthStyle	■										■		66
Healthy Achievers							■			■			66
Human Kinetics Publishers	■						■	■					66
Journeyworks Publishing							■						67
Melpomene Institute for Women's Health Research	■						■						67
National Association of Governor's Councils on Physical Fitness and Sports	■					■							67
National Youth Sports Safety Foundation Inc						■	■	■					67
Park Nicollet HealthSource							■						68
President's Council on Physical Fitness and Sports						■	■	■					68
Stanford Center for Research in Disease Prevention	■						■	■					68
Women's Sports Foundation	■	■	■			■	■					■	68

Additional Resources 69

Federal Agencies 70

■ ACA Council on Sports Injuries and Physical Fitness

2C Annapolis St
Annapolis, MD 21401
800-593-3222
Fax: 410-266-8124

National nonprofit organization whose mission is to advance chiropractic principles and education with practical applications of chiropractic sports medicine and exercise science to enhance performance and promote physical fitness.

Publications for Health Professionals
Journal of Sports Chiropractic and Rehabilitation, quarterly, free with membership; Sports Talk, quarterly, free with membership, $39.95/yr. Please contact for complete publications list.

■ Aerobics and Fitness Association of America

15250 Ventura Blvd, Ste 200
Sherman Oaks, CA 91403
Contact: Fitness Practitioner Dept, 800-968-7263
800-446-2322
818-905-0040
Fax: 818-990-5468
E-mail: afaa@earthlink.com
Web site: http://www.afaa.com

For-profit association that certifies individuals to become aerobics and step instructors, personal trainers, and weightroom instructors. Also specializes individuals in areas such as prenatal; youth and senior fitness; exercise and obesity; nutrition; and stress management.

Hotline or Toll-free Information Line
AFAA Fitness Triage Team Consumer Line: 800-YOUR-BODY (800-968-7263) (M–F 7:30AM–5:30PM PT) Operator assisted, referral service, answers questions, requests for materials.

Consumer or Patient Education Materials
Fitness Gets Personal Cards, 32 laminated flashcards, 4 main categories of health and fitness, $29.95. Please contact for complete catalog.

Publications for Health Professionals
Fitness and Theory, text, anatomy, physiology biomechanics of aerobics, $35; AFP Emerging Profession Resource, business strategies, client programming, health care, $65; Reference Manual, resource guide, specialty populations, $25. Please contact for complete publications list.

Classes and Conferences
Certification programs, training, workshops. Please contact for complete list and schedule.

Technical Assistance
Fitness Triage Team offers counseling and referral.

■ American College of Sports Medicine

401 W Michigan St
Indianapolis, IN 46202-3233
Mailing Address:
PO Box 1440
Indianapolis, IN 46206-1440
Contact: Susan Nelson
317-637-9200
Fax: 317-634-7817
E-mail: pipacsm@acsm.org
Web site: http://www.acsm.org

Nonprofit organization of more than 16,000 members in almost 60 countries that promotes and integrates scientific research, education, and practical applications of sports medicine and exercise science to maintain and enhance physical performance, fitness, health, and quality of life.

Consumer or Patient Education Materials
Pamphlets available: Fitting Fitness In; Play It Safe; Exercise Lite; Fit Over 40; free with SASE.

Publications for Health Professionals
Handbook for Team Physicians, for treatment of athletic injuries, $29.95; Health and Fitness Facilities Standards and Guidelines, essential guide, $39; Guidelines for Exercise Testing and Prescription, standards for rehabilitation and preventive exercise, $24.95.

■ American Medical Athletic Association

4405 East West Hwy, Ste 405
Bethesda, MD 20814
800-776-ARFA (800-776-2732)
301-913-9517
Fax: 301-913-9520
E-mail: arfarun@aol.com
Web site: http://www.arfa.org

Nonprofit association of physicians and allied health professionals whose mission is to educate and motivate fellow physicians and health care practitioners to disseminate information about aerobic exercise and nutrition to their patients, thereby enhancing the quality of their life.

Publications for Health Professionals
AMAA Quarterly, journal, sports medicine, research and discussion, $40.

Classes and Conferences
Marine Corps Marathon Sports Medicine Symposium, annually, 2 days, in October; New York City Sports

Medicine Seminar, 1 day, in November. Please contact for complete list and schedule.

American Running and Fitness Association

4405 East West Hwy, Ste 405
Bethesda, MD 20814
Contact: Barbara Baldwin, MPH
800-776-ARFA (800-776-2732)
301-913-9517
Fax: 301-913-9520
E-mail: arfarun@aol.com
Web site: http://www.arfa.org

Nonprofit educational association of exercisers, health professionals, and organizations who promote health and physical fitness for all Americans.

Special Campaigns, Events, or Programs
National Running and Fitness Week, in May, Posters, buttons, pamphlets, brochures, balloons, paycheck inserts, etc. Contact Bells International, 800-822-1923.

Consumer or Patient Education Materials
Your Child's Fitness—Practical Advice for Parents, book, $14.95; Brochures include: Fitness Is a Family Affair, fitness assessment quiz; Run! Your Way to Fitness, 12-week walk/run program; Fitness Is . . . Feeling Great!!, motivational tips and log sheet to get started. Free single copy with SASE, discounts available for quantity orders. Please contact for complete catalog.

Publications for Health Professionals
Running and FitNews, monthly newsletter, sports medicine and nutrition news, $25/yr; Resource Guide for Fitness and Health Promotion, manual, comprehensive listing of fitness organizations, seminar planning, etc, $40. Please contact for complete publications list.

Technical Assistance
Health and fitness writers available to write original pieces.

BioFitness Systems Inc

PO Box 337
Pompano Beach, FL 33061
800-895-5557
954-968-3195
E-mail: biofit@worldnet.att.net
Web site: http://www.biofitness.com

For-profit company offering an online, real-time health club that creates personalized professional-quality workout plans. Uses exercise science direct from professional literature to create 4-week personal and prescriptive workout plans as well as assessment testing for any resistance equipment or aerobic activity.

Electronic Information Resources
BioFitness Health Club® web site, http://www.biofitness.com
Offers exercise demonstrations with sequenced line action photos and text descriptions; exercise knowledge with reference bibliography; strength and conditioning assessment testing; exercise routines; workout planning.

Technical Assistance
Physical assessments, exercise knowledge, exercise demonstrations, and personal prescriptive workout planning available on BioFitness Health Club web site.

Corporate Fitness Midwest Inc.

11469 Olive Blvd, Ste 251
St Louis, MO 63141-7108
Contact: Harold Denlow
800-645-2535
314-994-7323
Fax: 314-994-1545
E-mail: cfm@welltech.com

For-profit full-service health promotion company with expertise in providing multi-level prevention and intervention programs for all types of fitness/wellness centers. Offers creative programs and services to build healthier people and organizations through healthier lifestyles.

Technical Assistance
Consultation on design, planning, and management of fitness/wellness centers; health promotion specialist available to plan and administer wellness programs.

Fitcorp

Prudential Center, Ste 200
800 Boylston St
Boston, MA 02199-8007
Contact: Laurie Selvaggio, 617-375-5600 x185
617-375-5600
Fax: 617-375-5649

For-profit company providing health promotion and fitness services delivered through network of public fitness centers or at private on-site centers.

Other Products and Services
The Fitcorp Wellness Benefit, state-of-the art fitness services and worksite health promotion planning, including: individual health profiles, health screenings, healthy lifestyle seminars, lifestyle management programs, health fairs. Can also help develop and manage private fitness centers.

■ Fitness Finders Inc

133 Teft Rd
PO Box 160
Spring Arbor, MI 49283
800-789-WALK (800-789-9255)
517-750-1500
Fax: 517-750-4584

For-profit company specializing in turnkey community outreach physical activity programs and other physical fitness products and services especially for youth.

Database or Statistical Information
Fitness for Youth Database, large compilation on youth fitness. Cost is variable.

Consumer or Patient Education Materials
Fitness books for children and adults. Please contact for complete catalog.

Publications for Health Professionals
Fit Mind and Body Bulletin, 9 issues/yr newsletter, current info on youth fitness, $20/yr; Aerobics with Fun, book, 1,100 physical activities for all age groups, $34.95. Please contact for complete publications list.

Classes and Conferences
GameAerobics®, 3 hrs over 2 days, utilization of games to enhance youth fitness, $100; Feelin' Good®, ½ day over 2 days, cardiovascular health/fitness for youth, $100.

Technical Assistance
Consulting services in program development.

Other Products and Services
Mileage Club Programs, 6- to 8-wk programs, complete kit including awards and incentives: Feelin' Good Mileage Club, elementary school students walk laps on playground to earn collectibles, $.80/child; Mega Mileage Club, teams of adults compete on walks, $34.95/group of 25; Families in Training, complete program for families, $19.95. Contact Beth Kuntzleman.

■ Health Education Services

PO Box 7126
Albany, NY 12224
518-439-7286
Fax: 518-439-7286 *51
Web site: http://www.hes.org

Nonprofit distributor of current health education, promotional publications, posters, and videos, most of which have been produced by the New York State Department of Health or the New York State Department of Environmental Conservation. (Health Education Services is a Division of Health Research Inc.)

Publications for Health Professionals
How to Promote Physical Fitness in Your Community, guide, $1. Please contact for complete publications list.

■ HealthStyle

11469 Olive Blvd, Ste 251
St Louis, MO 63141-7108
Contact: Lisa McKee
800-645-2535
314-994-7323
Fax: 314-994-1545
E-mail: healthstyle@welltech.com
Web site: http://www.welltech.com/healthstyle

National for-profit company that develops and distributes unique health and fitness incentive programs and products.

Other Products and Services
Spring into Motion™ and North Pole Expedition™, health and fitness incentive programs, $99 each; can also design customized incentive programs and products.

■ Healthy Achievers

22 Hayes Rd
Madbury, NH 03820-9511
603-743-3838
Fax: 603-749-7310
E-mail: ohshealthy@aol.com

Consulting firm specializing in worksite health promotion and occupational safety programs and materials.

Consumer or Patient Education Materials
Achieving an Active Lifestyle, complete education program kit with video and reproducible materials, $95. Please contact for complete catalog.

Technical Assistance
Consulting for corporate wellness programs and fitness center management and design.

■ Human Kinetics Publishers

1607 N Market St
PO Box 5076
Champaign, IL 61825-5076
Contact: Fulfillment Dept
800-747-4457
217-351-5076
Fax: 217-351-2674
E-mail: humank@hkusa.com
Web site: http://www.humankinetics.com/

Publisher of information in the field of physical activity; including health, fitness, adapted physical activity, nutrition, cardiopulmonary guidelines, sports medicine, physiology, and psychology of sport and exercise.

Consumer or Patient Education Materials
Free catalogs available for materials on specific areas: Fitness and Health Resources; Academic and Professional Resources; Physiology of Exercise and Sport; Sports Medicine; Sport and Exercise Psychology; and Children's Exercise & Sport. Please contact for copies.

Publications for Health Professionals
Quarterly journals include: Journal of Aging and Physical Activity, $40/yr; Adapted Physical Activity Quarterly, $40/yr; Pediatric Exercise Science, $45/yr. Please contact for complete publications list.

■ Journeyworks Publishing

736 Chestnut St
Santa Cruz, CA 95060
Mailing Address:
PO Box 8466
Santa Cruz, CA 95061-8466
800-775-1998
408-423-1400
Fax: 408-423-8102

Publisher of health promotion materials for clinics, hospitals, schools, and health departments covering a variety of topics including fitness, women's health, sexual abstinence, teen pregnancy prevention, STDs and HIV, mental wellness, tobacco use prevention, and smoking cessation.

Consumer or Patient Education Materials
I Walk because . . . ; 50 Great Reasons to Exercise; Exercise! Ten Tips to Get You Started; pamphlets, free review sample, pricing varies upon quantity ordered. Materials can be customized; Please contact for complete catalog.

■ Melpomene Institute for Women's Health Research

1010 University Ave
St Paul, MN 55104
Contact: Gloria Massey
612-642-1951
Fax: 612-642-1871
E-mail: melpomen@webspan.com
Web site: http://www.melpomene.org

Nonprofit research organization that helps women and girls of all ages link physical activity and health through research, publication, and education. Its resource center contains over 4,000 books and articles, including Melpomene's own research materials, on aging well, body image, girls and self-esteem, menopause, osteoporosis, larger women, and exercise and pregnancy.

Consumer or Patient Education Materials
Bodywise Woman, 320 pp book, information about physical activity and women's health, $16.95; Of Heroes, Hopes, and Level Playing Fields: A Collection of Insights and Observations on Physical Activity and Women, $10; Heroes: Growing Up Female and Strong, 50 min video and curriculum, focus on self-esteem and physical activity for adolescent girls, $29.95. Please contact for complete catalog.

■ National Association of Governor's Councils on Physical Fitness and Sports

201 S Capitol Ave, Ste 560
Indianapolis, IN 46225
Contact: Cindy Porteous
317-237-5630
Fax: 317-237-5632
E-mail: govcouncil@aol.com
Web site: http://www.fitnesslink.com/Govcouncil

Nonprofit organization whose mission is to improve quality of life by promoting physical fitness and healthy lifestyles.

Special Campaigns, Events, or Programs
National Employee Health and Fitness Day, 3rd Wednesday in May, posters, banners, T-shirts, and buttons available. Contact Cindy Porteous.

■ National Youth Sports Safety Foundation Inc

10 Meredith Cir
Needham, MA 02192-1946
Contact: Michelle Glassman
617-449-2499
Fax: 617-444-3288
E-mail: nyssf@aol.com

Nonprofit educational organization dedicated to reducing the number and severity of injuries youth sustain in sports activities. Also serves as an educational resource and clearinghouse for information for the country on safe sports participation.

Special Campaigns, Events, or Programs
National Youth Sports Safety Month, April, resource kit. Contact Michelle Glassman.

Consumer or Patient Education Materials
Individual Risk Factors, fact sheet, $2; Tips for Athletes, guidelines for safe sports participation, $2. Please contact for complete catalog.

Publications for Health Professionals
Sidelines, quarterly newsletter, $9.50/yr; Safety Quiz, questionnaire to help communities evaluate safety of sports programs, $2; Overuse Injuries: A Coach's Guide to Understanding Risk Factors, Recognizing Symptoms, and Guidelines for Prevention, $7. Please contact for complete publications list.

■ Park Nicollet HealthSource

3800 Park Nicollet Blvd
Minneapolis, MN 55416
Contact: Scott Laurent, Sales
800-372-7776
Fax: 612-993-1840

Nonprofit organization, a part of the Institute for Education and Research HealthSystem Minnesota, that develops and produces health promotion publications in self-care, health care consumerism, chronic conditions, and lifestyle education.

Consumer or Patient Education Materials
The Activity Pyramid, brochure, poster, and table tent; Building Your Activity Pyramid, book; Pricing varies upon quantity ordered. Materials can be customized; Please contact for complete catalog.

■ President's Council on Physical Fitness and Sports

701 Pennsylvania Ave NW, Ste 250
Washington, DC 20004
202-272-3421
Fax: 202-504-2064

Advises the President and the U.S. Secretary of Health and Human Services on efforts to promote physical activity, fitness, and sports for all Americans. Also works with schools, clubs, recreation agencies, and major employers on program design and implementation; and offers a variety of testing, recognition, and incentive programs for individuals, institutions, and organizations.

Special Campaigns, Events, or Programs
President's Challenge Physical Fitness Awards Program, earn Presidential recognition for long-term participation in one of 68 activities. Contact for complete information.

Consumer or Patient Education Materials
Fitness Fundamentals: Guidelines for Personal Exercise Programs; Pep Up Your Life: A Fitness Book for Seniors; Get Fit: A Handbook for Youth Ages 6–17; single copy free. Please contact for complete publications list.

Publications for Health Professionals
PCPFS Research Digest, quarterly, synopsis of science on specific topic; Surgeon General's Report on Physical Activity and Health-At-A-Glance (Summary), single copy free. Please contact for complete publications list.

■ Stanford Center for Research in Disease Prevention

Health Promotion Resource Center
1000 Welch Rd
Palo Alto, CA 94304-1885
Contact: SCRDP Distribution Center
415-723-0003
Fax: 415-725-6906
E-mail: distribution@scrdp.stanford.edu
Web site: http://www-med.Stanford.EDU:8/MedCenter/SCRDP/

Nonprofit educational resource center that produces and disseminates print and video materials on cardiovascular disease risk factors, injury prevention, and community health promotion.

Consumer or Patient Education Materials
Fresh Start: The Stanford Health & Fitness Program, 238 pp book, comprehensive exercise guide, $19.95; Walking Kit or Jogging Kit, self-help kits, $2.75 ea; The Exercise Book, booklet, helps couch potatoes choose a physical activity, $3.50. Materials can be customized; Please contact for complete catalog.

Publications for Health Professionals
Coming Alive: User's Guide for a Worksite Exercise Program, $19.50. Please contact for complete publications list.

■ Women's Sports Foundation

Eisenhower Park
East Meadow, NY 11554
800-227-3988
516-542-4700
Fax: 516-542-4716
E-mail: wosport@aol.com
Web site: http://www.lifetimetv.com/WoSport

National nonprofit educational, member-based organization dedicated to promoting the lifelong participation of all girls and women in sports and fitness, creating an educated public that encourages females' participation and supporting gender equality in sport.

Hotline or Toll-free Information Line
Women's Sports Foundation Sports Infoline: 800-227-3988 (M–F 9AM–5PM ET) Operator assisted, referral service, answers questions, requests for materials.

Clearinghouse or Resource Center
Women's Sports Foundation Library: 800-227-3988; Eisenhower Park, E Meadow, NY 11554; Open to the public, contains women's sports books, magazines, and articles.

Special Campaigns, Events, or Programs
National Girls and Women in Sports Day, 1st Thursday in February, Contact Special Projects Office.

Consumer or Patient Education Materials
A Balancing Act, guide, balancing family, career & social demands while staying healthy and active.

Grants, Funding, or Awards
Various research grants; scholarships and internships available.

ADDITIONAL RESOURCES

■ American Alliance for Health, Physical Education, Recreation, and Dance (AAHPERD)

1900 Association Dr
Reston, VA 20191
Contact: Publications Dept, 800-321-0789, PO Box 385, Oxon Hill, MD 20750-0385
800-213-7193
703-476-3400
Fax: 703-476-9527
Web site: http://www.aahperd.org

■ American Council on Exercise

5280 Oberlin Dr, Ste 102
San Diego, CA 92121-3787
800-825-3636
619-535-8227
Fax: 619-535-1778
Web site: http://www.acefitness.org

■ American Physical Therapy Association

1111 N Fairfax St
Alexandria, VA 22314
Contact: Public Relations Dept
800-999-2782
703-684-APTA (703-684-2782)
Fax: 703-684-7343
Web site: http://www.apta.org

■ Association of Hospital Health and Fitness

915 Elmwood Ave
Evanston, IL 60202
Mailing Address:
PO Box 6280
Evanston, IL 60204-6001
847-475-2332
Fax: 847-475-2112
E-mail: 102707.321@compuserve.com

■ The Benfield Group

8123 Delmar Blvd
St Louis, MO 63130
Contact: John Carlson, Director of Business Development
800-883-9665
314-862-4990
Fax: 314-862-4099

■ The Cooper Aerobics Center

12330 Preston Rd
Dallas, TX 75230
800-444-5764
972-239-7223
Fax: 972-239-6649

■ The Cooper Institute for Aerobics Research

12330 Preston Rd
Dallas, TX 75230
800-635-7050 x830
972-341-3200
Fax: 972-991-4626
E-mail: courses@cooperinst.org

■ Fitness Products Council

200 Castlewood Dr
North Palm Beach, FL 33408
Fax: 561-863-8984
Web site: http://www.sportlink.com/fitness

■ Healthworks

2501 SE Madison
Portland, OR 97214
503-232-3522

■ IDEA: International Association of Fitness Professionals

6190 Cornerstone Ct E, Ste 204
San Diego, CA 92121-3773
Contact: Member Services Representative
800-999-IDEA (800-999-4332)
619-535-8979
Fax: 619-535-8234
E-mail: ideafit@ix.netcom.com

■ **National Cattlemen's Beef Association**
444 N Michigan Ave
Chicago, IL 60611
Contact: C J Valenziano, Education Dept
800-848-5093
312-670-9227
E-mail: cow@ncanet.org
Web site: http://www.ncanet.org/

■ **National Coalition for Promoting Physical Activity**
401 W Michigan St
Indianapolis, IN 46206
317-637-0349
Fax: 317-634-7817
E-mail: natcoal@ncppa.org
Web site: http://www.ncppa.org/ncppa

■ **National Recreation and Park Association**
2775 S Quincy St, Ste 300
Arlington, VA 22206-2204
703-820-4940
Fax: 703-671-6772

■ **The Sports Club Company**
11100 Santa Monica Blvd, Ste 300
Los Angeles, CA 90025
Contact: Dr. Leinwohl
310-479-5200
Fax: 310-479-8350

■ **Walking Magazine**
9-11 Harcourt St
Boston, MA 02116
617-266-3322
Fax: 617-266-7373
E-mail: walking@cowles.com

■ **YMCA of the USA**
National Office
101 N Wacker Dr, Ste 1400
Chicago, IL 60606
Contact: Health and Fitness Dept
800-USA-YMCA
312-977-0031
Fax: 312-977-9063
Web site: http://www.ymcausa.org

■ **YWCA of the USA**
National Office
726 Broadway
New York, NY 10003
212-614-2700
Fax: 212-677-9716
Web site: http://www.ywca.org

FEDERAL AGENCIES

■ **Division of Nutrition and Physical Activity**
National Center for Chronic Disease Prevention & Health Promotion (NCCDPHP)
Centers for Disease Control and Prevention
4770 Buford Hwy NE, M/S K-46
Atlanta, GA 30341-3724
770-488-4721
Fax: 770-488-5473
Nutrition and Physical Activity Information Line: 888-232-4674

Provides leadership in promoting healthy dietary practices and moderate physical activity through epidemiology and behavioral research, health communications, surveillance, training, international assistance and policy development. Published the Physical Activity and Health: A Report of the Surgeon General.

■ **National Heart, Lung, and Blood Institute (NHLBI)**
National Institutes of Health
NIH/NHLBI/OPEC, Rm 4A-03
31 Center Dr, MSC 2480
Bethesda, MD 20892-2480
301-496-4236
Web site: http://www.nhlbi.nih.gov/nhlbi/nhlbi.htm

NHLBI Information Center
PO Box 30105
Bethesda, MD 20824-0105
301-251-1222
Fax: 301-251-1223

Oversees research, demonstration, prevention, education, control, and training activities in the fields of heart, lung, and blood diseases and education concerning these diseases. The Information Center offers materials on numerous topics, including exercise.

■ **National Institute of Arthritis and Musculoskeletal and Skin Diseases (NIAMS)**
National Institutes of Health
Bldg 31, Rm 4C-05
31 Center Dr, MSC 2350
Bethesda, MD 20892-2350
301-496-8188
Web site: http://www.nih.gov/niams/

NIAMS Information Clearinghouse
One AMS Circle
Bethesda, MD 20892-3675
301-495-4484
Fax: 301-587-4352
TTY: 301-565-2966

Conducts and supports basic, clinical, and epidemiologic research and research training and disseminates information on many debilitating diseases. Information available from the Clearinghouse includes bibliographies, reference sheets, and directories for professionals on many topics including physical exercise.

Substance Abuse

Organization	web site	hotline/toll-free information line	clearinghouse/resource center	electronic information resources	database/statistical information	special campaigns/events/programs	consumer/patient education materials	publications for health professionals	classes/conferences	technical assistance	other products/services	grants/funding/awards	Page No.
All Substances													
American Academy of Pediatrics	■						■						**75**
American Outreach Association				■			■			■			**75**
The BACCHUS and GAMMA Peer Education Network	■					■	■	■	■				**75**
The Bureau For At-Risk Youth	■						■					■	**75**
Channing L Bete Co Inc							■						**76**
Grafeeties and Company	■						■						**76**
International Commission for the Prevention of Alcoholism and Drug Dependency								■		■			**76**
Johnson Institute	■						■	■	■	■			**76**
Join Together: A National Resource for Communities Fighting Substance Abuse	■			■				■		■		■	**77**
Management Intervention Services								■	■	■	■		**77**
NASCO	■						■						**77**
National Asian Pacific American Families Against Substance Abuse	■						■	■	■	■			**77**
National Association of Alcoholism and Drug Abuse Counselors	■			■				■	■				**78**
National Clearinghouse for Alcohol and Drug Information (NCADI)	■	■		■	■	■	■	■			■	■	**78**
National Council on Alcoholism and Drug Dependence Inc (NCADD)	■	■				■	■	■					**79**
National Families in Action	■		■				■	■					**79**
National Family Partnership						■	■						**79**
National Parents' Resource Institute for Drug Education Inc (PRIDE)	■						■	■	■	■			**79**
National Prevention Network/National Association of State Alcohol and Drug Abuse Directors					■			■	■				**80**
Select Media							■	■					**80**

Organization	web site	hotline/toll-free information line	clearinghouse/resource center	electronic information resources	database/statistical information	special campaigns/events/programs	consumer/patient education materials	publications for health professionals	classes/conferences	technical assistance	other products/services	grants/funding/awards	Page No.
Alcohol and Other Drugs													
Al-Anon Family Groups Headquarters Inc		■						■					**80**
Alcoholics Anonymous	■						■	■					**80**
American Council on Alcoholism Inc		■					■	■	■	■			**81**
Drug Prevention Resources Inc							■			■			**81**
National Association for Native American Children of Alcoholics							■		■				**81**
National Center for Health Education	■						■			■			**81**
Rational Recovery Systems Inc	■						■	■					**82**
Women for Sobriety Inc	■						■		■		■		**82**
World Service Office of Narcotics Anonymous							■						**82**
Tobacco													
American Institute for Preventive Medicine	■								■				**82**
Americans for Nonsmokers' Rights	■				■		■	■		■			**83**
Anatomical Chart Company							■						**83**
Journeyworks Publishing							■						**83**
National Center for Tobacco-Free Kids		■								■			**83**
Oral Health America						■							**83**
QuitSmart Stop Smoking Resources							■	■	■	■			**84**
Smokenders Inc	■						■		■				**84**
STAT (Stop Teenage Addition to Tobacco)							■	■	■				**84**

Additional Resources **84**

Federal Agencies **86**

ALL SUBSTANCES

■ American Academy of Pediatrics

141 Northwest Point Blvd
PO Box 927
Elk Grove Village, IL 60007-0927
Contact: Publications Dept, 800-433-9016
847-228-5005
Fax: 847-228-1281
E-mail: kidsdocs@aap.org
Web site: http://www.aap.org

Nonprofit organization of 50,000 pediatricians dedicated to the health, safety, and well-being of infants, children, adolescents, and young adults. Activities include advocacy for children and youth; public education; research; professional education; membership service and advocacy for pediatricians. More than 30 committees develop positions and programs for interest areas including nutrition; pediatric AIDS; substance abuse; child abuse and neglect; children with disabilities.

Consumer or Patient Education Materials
Brochures include: Alcohol: Your Child and Drugs; Cocaine: Your Child and Drugs; Marijuana: Your Child and Drugs; Straight Talk About Smokeless Tobacco; $29.95/100. Please contact for complete catalog.

■ American Outreach Association

33 Beechwood Ct
Colorado Springs, CO 80918
Mailing Address:
PO Box 25042
Colorado Springs, CO 80936
Contact: Charles Prusch
719-592-1134
Fax: 719-592-1134

Nonprofit educational organization recognized by the federal government. Committed to early education of health and prevention of alcohol, tobacco, and other drug abuses.

Electronic Information Resources
Fax-on-Demand: 719-592-1134

Consumer or Patient Education Materials
Books, pamphlets, videotapes, posters, coloring books on topics including drugs, smoking, alcohol, inhalants, and steroids prevention. Donation required for shipping and handling costs. Please contact for complete catalog.

Technical Assistance
Project HOLD (Homes On the Lead against Drugs) intergenerational, home-based program; training and assistance with planning community awareness activities, presentations to schools.

■ The BACCHUS and GAMMA Peer Education Network

1909 E Evans Ave
Denver, CO 80210
Mailing Address:
PO Box 100430
Denver, CO 80250-0430
Contact: BACCHUS & GAMMA Materials Center, 352-377-5228, Fax: 352-372-6729, 2937 NE 19th Dr, Gainesville, FL 32609
303-871-0901
Fax: 303-871-0907
E-mail: bacgam@aol.com
Web site: http://www.bacchusgamma.org

National nonprofit network for college campus student peer educators who teach about alcohol abuse, impaired driving, sexual assault, healthy lifestyle choices, and other related student health issues. Chapters present a variety of educational programs, social events, and awareness campaigns to create positive campus environments.

Special Campaigns, Events, or Programs
Safe Spring Break Program, March, and National Collegiate Alcohol Awareness Week, October, Promotional materials and campaign kit. Please contact for complete information.

Consumer or Patient Education Materials
Pamphlets and videos.

Publications for Health Professionals
The BACCHUS Beat, monthly newsletter, college student health issues, $20.

Classes and Conferences
Annual General Assemby and educational conferences.

■ The Bureau For At-Risk Youth

135 Dupont St
PO Box 760
Plainview, NY 11803-0760
Contact: Customer Service Dept
800-99-YOUTH (800-999-6884)
516-349-5520
Fax: 516-349-5521
E-mail: info@at-risk.com
Web site: http://www.at-risk.com

Publisher and distributor of high-quality educational materials on at-risk children's issues.

Consumer or Patient Education Materials
Many videos, pamphlets, posters, booklets, books, other innovative products appropriate for use by educators, counselors, parents, health professionals, and children. Please contact for complete catalog.
Grants, Funding, or Awards
Annual Outdoor Prevention Mural Contest, open to all schools and organizations working to prevent alcohol and other drug use among today's youth. The winner will have all costs associated with producing mural paid by the Bureau. Contact 800-999-6884 x211 for an entry form.

■ Channing L Bete Co Inc

200 State Rd
S Deerfield, MA 01373-0200
800-628-7733 (Sales and Customer Service)
413-665-7611
Fax: 800-499-6464

Publisher of informational and educational booklets, videos, posters, calendars, books, and display racks. Booklets use a distinctive, condensed format—called scriptography—which combines key words and graphics to explain a variety of subjects and is appropriate for different age groups and reading levels.

Consumer or Patient Education Materials
Booklets, coloring and activities booklets, videos, and information center display. Topics include: alcohol, cocaine, marijuana, smoking. Some Spanish language available. Please contact for pricing and ask for the Patient Education catalog.

■ Grafeeties and Company

1730 Blake St, #400
Denver, CO 80202
Contact: Joyce Cranston
303-291-1011
Fax: 303-291-1113
E-mail: health@grafeeties.com
Web site: http://www.grafeeties.com

For-profit company offering materials that are fun and new ways of getting kids (of all ages) to wear and support preventive health messages.

Consumer or Patient Education Materials
No Butts About It, Tobacco Pollutes, brochure, second-hand smoke message, $1.40 ea; Kool Korners, to mount posters, with drug and smoking prevention messages, $.35 ea; Grafeeties® stickers, foam stickers, bumper stickers for shoes with prevention messages, $.35 set; prices are for order quantity of 1,000. Materials can be customized; Low literacy; Please contact for complete catalog.

■ International Commission for the Prevention of Alcoholism and Drug Dependency

12501 Old Columbia Pike
Silver Spring, MD 20904
Contact: Thomas R Neslund, Executive Director
301-680-6719
Fax: 301-680-6090
E-mail: 74617.2242@compuserve.com

Nonprofit voluntary organization that promotes the prevention and elimination of alcohol and drug dependency, including tobacco. Provides assistance and educational materials for community leaders to implement local prevention programs.

Publications for Health Professionals
The Reporter, quarterly newsletter, current trends in prevention, free.
Technical Assistance
Technical assistance and consultation with community groups, including seminars.

■ Johnson Institute

7205 Ohms Ln
Minneapolis, MN 55439-2159
Contact: Dee Stuart
800-231-5165
612-831-1630
Fax: 612-831-1631
E-mail: info@johnsoninstitute.com
Web site: http://www.johnsoninstitute.com

For-profit organization that provides products and services to schools, families, organizations, and communities to prevent and intervene with problems such as alcohol and drug abuse, violence, suicide, and emotional stress.

Consumer or Patient Education Materials
Books, booklets, software, CD-ROM products, $1.95 to $995. Materials can be customized; Low literacy; Please contact for complete catalog.
Publications for Health Professionals
Enabling in the Health Professional, booklet, how enabling influences an organization, $4.95; To Care Enough, book, how to intervene with a colleague, $24.95; Everything You Need to Know, book, complete resource on alcohol and drug issues, $24.95. Please contact for complete publications list.

Classes and Conferences
How to Train Families to Intervene, 2 days, $295.
Technical Assistance
Behavioral health survey measuring organizational risk for 24 factors; Student survey measuring school's risk for alcohol, drugs, violence, and other factors.

■ Join Together: A National Resource for Communities Fighting Substance Abuse

441 Stuart St, 6th Fl
Boston, MA 02116-9350
Contact: Shelley Barnes
617-437-1500
Fax: 617-437-9394
E-mail: info@jointogether.org
Web site: http://www.jointogether.org

National resource center for communities fighting substance abuse funded by a grant from the Robert Wood Johnson Foundation to the Boston University School of Public Health. Mission is to help coalitions overcome the barriers they face and to become more successful in their efforts.

Electronic Information Resources
Join Together Online, available on web site or call 617-437-1500 for a free start-up kit.
Publications for Health Professionals
Strategies, quarterly newsletter; FASA Update (news from Funders Against Substance Abuse); technical assistance guides; annual survey of community substance abuse prevention acitivity; single copies free, additional copies costs vary. Please contact for complete publications list.
Technical Assistance
Sponsors public policy panels; helps coalitions develop comprehensive strategies including media strategies and public awareness.
Grants, Funding, or Awards
National Leadership Fellows Program, 35 Fellows selected each year; Join Together Community Exchange Program, mail or fax request for an application.

■ Management Intervention Services

201 E 35th St, Ste 6A
New York, NY 10016-4278
Contact: Walter Scanlon
212-683-8419
Fax: 212-683-8449
E-mail: 71260.3171@compuserve.com

Consulting firm that provides consultation and training services on substance abuse/behavioral and employee assistance matters. Also provides structured family/workplace interventions for substance abuse/behavioral related matters.

Publications for Health Professionals
Alcoholism and Drug Abuse in the Workplace; textbook, $22.
Classes and Conferences
Substance Abuse, variable length, $200 and up; Employee Assistance Program, variable length, $300. Please contact for complete information.
Technical Assistance
Consulting with employers, treatment programs, managed care organizations, community organizations on issues and problems related to behavioral/substance abuse and the workplace/family.
Other Products and Services
Family and workplace alcoholism and drug abuse intervention services. Training on family and workplace intervention.

■ NASCO

901 Janesville Ave
Ft Atkinson, WI 53538-0901
Contact: Dan Christianson, Health Care Dept, 414-563-2446 x237
800-558-9595
414-563-2446
Fax: 414-563-8296
E-mail: lifeform@nascofa.com
Web site: http://www.nascofa.com

For-profit developer, producer, and distributor of health education products worldwide.

Consumer or Patient Education Materials
Complete curriculum, laminated chart and cards, posters, transparencies, folding displays, models, videotapes, computer programs. Topics include: street drugs, inhalants, alcohol, tobacco, $14–$450. Discounts available for quantity orders. Please contact for complete catalog.

■ National Asian Pacific American Families Against Substance Abuse

1887 Maplegate St
Monterey Park, CA 91755-6536
Contact: Frances Kuramoto
213-278-0031
Fax: 213-278-9078
E-mail: napafasn@igc.apc.org
Web site: http://www.emory.edu/NFIA/

Nonprofit membership organization dedicated to strengthening families and promoting culturally-competent substance abuse and related services for Asian and Pacific Islanders. Focuses on substance abuse and all of its related problems, including health care, gang and domestic violence, mental health, and poverty.

Consumer or Patient Education Materials
Various materials available. Materials can be customized; Low literacy; Chinese, Vietnamese, Korean, and Hmong languages available. Please contact for complete catalog.
Publications for Health Professionals
NAPAFASA Newsletter; informational materials. Please contact for complete publications list.
Classes and Conferences
National conferences. Please contact for complete list and schedule.
Technical Assistance
Technical assistance and training on substance abuse prevention and treatment services for Asian and Pacific Islander populations.

■ National Association of Alcoholism and Drug Abuse Counselors

1911 N Fort Myer Dr, Ste 900
Arlington, VA 22209
Contact: Terri Mitchell, Publications, 703-741-7686 x126
800-548-0497
703-741-7686
Fax: 703-741-7698
E-mail: naadac@internetmci.com
Web site: http://www.naadac.org

Nonprofit professional membership organization dedicated to the needs and advancement of alcoholism and drug abuse counselors.

Electronic Information Resources
Fax-on-Demand: 800-441-4528, Fact sheets, position statements, publications listing available at no cost.
Publications for Health Professionals
NAADHC Newsletter, bimonthly, membership information, free with membership; The Counselor, bimonthly magazine, current research, events; free with membership or $42/yr.
Classes and Conferences
Annual conference, 4 days, workshops, exhibits, technology center.

■ National Clearinghouse for Alcohol and Drug Information (NCADI)

PO Box 2345
Rockville, MD 20847-2345
800-729-6686
301-468-2600
Fax: 301-468-6433
TDD: 800-487-4889
E-mail: info@prevline.health.org
Web site: http://www.health.org

Federally supported clearinghouse that serves as the central repository for the latest information on all aspects of substance abuse; answers questions; and designs, implements, and evaluates innovative knowledge transfer and communications strategies. Includes information from SAMHSA's Center for Substance Abuse Prevention and Center for Substance Abuse Treatment, the National Institute on Drug Abuse and the National Institute on Alcohol Abuse and Alcoholism.

Hotline or Toll-free Information Line
National Clearinghouse for Alcohol and Drug Information Line: 800-729-6686 24-hr automated line; information specialists available M–F 8AM–7PM ET; answers questions, referral service, requests for materials.
Electronic Information Resources
PREVline: http://www.health.org, free online data system providing direct access to information on prevention programs, current literature and research, new funding sources, survey data, and government and legislative updates. Offers a calendar of events and number of directories of programs, organizations, and resource people and complete NCADI publications catalog.
Database or Statistical Information
Prevention Materials Database (PMD), current collection of substance abuse materials developed by public and private agencies, disk $12/full release, $5/update; customized searches in the form of annotated bibliographies from alcohol and other drug databases.
Special Campaigns, Events, or Programs
Many substance abuse special campaigns and initiatives, call for complete information.
Consumer or Patient Education Materials
Free materials including fact sheets, brochures, pamphlets, posters, and video tapes; many available for racial and ethnic populations tailored for use by parents, teachers, youth, communities, and prevention professionals. Please contact for complete catalog.
Publications for Health Professionals
The Prevention Pipeline, bimonthly journal, latest prevention news and research findings, $20/yr. Please contact for complete publications list.
Other Products and Services
Prevention Dollars at Work, computer software program, results and expenses for specific prevention projects, $24.

Grants, Funding, or Awards
Disseminates Federal grant announcements and application kits for alcohol, tobacco, and other drug prevention programs, treatment, and research funding opportunities. Contact for complete information or available from PREVline.

■ National Council on Alcoholism and Drug Dependence Inc (NCADD)

12 W 21st St
New York, NY 10010
Contact: Public Information Dept
212-206-6770
Fax: 212-645-1690
E-mail: national@ncadd.org
Web site: http://www.ncadd.org

Nonprofit voluntary health organization with more than 128 affiliates in the U.S. providing education, information, help and hope in the fight against the chronic, often fatal disease of alcoholism and other drug addictions. Advocate for prevention, intervention, research, and treatment programs.

Hotline or Toll-free Information Line
NCADD Hope Line: 800-NCA-CALL (800-622-2255) 24-hr automated, referral service, requests for materials.
Special Campaigns, Events, or Programs
Alcohol Awareness Month and Alcohol-Free Weekend, April, awareness kit includes poster, brochures, camera-ready materials, $10. Contact Public Information Dept, 212-206-6770.
Consumer or Patient Education Materials
Fact sheets, $.20 each; Pamphlets $.50–$1 each; Posters, $1 each. Some Spanish languages available. Please contact for complete catalog.
Publications for Health Professionals
The Alcoholism Report, monthly newsletter, public policy news, $97/yr; NCADD Amethyst, quarterly, prevention and treatment information, $50/yr. Please contact for complete publications list.

■ National Families in Action

2296 Henderson Mill Rd, Ste 300
Atlanta, GA 30345
Contact: Circulation Dept
770-934-6364
Fax: 770-934-7137
Web site: http://www.emory.edu/nfia/

Nonprofit drug education and prevention organization that develops and tests programs and techniques to enable individuals and communities to make a difference; builds coalitions and collaborates with other groups; trains professional and volunteer trainers; and provides accurate information.

Clearinghouse or Resource Center
NFIA Drug Information Center: 770-934-6364; houses more than 500,000 documents on substance abuse, organized in more than 1,000 subject categories.
Consumer or Patient Education Materials
Pamphlets; posters; videotapes; brochures include Crack Update and Inhalant Update, $1 ea or $35/100 copies; Twelve Tips for Helping Your Child Stay Drug-Free, reference card available in Spanish, $15/100 copies. Please contact for complete catalog.
Publications for Health Professionals
Drug Abuse Update, quarterly magazine, digest abstracts current medical literature, reviews and articles, $30/yr; Drug Abuse Update for Kids, 4 issues/school yr, format for grades 4–6, harmful effects of drugs reinforced with discussion questions and games, $10/yr; You Have the Right to Know, curriculum series, explains how the brain works and how specific drugs affect the brain, $10. Please contact for complete publications list.

■ National Family Partnership

11159B South Towne Sq
St Louis, MO 63123
Contact: Olive O'Donnell
314-845-1933
Fax: 314-845-2117
E-mail: redrib@aol.com

Nonprofit organization of state, community, and individual partners whose mission is to help the young people of the U.S. achieve their full potential through the prevention of substance abuse.

Special Campaigns, Events, or Programs
Red Ribbon Week, in October, educational materials. Contact for complete information.
Consumer or Patient Education Materials
Parenting brochures and information; Tips for Teens, substance abuse prevention topics, free. Please contact for complete catalog.

■ National Parents' Resource Institute for Drug Education Inc (PRIDE)

3610 DeKalb Technology Pkwy, Ste 106
Atlanta, GA 30340
Contact: Sarah Ellsworth
770-458-9900
Fax: 770-458-5030
Web site: http://www.prideusa.org

Nonprofit organization devoted to alcohol, tobacco, and other drug prevention that offers programs for parents, youth, educators, businesses, and governments. Also is part of the World Health Organization (WHO) Global Initiative on Primary Prevention of Substance Abuse.

Consumer or Patient Education Materials
Videos and other materials. Please contact for complete catalog.
Publications for Health Professionals
International newsletter about drug abuse prevention issues. Please contact for complete publications list.
Classes and Conferences
PRIDE World Drug Conference, 3 days. Please contact for complete information.
Technical Assistance
Training programs for youth and parents; questionnaires to monitor student drug abuse; research activities.

■ National Prevention Network/National Association of State Alcohol and Drug Abuse Directors

444 N Capitol St NW, Ste 642
Washington, DC 20001
Contact: Lynette Greenwood
202-783-6868
Fax: 202-783-2704
E-mail: jgus@sso.org

Nonprofit membership association of officials of state alcohol and drug abuse agencies.

Database or Statistical Information
State Alcohol and Drug Abuse Profile (SADAP), book, provides state-by-state data on funding of programs, policy needs, and numbers of clients served; $45–$60.
Publications for Health Professionals
State Substance Abuse Quarterly, newsletter, $100; Prevention White Paper, annual, $10. Please contact for complete publications list.
Classes and Conferences
Annual Prevention Research Conference, Fall. Contact Director of Prevention Services for complete information.

■ Select Media

60 Warren St, 5th Fl
New York, NY 10007
Contact: Rebecca Chertok
800-707-6334
212-732-4437
Fax: 212-732-4439
E-mail: selmedbw@interport.net

For-profit distributor of educational films, videos, and CD-ROMs specializing in health and social issues.

Consumer or Patient Education Materials
An Alphabetter Answer, 31-min video, early drug use intervention for grades 3–6, $39.95; Safe Spaces, video with guide, drug and alcohol prevention for special needs and drug exposed K–2 children, $95; What Would You Do?, video with guide, help students develop decision-making and problem-solving skills, grades K–2, $95. Please contact for complete catalog.
Publications for Health Professionals
Teaching Healthy Choices, video, to train teachers, counselors, and administrators to implement Project Healthy Choices grades K–2, $95. Please contact for complete publications list.

ALCOHOL AND OTHER DRUGS

■ Al-Anon Family Groups Headquarters Inc

1600 Corporate Landing Pkwy
Virginia Beach, VA 23456-5617
Contact: Phyllis A Mullaney
800-356-9996
757-563-1600
Fax: 757-563-1655

International nonprofit fellowship organization of people whose lives have been affected by someone else's drinking. Al-Anon Family Groups, which includes Alateen for younger members, provides shared experience, strength, and hope allowing common problems to be solved.

Hotline or Toll-free Information Line
Al-Anon Meeting Information Line: 800-344-2666 (M–F 9AM–5PM ET); General Information: 800-356-9996 (M–F 9AM–5PM ET)
Publications for Health Professionals
Al-Anon Speaks Out, semiannual newsletter, community resource for professionals, free.

■ Alcoholics Anonymous

475 Riverside Dr
New York, NY 10115
Mailing Address:
Grand Central Station
PO Box 459
New York, NY 10163
Contact: General Service Office
212-870-3400
Fax: 212-870-3003
TDD: 212-870-3199

Web site: http://www.alcoholics-anonymous.org

A worldwide nonprofit fellowship of sober alcoholics, whose recovery is based on Twelve Steps; no dues or fees, self-supporting through voluntary, small contributions of members, accepts no outside funds; not affiliated with any other organization; primary purpose: to carry the AA message to alcoholic who still suffers.

Consumer or Patient Education Materials
Books, booklets, pamphlets, flyers, fact sheets, films, tape cassettes are available; costs vary. Please contact for complete catalog.

Publications for Health Professionals
Single copies of pamphlets and flyers available to anyone with a professional interest in AA program at no cost. Please contact for complete publications list.

■ American Council on Alcoholism Inc

2522 St Paul St
Baltimore, MD 21218
Contact: Robert G Kirk, 410-889-0100
800-527-5344
410-889-0100
Fax: 410-889-0297

National nonprofit organization dedicated to educating the public to view alcoholism and problem drinking as conditions that are responsive to intervention and treatment. Emphasizes the importance of scientific research, employee assistance programs in the workplace; channeling resources to educate the public; discouraging alcohol abuse; and treating individuals suffering from alcholism.

Hotline or Toll-free Information Line
American Council on Alcoholism Information Line: 800-527-5344 (M–F 9AM–5PM ET) Referral service, answers questions, request for materials.

Consumer or Patient Education Materials
Pamphlets and fact sheets, free single copy. Please contact for complete catalog.

Publications for Health Professionals
ACA News, monthly newsletter; research reviews, document critiques. Please contact for complete publications list.

Classes and Conferences
Driver Alcohol Training and Evaluation School, 6 weeks, for DWI clients, $125. Please contact for complete list and schedule.

Technical Assistance
Employee assistance program consultants.

■ Drug Prevention Resources Inc

5525 N MacArthur Blvd, Ste 450
Irving, TX 75038
Contact: Kay Maxwell or Nancy Feaster
800-989-3774
972-518-1821
Fax: 972-550-1477

Nonprofit organization that provides drug prevention education and alternative activities in a variety of settings including public housing authorities and churches.

Consumer or Patient Education Materials
Drug Education Display Kit with Education Manual, drugs arranged in subgroups for ease of use, $219, Spanish overlay available, $25; Marijuana awareness wafers, 5 per pkg, $1.50/pkg; brochures, $.30 each. Please contact for complete catalog.

Technical Assistance
Assistance with drug elimination strategies provided to public housing authorities, and available to other entities, with focus on community development.

■ National Association for Native American Children of Alcoholics

1402 Third Ave, Ste 1110
Seattle, WA 98101
Contact: Annette Squetimkin-Anquoe
206-467-7686
Fax: 206-467-7689
E-mail: nanacoa@aol.com

Nonprofit association that promotes awareness of the needs of Native American children of alcoholics. Develops educational and supportive material for Native American communities and provides information about substance abuse resources and materials.

Consumer or Patient Education Materials
RESPECT Handbook, guide for caregivers who work with children of alcoholics, $20; Hope for Native American Children of Alcoholics, 30-min video, about intergenerational alcoholism, $50.

Classes and Conferences
Annual conference, 3½ days, national event, $165.

■ National Center for Health Education

72 Spring St, Ste 208
New York, NY 10012-4019
Contact: Urvi R Dalal, 212-334-9470 x25
212-334-9470
Fax: 212-334-9845
Web site: http://www.nche.org

Nonprofit organization dedicated to leading the nation in the implementation of life-long comprehensive health education. Designs and disseminates Growing Healthy®, a comprehensive school health education curriculum for students in grades K–6, which teaches students skills that will enable them to adopt healthy attitudes and behaviors. Call WRS Group Inc at 800-551-3488 for Growing Healthy and National Health Education Week materials.

Consumer or Patient Education Materials
Helping Children Stay Off Drugs, handbook, $1.99. Please contact for complete catalog.
Technical Assistance
Technical assistance available for comprehensive school health education, teacher training, and Growing Healthy.

■ Rational Recovery Systems Inc

PO Box 800
Lotus, CA 95651
Contact: Lois Trimpey, 916-621-2667
800-303-CURE (800-303-2873)
916-621-4374
Fax: 916-622-4296
E-mail: rr@rational.org
Web site: http://www.rational.org/recovery

For-profit organization offering the concept of immediate self-recovery from substance addiction through planned abstinence put into practice by using an easily-learned thinking skill called Addictive Voice Recognition Technique® (AVRT).

Consumer or Patient Education Materials
Rational Recovery, book, complete program description, $12; Final Fix, audiotapes, 3 hrs recorded sessions, $39.95.
Publications for Health Professionals
Journal of Rational Recovery, bimonthly, for health professionals and general public, $25/yr. Please contact for complete publications list.

■ Women for Sobriety Inc

109 W Broad St
PO Box 618
Quakertown, PA 18951-0618
Contact: Dr. Jean Kirkpatrick
215-536-8026
Fax: 215-536-8026
E-mail: wfsobriety@aol.com
Web site: http://www.mediapulse.com/wfs/

Nonprofit self-help program for women alcoholics.

Consumer or Patient Education Materials
Monthly newsletter for women alcoholics, $8.95; Program booklet, $3; So You Want to Quit, tape. Please contact for complete catalog.
Classes and Conferences
Annual conference, 3 days, at Cedar Crest College, PA, $145. Please contact for complete list and schedule.
Other Products and Services
Pen pal program.

■ World Service Office of Narcotics Anonymous

19737 Nordhoff Pl
Chatsworth, CA 91311
Contact: Julie Kirkpatrick, 818-773-9999 x1-121
818-773-9999
Fax: 818-700-0700

Nonprofit organization offering support and a 12-step program for recovering addicts. The mission of the World Service Office is to provide the services and support that facilitate the continued growth and development of the fellowship of Narcotics Anonymous worldwide.

Consumer or Patient Education Materials
Narcotics Anonymous, The Basic Text of Recovery, $9.25; It Works How and Why, book, $7.30; An Introductory Guide to Narcotics Anonymous, book plus 10 pamphlets, $1.60. Please contact for complete catalog.

TOBACCO

■ American Institute for Preventive Medicine

30445 Northwestern Hwy, Ste 350
Farmington Hills, MI 48334-3102
Contact: Order Dept, 810-539-1800 x239
800-345-2476
810-539-1800
Fax: 810-539-1808
E-mail: aipm@healthy.net
Web site: http://aipm.healthy.net

International for-profit developer and provider of health promotion programs, self-help kits, and self-care publications. Works with over 5,000 corporations, HMOs, and hospitals to reduce health care costs, lower absenteeism, and improve morale. Services include those for self-care, smoking cessation, weight control, stress management, self-esteem enhancement, prenatal education, fitness center management, nutrition, and EAP education.

Classes and Conferences
Smokeless, 8 sessions, teaches people to become permanent nonsmokers; Group Program and Guided Self-Help Kit also available. Please contact for pricing and complete list.

■ Americans for Nonsmokers' Rights

2530 San Pablo Ave, Ste J
Berkeley, CA 94702
510-841-3032
Fax: 510-841-3071
Web site: http://www.no-smoke.org

National nonprofit public interest group works to protect the right of nonsmokers to smokefree air. Its educational arm, The American Nonsmokers' Rights Foundation, promotes smoking prevention and education about smoking, passive smoke, and the tobacco industry.

Database or Statistical Information
National database of local tobacco control ordinances (clean indoor air, youth access to tobacco, advertising and promotion, tobacco excise tax); negotiable cost. Contact Elva Yanez.
Consumer or Patient Education Materials
How to Butt In: Teens Take Action Guidebook, 20 pp booklet, to help youth interested in local community action, $4.95.
Publications for Health Professionals
ANR Update, quarterly newsletter, analysis and information on current tobacco control issues, $55/yr; Death in the West, curriculum guide; Secondhand Smoke, curriculum guide.
Technical Assistance
Conducts Teens as Teachers training, a smoking prevention program to reach elementary school students.

■ Anatomical Chart Company

8221 N Kimball
Skokie, IL 60076-2956
800-621-7500 (Order Dept)
847-679-4700
Fax: 847-674-0211

Mail order company catering to the professional or student in need of biological or scientific charts and models of the human anatomy.

Consumer or Patient Education Materials
Dangers of Smoking Demonstration Models including: smoking during pregnancy, chewing tobacco, secondhand smoke, $95–$210; Charts and posters illustrating harmful effects including: alcohol, marijuana, steroids, inhalants, $10.95–$23.95; The ABC's of Smoking, booklet, $1.50 ea. Please contact for complete catalog.

■ Journeyworks Publishing

736 Chestnut St
Santa Cruz, CA 95060
Mailing address:
PO Box 8466
Santa Cruz, CA 95061-8466
800-775-1998
408-423-1400
Fax: 408-423-8102

Publisher of health promotion materials for clinics, hospitals, schools, and health departments covering a variety of topics including fitness, women's health, sexual abstinence, teen pregnancy prevention, STDs and HIV, mental wellness, tobacco use prevention, and smoking cessation.

Consumer or Patient Education Materials
Tobacco use prevention and smoking cessation pamphlets, free review sample, pricing varies upon quantity ordered. Materials can be customized; Please contact for complete catalog.

■ National Center for Tobacco-Free Kids

1707 L St, Ste 800
Washington, DC 20036
202-296-5469
Fax: 202-296-5427

Largest nonprofit initiative ever undertaken to decrease youth tobacco use in the U.S. and serving as a focal point for anti-tobacco lobbying efforts.

Hotline or Toll-free Information Line
Campaign for Tobacco-Free Kids Request Line: 800-284-KIDS (800-284-5437) 24-hr automated, to request Action Kit.
Technical Assistance
Campaign for Tobacco-Free Kids; technical assistance and educational outreach; also serves as clearinghouse for information about anti-tobacco programs.

■ Oral Health America

410 N Michigan Ave, Ste 352
Chicago, IL 60611-4211
Contact: Bryan McGuire, Manager of Programs
800-523-3438
312-836-9900
Fax: 312-836-9986

National independent nonprofit foundation whose programs help motivate people to seek dental care, assist the forgotten in obtaining care, support dental education and research, and advance the art and science of dentistry (previously known as America's Fund For Dental Health).

Special Campaigns, Events, or Programs
National Spit Tobacco Education Program, year-round and during baseball season, sponsored in cooperation with Major League Baseball. Brochures, posters, videotapes; contact Brendan Ratliff.

■ QuitSmart Stop Smoking Resources

4614 Arrowhead Tr
Hillsborough, NC 27278
Mailing Address:
PO Box 99016 Duke Station
Durham, NC 27708-9016
888-73-SMART (888-737-6278)
919-644-0736
Fax: 919-644-0736

For-profit company with over 600 certified QuitSmart facilitators across the U.S. that conducts Quit Smoking Clinics for organizations and individual smokers using a proven, cost-effective 3-session system to help smokers quit.

Consumer or Patient Education Materials
QuitSmart Stop Smoking Kit, stop smoking book, hypnosis tape, and cigarette substitute, $25.95; QuitSmart Stop Smoking Guide: With the QuitSmart System It's Easier Than You Think, book, $8.99.

Publications for Health Professionals
QuitSmart Leader Manual, stop smoking information for health professionals, $75.

Classes and Conferences
QuitSmart Trainer Certification Seminar, 1½ days, latest in smoking cessation techniques and how to promote it, $220. Please contact for complete list and schedule.

Technical Assistance
Consulting on smoking cessation in worksites and organizations.

■ Smokenders Inc

800 Connecticut Ave
Norwalk, CT 06854
Contact: Mitch Firger
800-828-4357
203-851-1835
Fax: 203-851-1259
E-mail: info@smokenders.com
Web site: http://www.smokenders.com

National for-profit provider of smoking cessation products and services for individuals, groups, corporations, and health plans. Implements live seminars and provides self-study kits and assessment surveys to determine who is ready to quit.

Consumer or Patient Education Materials
Learn How to Quit Kit, audiotape and workbook, seminar on tape, $129.

Classes and Conferences
Seminars, 1 to 1½ hour weekly meeting for 6 to 7 weeks, $325. Please contact for complete information.

■ STAT (Stop Teenage Addiction to Tobacco)

511 E Columbus Ave
Springfield, MA 01105-2556
Contact: Laura Mullen or Jeannine Berger
413-732-7828
Fax: 413-732-4219

Nonprofit organization whose mission is to stop childhood and teenage addiction to tobacco by using a combination of activism, advocacy, education, and networking. Works to eliminate the availability of tobacco to minors, regulate tobacco advertising and promotion, make the public aware of the marketing practices of the tobacco industry, and conduct other related actions.

Consumer or Patient Education Materials
Kids Say Don't Smoke Book, $5.95; STAT Spit Tobacco Speaker's Guide & Slide Collection, $100; videos, posters, T-shirts, stickers also available. Please contact for complete catalog.

Publications for Health Professionals
The STAT Tobacco-Free Youth Resource Catalog, comprehensive guide to tobacco-related materials and curricula with special focus on teens, $25; STAT Community Organizers Manual, how-to guide for community coalition building, $25; Speaker Guide and Slide Collection, 244 slides and instructional text, guided tour of 60 yrs of tobacco advertising, $200. Please contact for complete publications list.

Classes and Conferences
Annual conference, 2 days, international meeting.

ADDITIONAL RESOURCES

■ Action on Smoking and Health (ASH)

2013 H St NW
Washington, DC 20006
202-659-4310
Web site: http://ash.org

■ American Association for Respiratory Care
11030 Ables Ln
Dallas, TX 75229-4593
214-243-2272
Fax: 214-484-2720
Web site: http://www.aarc.org

■ American College Health Association
PO Box 28937
Baltimore, MD 21240-8937
410-859-1500
Fax: 410-859-1510
E-mail: ACHA@access.digex.net
Web site: http://www.clbalt.com/acha.org/

■ American Lung Association
National Office
1740 Broadway
New York, NY 10019-4374
Mailing Address:
GPO Box 596
New York, NY 10016-0596
Contact: Call 800-LUNG-USA (800-586-4872) to reach a local chapter
212-315-8700
Web site: http://www.lungusa.org

■ Coalition on Smoking or Health
1150 Connecticut Ave NW, Ste 820
Washington, DC 20036
202-452-1184

■ Community Anti-Drug Coalitions of America
901 N Pitt St, Ste 300
Alexandria, VA 22314
800-54-CADCA (800-542-2322)
703-706-0560
Fax: 703-706-0565

■ Group Health Cooperative of Puget Sound
Center for Health Promotion
1730 Minor Ave, Ste 1520
Seattle, WA 98101-1448
206-287-4320

■ Hazelden
15251 Pleasant Valley Rd
PO Box 176
Center City, MN 55012-0176
800-328-9000
612-257-4010
Fax: 612-257-1331

■ The Health Connection
55 W Oak Ridge Dr
Hagerstown, MD 21740
800-548-8700
301-790-9735
Fax: 301-790-9733

■ Higher Education Center for Alcohol and Other Drug Prevention
55 Chapel St
Newton, MA 02158-1060
800-676-1730
Fax: 617-969-5979
E-mail: HigherEdCtr@edc.org
Web site: http://www.edc.org/hec/

■ Just Say No International
2101 Webster St, Ste 1300
Oakland, CA 94612
800-258-2766
510-451-6666

■ The Learning Partnership
PO Box 199
Pleasantville, NY 10570-0199
800-551-7672
914-769-0055
Fax: 914-769-5676

■ National Assembly of National Voluntary Health and Social Welfare Organizations
1319 F St, Ste 601
Washington, DC 20004
202-347-2080
Fax: 202-939-4517
E-mail: nassembly@aol.com
Web site: http://www.nassembly.org

■ National Association for Families and Addictions and Research and Education
200 N Michigan Ave, Ste 300
Chicago, IL 60601
312-541-1272
Fax: 312-541-1271

■ National Association on Drug Abuse Problems
355 Lexington Ave, Second Fl
New York, NY 10017
Contact: Scott Stepp, Director of Development
212-986-1170
Fax: 212-697-2939
National Cocaine Hotline
800-COCAINE (800-262-2463)

■ **National Federation of State High School Associations**
11724 NW Plaza Cir
PO Box 20626
Kansas City, MO 64195-0626
Contact: Healthy Lifestyles Program
816-464-5400
Fax: 816-464-5571

■ **National Women's Resource Center**
515 King St, Ste 410
Alexandria, VA 22314
800-354-8824
703-836-8761
Fax: 703-836-7256
E-mail: nwrc@smtp.nafare.com
Web site: http://www.nwrc.org

■ **Partnership for a Drug-Free America**
405 Lexington Ave
New York, NY 10174
212-922-1560
Fax: 212-922-1570
Web site: http://www.drugfreeamerica.org

■ **Project ALERT**
c/o BEST Foundation
725 S Figueroa St
Los Angeles, CA 90017
800-ALERT-10 (800-253-7810)
213-623-0580
Fax: 213-623-0585
Web site: http://www.projectalert.best.org

FEDERAL AGENCIES

■ **Center for Substance Abuse Prevention (CSAP)**
Substance Abuse and Mental Health Services Administration
Rockwall 2 Bldg, Rm 9D-10
5600 Fishers Ln
Rockville, MD 20857
301-443-0365
Division of State Prevention Systems Programs: 301-443-7942
CSAP National Workplace Helpline: 800-843-4971
Web site: http://www.samhsa.gov/csap/csap.htm

Leads the federal efforts in prevention and intervention of alcohol, tobacco, and other drug abuse. Promotes the development of comprehensive prevention systems suited to community, state, national, and international needs. The Regional Alcohol and Drug Awareness Resource (RADAR) Network is an international communications network that distributes prevention information and includes an electronic communications system known as PREVline (301-770-0850 or via the Web: www.health.org). Other publications, materials, and program information is made available through the National Clearinghouse for Alcohol and Drug Information (NCADI): 800-729-6686.

■ **Center for Substance Abuse Treatment (CSAT)**
Substance Abuse and Mental Health Services Administration
Rockwall 2 Bldg, Ste 840
5600 Fishers Ln
Rockville, MD 20857
Communications Office: 301-443-5052
National Drug and Alcohol Treatment Routing Service: 800-662-HELP (800-662-4357)
Web site: http://www.samhsa.gov/csat/csat.htm

Leads the federal efforts to expand the capabilities of the nation's treatment effort; works cooperatively across the private and public treatment spectrum to identify, develop, and support policies, approaches, and programs that enhance and expand treatment services. Publications and grant information are disseminated through the National Clearinghouse for Alcohol and Drug Information (NCADI): 800-729-6686.

■ **National Heart, Lung, and Blood Institute (NHLBI)**
National Institutes of Health
NIH/NHLBI/OPEC, Rm 4A-03
31 Center Dr, MSC 2480
Bethesda, MD 20892-2480
301-496-4236
Web site: http://www.nhlbi.nih.gov/nhlbi/nhlbi.htm

NHLBI Information Center
PO Box 30105
Bethesda, MD 20824-0105
301-251-1222
Fax: 301-251-1223

Oversees research, demonstration, prevention, education, control, and training activities in the fields of heart, lung, and blood diseases and education concerning these diseases. The Information Center offers materials on numerous topics, including smoking.

■ **National Highway Traffic Safety Administration (NHTSA)**
U.S. Department of Transportation
400 Seventh St SW
Washington, DC 20590
Public Inquiries: 202-366-9550
Web site: http://www.nhtsa.dot.gov

Responsible for reducing deaths, injuries, and economic losses resulting from motor vehicle crashes. Provides technical and financial assistance to state and local governments and awards grants for highway safety and to help combat drunk driving. Also works with private organizations to promote safety programs. Information available from NHTSA regional offices. (Regional office number available from State and Community Services at 202-366-2121.)

■ **National Institute on Alcohol Abuse and Alcoholism (NIAAA)**
National Institutes of Health
6000 Executive Blvd, Ste 409
Bethesda, MD 20892-7003
Public Information Office: 301-443-3860
Fax: 301-480-1726
Web site: http://www.niaaa.nih.gov

Supports and conducts biomedical and behavioral research on the causes, consequences, treatment, and prevention of alcoholism and alcohol-related problems. Provides leadership in the national effort to reduce the severe and often fatal consequences of these problems. NIAAA publications and materials are available from the National Clearinghouse for Alcohol and Drug Information (NCADI).

■ **National Institute on Drug Abuse (NIDA)**
National Institutes of Health
5600 Fishers Ln, Rm 10A-39
Rockville, MD 20857
Public Information Office: 301-443-1124
Web site: http://www.nida.nih.gov/

Conducts research into the incidence and prevalence of drug abuse, its causes and consequences, and improved approaches to prevention and treatment of drug abuse. NIDA publications and materials are available from the National Clearinghouse for Alcohol and Drug Information (NCADI).

■ **Oral Health Program, Divison of Cancer Prevention and Control**
National Center for Chronic Disease Prevention & Health Promotion (NCCDPHP)
Centers for Disease Control and Prevention
4770 Buford Hwy NE, M/S F-10
Atlanta, GA 30341-3724
770-488-3038
Fax: 770-488-3065
Web site: http://www.cdc.gov/nccdphp/oh

Serves as a national resource for activities to prevent oral diseases and improve oral health; provides information on the oral effects of tobacco use. Also provides consultation and technical assistance to state and local health agencies and works with health professionals on issues related to the promotion of oral health.

■ **Office of National Drug Control Policy (ONDCP)**
750 17th St NW
Washington, DC 20006
202-395-6618

Established by Act of Congress and is organized with the Executive Office of the President. Authorized to develop and coordinate the policies, goals, and objectives of the nation's drug control program for reducing the use of illicit drugs; and also treatment and prevention. Information and publications are available from the ONDCP Drugs and Crime Clearinghouse, a component of the National Criminal Justice Reference Service (800-666-3332).

■ **Office on Smoking and Health**
National Center for Chronic Disease Prevention & Health Promotion (NCCDPHP)
Centers for Disease Control and Prevention
4770 Buford Hwy NE, M/S K-50
Atlanta, GA 30341-3714
770-488-5705
Fax: 770-488-5939
Smoking, Tobacco, and Health Information Line: 800-232-1311

Develops and distributes the annual Surgeon General's report on smoking and health, coordinates a national public information and education program on tobacco use and health, and coordinates tobacco education and research efforts within the Department of Health and Human Services and throughout the federal and state governments.

■ Safe and Drug Free Schools Program

U.S. Department of Education
1250 Maryland Ave SW, Rm 603
Washington, DC 20202
Mailing address:
600 Independence Ave SW, PRTL Rm 604
Washington, DC 20202-6123
800-624-0100
202-260-3954
Fax: 202-260-7767
Web site: http://www.ed.gov

Responds to the continuing crisis of violence and drugs in schools by supporting comprehensive school- and community-based drug abuse and violence prevention programs; allows school districts flexibility to design their own programs. Materials are available without charge by calling 800-624-0100 or writing to the office.

■ Substance Abuse and Mental Health Services Administration (SAMHSA)

Office of Public Health and Science
U.S. Dept of Health & Human Services
Parklawn Bldg, Rm 13C-05
5600 Fishers Ln
Rockville, MD 20857
Public Affairs: 301-443-8956
Information Line: 301-443-3783
Funding Opportunites: Bulletin Board Service:
800-424-2294 (9600,N,8,1)
Web site: http://www.samhsa.gov

Agency whose mission is to assure that quality substance abuse and mental health services are available to the people who need them and to ensure that prevention and treatment knowledge is used more effectively in the general health care system. Is composed of three centers: Center for Mental Health Services, Center for Substance Abuse Prevention, and Center for Substance Abuse Treatment.

Wellness Professional Resources

Products/Services Offered

Organization	web site	hotline/toll-free information line	clearinghouse/resource center	electronic information resources	database/statistical information	special campaigns/events/programs	consumer/patient education materials	publications for health professionals	classes/conferences	technical assistance	other products/services	grants/funding/awards	Page No.
American Academy of Family Physicians	■						■	■					**91**
American Association for Health Education	■						■	■					**91**
American Business Publishing								■					**91**
American College of Preventive Medicine	■							■	■				**91**
American Journal of Health Promotion								■	■				**91**
American Public Health Association	■			■		■		■	■				**92**
Association for Worksite Health Promotion	■							■	■			■	**92**
Association of State and Territorial Health Officials (ASTHO)	■										■		**92**
Association of Teachers of Preventive Medicine	■							■	■			■	**93**
Center for Training in Mind/Body Medicine									■	■			**93**
Feistritzer Publications								■					**93**
The Healthcare Forum	■							■	■				**93**
National Association for Healthcare Quality	■					■		■	■				**93**
National Association of Women's Health Professionals								■	■	■	■		**94**
National Head Start Association	■							■	■				**94**
The National Managed Health Care Congress									■				**94**
National Wellness Information Resource Center	■				■			■					**95**
National Wellness Institute Inc	■							■	■				**95**
OVID Technologies Inc	■				■								**95**
PNG Publications								■					**95**
Research!America	■	■						■					**95**

Products/Services Offered

Organization	web site	hotline/toll-free information line	clearinghouse/resource center	electronic information resources	database/statistical information	special campaigns/events/programs	consumer/patient education materials	publications for health professionals	classes/conferences	technical assistance	other products/services	grants/funding/awards	Page No.
Wellness Councils of America (WELCOA)				■				■	■	■			96
Wellsource Inc	■								■				96
WellTech International	■									■			96

Additional Resources 97

Federal Agencies 99

American Academy of Family Physicians

8880 Ward Pkwy
Kansas City, MO 64114-2797
Contact: Jacqelyn B Admire, MSPH, 800-274-2237 x5510
800-274-2237
816-333-9700
Fax: 816-333-9855
E-mail: fp@aafp.org
Web site: http://www.aafp.org

National nonprofit association that is the advocate for family physicians, the medical specialty of family practice, their patients, and the American public.

Consumer or Patient Education Materials

Personal Health Guide; Child Health Guide, booklets, enable patient to actively participate in preventive care, $1.75 ea.

Publications for Health Professionals

American Family Physician, monthly journal, $11/issue; Clinicians Handbook, reference, is useful text for health professions students of all disciplines, $25. Please contact for complete publications list.

American Association for Health Education

1900 Association Dr
Reston, VA 20191-1599
800-213-7193
703-476-3437
Fax: 703-476-6638
E-mail: aahe@aahperd.org
Web site: http://www.aahperd.org/aahe.html

National, nonprofit organization whose mission is to advance health by encouraging, supporting, and assisting health professionals concerned with health promotion through education and other systematic strategies.

Consumer or Patient Education Materials

What Every Parent Should Know About Health Education, pamphlet. Please contact for complete catalog.

Publications for Health Professionals

Journal of Health Education, bimonthly; HE-XTRA, newsletter 5 times/yr; free with membership. Please contact for complete publications list.

American Business Publishing

3100 Highway 138
PO Box 1442
Wall Township, NJ 07719-1442
800-516-4343
908-681-1133
Fax: 908-681-0490
E-mail: 75673.624@compuserve.com

Publisher of information for wellness program professionals.

Publications for Health Professionals

Wellness Program Management Advisor, monthly newsletter, effective management strategies for wellness programs, $227/yr; How Employers Are Saving Through Wellness and Fitness Programs, book, case studies, trends and analysis, and implementation, $84.25; Monitoring the Effectiveness of Worksite Wellness Programs, in-depth study on impact of wellness programs and prevalence of specific types of programs, $99. Please contact for complete publications list.

American College of Preventive Medicine

1660 L St NW, Ste 206
Washington, DC 20036-5603
Contact: Melissa Devlin
202-466-2044
Fax: 202-466-2662
E-mail: info@acpm.org
Web site: http://www.acpm.org/acpm

National nonprofit professional organization of physician specialists who practice preventive medicine. Advances the science and practice of disease prevention and health promotion, and provides leadership in research, professional education, development of public policy, and enhancement of standards for preventive medicine.

Publications for Health Professionals

ACPM News, quarterly newsletter, updates on legislative issues affecting preventive medicine, $25/yr; American Journal of Preventive Medicine, bimonthly, covers all aspects of practice, teaching, and research in preventive medicine. Please contact for pricing and complete publications list.

Classes and Conferences

Prevention, 4-day conference co-sponsored with the Association of Teachers of Preventive Medicine, annual national disease and health promotion meeting. Please contact for complete information.

American Journal of Health Promotion

1660 Cass Lake Rd, Ste 104
Keego Harbor, MI 48320-1036
810-682-0707
Fax: 810-682-1212

Publisher and promoter of health promotion publications, conferences, seminars, and workshops.

Publications for Health Professionals

American Journal of Health Promotion, bimonthly, peer-reviewed scientifc, $69/yr; Art of Health Promotion Newsletter, bimonthly, for health promotion practitioners, included with journal subscription; Design of Workplace Health Promotion Programs, workbook, framework for designing and implementation, $19.95.

Classes and Conferences

Annual Art and Science of Health Promotion Conference, 1 week in late Feb or early March, covering all aspects of health promotion; intensive tranining seminars and pre-conference workshops available. Contact Steve Hawks, Conference Director, 800-627-0629 for complete information.

■ American Public Health Association

1015 15th St NW
Washington, DC 20005
Contact: Publication Sales, 301-893-1894, PO Box 753, Waldorf, MD 20604-0753
202-789-5600
TDD: 202-789-6573
Web site: http://www.apha.org

National nonprofit multi-disciplinary association of professionals in public health and related fields that works to protect and promote personal and environmental health. Develops standards, promulgates recommended rules, and publishes pamphlets, books, model codes, and educational materials.

Electronic Information Resources

Fax-on-Demand: 202-274-4577

Special Campaigns, Events, or Programs

National Public Health Week, April, contact Katherine S McCarter.

Publications for Health Professionals

American Journal of Public Health, monthly journal, articles covering many areas of public health, $100–$160/yr; The Nation's Health, 11 issues/yr newspaper, reports on current developments and issues, $15/yr. Please contact for complete publications list.

Classes and Conferences

Annual meeting and exhibition, scientific and professional sessions, commercial exhibits. Please contact for complete list and schedule.

■ Association for Worksite Health Promotion

60 Revere Dr, Ste 500
Northbrook, IL 60062
Contact: Corie Louie, Membership Director
847-480-9574
Fax: 847-480-9282
E-mail: awhp@awhp.com
Web site: http://www.awhp.com

Nonprofit organization whose mission is to advance worksite health promotion throughout the world and dedicated to enhancing the personal and organizational health and well-being of employees and their families. Works to achieve mission by: advocating the value of worksite health promotion to business and government leaders; supporting health promotion professionals through education; providing resources to worksite health promotion professionals; and serving as a catalyst to advance research and learning in the field.

Publications for Health Professionals

Worksite Health, quarterly journal, $45–$60/yr; Action, bimonthly newsletter, $25/yr.

Classes and Conferences

Annual international conference, 4 days, educational and trade show, $345–$525; Eight regional conferences, 2½ days, educational, $100–$300. Please contact for complete list and schedule.

Grants, Funding, or Awards

Student scholarships and research committee grants. Contact central office.

■ Association of State and Territorial Health Officials (ASTHO)

415 Second St NE, Ste 200
Washington, DC 20002
202-546-5400
Fax: 202-544-9349
Web site: http://www.astho.org

Nonprofit association that represents the public health agencies of each of the U.S. states and territories whose mission is to formulate and influence national health policy and serve state health departments in the development and implementation of programs and policies to promote health and prevent disease. Also engages in a wide variety of legislative, scientific, educational, and programmatic issues and activities on behalf of public health. Currently has 16 affiliate groups representing directors of divisions with the state health departments.

Other Products and Services

Information published includes newsletters, surveys, resource lists, and white papers from cooperative special projects guided by ASTHO committees.

■ Association of Teachers of Preventive Medicine

1660 L St NW, Ste 208
Washington, DC 20036
202-463-0550
Fax: 202-463-0555
E-mail: info@atpm.org
Web site: http://www.atpm.org/atpm.htm

Nonprofit organization whose mission is to ensure the primacy and excellence of individual and community health promotion and disease prevention in the education of physicians and other health professionals. Also promotes the exchange of ideas among its members, provides leadership, and promotes national advocacy on behalf of its members.

Publications for Health Professionals

American Journal of Preventive Medicine, bimonthly, covers all aspects of practice, teaching, and research in preventive medicine. Please contact for pricing and complete publications list.

Classes and Conferences

Prevention, 4-day conference co-sponsored with the American College of Preventive Medicine, annual national disease and health promotion meeting. Please contact for complete information.

Grants, Funding, or Awards

Research grants for medical schools and schools of public health.

■ Center for Training in Mind/Body Medicine

Mind/Body Medical Institute
1 Deaconess Rd
Boston, MA 02215
Contact: Marilyn Wilcher, Program Director, 617-632-7375
617-632-9530 x107
Fax: 617-632-9545
E-mail: mwilcher@nedhmail.nedh.harvard.edu

Nonprofit, scientific and educational organization prepares health care professionals to implement health management outpatient clinics utilizing mind/body interventions. Programs cover all aspects of practice of mind/body medicine with emphasis on multidisciplinary interventions including the relaxation response. Conducted at Harvard Medical School under direction of Herbert Benson, MD.

Classes and Conferences

Training programs for cancer, cardiovascular rehabilitation and risk reduction, HIV/AIDS, chronic pain, infertility, insomnia, and medical symptom reduction. Customized training programs offered to health care providers who are planning to incorporate mind/body interventions into their medical practice. $1,200–$50,000. Please contact for complete list and schedule.

Technical Assistance

Consulting offered on clinical, administrative, and marketing issues.

■ Feistritzer Publications

4401A Connecticut Ave NW, #212
Washington, DC 20008
Contact: David T Chester, Publisher
202-362-3444
Fax: 202-362-3493

Publisher of health education newsletter.

Publications for Health Professionals

Health Education Reports, 24 issues/yr newsletter, covers fields of health education, promotion, prevention, resources, and events, $198.

■ The Healthcare Forum

425 Market St, 16th Fl
San Francisco, CA 94105
Contact: Brenda Whitney, 415-356-4400
415-356-4300
Fax: 415-356-9300
E-mail: thf@healthonline.com
Web site: http://www.healthonline.com.thf.htm

Nonprofit leadership center and hospital membership organization with members in the U.S. and countries around the world. It is a resource in education and applied research at the forefront of new leadership thinking, organizational learning, and mastering change.

Publications for Health Professionals

Healthcare Forum Journal, bimonthly, for senior health care executives, $55/yr.

Classes and Conferences

Annual Healthier Communities Summit, 3 days, international conference. Call 415-356-4400 for complete information.

■ National Association for Healthcare Quality

4700 W Lake Ave
Glenview, IL 60025-1485
800-966-9392
847-375-4720

Fax: 847-875-4777
E-mail: info@nahq.org
Web site: http://www.nahq.com

Nonprofit organization for health care quality professionals comprised of more than 7,000 individual members and 100 institutional members. Goal is to promote the continuous improvement of quality in health care by providing educational and development opportunities for professionals at all management levels and within all health care settings.

Special Campaigns, Events, or Programs
National Healthcare Quality Week, 3rd week in October, products catalog. Contact Eden Essex.

Publications for Health Professionals
Journal for Healthcare Quality, bimonthly; NAHQ News, quarterly newsletter, free with membership.

Classes and Conferences
Managed Care Course, 2 days, Building an Integrated QI Program in Managed Care, $325–$430.

■ National Association of Women's Health Professionals

175 W Jackson Blvd, Ste A-1711
Chicago, IL 60604-9674
Contact: C Coglianese
312-786-1468
Fax: 312-786-0376

Nonprofit interdisciplinary membership association for professionals who influence health care for women. Promotes excellence and provides leadership, resources, and collegial support to professionals who influence and champion quality health care for women and their communities.

Publications for Health Professionals
Business of Women's Health, one-time compilation of articles on management, strategic planning, marketing for women's health services, $45; Focus, quarterly newsletter, provides information specific to needs of those responsible for women's health programs, included with membership; audiotapes, covers range of women's health topics, $10–$12. Please contact for complete publications list.

Classes and Conferences
Annual Women's Health Conference, 3–4 days, addresses both clinical and business aspects of women's health, $415–$595. Please contact for complete list and schedule.

Technical Assistance
Members can access women's health experts who share information, offer site visits, and provide resources in outcomes measurement, managed care contracting, strategic planning, clinical issues, educational programming, and more.

Other Products and Services
Peer mentor program, faxed briefings on women's health.

■ National Head Start Association

1651 Prince St
Alexandria, VA 22314
Contact: Publications Dept, 800-687-5044
703-739-0875
Fax: 703-739-0878
Web site: http://www.nhsa.org

Nonprofit organization dedicated exclusively to serving the needs of the Head Start Community. Mission includes advocating in the government, business, and private sectors; working to improve quality and expand enrollment through increased funding; and providing training and professional development for members.

Publications for Health Professionals
Linking the Pieces Together, newsletter, information about partnerships, $40; Child and Family National Resource Directory, $9; Head Start Yellow Pages, 3rd edition, annual directory, $25. Please contact for complete publications list.

Classes and Conferences
Annual conference, 1 week in May; Parent Training Conference, 1 week in December. Contact Conference Dept, 703-739-0875.

■ The National Managed Health Care Congress

70 Blanchard Rd, Ste 4000
Burlington, MA 01803
Contact: Amy R Pavel, Public Relations Manager, 617-505-8167
888-44-NMHCC (888-446-6422)
617-505-8000
Fax: 617-270-6004
E-mail: register@nmhcc.com

For-profit conference producer of the nation's largest, most diverse educational forum for all constituents in the managed health care industry—purchasers, providers, payors, and suppliers. Offers distinguished faculty, in-depth symposia, diverse industry tracks, and large exhibition hall.

Classes and Conferences
The National Managed Health Care Congress, 4 days. Please contact for complete list and schedule.

■ National Wellness Information Resource Center

Fisher Institute for Wellness, Ball State University
2000 University Ave
Muncie, IN 47306-0210
Contact: Debbie J Sheller
888-935-5278
317-285-8121
317-285-8259
Fax: 317-285-8237
E-mail: 00djsheller@bsuvc.bsu.edu
Web site: http://www.bsu.edu/up/wellness/nwirc.html

Nonprofit educational resource center that assists wellness and health promotion professionals in their professional development by providing resources, information, and networking opportunities in higher education.

Database or Statistical Information

Database information available on wellness trends and programming in higher education.

Publications for Health Professionals

Wellness Connections, bimonthly newsletter, covering wellness in higher education, free with membership; NWIRC Directory, every 2 yrs, colleges and universities offering wellness and health promotion programs, $15.

■ National Wellness Institute Inc

1045 Clark St, Ste 210
PO Box 827
Stevens Point, WI 54481-0827
Contact: Krista Wittkopf
800-243-8694
715-342-2969
Fax: 715-342-2979
E-mail: nwi@wellnessnwi.org
Web site: http://www.wellnessnwi.org/

Nonprofit organization whose mission is to help individuals lead better lives by serving a worldwide network of health promotion and wellness professionals and organizations by providing professional education; furnishing information and resources; developing and distributing wellness related products and services, research, and national and international leadership. The National Wellness Association is the membership division of the Institute.

Publications for Health Professionals

Health Issues Update, quarterly, newsletter for NWA professional members.

Classes and Conferences

National Wellness Conference, 8 days, educational seminars and workshops, networking. Please contact for complete information.

■ OVID Technologies Inc

333 Seventh Ave
New York, NY 10001
Contact: Ilyssa Greene, 212-563-3006 x344
800-950-2035
212-563-3006
Fax: 212-563-3784
E-mail: sales@ovid.com or igreene@ovid.com
Web site: http://www.ovid.com

Software company providing platform-independent online access to more than 80 bibliographic and full text databases for academic, biomedical, and scientific research that are available via the Internet or dial-up communications. Fixed-fee or pay-as-you-go pricing options are available.

Database or Statistical Information

Combined Health Information Database (CHID), composed of a number of subfiles produced by separate federal agencies, topics covered include: health promotion and education, disease prevention, maternal and child health.

■ PNG Publications

PO Box 4593
Morgantown, WV 26504-4593
Contact: Penny N Glover
304-293-4699
Fax: 304-293-4693

Publisher of American Journal of Health Behavior™ (formerly Health Values), which was developed to improve the approach of health education, health promotion, and other multi-disciplinary health efforts by fostering a better understanding of the multidimensional nature of both individuals and social systems as it relates to health behavior.

Publications for Health Professionals

American Journal of Health Behavior™, bimonthly, peer-reviewed, $64/yr individual, $99/yr institutional.

■ Research!America

1522 King St
Alexandria, VA 22314
Contact: Keri J Sperry
800-FON-CURE (800-366-2873)
703-739-2577

Fax: 703-739-2372
E-mail: researcham@aol.com
Web site: http://www.nicom.com/~ramerica

National nonprofit membership-based public education and advocacy alliance of more than 350 academic institutions, corporations, hospitals, professional societies, voluntary health agencies, and individuals. Objective is to increase awareness of the value of medical research and its significance in improving the quality of life for all, and to make medical research a much higher national priority.

Hotline or Toll-free Information Line
Research!America Information Line: 800-FON-CURE (800-366-2873) (M–F 9AM–5:30PM ET) Operator assisted, referral service, requests for materials.

Publications for Health Professionals
Membership Matters, monthly newsletter, news for medical research advocate, free with membership; Odds Brochure, advocacy tips for medical research, free. Please contact for complete publications list.

■ Wellness Councils of America (WELCOA)

Community Health Plaza
7101 Newport Ave, Ste 311
Omaha, NE 68152-2100
402-572-3590
Fax: 402-572-3594
E-mail: welcoa@neonramp.com

National nonprofit membership organization dedicated to promoting healthier lifestyles for all Americans, especially through health promotion activities at the workplace—has a nationwide network of locally affiliated Wellness Councils and direct network members serving corporate members and their employees. Acts as a national clearinghouse and information center on corporate health promotion for companies everywhere.

Electronic Information Resources
Fax-on-Demand: 402-498-9805 code 100 (must call from your fax machine phone); Cost-benefits summary of corporate health promotion programs (document #101); list of America's healthiest companies (document #102).

Publications for Health Professionals
How-to guidebooks for health planners include: Healthy, Wealthy & Wise, $95; Health Fairs, $30; HealthTrip incentive campaign, $89. Please contact for complete publications list.

Classes and Conferences
Fundamentals of Workplace Health Promotion, 1–2 days, covers basics; other seminars and workshops; fee varies. Please contact for complete list and schedule.

Technical Assistance
Technical assistance available and included with membership.

■ Wellsource Inc

15431 SE 82nd Dr, Ste D
PO Box 569
Clackamas, OR 97015
Contact: Area sales representative
800-533-9355
503-656-7446
Fax: 503-650-0880
E-mail: well@wellsource-in.com
Web site: http://www.wellsource-inc.com

International consulting firm that develops software systems, health risk appraisals (HRA); offers training and support for managing risk factors, tracking health outcomes; and serves health promotion professionals.

Classes and Conferences
Wellness and Prevention Systems Training Seminars, 2½ days, designed for directors of health promotion programs. Please contact for complete list and schedule.

■ WellTech International

PO Box 411183-251
St Louis, MO 63141
Contact: Geoff Allen
314-995-9838
Fax: 314-994-1545
E-mail: info@welltech.com
Web site: http://www.welltech.com

Consulting firm that provides Internet presence and resources to companies and professionals associated with health promotion. Team of health promotion, information management, and interactive media specialists provides service and quality to an online presence. WellTech's web site provides free access to information and resources for health promotion professionals.

Technical Assistance
Consulting on Internet and Intranet site development.

ADDITIONAL RESOURCES

American Chiropractic Association
1701 Clarendon Blvd
Arlington, VA 22209
Contact: Communications Dept
800-986-INFO (800-986-4636)
703-276-8800
Fax: 703-243-2593
E-mail: amerchiro@aol.com
Web site: http://www.cais.net/aca

American College Health Association
PO Box 28937
Baltimore, MD 21240-8937
410-859-1500
Fax: 410-859-1510
E-mail: ACHA@access.digex.net
Web site: http://www.clbalt.com/acha.org/

American College of Epidemiology
401 E Jefferson St, Ste 205
Rockville, MD 20850
Mailing Address:
PO Box 10639
Rockville, MD 20849
Contact: Mary Cassidy
301-251-0594
Fax: 301-279-6749
E-mail: epiinfo@amcollepi.org

American College of Nurse Practitioners
1090 Vermont Ave NW, Ste 800
Washington, DC 20005
Contact: Nancy J Sharp
202-408-7050
Fax: 202-408-0902
E-mail: acnp@aol.com
Web site: http://www.nurse.org/acnp

American Medical Association
515 N State St
Chicago, IL 60610
Contact: Publications and Customer Service, 800-621-8335
312-464-5000
Web site: http://www.ama-assn.org

American Osteopathic Association
142 E Ontario St
Chicago, IL 60611
800-621-1773
312-280-5800
Fax: 312-280-3860
Web site: http://www.am-osteo-assn.org

Association of Hospital Health and Fitness
915 Elmwood Ave
Evanston, IL 60202
Mailing Address:
PO Box 6280
Evanston, IL 60204-6001
847-475-2332
Fax: 847-475-2112
E-mail: 102707.321@compuserve.com

Association of Schools of Public Health
1660 L St NW, Ste 204
Washington, DC 20036
Contact: Carol Madkins
202-296-1099
Fax: 202-296-1252

Council on Education for Public Health
1015 15th St NW, Ste 402
Washington, DC 20005
202-789-1050
Fax: 202-789-1895

Employee Assistance Society of North America
PO Box 634
New Hope, PA 18938-0634
215-891-9538
Fax: 215-891-9539

Health Resources Publishing
Brinley Professional Bldg
3100 Hwy 138
Wall Township, NJ 07719-1442 07719
800-516-4343
Fax: 908-681-0490
E-mail: mcic@monmouth.com
Web site: http://www.themcic.com

Infoline
225 Turnpike Rd
Southborough, MA 01772-1749
Contact: IBC USA Conferences Inc
508-481-6400
Fax: 508-481-7911

■ **Institute for Healthcare Improvement**
135 Francis St
Boston, MA 02215
617-754-4800
Fax: 617-754-4848

■ **International Quality and Productivity Center**
150 Clove Rd
PO Box 401
Little Falls, NJ 07424-0401
800-882-8684
201-256-0211
Fax: 201-256-0205
E-mail: info@iqpc.com
Web site: http://www.iqpc.com

■ **National Academy for State Health Policy**
50 Monument Square, Ste 502
Portland, ME 04101
207-874-6524
Fax: 207-874-6527
E-mail: 73612.316@compuserve.com

■ **National Association of County & City Health Officials (NACHO)**
440 First St NW, Ste 500
Washington, DC 20001
202-783-5550
Fax: 202-783-1583
Web site: http://www.naccho.org

■ **National Association of State Boards of Education**
1012 Cameron St
Alexandria, VA 22314
703-684-4000
Fax: 703-836-2313
Web site: http://www.nasbe.org

■ **The National Business Coalition on Health**
1015 18th St NW, Ste 450
Washington, DC 20036
202-775-9300
Fax: 202-775-1569
Web site: http://www.nbch.org/nbch/

■ **National Health Council**
1730 M St NW, Ste 500
Washington, DC 20036-4505
Contact: Publications
202-785-3910
Fax: 202-785-5923
Web site: http://www.housecall.com/sponsors/nhc/index.html

■ **The National Public Health and Hospital Institute**
1212 New York Ave NW, Ste 800
Washington, DC 20005
202-408-0229
Fax: 202-408-0235
E-mail: naph@naph.org
Web site: http://www.naph.org/NPHHI.html

■ **National Rural Health Association**
One W Armour Blvd, Ste 301
Kansas City, MO 64111
816-756-3140
Fax: 816-756-3144
E-mail: mail@nrharural.org
Web site: http://www.NRHArural.org

■ **Partnership for Prevention**
1220 19th St NW, Ste 405
Washington, DC 20036
Contact: Diane Hawkins
202-833-0009
Fax: 202-833-0113

■ **Preventive Medicine Research Institute**
900 Bridgeway, Ste 1
Sausalito, CA 94965
800-775-PMRI (800-775-7674)
415-332-2525
Fax: 415-332-5730

■ **Society for Public Health Education Inc**
1015 15th St NW, Ste 410
Washington, DC 20005
202-408-9804
Fax: 202-408-9815
E-mail: sopheauld@aol.com

■ **U.S. Conference of Local Health Officers**
1620 Eye St, Ste 400
Washington, DC 20006
202-293-7330
Fax: 202-293-2352
Web site: http://www.usmayors.org/uscm

FEDERAL AGENCIES

■ Bureau of Health Professions (BHPr)

Health Resources and Services Administration
Parklawn Bldg, Rm 8-05
5600 Fishers Ln
Rockville, MD 20857
301-443-1590

Provides national leadership in supporting the development and use of the nation's health personnel and serves as a focus for selected issues of quality assurance and medical malpractice. Supports health professions and nursing education in areas of high national priority, such as primary care workforce development, health care for minorities and the underserved, strengthened education concerning HIV/AIDS and substance abuse, and health care of the elderly.

■ Public Health Practice Program Office (PHPPO)

Centers for Disease Control and Prevention
1600 Clifton Rd NE, M/S E-20
Atlanta, GA 30333
404-639-1938
Fax: 404-639-1920
Information Network for Public Health Officials (INPHO): http//www.cdc.gov/inpho/inpho.htm
Web site: http://www.cdc.gov/phppo/phppo.htm

Mission of this office is to strengthen the community practice of public health.

Health and Injury Protection

Environmental Health 103
Food and Drug Safety 111
Occupational Safety and Health 117
Oral Health 125
Unintentional Injuries 129
Violence-related Injuries 137

Environmental Health

Products/Services Offered

Organization	web site	hotline/toll-free information line	clearinghouse/resource center	electronic information resources	database/statistical information	special campaigns/events/programs	consumer/patient education materials	publications for health professionals	classes/conferences	technical assistance	other products/services	grants/funding/awards	Page No.
Alliance To End Childhood Lead Poisoning	■						■	■					104
American Conference of Governmental Industrial Hygienists	■						■	■					104
Americans for Nonsmokers' Rights	■				■		■	■		■			104
Chemical Injury Information Network								■					104
Environmental Health Center	■	■	■			■					■		105
Health Education Services	■						■						105
IAQ Publications	■							■	■				105
Industrial Health Foundation Inc										■			105
National Environmental Health Association	■			■			■	■	■	■	■	■	105
National Pediculosis Association	■					■	■	■		■	■		106
Occupational Health Strategies Inc										■	■		106
Rachel Carson Council Inc							■	■		■			106

Additional Resources 107

Federal Agencies 108

■ Alliance To End Childhood Lead Poisoning

227 Massachusetts Ave NE, Ste 200
Washington, DC 20002
202-543-1147
Fax: 202-543-4466
E-mail: aeclp@aeclp.org
Web site: http://www.aeclp.org

National nonprofit public interest organization created to launch a comprehensive attack on the epidemic of childhood lead poisoning. Mission is to frame the national agenda, formulate innovative approaches, and bring critical resources to bear—scientific and technical knowledge, public policy, economic forces, other organizations, and community leaders—to prevent childhood lead poisoning. Encompasses three major areas of activity: education, policy support, and advocacy.

Consumer or Patient Education Materials

Slide Show on Lead Hazard Disclosure, overview of new requirements for broad range of audiences; Slide Show for Rental Property Owners and Managers; Slide Show for Tenants; all with accompanying script. $50–$95. Low literacy; Please contact for complete catalog.

Publications for Health Professionals

Alliance Alert, bimonthly newsletter, brief reviews of developments, reference for more information, free with donation; Resource Handbook for Lead Hazard Control, reference guide, easy-to-use guide to new federal lead hazard regulations for public inquiries, $60; Childhood Lead Poisoning: Blueprint for Prevention, booklet, essential resource for educating policymakers, $4. Please contact for complete publications list.

■ American Conference of Governmental Industrial Hygienists

1330 Kemper Meadow Dr
Cincinnati, OH 45240
513-742-2020
Fax: 513-742-3355
E-mail: acgih_pubs@pol.com
Web site: http://www.acgih.org

Nonprofit membership organization of professionals or students in the fields of occupational or environmental health that promotes excellence in environmental and occupational health; provides technical information of the highest quality; benefits the health and well-being of people worldwide; and serves the membership and continually improves the organization, including its financial and human resources.

Consumer or Patient Education Materials

Heat Stress posters and slides, demonstrates how to recognize and prevent heat stress. Please contact for complete catalog.

Publications for Health Professionals

Various materials available including monitoring indoor air quality. Please contact for complete publications list.

■ Americans for Nonsmokers' Rights

2530 San Pablo Ave, Ste J
Berkeley, CA 94702
510-841-3032
Fax: 510-841-3071
Web site: http://www.no-smoke.org

National nonprofit public interest group works to protect the right of nonsmokers to smokefree air. Its educational arm, The American Nonsmokers' Rights Foundation, promotes smoking prevention and education about smoking, passive smoke, and the tobacco industry.

Database or Statistical Information

National database of local tobacco control ordinances (clean indoor air, youth access to tobacco, advertising and promotion, tobacco excise tax); negotiable cost. Contact Elva Yanez.

Consumer or Patient Education Materials

Clearing the Air, 44 pp guide, step-by-step process of organizing for and passing a local clean indoor air ordinance, $8.95.

Publications for Health Professionals

ANR Update, quarterly newsletter, analysis and information on current tobacco control issues, $55/yr.

Technical Assistance

Conducts trainings and presentations on policy and media advocacy related to passing laws to protect nonsmokers from secondhand smoke in public and workplaces.

■ Chemical Injury Information Network

PO Box 301
White Sulphur Springs, MT 59645-0301
406-547-2255
Fax: 406-547-2255

Nonprofit support and advocacy organization for the chemically injured, especially suffering from multiple chemical sensitivities. Focuses on education, research, and the empowerment of the chemically disabled.

Publications for Health Professionals

Our Toxic Times, monthly, covers chemical health issues, by donation.

■ Environmental Health Center

1019 19th St NW, Ste 401
Washington, DC 20036
202-293-2270
Fax: 202-293-0032
E-mail: ehc@cais.com
Web site: http://nsc.org

A division of the nonprofit, nongovernmental National Safety Council to foster improved public understanding of significant health risks and challenges facing modern society. Operates the National Radon Hotline and the National Lead Information Center.

Hotline or Toll-free Information Line

National Lead Information Center Hotline: 800-LEAD-FYI (800-532-3394) 24-hr automated line, request for information packet
Radon Hotline: 800-SOS-RADON (800-767-7236) 24-hr automated line, request for information packet, answers questions

Clearinghouse or Resource Center

National Lead Information Center Clearinghouse: 800-424-LEAD (800-424-5323) or 202-883-1071; Specialist available (M–F 8:30AM–5PM ET) to answer questions or provide detailed information.

Special Campaigns, Events, or Programs

Radon Awareness Week, October, contact 800-55-RADON (800-557-2366) or write the Indoor Air Quality Program, National Safety Council/EHC, PO Box 33435, Washington, DC 20033-0435

Other Products and Services

Computer-Aided Management of Emergency Operations (CAMEO) software, includes database of 4,700 hazardous chemicals with emergency response and safety data, $375 for government entities; $1,050 for industry/commercial users.

■ Health Education Services

PO Box 7126
Albany, NY 12224
518-439-7286
Fax: 518-439-7286 *51
Web site: http://www.hes.org

Nonprofit distributor of current health education, promotional publications, posters, and videos, most of which have been produced by the New York State Department of Health or the New York State Department of Environmental Conservation (Health Education Services is a Division of Health Research Inc).

Consumer or Patient Education Materials

Environmental Health Information Kit, citizen and community guide to dealing with toxic chemicals in the home and environment, $1.50; storage of petroleum and hazardous substances; lead poisoning. Some Spanish languages available. Please contact for complete catalog.

■ IAQ Publications

2 Wisconsin Cir, Ste 430
Chevy Chase, MD 20815
Contact: Monique Henderson
800-394-0115
301-913-0115
Fax: 301-913-0119
E-mail: iaqpubs@aol.com
Web site: http://www.iaqpubs.com

Publisher specializing in indoor air quality, healthy building management, and lead poisioning prevention media.

Publications for Health Professionals

The Indoor Air Quality Directory, 370 pp book, $100; Federal Indoor Air Quality Information Library, reference collection of 19 publications, $250; Lead Detection & Abatement Directory, 333 pp book, $100. Please contact for complete publications list.

Classes and Conferences

Annual conferences on indoor air quality and lead detection. Please contact for complete list and schedule.

■ Industrial Health Foundation Inc

34 Penn Circle W
Pittsburgh, PA 15206
412-363-6600
Fax: 412-363-6605

National nonprofit member-oriented organization dedicated to the advancement of healthful working conditions in industry.

Technical Assistance

Toxicology consultation available.

■ National Environmental Health Association

720 S Colorado Blvd, Ste 970 South
Denver, CO 80222-1925
Contact: Customer Service
303-756-9090
Fax: 303-691-9490
E-mail: beckyr@csn.net
Web site: http://www.neha.org/~beckyr

Nonprofit organization whose mission is to advance the environmental health and protection professional for the purpose of providing a healthful environment for all.

Electronic Information Resources
Fax-on-Demand: 303-756-9090 (option 5), no charge for information.

Consumer or Patient Education Materials
OSHA Refresher Course, computer-based training, designed to meet 8 hrs of requirements, $129; Fundamental Toxicology and Risk Assessment, computer-based training, geared for those with little or no background, $250–$375. Please contact for complete catalog.

Publications for Health Professionals
Journal of Environmental Health, 10 times/yr, $90/yr; Disaster Field Manual, booklet, practical guide for what needs to be done during a natural or unnatural disaster, $35–$45. Please contact for complete publications list.

Classes and Conferences
Annual Educational Conference and Exhibition, 5 days, workshops and commercial exhibits, $349–$449; Radon/Indoor Air Outreach, 1 day, overview and how to implement program, free; Radon Resistant New Construction, 1 day, technical review of techniques, free; Health Risk Communication Workshop, 1 day, training on key principles of risk communication, free. Please contact for complete list and schedule.

Technical Assistance
Technical sections available for many topics including: general environmental health, institutional environmental health, hazardous and toxic substances, injury prevention, occupational health, food protection.

Other Products and Services
Credentialing, $50–$110 (members), $95–$175 (nonmembers)

Grants, Funding, or Awards
NEHA Scholarship. Contact Veronica White by mail at main address.

■ National Pediculosis Association

50 Kearney Rd
Needham, MA 02194
Mailing Address:
PO Box 610189
Newton, MA 02161-0189
Contact: Linda Menditto, 617-449-6487 x108
617-449-6487
Fax: 617-449-8129
Web site: http://www.headlice.org

Nonprofit health education agency dedicated to protecting children and their families from potentially harmful lice and scabies pesticidal treatments.

Special Campaigns, Events, or Programs
National Pediculosis Prevention Month, September, prevention packet. Contact Linda Menditto.

Consumer or Patient Education Materials
Handouts, books, videos. Please contact for complete catalog.

Publications for Health Professionals
Progress, 3 to 4 times annually, current information, free with membership; screening tools. Please contact for complete publications list.

Technical Assistance
Consultation available.

Other Products and Services
NPA National Reporting Registry, 800-446-4NPA (800-446-4672), for reporting lice and scabies outbreaks, treatment failures, and adverse reactions to treatments.

■ Occupational Health Strategies Inc

901 Preston Ave, Ste 400
Charlottesville, VA 22903-4491
Contact: Linda David
804-977-3784
Fax: 804-977-8570
E-mail: kwp@cstone.net

National consulting firm who provides planning, design, and evaluation of corporate-wide occupational and environmental health policies, procedures, programs, and strategies to corporations and health care providers.

Technical Assistance
Performs health data analysis.

Other Products and Services
Builds customized microcomputer software.

■ Rachel Carson Council Inc

8940 Jones Mill Rd
Chevy Chase, MD 20815-4700
Contact: Dr. Diana Post
301-652-1877
Fax: 301-951-7179
E-mail: rccouncil@aol.com

Nonprofit organization that provides scientifically accurate information about pesticides, alternatives, and other environmental contaminants to help society realize Rachel Carson's vision of a healthy and diverse environment.

Consumer or Patient Education Materials
Alternative Pest Controls, chemical alternatives and non-toxic control for gardening, $4; Pesticides and Lawns, toxicity of commonly used garden pesticides, $4; The Other Road to Flea Control, less toxic methods of flea control, $4. Please contact for complete catalog.

Publications for Health Professionals
Basic Guide to Pesticides, book, pesticide toxicity and references, $39.50.

Technical Assistance
Consulting on pesticide toxicity, alternative less-toxic methods.

ADDITIONAL RESOURCES

■ American Lung Association
National Office
1740 Broadway
New York, NY 10019-4374
Mailing Address:
GPO Box 596
New York, NY 10016-0596
Contact: Call 800-LUNG-USA (800-586-4872) to reach a local chapter
212-315-8700
Web site: http://www.lungusa.org

■ American Water Works Association
6666 W Quincy Ave
Denver, CO 80235-3098
Contact: AWWA Bookstore, 800-926-7337
303-794-7711
Fax: 303-794-7310
Web site: http://www.awwa.org

■ American Water Works Association Research Foundation
6666 W Quincy Ave
Denver, CO 80235-3098
303-347-6100
Fax: 303-730-0851
Web site: http://www.awwarf.com

■ Children's Environmental Health Network
5900 Hollis St, Ste E
Emeryville, CA 94608
Contact: Joy Carlson, Director
510-450-3818
Fax: 510-450-3773
E-mail: cehn@aimnet.com
Web site: http://www.cehn.org

■ Environmental Action Foundation
6930 Carroll Ave, Ste 600
Takoma Park, MD 20912
301-891-1100

■ Environmental Defense Fund
257 Park Ave S, 16th Fl
New York, NY 10010
Contact: Public Information, Washington DC, 202-387-3500
800-684-3322
212-505-2100
Fax: 212-505-0892
E-mail: members@edf.org
Web site: http://www.edf.org

■ Government Institutes
4 Research Pl
Rockville, MD 20850
Contact: Tom Sullivan
301-921-2355
Fax: 301-921-0373
Web site: http://www.govinst.com

■ National Center for Environmental Health Strategies Inc
1100 Rural Ave
Voorhees, NJ 08043
609-429-5358
E-mail: wjrd37a@prodigy.com

■ National Center for Lead-Safe Housing
10227 Wincopin Cir, Ste 205
Columbia, MD 21044
Contact: Evelyn Bloomer
410-992-0712
Fax: 410-715-2310

■ National Pesticide Telecommunications Network
333 Weniger
Oregon State University
Corvallis, OR 97331-6502
800-858-7378
Fax: 541-737-0761
Web site: http://ace.orst.edu/info/nptn

■ Natural Resources Defense Council
40 W 20th St, 11th Fl
New York, NY 10011
Contact: Publications Dept, 212-727-4486
212-727-2700
Fax: 212-727-1773
E-mail: NRDCinfo@NRDC.org
Web site: http://www.nrdc.org

■ NSF International
National Sanitation Foundation
3475 Plymouth Rd
PO Box 130140
Ann Arbor, MI 48113-0140
800-NSF-MARK (800-673-8010)
Fax: 313-769-0109
E-mail: info@nsf.org
Web site: http://www.nsf.org

■ Water Environment Federation
601 Wythe St
Alexandria, VA 22314-1994
Contact: Member Services Dept
800-666-0206
703-684-2452
Fax: 703-684-2492
Web site: http://www.wef.org

■ Water Quality Association
4151 Naperville Rd
Lisle, IL 60532
800-749-0234
630-505-0160
Fax: 630-505-9637
E-mail: info@mail.wqa.org
Web site: http://www.wqa.org

FEDERAL AGENCIES

■ Agency for Toxic Substances and Disease Registry (ATSDR)
Office of Public Health and Science
U.S. Dept of Health & Human Services
1600 Clifton Rd NE, MSC E-29
Atlanta, GA 30333
Information Center: 404-639-6357
Fax: 404-639-6359
Web site: http://atsdr1.atsdr.cdc.gov:8080/astdrhome.html

Agency that works with CDC to prevent exposure to hazardous substances from waste sites. Conducts public health assessments, health studies, surveillance activities, and health education training at waste sites on the EPA's National Priorities List. Toxicology profiles and reports are available from the Information Center.

■ Environmental Health Clearinghouse
2605 Meridian Pkwy, Ste 115
Durham, NC 27713
800-NIEHS-94 (800-643-4794)
919-361-0570 (callers outside the U.S.)
Fax: 919-361-9408
E-mail: envirohealth@niehs.nih.gov
Web site: http:infoventures.com/e-hlth/

An information and referral service sponsored by the National Institute of Environmental Health Sciences (NIEHS). Information available on environmental health effects, worker exposure, hazardous waste sites, chemical spills and releases, and information for schools and students. Information specialists are available M–F 9AM–8PM ET (the hours that the clearinghouse is open to the public).

■ HUD User
U.S. Department of Housing and Urban Development
PO Box 6091
Rockville, MD 20849
800-245-2691
301-251-5154
Fax: 301-251-5767
TDD: 800-483-2209
E-mail: huduser@aspensys.com
Web site: http://www.huduser.org

Offers an excellent selection of training kits, manuals, and guidelines for public housing officials and others on the assessment, control, and abatement of lead-based paint hazards in residential buildings.

■ National Center for Environmental Health (NCEH)

Centers for Disease Control and Prevention
4770 Buford Hwy NE, M/S F-29
Atlanta, GA 30341-3724
770-488-7030
Division of Environmental Hazards & Health Effects: 404-488-7300
E-mail: ncehinfo@cehodl.em.cdc.gov
Web site: http://www.cdc.gov/nceh/ncehhome.htm

NCEH's mission is to provide national leadership, through science and service, to promote health and quality of life by preventing and controlling disease, birth defects, disability, and death resulting from interactions between people and their environment. The Division of Environmental Hazards & Health Effects studies and recommends ways of controlling or preventing health problems associated with human exposure to lead, radiation, air pollution, and other toxicants, as well as to hazards resulting from technologic or natural disasters.

■ National Institute of Environmental Health Sciences (NIEHS)

National Institutes of Health
PO Box 12233
Research Triangle Park, NC 27709
Communications Office: 919-541-3665
National Toxicology Program: 919-541-3419
Web site: http://www.niehs.nih.gov

Conducts and supports research and training on the human health effects of environmental agents and on the prevention of, intervention in, and treatment of environmentally related disease and dysfunction. NIEHS is the headquarters agency for the National Toxicology Program (NTP).

■ Toxicology Information Response Center

Oak Ridge National Laboratory
1060 Commerce Park, MS-6480
Oak Ridge, TN 37830
423-576-1746
Fax: 423-574-9888

Provides information and reference devices on individual chemicals and a wide variety of toxicology-related and environmental topics. Provides fee-based services such as comprehensive literature packets tailored to individual requests.

■ U.S. Environmental Protection Agency (EPA)

Public Information Center
401 M St SW, Rm 3404
Washington, DC 20013-7133
202-260-2080
Fax: 202-260-6257
EPA Safe Drinking Water Hotline: 800-426-4791 (M–F 9AM–5PM ET)
Office of Water Resource Center: 202-260-7786
Web site: http://www.epa.gov

Indoor Air Quality Information Clearinghouse
PO Box 37133
Washington, DC 20013-7133
800-438-4318; 202-484-1307
Fax: 202-484-1510

The public information center offers public information materials on such topics as hazardous wastes, radon, indoor air quality, asbestos, air and water pollution, pesticides, and drinking water. Open to the public M–F 10AM–4PM ET (except federal holidays). Responds to mail and telephone inquiries.

Food and Drug Safety

Products/Services Offered

Organization	web site	hotline/toll-free information line	clearinghouse/resource center	electronic information resources	database/statistical information	special campaigns/events/programs	consumer/patient education materials	publications for health professionals	classes/conferences	technical assistance	other products/services	grants/funding/awards	Page No.
American Council on Science and Health	■						■						**112**
American Dietetic Association	■						■	■					**112**
Center for Science in the Public Interest	■							■					**112**
Council on Family Health							■	■					**112**
National Consumers League		■					■	■					**112**
National Council on Patient Information and Education						■	■	■	■				**113**
STOP—Safe Tables Our Priority	■						■			■			**113**
U.S. Pharmacopeia	■				■		■	■			■		**113**

Additional Resources **114**

Federal Agencies **114**

■ American Council on Science and Health

1995 Broadway, 2nd Fl
New York, NY 10023-5860
Contact: Judy D'Agostino
212-362-7044
Fax: 212-362-4919
E-mail: acsh@acsh.org
Web site: http://www.acsh.org

National nonprofit independent consumer-education consortium concerned with issues related to food, chemicals, pharmaceuticals, lifestyle, the environment and human health.

Consumer or Patient Education Materials

Priorities, quarterly magazine, included with membership; Eating Safely: Avoiding Foodborne Illness, booklet, $3.85, discounts available for quantity orders. Please contact for complete publications list.

■ American Dietetic Association

216 W Jackson Blvd, Ste 800
Chicago, IL 60606-6995
Contact: Customer Service, 312-899-0040 x5000
312-899-0040
Fax: 312-899-1757
Web site: http://www.eatright.org

Nonprofit organization of food and nutrition professionals in the U.S. whose mission is to serve the public through the promotion of optimal nutrition, health, and well-being. Members include clinical and community dietetics professionals, food service managers, educators, researchers, dietetic technicians, and students. Covers a wide range of practice areas and special interests, including diet counseling for weight control, cholesterol reduction, diabetes, renal, and other health concerns.

Consumer or Patient Education Materials

Safe Cooking for Safe Eating: Tips on Proper Food Preparation; Safe Keeping for Safe Eating: Tips on Proper Food Storage, pamphlets, $6.25 for 25. Please contact for complete catalog.

Publications for Health Professionals

Food Safety for Professionals: A Reference and Study Guide, 101 pp book, includes preventive food service practices, $17. Please contact for complete publications list.

■ Center for Science in the Public Interest

1875 Connecticut Ave NW, Ste 300
Washington, DC 20009-5728
202-332-9110
Fax: 202-265-4954
E-mail: cspi@essential.org
Web site: http://www.cspinet.org

Nonprofit education and advocacy organization that focuses primarily on improving the safety and nutritional quality of the foods we buy and eat, and on reducing the carnage caused by alcoholic beverages.

Publications for Health Professionals

Nutrition Action Healthletter, nutrition and food safety issues, $24/yr. Please contact for complete publications list.

■ Council on Family Health

225 Park Ave S, Ste 1700
New York, NY 10003
Contact: Dianne Concannon
212-598-3617
Fax: 212-598-3665

National nonprofit organization dedicated to educating consumers about the proper use of nonprescription and prescription medicines, home safety, and personal health.

Consumer or Patient Education Materials

Various booklets, pamphlets, and brochures including: The Medicine Label . . . Your Road Map to Good Health; How to Prevent Drug Interactions; Medicines and You: A Guide for Older Americans. Free single copy; Low literacy; Some Spanish languages available. Please contact for complete catalog.

Publications for Health Professionals

Public service announcements, free. Please contact for complete publications list.

■ National Consumers League

1701 K St NW, Ste 1200
Washington, DC 20006
Contact: Theresa Smith
202-835-3323
Fax: 202-835-0747

Nonprofit private organization representing consumers and workers through advocacy, research, and education in areas including health care, food and drug safety, fire safety, and the environment.

Hotline or Toll-free Information Line

National Fraud Information Center Hotline: 800-876-7060 (M–F 9AM–5PM ET) Operator assisted, referral service, answers questions.

Consumer or Patient Education Materials

Take Care with Over-the-Counter Medications, series of 6 brochures, describes safe OTC drug use for low-literacy consumers, $1; Food and Drug Interactions, brochure, available in Spanish, $1; From Market to Mealtime: What You Should Know About Meat, Poultry, and Seafood, brochure, $.50. Please contact for quantity discount pricing and complete publications list.

Publications for Health Professionals

NCL Bulletin, bimonthly newsletter, updates including health care issues, included with membership.

■ National Council on Patient Information and Education

666 11th St NW, Ste 810
Washington, DC 20001-4542
Contact: Colleen Dill, Office Manager
202-347-6711
Fax: 202-638-0773

Nonprofit coalition of over 350 member organizations committed to improving communication between health care professionals and patients about prescription medicines. Goal is to encourage patients to work with their health care providers and to follow their medication therapy safely and effectively.

Special Campaigns, Events, or Programs

Talk About Prescriptions Month, October, planning guide, poster, badge, camera-ready artwork set. Contact Colleen Dill.

Consumer or Patient Education Materials

Prescription Medicines and You: A Consumer Guide, 16 pp booklet, offers 3 steps to better medicine use, $25 for 50 booklets; The Active Consumer: Getting the Most from Your Medicines, brochure, $20 for 100 copies; Get the Answers Wallet Card, to keep personal record, $12 for 100. Materials can be customized; Low literacy; Some Spanish languages available. Please contact for complete catalog.

Publications for Health Professionals

Directory of Prescription Medicine Information and Education Products, Programs and Services, 42 pp book, $25 member, $40 nonmember; The Medicine Check-Up Kit for Health Care Professionals, especially to support outreach activities, $45; Brown Bag Medicine Review Kit, for helping older patients and multiple medicine users avoid harmful drug interactions, $45. Please contact for complete publications list.

Classes and Conferences

National Conference on Prescription Medicine Information and Education, biennial (odd number years), policy discussions, workshops, poster sessions, and exhibits. Contact Colleen Dill.

■ STOP—Safe Tables Our Priority

PO Box 4442
Oceanside, CA 92052-4442
Contact: Rainer Mueller, President
800-350-STOP (800-350-7867)
619-439-2969
Fax: 619-439-1696
Web site: http://www.stop-usa.com

Nonprofit voluntary organization dedicated to preventing and properly testing foodborne illnesses and leading the fight to improve the nation's meat supply.

Consumer or Patient Education Materials

STOP NOW!, quarterly newsletter, current and international information; E. coli 0157:H7 Information, brochure; Tips on Foodborne Illness Prevention for Consumers, information sheet; single copy free.

Technical Assistance

Referral to medical professionals, physicians, and support groups.

■ U.S. Pharmacopeia

12601 Twinbrook Pkwy
Rockville, MD 20852
Contact: Marketing Dept, 301-816-8207
800-822-8772
301-881-0666
Fax: 301-816-8236
Web site: http://www.usp.org

Nonprofit organization that promotes public health by establishing and disseminating officially recognized standards of quality and authoritative information for the use of medicines and other health care technologies by health professionals, patients, and consumers.

Database or Statistical Information

USP Database Licensing, USP databases can be adapted to a number of electronic formats that can be easily accessed by practitioners, researchers, patients, and consumers. Cost is based on type and use of the database.

Consumer or Patient Education Materials

USP DI Volume II, Advice for the Patient, annual book, simplified monographs corresponding to listings in USP DI Volume I, $125; USP DI Patient Education Leaflets, customized quantity orders available. Please contact for complete catalog.

Publications for Health Professionals

USP DI Volume I, Drug information for the Health Care Professional, annual book, contains medically accepted uses of more than 10,000 generic and brand name drug products, $125. Please contact for complete publications list.

Other Products and Services

MedCoach™, Windows- and DOS-based software program, allows creating and customizing patient drug education leaflets, $395/yr.

ADDITIONAL RESOURCES

■ National Association of Chain Drug Stores

413 N Lee St
PO Box 1417-D49
Alexandria, VA 22313-1480
703-549-3001
Fax: 703-836-4869

■ National Community Pharmacists Association

205 Daingerfield Rd
Alexandria, VA 22314
703-683-8200
Fax: 703-683-3619

■ Nonprescription Drug Manufacturers Association

1150 Connecticut Ave NW, Ste 1200
Washington, DC 20036
202-429-9260
Fax: 202-223-6835

■ Public Citizen

1600 20th St NW
Washington, DC 20009-1001
Contact: Health Research Group
202-588-1000
Web site: http://www.citizen.org

■ Public Voice for Food and Health Policy

1101 14th St NW, Ste 710
Washington, DC 20005
Contact: Jennifer Zavolinsky, Communications Coordinator
202-371-1840
Fax: 202-371-1910
E-mail: pvoice@ix.netcom.com
Web site: http://www.publicvoice.org/pvoice.html

FEDERAL AGENCIES

■ Center for Devices & Radiological Health (CDRH)

U.S. Food and Drug Administration
9200 Corporate Blvd, MSC HFZ-1
Rockville, MD 20850
301-443-4690
Consumer Information Service: 301-443-4190
Fax: 301-443-9535
Fax-on-Demand: 800-899-0381
Web site: http://www.fda.gov/cdrh

Responsible for communicating with consumers, health professionals, and other government agencies on issues relating to medical devices, radiation-emitting products, and mammography facilities.

■ Center for Drug Evaluation and Research (CDER)

U.S. Food and Drug Administration
5600 Fishers Ln, HFD-700
Rockville, MD 20857
301-827-4573
Fax-on-Demand and Inquiries: 800-342-2722
Web site: http://www.fda.gov/cder

Develops responses to drug information requests under FDA's procedural regulations. Materials are available on specific pharmaceuticals, drug labeling, and for consumer education.

■ Center for Food Safety and Applied Nutrition (CFSAN)

U.S. Food and Drug Administration
200 C St SW, M/S HFS-55
Washington, DC 20204
Consumer Education Staff: 202-205-5004
General Inquiries and Seafood Hotline: 800-FDA-4010 (800-332-4010)
Office of Food Labeling (Division of Technical Evaluation): 202-205-5483
Web site: http://vm.cfsan.fda.gov/list.html

Regulates all food and cosmetic products other than meat and poultry. Responsible for food safety, nutrition, food labeling, and economic fraud.

■ Food Safety and Inspection Service (FSIS)

U.S. Department of Agriculture
1400 Independence Ave SW, Rm 1175-South
Washington, DC 20250
202-720-7943
Fax: 202-720-1843
USDA Meat and Poultry Hotline: 800-535-4555 and 202-720-3333
Web site: http://www.usda.gov/agency.fsis/homepage.htm

Responsible for ensuring that meat, poultry, and egg products are safe, wholesome, and accurately labeled. FSIS produces a wide variety of pamphlets and other educational materials on such topics as food safety, food poisoning, labels on meat and poultry products, food additives, food labeling, sodium, herbs, and the food inspection program.

■ U.S. Food and Drug Administration (FDA)

Office of Public Health and Science
U.S. Dept of Health & Human Services
5600 Fisher Ln, HFE-88
Rockville, MD 20857
Office of Consumer Affairs Inquiries Information Line: 800-532-4440; 301-827-4420 (M–F 10AM–4PM ET)
Office of Health Affairs, Medicine Staff: 301-443-5470
Web site: http://www.fda.gov/

Public health agency, charged with protecting American consumers by enforcing the Federal Food, Drug, and Cosmetic Act and several related public health laws. Answers questions on food and cosmetics. Publications available on federal regulations, drug development process, drug labeling, and pharmaceuticals.

Occupational Safety and Health

Products/Services Offered

Organization	web site	hotline/toll-free information line	clearinghouse/resource center	electronic information resources	database/statistical information	special campaigns/events/programs	consumer/patient education materials	publications for health professionals	classes/conferences	technical assistance	other products/services	grants/funding/awards	Page No.
American Association of Occupational Health Nurses Inc	■							■	■				118
American College of Occupational and Environmental Medicine	■			■				■	■	■		■	118
American Conference of Governmental Industrial Hygienists	■						■	■					118
Back School of Atlanta							■	■	■	■			118
The Center to Protect Workers' Rights	■						■			■		■	119
Genium Publishing Corporation	■							■			■		119
Health Examinetics Inc										■			119
Healthy Achievers							■		■	■			119
HIN Inc (The Health Information Network)							■						120
IAQ Publications	■							■	■				120
Industrial Health Foundation Inc										■	■		120
The Joyce Institute									■				120
National Campaign for Healthcare Worker Safety	■								■	■			120
National Safety Council	■		■					■	■	■			121
Occupational Health Strategies Inc								■		■	■		121
Park Nicollet HealthSource							■						121
Prevention Plus Inc							■			■			121
SAVANT Audiovisuals Inc							■						122
Spine Education Center Inc							■		■	■			122

Additional Resources 122

Federal Agencies 123

■ American Association of Occupational Health Nurses Inc

50 Lenox Pointe
Atlanta, GA 30324-3176
Contact: Information Resources, 404-262-1162 x100 or 101
404-262-1162
Fax: 404-262-1165
Web site: http://www.aaohn.org

National nonprofit for registered nurses who provide on-the-job health care for the nation's workers. This specialized practice is devoted to health promotion and prevention of illness and injury in the work environment.

Publications for Health Professionals
AAOHN News, monthly newsletter, free with membership, $12/yr; Guidelines for an Occupational Health & Safety Service, $55; Ergonomics . . . Creating a Healthier Workplace for a Healthier Bottom-line, 18-min video, $150 (member price). Please contact for complete publications list.

Classes and Conferences
Annual conference, 7–8 days, educational programs and trade show. Contact Professional Affairs, 404-262-1162 x821.

■ American College of Occupational and Environmental Medicine

55 W Seegers Rd
Arlington Heights, IL 60005-3919
Contact: Publications Dept, 847-228-6850 x189
847-228-6850
Fax: 847-228-1856
Web site: http://www.acoem.org

International nonprofit organization of occupational and environmental physicians dedicated to promoting and protecting the health of workers through preventive services, clinical care, research, and educational programs.

Electronic Information Resources
INSTA-Facts: 800-226-3626, fax-on-demand service includes position papers, news releases, publications, membership information. Cost varies, some free.

Publications for Health Professionals
Manager's Guide to Occupational Health Services, book, $20; ACOEM Report, monthly newsletter; Journal of Occupational and Environmental Medicine, monthly, scientific information. Please contact for complete publications list.

Classes and Conferences
American Occupational Health Conference, 1 week, nation's largest meeting of occupational health professionals; State-of-the-Art Conference, 4 days, scientific meeting; 2-day training courses in MRO, disability, occupational medicine, environmental medicine. Please contact for complete list and schedule.

Technical Assistance
Volunteer committees of physicians in all aspects of occupational medicine.

Grants, Funding, or Awards
Corporate Health Achievement Award, Contact Susanna Matthew, 804-970-7744; Bacon Foundation for research.

■ American Conference of Governmental Industrial Hygienists

1330 Kemper Meadow Dr
Cincinnati, OH 45240
513-742-2020
Fax: 513-742-3355
E-mail: acgih_pubs@pol.com
Web site: http://www.acgih.org

Nonprofit membership organization of professionals or students in the fields of occupational or environmental health that promotes excellence in environmental and occupational health; provides technical information of the highest quality; benefits the health and well-being of people worldwide; and serves the membership and continually improves the organization, including its financial and human resources.

Consumer or Patient Education Materials
Various materials available on ergonomics and workplace safety. Please contact for complete catalog.

Publications for Health Professionals
Essentials of Modern Hospital Safety I, II, and III, books, major occupation health issues in hospitals. Please contact for complete publications list.

■ Back School of Atlanta

1465 Northside Dr NW, Ste 217
Atlanta, GA 30318-4225
Contact: Ronald W. Porter
800-783-7536
404-355-7756
Fax: 404-355-3907

National for-profit consulting firm providing assistance to occupational health and safety professionals in the development and implementation of cumulative trauma injury prevention and ergonomic awareness programs. Training is provided to supervisors and managers on-site and directly to employees.

Consumer or Patient Education Materials
Prevention slides for trainers, slide program to assist in providing injury prevention training, $360. Materials can be customized; Low literacy; Please contact for complete catalog.
Publications for Health Professionals
Reducing the Cost of Pain, workshop manual for providing injury prevention training, $150. Please contact for complete publications list.
Classes and Conferences
Cumulative Trauma and Ergonomics, 2 days, Train-the-Trainer workshop, $395; Worksite Analysis, 2½ days, hands-on ergonomic worksite training, $575. Please contact for complete list and schedule.
Technical Assistance
Worksite ergonomic analysis; Train-the-Trainer programs; Employee training; Audio-visual program development.

■ The Center to Protect Workers' Rights

111 Massachusetts Ave NW
Washington, DC 20001
Contact: Jane Seegal, 202-962-8493
202-962-8490
Fax: 202-962-8499
E-mail: cpwr@cpwr.com
Web site: http://www.cpwr.com

Nonprofit research arm of the Building and Construction Trades Department of the AFL-CIO. Goal is to produce and disseminate useful information about the construction industry and its labor market; quality of life for workers and their families; and the construction workplace.

Consumer or Patient Education Materials
Pocket size hazard alert cards, $.10 ea; reports, videos, and brochures, $5–$10. Please contact for complete catalog.
Technical Assistance
Industrial hygiene assistance; occupational safety and health consulting and advice.
Grants, Funding, or Awards
Small studies grant program for research in the construction industry. Contact Pete Stafford, 202-962-8490.

■ Genium Publishing Corporation

One Genium Plaza
Schenectady, NY 12304-4690
800-243-6486
518-377-8854
Fax: 518-377-1891
Web site: http://www.chemweek.com/genium/

Publisher of books, training booklets, software, and videotape programs to help organizations work safely with hazardous chemicals.

Publications for Health Professionals
MSDS Collection on CD-ROM, reference, contains over 1,000 custom written material safety data sheets, $499 and $159 yearly for updates; books, booklets, videotapes. Please contact for complete publications list.
Other Products and Services
MSDS Hotline Service, subscription service that provides material safety data sheets as needed, request made by phone M–F 8AM–5PM ET, 25 sheets for $99/yr.

■ Health Examinetics Inc

10920 Via Frontera
San Diego, CA 92127-1704
Contact: Bruce H Meyer, 800-232-2332 x312
800-232-2332
619-485-0933
Fax: 619-485-8133
E-mail: lowercosts@healthex.com

For-profit company providing health services nationwide. Programs are designed to assist corporations, labor, governmental agencies, school districts, and associations in controlling health care costs.

Technical Assistance
Consulting; occupational medical surveillance including hearing conservation, respirator evaluations, and fit testing.

■ Healthy Achievers

22 Hayes Rd
Madbury, NH 03820-9511
603-743-3838
Fax: 603-749-7310
E-mail: ohshealthy@aol.com

Consulting firm specializing in worksite health promotion and occupational safety programs and materials.

Consumer or Patient Education Materials
Achieving a Healthy Back and Preventing Repetitive Motion Injuries, complete education program kits with video and reproducible materials, $95. Please contact for complete catalog.
Classes and Conferences
OSHA Training Programs, employee training for compliance, length varies. Please contact for complete list and schedule.

Technical Assistance
Consulting for occupational health and safety programs and services.

■ HIN Inc (The Health Information Network)

231 Market Place, #331
San Ramon, CA 94583-9800
Contact: Lois Kamoroff
800-HIN-1121 (800-446-1121)
510-551-4800
Fax: 510-551-4808

Medical publishing company of patient education booklets in easy-to-read, understandable text and with full-color medical illustrations; authored and edited by medical experts.

Consumer or Patient Education Materials
Back Pain; Carpal Tunnel Syndrome, booklets, $36.25 for 25 copies, discounts available for quantity orders. Materials can be customized; Please contact for complete catalog.

■ IAQ Publications

2 Wisconsin Cir, Ste 430
Chevy Chase, MD 20815
Contact: Monique Henderson
800-394-0115
301-913-0115
Fax: 301-913-0119
E-mail: iaqpubs@aol.com
Web site: http://www.iaqpubs.com

Publisher specializing in indoor air quality, healthy building management, and lead poisioning prevention media.

Publications for Health Professionals
Safety & Health Today, monthly newsletter, safety and health issues in the workplace, $325/yr. Please contact for complete publications list.
Classes and Conferences
Annual conference on safety and health. Please contact for complete information.

■ Industrial Health Foundation Inc

34 Penn Circle W
Pittsburgh, PA 15206
412-363-6600
Fax: 412-363-6605

National nonprofit member-oriented organization dedicated to the advancement of healthful working conditions in industry.

Technical Assistance
Industrial hygiene surveys; AIHA-accredited analytical laboratory.
Other Products and Services
Material safety data sheet development and review; literature searches.

■ The Joyce Institute

1313 Plaza 600 Bldg
Seattle, WA 98101
Contact: Marilyn Joyce
800-645-6045
206-441-6745
Fax: 206-441-6750
E-mail: Joyce.Marilyn@adlittle.com

A unit of Arthur D Little that provides a full range of ergonomics planning, consulting, and training services to more than 750 companies, government agencies, hospitals, and associations throughout the U.S., United Kingdom, Mexico, Europe, and Asia.

Classes and Conferences
Various seminars and workshops available. Please contact for complete information.

■ National Campaign for Healthcare Worker Safety

44 N Queen St
Lancaster, PA 17603
Contact: Lynda Arnold, RN
717-299-0228
Fax: 717-299-0244
Web site: http://www.healthcaresafety.com

Nonprofit organization whose goal is to promote awareness of occupational exposure to bloodborne pathogens and to advocate for the use of protected intravenous catheters and protected blood drawing devices by all of America's health care workers.

Classes and Conferences
Presentations available from keynote to workshops including: It Could Happen to You, 1 hr, personal perspective speaker; Reality Is Hard to Ignore, 1 hr, issue overview, by donation. Please contact for complete list and schedule.
Technical Assistance
Campaign packets, certificate-like pledges, statistical data, overview of safety devices.

National Safety Council

1121 Spring Lake Dr
Itasca, IL 60143-3201
Contact: Customer Service, 800-621-7619
Fax: 630-285-0797
800-621-7619
630-285-1121
Fax: 630-285-1315
Web site: http://nsc.org

Nonprofit, non-governmental, public service organization dedicated to improving the safety, health, and environmental well-being of all people. Its mission is to educate and influence society to adopt safety, health, and environmental policies, practices, and procedures that prevent and mitigate human suffering and economic losses arising from preventable causes.

Clearinghouse or Resource Center
National Safety Council Library: 630-775-2199; Fax: 630-285-0242; contains one of the world's largest sources of safety and health information.

Publications for Health Professionals
Safety and Health, monthly magazine; Today's Supervisor, monthly, 16 pp digest; Safeworker, 16 pp, pamphlet. Please contact for complete publications list.

Classes and Conferences
Safety Training Institute, educational classes for safety and health professionals, call 800-621-7615 x2356 for complete list and schedule.

Technical Assistance
Consulting services include safety and health program audits, employee surveys, ergonomic surveys, management training programs, risk communication plans and overall needs analysis. Employee safety program benchmarking surveys, call 800-621-7615 x2367.

Occupational Health Strategies Inc

901 Preston Ave, Ste 400
Charlottesville, VA 22903-4491
Contact: Linda David
804-977-3784
Fax: 804-977-8570
E-mail: kwp@cstone.net

National consulting firm who provides planning, design, and evaluation of corporate-wide occupational and environmental health policies, procedures, programs, and strategies to corporations and health care providers.

Publications for Health Professionals
Directory of Occupational Health and Safety Software, annual, detailed descriptions of over 100 programs, $75.

Technical Assistance
Performs health data analysis.

Other Products and Services
Develops occupational health information systems; builds customized microcomputer software.

Park Nicollet HealthSource

3800 Park Nicollet Blvd
Minneapolis, MN 55416
Contact: Scott Laurent, Sales
800-372-7776
Fax: 612-993-1840

Nonprofit organization, a part of the Institute for Education and Research HealthSystem Minnesota, that develops and produces health promotion publications in self-care, health care consumerism, chronic conditions, and lifestyle education.

Consumer or Patient Education Materials
Cumulative Trauma: Reducing the Risk; Office Ergonomics: Working in Comfort: A User's Guide to Office Ergonomics and Body Mechanics, booklets, $1.60; Take a Break Series, easy-to-use card reminders to ease muscle fatigue, $1.25; Discounts available for quantity orders. Materials can be customized; Please contact for complete catalog.

Prevention Plus Inc

5775 Wayzata Blvd, Ste 700
Minneapolis, MN 55416
Contact: Todd Bruchert, Sales Manager
800-887-2282
612-525-2255
Fax: 612-546-7549

Consulting firm that specializes in back injury prevention, CTD prevention, and loss control services. Also offers a variety of process support products including videos and manuals.

Consumer or Patient Education Materials
Videos include: A Bit About Backs, practical and humorous look at back care, $279; The Lighter Side of Lifting, practical and humorous look at lifting, $179; Back In Step, practical guide to recovery from back pain, $129. Materials can be customized; Low literacy; Please contact for complete catalog.

Technical Assistance
Consulting services in the areas of back injury prevention, CTD prevention, and loss control.

■ SAVANT Audiovisuals Inc

801 E Chapman Ave, #101
Fullerton, CA 92831
Mailing Address:
PO Box 3670
Fullerton, CA 92834
Contact: Valerie Sloane
800-472-8268
714-870-7880
Fax: 714-526-7400

For-profit producer and distributor of audiovisual and computer-based safety training programs for compliance with OSHA chemical hazard and biohazard regulations.

Consumer or Patient Education Materials

Protecting Yourself Against Bloodborne Diseases, computer-based training program, $495; videotapes, manuals, or computer disks also available. Some Spanish languages available. Please contact for complete catalog.

■ Spine Education Center Inc

9705 Harry Hines Blvd, Ste 102
Dallas, TX 75220-5700
Mailing Address:
PO Box 542376
Dallas, TX 75354-2376
Contact: Nancy Selby
214-956-0211
Fax: 214-956-7251

National consulting firm that designs programs to educate employees about back care, best work practices, and proactive safety practices; customized for a client or a group of clients with similar challenges.

Consumer or Patient Education Materials

SpineSense, back education for health care workers, computer-based training program, $595, or compact disc interactive program, $495; booklets available include: anatomy and body mechanics, stretching and strengthening, $1.25. Materials can be customized; Spanish languages available. Please contact for complete catalog.

Classes and Conferences

Training-the-Trainer, 2–8 hrs, training for successful program implementation. Please contact for complete list and schedule.

Technical Assistance

Consulting, job assessment, ergonomic evaluation.

ADDITIONAL RESOURCES

■ American Industrial Hygiene Association

2700 Prosperity Ave, Ste 250
Fairfax, VA 22031-4319
703-849-8888
Fax: 703-207-3651
E-mail: infonet@aiha.org
Web site: http://www.aiha.org

■ Business & Legal Reports Inc

39 Academy St
Madison, CT 06443-1513
800-727-5257 (Order Dept)
203-245-7448
Fax: 203-245-2559
E-mail: BLRblr@aol.com
Web site: http://www.safetyonline.net/blr

■ DuPont Company

Rt 141 and Rt 48
Barley Mill Plaza, #23
Wilmington, DE 19880
Contact: Training Materials
800-532-SAFE (800-532-7233)
Fax: 888-644-7233

■ Krames Communications

1100 Grundy Ln
San Bruno, CA 94066-3030
800-333-3032 (Order Dept)
415-742-0400
Fax: 415-244-4512

■ LRP Publications

747 Dresher Rd, Ste 500
PO Box 980
Horsham, PA 19044-0980
800-341-7874
Fax: 215-784-9639
Web site: http://www.lrp.com

■ National Coalition on Ergonomics

7485 Rush River Dr, Ste 710-141
Sacramento, CA 95831
Contact: Al Lundeen
916-774-9750
Fax: 916-774-9777
E-mail: aplundeen@aol.com

■ **Safety Shorts Production Inc**
2960 N 23rd St
La Porte, TX 77571
800-458-2236
281-470-9990
Fax: 281-470-8653

■ **Society for Occupational and Environmental Health**
6728 Old McLean Village Dr
McLean, VA 22101
703-556-9222
Fax: 703-556-8729
E-mail: degnon@aol.com

■ **Tel-A-Train Inc**
309 N Market St
Chattanooga, TN 37405
800-251-6018
423-266-0113
Fax: 423-267-2555
Web site: http://www.telatrain.com

FEDERAL AGENCIES

■ **National Institute for Occupational Safety and Health (NIOSH)**
Centers for Disease Control and Prevention
4676 Columbia Pkwy
Cincinnati, OH 45226-1998
513-533-8328
Toll-free technical information: 800-35-NIOSH (800-356-4674)
Web site: http://www.cdc.gov/niosh/homepage.html

The federal institute responsible for conducting research and making recommendations for the prevention of work-related illnesses and injuries. Identifies the causes of work-related diseases and injuries and the potential hazards of new work technologies and practices; determines new and effective ways to prevent workers from chemicals, machinery, and hazardous working conditions. Callers may request information about NIOSH activities, order its publications, or request information about any aspect of occupational safety and health from the toll-free number. Automated recorded information and fax information 24 hrs/day, technical information specialist 9AM–4PM ET, publications representatives 1PM–4PM ET. Materials on hand are provided free of charge.

■ **Occupational Safety and Health Administration (OSHA)**
U.S. Department of Labor
200 Constitution Ave NW, Rm N-3647
Washington, DC 20210
Public Affairs: 202-219-8151
Web site: http://www.osha.gov

OSHA Publications Office
U.S. Dept of Labor
200 Constitution Ave NW, Rm N-3101
Washington, DC 20210
202-219-4667
Fax: 202-219-9266

Federal agency whose mission is to save lives, prevent injuries and protect the health of America's workers. Encourages employers and employees to reduce workplace hazards and implement safety programs. Maintains a reporting and record-keeping system to monitor job-related injuries and illnesses. Develops and enforces mandatory job safety and health standards and distributes training programs. Distributes print and audiovisual materials, some in Spanish.

■ **Office of Safety, Health, and Working Conditions**
Bureau of Labor Statistics (BLS), U.S. Dept of Labor
2 Massachusetts Ave NE, Rm 3180
Washington, DC 20212
202-606-6179
Publications: 202-606-7828
Fax-on-Demand: 202-606-6325
Web site: http://stats.bls.gov/oshhome.htm

Provides occupational injury rates by industry and historical fatality data.

Oral Health

Products/Services Offered

Organization	web site	hotline/toll-free information line	clearinghouse/resource center	electronic information resources	database/statistical information	special campaigns/events/programs	consumer/patient education materials	publications for health professionals	classes/conferences	technical assistance	other products/services	grants/funding/awards	Page No.
American Dental Association						■	■	■					**126**
Channing L Bete Co Inc							■						**126**
Oral Health America								■				■	**126**

Additional Resources **126**

Federal Agencies **127**

■ American Dental Association

211 E Chicago Ave
Chicago, IL 60611-2678
Contact: Catalog Sales Dept, 800-947-4746
312-440-2500
E-mail: http://www.ada.org

Nonprofit organization representing dentistry in the U.S. whose goal is to encourage the improvement of the health of the public and to promote the art and science of dentistry. Works to achieve this through research, education, communication, legislation, and many other activities.

Special Campaigns, Events, or Programs
National Children's Dental Health Month, February, starter kit includes: stencils, crayons, brochures, planning guide, poster, and stickers. Contact Catalog Sales for price and to order.

Consumer or Patient Education Materials
Booklets, manuals, and audiovisual materials. Please contact for complete catalog.

Publications for Health Professionals
The Journal of the American Dental Association; ADA News; Index to Dental Literature. Please contact for complete publications list.

■ Channing L Bete Co Inc

200 State Rd
S Deerfield, MA 01373-0200
800-628-7733 (Sales and Customer Service)
413-665-7611
Fax: 800-499-6464

Publisher of informational and educational booklets, videos, posters, calendars, books, and display racks. Booklets use a distinctive, condensed format—called scriptography—which combines key words and graphics to explain a variety of subjects and is appropriate for different age groups and reading levels.

Consumer or Patient Education Materials
Booklets include topics: periodontal disease, tots and tooth care, coloring and activities for children. Please contact for pricing and ask for the Patient Education catalog.

■ Oral Health America

410 N Michigan Ave, Ste 352
Chicago, IL 60611-4211
Contact: Bryan McGuire, Manager of Programs
800-523-3438
312-836-9900
Fax: 312-836-9986

National independent nonprofit foundation whose programs help motivate people to seek dental care, assist the forgotten in obtaining care, support dental education and research, and advance the art and science of dentistry. (Previously known as America's Fund for Dental Health)

Publications for Health Professionals
Oral Health Advocate, 2–3 times/yr newsletter, free.

Grants, Funding, or Awards
Funding for 2-yr pilot projects, 1-yr demonstration projects, and program development projects. Contact Brendan Ratliff for more information.

ADDITIONAL RESOURCES

■ American Association of Public Health Dentistry

10619 Jousting Ln
Richmond, VA 23235
804-272-8344
Fax: 804-272-0802
E-mail: natoss@aol.com

■ American Dental Hygienists' Association

444 N Michigan Ave, Ste 3400
Chicago, IL 60611
Contact: Communications Dept
800-243-ADHA (800-243-2342)
312-440-8900
Fax: 312-440-8929
Web site: http://www.adha.org

■ American Society of Dentistry for Children

875 N Michigan Ave, Ste 4040
Chicago, IL 60611-1901
800-637-ASDC (800-637-2732)
312-943-1244
Fax: 312-943-5341
Web site: http://cudental.creighton.edu/asdc

■ Dental Health Foundation

4340 Redwood Hwy, #319
San Rafael, CA 94903
415-499-4648
Fax: 415-499-4681

FEDERAL AGENCIES

■ National Institute of Dental Research (NIDR)

National Institutes of Health
Bldg 31, Rm 2C-35
31 Center Dr, MSC 2290
Bethesda, MD 20892-2290
Public Inquiries: 301-496-4261
Fax: 301-496-9988
Web site: http://www.nidr.nih.gov

National Oral Health Information Clearinghouse (NOHIC)
1 NOHIC Way
Bethesda, MD 20892-3500
301-402-7364
Fax: 301-907-8830
E-mail: nidr@aerie.com

Conducts and supports research on dental health and disseminates information to improve dental health. Posters and professional materials on school fluoride programs, as well as consumer-oriented pamphlets on dental health, fluoride treatment, canker sores, dry mouth, periodontal disease, dental sealants, and pain research available from the Clearinghouse.

■ Oral Health Program, Divison of Cancer Prevention and Control

National Center for Chronic Disease Prevention & Health Promotion (NCCDPHP)
Centers for Disease Control and Prevention
4770 Buford Hwy NE, M/S F-10
Atlanta, GA 30341-3724
770-488-3038
Fax: 770-488-3065
Web site: http://www.cdc.gov/nccdphp/oh

Serves as a national resource for activities to prevent oral diseases and improve oral health; provides information on fluoridation, oral cancer, dental sealants, baby bottle tooth decay, infectious disease transmission in dentistry, and oral effects of tobacco use. Also provides consultation and technical assistance to state and local health agencies and works with health professionals on issues related to the promotion of oral health.

Unintentional Injuries

Products/Services Offered

Organization	web site	hotline/toll-free information line	clearinghouse/resource center	electronic information resources	database/statistical information	special campaigns/events/programs	consumer/patient education materials	publications for health professionals	classes/conferences	technical assistance	other products/services	grants/funding/awards	Page No.
American Academy of Pediatrics	■						■	■					**130**
American Trauma Society	■	■				■	■	■	■				**130**
Association for the Advancement of Automotive Medicine							■	■					**130**
Bicycle Helmet Safety Institute	■			■	■		■	■		■			**130**
Channing L Bete Co Inc							■						**131**
FastMark Inc							■						**131**
Harvard Injury Control Center	■							■	■	■			**131**
Health Education Services	■						■						**131**
HIN Inc (The Health Information Network)							■						**132**
Juvenile Products Manufacturers Association						■	■						**132**
National Consumers League							■						**132**
National Safety Council	■		■				■	■	■	■			**132**
National Youth Sports Safety Foundation Inc							■	■					**132**
Poison Prevention Week Council						■							**133**
Progressive Farmer Magazine										■			**133**
Safe Ride News Publications Inc	■							■					**133**
Safety By Design Ltd						■	■		■	■			**133**
Think First Foundation	■						■	■					**133**
University of North Carolina Injury Prevention Research Center	■							■		■			**134**

Additional Resources **134**

Federal Agencies **136**

■ American Academy of Pediatrics

141 Northwest Point Blvd
PO Box 927
Elk Grove Village, IL 60007-0927
Contact: Publications Dept, 800-433-9016
847-228-5005
Fax: 847-228-1281
E-mail: kidsdocs@aap.org
Web site: http://www.aap.org

Nonprofit organization of 50,000 pediatricians dedicated to the health, safety, and well-being of infants, children, adolescents, and young adults. Activities include advocacy for children and youth; public education; research; professional education; membership service and advocacy for pediatricians. More than 30 committees develop positions and programs for interest areas including nutrition; pediatric AIDS; substance abuse; child abuse and neglect; children with disabilities.

Consumer or Patient Education Materials
TIPP®—The Injury Prevention Program covers childhood injuries, injury hazards, bicycle safety; safety survey questionnaire and age-related safety sheets. Please contact for pricing and complete catalog.

Publications for Health Professionals
Handbook of Common Poisonings in Children, book, $44.95; Injury Control for Children and Youth, book, $42.95. Please contact for complete publications list.

■ American Trauma Society

8903 Presidential Pkwy, Ste 512
Upper Marlboro, MD 20772-2656
Contact: Diane Colomo
800-556-7890
301-420-4189
Fax: 301-420-0617
E-mail: atstrauma@aol.com
Web site: http://www.amtrauma.org

Nonprofit voluntary organization dedicated to the prevention of trauma and the improvement of trauma care. Also works to increase public awareness of the term "trauma"; to initiate, promote and/or coordinate prevention programs and activities; to advance trauma care throughout the nation through advocacy for development of comprehensive trauma systems.

Hotline or Toll-free Information Line
American Trauma Society Information Line: 800-556-7890 (M-F 8:30AM-4:30PM ET) Operator assisted, answers questions, request for materials.

Special Campaigns, Events, or Programs
Trauma Awareness Month, May, media and press kit, brochure. Contact John Phillips.

Consumer or Patient Education Materials
Various buttons, patches, stickers; Posters include burn injury prevention and bicycle helmet safety; Brochures, reference cards, and manuals include Keep Playgrounds Fun & Safe; Driving Safely Is No Accident; If You Arrive First At An Accident. Please contact for pricing and complete catalog.

Publications for Health Professionals
Troo the Traumaroo Safety Program, injury prevention program for young children, videotape, facilitator's guide, posters, activity books, achievement stickers, $250 institutional members; $750 non-institutional member. Please contact for complete publications list.

Classes and Conferences
Trauma Coordinator Care Course, 1½ days, coordination of trauma centers, $240–$300.

■ Association for the Advancement of Automotive Medicine

2340 Des Plaines Ave, Ste 106
Des Plaines, IL 60018
847-390-8927
Fax: 847-390-9962

Nonprofit international multidisciplinary organization of professionals committed to reducing motor vehicle trauma and improving highway safety. Encourages and promotes the growth and dissemination of knowledge in traffic and vehicular safety.

Consumer or Patient Education Materials
Traffic Injury: The Medicine-Engineering Link, 30-min video, explores forces involved and mechanisms of injury in traffic crashes, $80.

Publications for Health Professionals
Inroads, quarterly newsletter, research info and other highway safety news; Traffic Lines, periodically, legislative, policy and legal developments affecting highway safety, $75 for both publications; Accident Analysis & Prevention, bimonthly journal, scientific journal, included with membership.

■ Bicycle Helmet Safety Institute

4611 Seventh St S
Arlington, VA 22204-1419
Contact: Randy Swart
703-486-0100
Fax: 703-486-0100
E-mail: helmets@bhsi.org
Web site: http://www.bhsi.org

A helmet advocacy program and technical resource whose volunteers run a clearinghouse to provide helmet information and work on the ANSI and ASTM helmet standards committees.

Electronic Information Resources
Fax-on-Demand: 703-486-0100, no cost.
Database or Statistical Information
Compilation of statistics on helmet effectiveness, nominal charge.
Consumer or Patient Education Materials
Consumer's Guide to Bicycle Helmets, pamphlet, why and how to buy a helmet, $.15 ea; Must I Buy a Bicycle Helmet for My Child?, pamphlet, for parents, $.15 ea.
Publications for Health Professionals
Helmet Update, periodic newsletter, developments in helmets and standards, free; also available: resource lists, technical studies, standards information, and a toolkit for helmet program developers. Please contact for complete publications list.
Technical Assistance
Press briefings.

■ Channing L Bete Co Inc

200 State Rd
S Deerfield, MA 01373-0200
800-628-7733 (Sales and Customer Service)
413-665-7611
Fax: 800-499-6464

Publisher of informational and educational booklets, videos, posters, calendars, books, and display racks. Booklets use a distinctive, condensed format—called scriptography—which combines key words and graphics to explain a variety of subjects and is appropriate for different age groups and reading levels.

Consumer or Patient Education Materials
Booklets and coloring and activity booklet. Topics include: bicycle helmets, fire hazards, lead poisoning, poisons, safety belts. Some Spanish language available. Please contact for pricing and ask for the Patient Education catalog.

■ FastMark Inc

125 University Ave, Ste 250
Palo Alto, CA 94301
Contact: Leah Jacobs, Marketing Manager
800-406-2035
415-327-7760
Fax: 415-327-7734
E-mail: fastmark.com

Publisher of first aid and wellness reference guides using a patented laminated format that allows thickly laminated products to lie flat when folded. Health topics include: women's health, children's health, seniors' health, allergies/asthma, diabetes, heart disease, fitness, nutrtition, and stress management.

Consumer or Patient Education Materials
FastAid, The Easy First Aid Guide, 5-panel folded laminated brochure, covers 27 conditions and 4 emergency techinques including CPR and rescue breathing. Pricing varies upon quantity ordered; Materials can be customized; Spanish languages available. Please contact for complete catalog.

■ Harvard Injury Control Center

718 Huntington Ave
Boston, MA 02115
Contact: Jane Lee, Research Asst, 617-432-4346
617-432-2123
Fax: 617-432-0190
E-mail: jlee@hsph.harvard.edu
Web site: http://www.harvard.hsph/organizations/hcra/hicc.html

National nonprofit education and research organization that contributes to the scientific knowledge about how to prevent and reduce unintentional injuries and violence in the home, the workplace, and the community.

Publications for Health Professionals
Journal articles and books. Please contact for complete publications list.
Classes and Conferences
Graduate level courses at the Harvard School of Public Health; Seminar Series. Please contact for complete list and schedule.
Technical Assistance
Also provides training and technical assistance on injury prevention and control to government agencies and public health professionals and groups.

■ Health Education Services

PO Box 7126
Albany, NY 12224
518-439-7286
Fax: 518-439-7286 *51
Web site: http://www.hes.org

Nonprofit distributor of current health education, promotional publications, posters, and videos, most of which have been produced by the New York State Department of Health or the New York State Department of Environmental Conservation. (Health Education Services is a Division of Health Research Inc.)

Consumer or Patient Education Materials
Find the Safety Hazards, poster, 40 common home hazards, $1; How to Prevent Injuries to Children, $15 for 100 copies; Poison Proof Your Home, $12 for 100 copies. Please contact for complete catalog.

■ HIN Inc (The Health Information Network)

231 Market Place, #331
San Ramon, CA 94583-9800
Contact: Lois Kamoroff
800-HIN-1121 (800-446-1121)
510-551-4800
Fax: 510-551-4808

Medical publishing company of patient education booklets in easy-to-read, understandable text and with full-color medical illustrations; authored and edited by medical experts.

Consumer or Patient Education Materials
Preventing Childhood Injuries, booklet, $33.75 for 25 copies, discounts available for quantity orders. Materials can be customized; Please contact for complete catalog.

■ Juvenile Products Manufacturers Association

236 Route 38 W, Ste 100
Moorestown, NJ 08057
Contact: Safety Information
609-231-8500
Fax: 609-231-4664

Trade association of more than 250 companies in the U.S., Mexico, and Canada who manufacture and/or import juvenile products such as cribs, car seats, strollers, bedding, and a wide range of accessories and decorative items.

Special Campaigns, Events, or Programs
Baby Safety Month, September, information kit about baby safety.

Consumer or Patient Education Materials
Safe and Sound for Baby, 16 pp guide, safe use and selection of juvenile products, free single copy with SASE, also available in Spanish.

■ National Consumers League

1701 K St NW, Ste 1200
Washington, DC 20006
Contact: Theresa Smith
202-835-3323
Fax: 202-835-0747

Nonprofit private organization representing consumers and workers through advocacy, research, and education in areas including health care, food and drug safety, fire safety, and the environment.

Consumer or Patient Education Materials
Be Cool About Fire Safety, 15-min video, for children 5–9 includes tips on escape plans, smoke detectors, and more, $20.

■ National Safety Council

1121 Spring Lake Dr
Itasca, IL 60143-3201
Contact: Customer Service, 800-621-7619; Fax: 630-285-0797
800-621-7619
630-285-1121
Fax: 630-285-1315
Web site: http://nsc.org

Nonprofit, non-governmental, public service organization dedicated to improving the safety, health, and environmental well-being of all people. Its mission is to educate and influence society to adopt safety, health, and environmental policies, practices, and procedures that prevent and mitigate human suffering and economic losses arising from preventable causes.

Clearinghouse or Resource Center
National Safety Council Library: 630-775-2199; Fax: 630-285-0242; contains one of the world's largest sources of safety and health information.

Consumer or Patient Education Materials
Family Safety and Health, quarterly periodical; Safedriver, monthly 8 pp pamphlet. Please contact for complete catalog.

Publications for Health Professionals
Traffic Safety, bimonthly magazine, for traffic professionals. Please contact for complete publications list.

Classes and Conferences
Defensive driving courses; aquatics training; First Aid Insititute; Call 800-621-6244.

Technical Assistance
Highway Traffic Safety Division: 630-775-2385.

■ National Youth Sports Safety Foundation Inc

10 Meredith Cir
Needham, MA 02192-1946
Contact: Michelle Glassman
617-449-2499
Fax: 617-444-3288
E-mail: nyssf@aol.com

Nonprofit educational organization dedicated to reducing the number and severity of injuries youth sustain in sports activities. Also serves as an educational resource and clearinghouse for information for the country on safe sports participation.

Consumer or Patient Education Materials
Fact sheets on Helmets, Head Injuries, Eye Injuries, $2. Please contact for complete catalog.

Publications for Health Professionals
National Guide to Injury Reporting Systems, $2.50; Injury Guidelines, $2. Please contact for complete publications list.

■ Poison Prevention Week Council

PO Box 1543
Washington, DC 20013
Contact: Ken Giles, please contact by mail
301-504-0580 x1184
Fax: 301-504-0399

National nonprofit coordinator of annual observance of National Poison Prevention Week. Objective is to alert Americans to the problem of accidental poisonings and to take preventive steps such as using child-resistant packaging; locking up medicines and chemicals; and having the local poison control center's phone number.

Special Campaigns, Events, or Programs
National Poison Prevention Week, 3rd full week in March, beginning on Sunday, free packet of publications on poison prevention. Send postcard to above address.

■ Progressive Farmer Magazine

2100 Lakeshore Dr
Birmingham, AL 35209
Contact: Susan Reynolds
800-366-4712
205-877-6000
Fax: 205-877-6450
E-mail: pffarmer@aol.com

Publisher who provides training for sponsors of Farm Safety Day Camps for Kids. A Progressive Farmer Foundation has been established to accept funds towards this program.

Technical Assistance
Training to local coordinators to work with others in their community to sponsor Farm Safety Day Camps for Kids, a one-day event. Please contact for application.

■ Safe Ride News Publications Inc

5223 NE 187th St
Lake Forest Park, WA 98155
Contact: Chung Ho Lee
206-364-5696
Fax: 206-364-5992
E-mail: willapa@nwlink.com
Web site: http://www.twbc.com

Publisher of information for child safety advocates to protect children in traffic.

Publications for Health Professionals
Safe Ride News, quarterly newsletter, technical information regarding child passenger safety, $25/yr.

■ Safety By Design Ltd

PO Box 4312
Great Neck, NY 11023
Contact: Randi Leifer RN
516-488-5395

National consulting firm offering services and products promoting child safety and wellness.

Special Campaigns, Events, or Programs
National Childhood Injury Prevention Week, 1st week in September, informational and promotional items. Please contact Safety By Design, Ltd, Attn: NCIPW.

Consumer or Patient Education Materials
Safety Synergy® Kit, complete do-it-yourself guide to finding and fixing potential hazards around the home; brochures, pamphlets, and full promotional product line for child health and wellness. Materials can be customized; Low literacy; Please contact for complete catalog.

Classes and Conferences
Seminars and workshops available, variable length. Please contact for complete information.

Technical Assistance
Consulting available for curriculum and programming; guest speaker and conference presenter.

■ Think First Foundation

22 S Washington St
Park Ridge, IL 60068
Contact: Susan C Morton
800-THINK-56 (800-844-6556)
847-692-2740
Fax: 847-692-2394
E-mail: thinkfirst@aans.org
Web site: http://www.thinkfirst.org

Nonprofit organization whose mission is to prevent brain and spinal cord injuries through the education of individuals, community leaders, and the creators of public policy.

Consumer or Patient Education Materials
Think First for Kids, curriculum for grades 1–3, injury prevention, $249; On the Edge, video, testimony from kids who have sustained TBI/SCI, $65. Other materials available. Spanish and French languages available. Please contact for complete catalog.

Publications for Health Professionals
Prevention Pages, 3 times/yr newsletter, free.

■ University of North Carolina Injury Prevention Research Center

CB #7505, Chase Hall
Chapel Hill, NC 27599-7505
Contact: Janet Heath
919-966-2251
Fax: 919-966-0466
E-mail: iprc@unc.edu
Web site: http://www.sph.unc.edu/iprc/

Free-standing University Center with the Division of Health Affairs whose mission is to stimulate and participate in interdisciplinary research and to facilitate the translation of research into injury control policies and programs for prevention, acute care, and rehabilitation at the state, regional, and national levels.

Publications for Health Professionals

IPRC News, quarterly newsletter, latest info on practice and research, free; You Can Make The Difference Preventing Injuries in Your Community, manual, assists communities in reducing injuries, $12. Please contact for complete publications list.

Technical Assistance

Consulting, continuing education, program evaluation in areas of violence prevention and injury control.

ADDITIONAL RESOURCES

■ AAA Foundation for Traffic Safety

1440 New York Ave NW, Ste 201
Washington, DC 20005
202-638-5944
Fax: 202-638-5943
Web site: http://www.aaafts-org/aaa

■ American Association of Poison Control Centers

3201 New Mexico Ave NW, Ste 310
Washington, DC 20016
Contact: Roseann Soloway, Administrator
202-362-7217
Fax: 202-362-8377
Web site: http://198.79.220.3/aapc/aapc.htm

■ American Automobile Association (AAA)

Traffic Safety Department
1000 AAA Dr M/S 76
Heathrow, FL 32746-5063
Contact: Mark L Edwards, Managing Director
407-444-7909

■ American Coalition for Traffic Safety Inc

1110 N Glebe Rd, Ste 1020
Arlington, VA 22201
703-243-7501
Fax: 703-243-2806

■ Brain Injury Association Inc

1776 Massachusetts Ave NW, Ste 100
Washington, DC 20036-1904
202-296-6443
Fax: 202-296-8850
Web site: http://www.bia.usa.org

■ CAR SAFE Inc

Community Auto Restraint Safety and Family Education
417 Associated Rd, #A-254
Brea, CA 92621
800-993-7472 (in-state)
714-993-7472
Fax: 714-528-5833

■ Children's Safety Network National Injury and Violence Prevention Resource Center

CSR Incorporated
1400 Eye St NW, Ste 200
Washington, DC 20005
Contact: Diane Dougherty, Director
202-842-4450
Fax: 202-842-0418
E-mail: chldsafe@erols.com

■ Citizens Against Drug Impaired Drivers

PO Box 17705
Milwaukee, WI 53217
414-352-2043
Fax: 414-352-7080
Web site: http://www.candid.org

■ CWE Inc

19 Charles St
Medford, NJ 08052
Mailing Address:
PO Box 146
Hainesport, NJ 08036
Contact: John J Anderson
609-667-3997
609-659-0625
Fax: 609-654-9714

■ **DuPont Company**
Rt 141 and Rt 48
Barley Mill Plaza, #23
Wilmington, DE 19880
Contact: Training Materials
800-532-SAFE (800-532-7233)
Fax: 888-644-7233

■ **Fire and Injury Prevention Association**
1259 Courthouse Rd, Ste 204
Stafford, VA 22554
Mailing Address:
PO Box 2320
Stafford, VA 22555
800-435-0005
540-657-9375
Fax: 540-657-9471
Web site: http://www.afem.org/afem

■ **Insurance Institute for Highway Safety**
1005 N Glebe Rd, Ste 800
Arlington, VA 22201
703-247-1500
Fax: 703-247-1678
Web site: http://hwysafety.org

■ **Learn Not To Burn® Foundation**
One Batterymarch Pk
PO Box 9101
Quincy, MA 02269-9101
617-984-7285

■ **Mothers Against Drunk Driving (MADD)**
511 E John Carpenter Fwy, Ste 700
Irving, TX 75062-8187
800-GET-MADD (800-438-6233)
214-744-6233
Fax: 214-869-2207
Web site: http://www.madd.org

■ **National Commission Against Drunk Driving**
1900 L St NW, Ste 705
Washington, DC 20036
Contact: ADDY (Alcohol, Drunk Driving and You), 800-972-4636, 710 11th Ave, Ste 110, Greely, CO 80631
202-452-6004
Fax: 202-223-7021
Web site: http://www.ncadd.com

■ **National Fire Protection Association**
One Batterymarch Pk
PO Box 9101
Quincy, MA 02269-9101
Contact: Publications, 800-344-3555
617-770-3000
Fax: 617-770-0200
TDD: 617-984-7880

■ **The National Program for Playground Safety**
203 East Gym
University of Northern Iowa
Cedar Falls, IA 50614
800-554-PLAY (800-554-7529)
319-273-2416
Fax: 319-273-5833
Web site: http://www.uni.edu/coe/playground

■ **National SAFE KIDS Campaign**
111 Michigan Ave NW
Washington, DC 20010
202-662-0600

■ **National Safety Belt Coalition**
1019 19th St NW, Ste 401
Washington, DC 20036
202-296-6263
Fax: 202-293-0032

■ **Safety Shorts Production Inc**
2960 N 23rd St
La Porte, TX 77571
800-458-2236
281-470-9990
Fax: 281-470-8653

■ **Students Against Driving Drunk (SADD)**
PO Box 800
Marlboro, MA 01752
Contact: Mary Lou Vanzini, 508-481-3568 #2
800-886-2972 (Order Dept)
508-481-3568
Fax: 508-481-5759

FEDERAL AGENCIES

■ Indian Health Service (IHS)

Office of Environmental Health & Engineering
Injury Prevention Program
12300 Twinbrook Pkwy, Ste 610
Rockville, MD 20852
301-443-1054
Web site: http://www.tucson.ihs.gov

Mission is to decrease the incidence of severe injuries and death to the lowest possible level and increase the ability of tribes to address their injury problems. Primary emphasis is directed to the greatest cause, which are motor vehicle crashes. Other projects focus on preventing injuries to the elderly as a result of falling, the use of motorcycle and bicycle helmets to reduce traumatic brain injury, and drowning prevention.

■ National Center for Injury Prevention and Control (NCIPC)

Centers for Disease Control and Prevention
4770 Buford Hwy NE, M/S K-63
Atlanta, GA 30341
NCIPC Automated Information Line: 770-488-4677
Web site: http://www.cdc.gov/ncipc/ncipchm.htm

Lead federal agency for injury prevention working closely with other federal agencies; national, state, and local organizations; state and local health departments; and research insitutitons. Works to reduce morbidity, disability, mortality, and costs associated with injuries outside the workplace.

■ National Highway Traffic Safety Administration (NHTSA)

U.S. Department of Transportation
400 Seventh St SW
Washington, DC 20590
Public Inquiries: 202-366-9550
Auto Safety Hotline: 800-424-9393 (202-366-0123 in D.C.)
Web site: http://www.nhtsa.dot.gov

Responsible for reducing deaths, injuries, and economic losses resulting from motor vehicle crashes. Provides technical and financial assistance to state and local governments and awards grants for highway safety and to help combat drunk driving. Also works with private organizations to promote safety programs. Information available from NHTSA regional offices. (Regional office number available from State and Community Services at 202-366-2121.)

■ National Injury Information Clearinghouse

U.S. Consumer Product Safety Commission (CPSC)
4330 East West Hwy
Bethesda, MD 20814
Mailing Address:
CPSC
Washington, DC 20207
301-504-0424
Fax: 301-504-0025

Division of the U.S. Consumer Product Safety Commission (CPSC) that collects, investigates, analyzes, and disseminates injury data and information relating to the causes and prevention of death, injury, and illness associated with consumer products. It compiles data obtained from accident investigation reports, consumer complaints, reported incidents, death certificates, news clips, and the CPSC-operated National Electronic Injury Surveillance System (NEISS).

■ Office of Boating Safety

U.S. Coast Guard, Department of Transportation
2100 Second St SW, G-OPB, Rm 3100
Washington, DC 20593-0001
202-267-1077
Fax: 202-267-4285
Coast Guard Customer Information Line: 800-368-5647
Boat/U.S. Foundation for Boating Safety CourseLine: 800-336-2628

Assists the public on boating safety, answers technical questions and distributes literature.

■ U.S. Consumer Product Safety Commission (CPSC)

Washington, DC 20207
301-504-0580
Fax: 301-504-0399
TDD: 800-638-8270
CPSC Hotline: 800-638-CPSC (800-638-2772)
E-mail: info@cpsc.gov
Web site: http://www.cpsc.gov

Established to reduce injuries and deaths resulting from the use of consumer products. Assists consumers in evaluating the comparative safety of products and conducts information and education programs to increase consumer awareness of dangerous products. CPSC operates the National Electronic Injury Surveillance System (NEISS), which monitors a statistical sample of hospital emergency rooms for injuries associated with consumer products.

Violence-related Injuries

Organization	web site	hotline/toll-free information line	clearinghouse/resource center	electronic information resources	database/statistical information	special campaigns/events/programs	consumer/patient education materials	publications for health professionals	classes/conferences	technical assistance	other products/services	grants/funding/awards	**Page No.**
American Academy of Pediatrics	■						■	■					**139**
Center to Prevent Handgun Violence	■						■	■					**139**
Channing L Bete Co Inc							■						**139**
Child Find of America Inc		■				■	■						**139**
Child Welfare League of America	■							■					**140**
Committee for Children		■						■	■	■			**140**
The Educational Fund to End Handgun Violence	■						■		■	■			**140**
Family Violence Prevention Fund	■	■					■	■		■			**140**
Harvard Injury Control Center	■							■	■	■			**141**
Intermedia	■						■						**141**
Kempe National Center for the Prevention and Treatment of Child Abuse and Neglect	■						■	■	■	■			**141**
National Association of State Units on Aging			■				■						**141**
National Center for Health Education	■						■			■			**142**
National Committee for the Prevention of Elder Abuse								■		■			**142**
National Committee to Prevent Child Abuse	■	■				■	■	■	■	■			**142**
National Crime Prevention Council						■	■	■		■			**143**
National Head Start Association	■							■					**143**
National Safe Workplace Institute	■							■		■			**143**
National School Safety Center			■					■					**143**
Physicians for a Violence-Free Society							■	■	■				**144**

Organization	web site	hotline/toll-free information line	clearinghouse/resource center	electronic information resources	database/statistical information	special campaigns/events/programs	consumer/patient education materials	publications for health professionals	classes/conferences	technical assistance	other products/services	grants/funding/awards	Page No.
Select Media							■	■					**144**
Youth Development International		■											**144**

Additional Resources **144**

Federal Agencies **146**

■ American Academy of Pediatrics

141 Northwest Point Blvd
PO Box 927
Elk Grove Village, IL 60007-0927
Contact: Publications Dept, 800-433-9016
847-228-5005
Fax: 847-228-1281
E-mail: kidsdocs@aap.org
Web site: http://www.aap.org

Nonprofit organization of 50,000 pediatricians dedicated to the health, safety, and well-being of infants, children, adolescents, and young adults. Activities include advocacy for children and youth; public education; research; professional education; membership service and advocacy for pediatricians. More than 30 committees develop positions and programs for interest areas including nutrition; pediatric AIDS; substance abuse; child abuse and neglect; children with disabilities.

Consumer or Patient Education Materials
Child Sexual Abuse: What It Is and How to Prevent It, brochure, recognizing and reporting abuse, and prevention plan geared to children aged 18 mos to 18 yrs, $29.95/100. Please contact for complete catalog.

Publications for Health Professionals
A Guide to References and Resources in Child Abuse and Neglect, 197 pp book, $29.95. Please contact for complete publications list.

■ Center to Prevent Handgun Violence

1225 Eye St NW, Ste 1100
Washington, DC 20005
202-289-7319
Fax: 202-408-1851
Web site: http://www.hci-cphv.org

Nonprofit organization whose mission is to prevent gun-related violence, injuries, and deaths so people can live in a safer America.

Consumer or Patient Education Materials
Posters; Safety Tips, bookmarker; Fact cards and fact sheets include: Steps Parents Can Take to Reduce Children's Risks; Children and Firearms; Firearms and Youth Suicide. Free. Spanish languages available. Please contact for complete catalog.

Publications for Health Professionals
Steps to Prevent (STOP) Firearm Injury, partnership project with American Academy of Pediatrics, national education campaign, materials free to health professionals; Straight Talk About Risks (STAR): A Pre-K–12 Curriculum for Preventing Gun Violence, comprehensive 200 pp, $13.90 for review copy; Handgun Safety Guidelines, brochure, free. Materials available in Spanish. Please contact for complete publications list.

■ Channing L Bete Co Inc

200 State Rd
S Deerfield, MA 01373-0200
800-628-7733 (Sales and Customer Service)
413-665-7611
Fax: 800-499-6464

Publisher of informational and educational booklets, videos, posters, calendars, books, and display racks. Booklets use a distinctive, condensed format—called scriptography—which combines key words and graphics to explain a variety of subjects and is appropriate for different age groups and reading levels.

Consumer or Patient Education Materials
Booklets. Topics include: child, family, elder, and partner abuse; child neglect; preventing violence in health-care facilities. Some Spanish language available. Please contact for pricing and ask for the Patient Education catalog.

■ Child Find of America Inc

243 Main St
PO Box 277
New Paltz, NY 12561-0277
Contact: Michael Messner, 914-255-1848
800-I-AM-LOST (800-426-5678)
914-255-1848
Fax: 914-255-5706

National nonprofit charity whose mission is to locate missing children through active investigation, prevent child abduction through education, and resolve incidents of parental abduction through mediation.

Hotline or Toll-free Information Line
Child Find of America: 800-I-AM-LOST (800-426-5678) (to locate missing children); 800-A-WAY-OUT (800-292-9688) (parental abduction mediation) (M–F 9AM–5PM ET)

Special Campaigns, Events, or Programs
National Missing Children's Day, May 25.

Consumer or Patient Education Materials
Brochures include Shopping Safely: How to Keep Your Child Safe and Protect Your Child: 9 Rules to Keep Your Child Safe From Abduction; videotapes include: Safety Game and Be Smart-Stay Safe. Please contact for pricing and complete list.

■ Child Welfare League of America

440 First St NW, Ste 310
Washington, DC 20001-2085
Contact: Publications Dept
202-638-2952
Fax: 202-638-4004
Web site: http://www.cwla.org

National nonprofit organization that unites almost 1,000 public and private agencies devoted to the well-being of children. Established to guard children's rights and serve children's needs.

Publications for Health Professionals

Children's Voice, quarterly newsmagazine, child and family service news, policy, practice and issues, $50/yr; Children's Monitor, 10 issues/yr newsletter, covers federal public policy issues. $55.00; Child Welfare Journal, bimonthly, child welfare theory, research and practice, $77. Please contact for complete publications list.

■ Committee for Children

2203 Airport Way S, Ste 500
Seattle, WA 98134-2027
Contact: Client Support Services
800-634-4449
206-343-1223
Fax: 206-343-1445

Nonprofit organization that develops educational materials for the prevention of child abuse and youth violence.

Hotline or Toll-free Information Line

Committee for Children Information Line: 800-634-4449 (M–F 8AM–5PM PT) Answers questions and requests for materials.

Publications for Health Professionals

Prevention Update, quarterly newsletter, for school and community leaders, free; Second Step: A Violence Prevention Curriculum, Grades pre-K to 9th, teaches social skills for violence prevention, $295; additional brochures on programs for violence prevention. Please contact for complete publications list.

Classes and Conferences

Safe by Design, 1 day, school-community training for safe schools, $150. Please contact for complete list and schedule.

Technical Assistance

Free consultation for program implementation of violence prevention efforts.

■ The Educational Fund to End Handgun Violence

1000 16th St NW, Ste 603
Washington, DC 20036-5705
202-530-5888
Fax: 202-530-0331
E-mail: edfund@aol.com
Web site: http://www.gunfree.inter.net

Nonprofit educational charity dedicated to ending firearm violence, particularly as it affects children and seeks to curb this violence through education, litigation, and research. Also serves as an information resource for researchers, educators, journalists, attorneys, legislators, and the general public.

Consumer or Patient Education Materials

Ceasefire Action Network Newsletter, bimonthly newsletter, regular forum for sharing information. By donation, but not required.

Classes and Conferences

Citizen's Conference to Stop Gun Violence, each Fall, seminars and workshops, sharing of strategies. Please contact for complete information.

Technical Assistance

Ceasefire Action Network (CAN), provides a clearinghouse of information, advice, and ideas for helping citizens make a greater impact in their local communities; Hands Without Guns, public health and education campaign designed to recognize, celebrate, and promote local efforts to reduce gun violence.

■ Family Violence Prevention Fund

Health Resource Center on Domestic Violence
383 Rhode Island St, Ste 304
San Francisco, CA 94103-5133
Contact: Suzie Jacinthe
888-Rx-ABUSE (888-792-2873)
415-252-8900
Fax: 415-252-8991
E-mail: health@fvpf.org
Web site: http://www.fvpf.org/health

Nonprofit organization provides resource and training materials, technical assistance, and information and referral to health care and domestic violence professionals interested in developing a comprehensive response to domestic violence in the health care setting (e.g., routine screening, protocols, regular staff trainings, and resource materials). Also serves government agencies, researchers, and policymakers.

Hotline or Toll-free Information Line

Health Resource Center on Domestic Violence Information Line: 888-Rx-ABUSE (888-792-2873)

(M–F 9AM–5PM PT) Automated line, referral service, answers questions, request materials.

Consumer or Patient Education Materials
Posters for waiting rooms, $3 ea; pocket Safety Information Card, $.20; Exit Instructions, flyer, free. Materials can be customized; Some Spanish, Tagalog, Chinese, Vietnamese, Korean, Russian, Serbo-Croatian, Arabic languages available. Please contact for complete catalog.

Publications for Health Professionals
Information Packets, 20–40 pp, introduction to health care response to domestic violence for various medical specialties, free to $9; Improving the Health Care Response to Domestic Violence, 250 pp manual, comprehensive resource manual, $50; Health Alert, 2 times/yr newsletter, media advocacy ideas, free. Please contact for complete publications list.

Technical Assistance
Information specialist available to answer questions about domestic violence and an appropriate health care response through the toll-free line.

■ Harvard Injury Control Center

718 Huntington Ave
Boston, MA 02115
Contact: Jane Lee, Research Asst, 617-432-4346
617-432-2123
Fax: 617-432-0190
E-mail: jlee@hsph.harvard.edu
Web site: http://www.harvard.hsph/organizations/hcra/hicc.html

National nonprofit education and research organization that contributes to the scientific knowledge about how to prevent and reduce unintentional injuries and violence in the home, the workplace, and the community.

Publications for Health Professionals
Journal articles and books. Please contact for complete publications list.

Classes and Conferences
Graduate level courses at the Harvard School of Public Health; Seminar Series. Please contact for complete list and schedule.

Technical Assistance
Also provides training and technical assistance on injury prevention and control to government agencies and public health professionals and groups.

■ Intermedia

1300 Dexter Ave N
Seattle, WA 98109
Contact: Susan Hoffman
800-553-8336
206-284-2995
800-553-1655 (toll-free fax)
Fax: 206-283-0778
E-mail: shoffman@intermedia-inc.com
Web site: http://www.intermedia-inc.com

Publisher and distributor of video products for education and training needs on topics of social interest to customers in the U.S. and Canada.

Consumer or Patient Education Materials
Videos include: Hostages at Home; Reporting Child Abuse. Please contact for complete catalog.

■ Kempe National Center for the Prevention and Treatment of Child Abuse and Neglect

1205 Oneida St
Denver, CO 80220
Contact: Susan Hiatt, PhD
303-321-3963
Fax: 303-329-3523
Web site: http://electricstores.com/kempe/default.htm

Nonprofit organization providing a clinically based resource for training, consultation, program development and evaluation, and research in all forms of child abuse and neglect. It is committed to multidisciplinary approaches to improve the recognition, treatment, and prevention of all forms of abuse and neglect.

Consumer or Patient Education Materials
Various books, booklets, information packages, and videos. Please contact for complete catalog.

Publications for Health Professionals
Various materials available, including articles. Please contact for complete publications list.

Classes and Conferences
Annual Child Abuse and Neglect Symposium, 4 days, contact Isabel S Schulz; Professional education, workshops, and seminars, contact for complete list and schedule.

Technical Assistance
Consultation on program development of scientifically-based home visitation programs available on a contracted basis.

■ National Association of State Units on Aging

1225 I St NW, Ste 725
Washington, DC 20005
Contact: Cindy Wellons
202-898-2578
Fax: 202-898-2583
E-mail: staff@nasua.org

Nonprofit public interest organization that provides information, technical assistance, and professional development support to its members—the 57 state and territorial government agencies on aging. Works to promote social policy at the federal and state levels responsive to the needs of older Americans.

Clearinghouse or Resource Center
National Resource Center on Elder Abuse: 202-898-2578; 1225 I St NW, Ste 725, Washington, DC 20005; Broad range of publications, studies, technical assistance, and consumer education documents related to abuse, neglect, and exploitation, as well as coordination with health and law enforcement systems. (Operated in collaboration with America Public Welfare Association.)

Consumer or Patient Education Materials
Abuse booklet, English and Spanish, free.

■ National Center for Health Education

72 Spring St, Ste 208
New York, NY 10012-4019
Contact: Urvi R Dalal, 212-334-9470 x25
212-334-9470
Fax: 212-334-9845
Web site: http://www.nche.org

Nonprofit organization dedicated to leading the nation in the implementation of life-long comprehensive health education. Designs and disseminates Growing Healthy®, a comprehensive school health education curriculum for students in grades K–6, which teaches students skills that will enable them to adopt healthy attitudes and behaviors. Call WRS Group Inc at 800-551-3488 for Growing Healthy and National Health Education Week materials.

Consumer or Patient Education Materials
Preventing Violence: Parents and Caregivers Can Make a Difference, pamphlet, handbook to confront the rise of violence, $4. Please contact for complete catalog.

Technical Assistance
Technical assistance available for comprehensive school health education, teacher training, and Growing Healthy.

■ National Committee for the Prevention of Elder Abuse

c/o Institute on Aging Memorial Hospital
119 Belmont St
Worcester, MA 01605
Contact: Rosalie S Wolf
508-793-6166
Fax: 508-793-6906

Nonprofit group established to promote a greater understanding of the problem of elder abuse and the development of services to protect older persons and disabled adults or reduce the likelihood of their abuse and neglect. Program includes outreach, research, advocacy, public awarenesss, and training.

Publications for Health Professionals
Journal of Elder Abuse and Neglect, quarterly, indepth information on topic, free with membership or $30/yr.

Technical Assistance
Technical assistance provided on a case-by-case basis with regard to elder mistreatment research, service programs, policies.

■ National Committee to Prevent Child Abuse

332 S Michigan Ave, Ste 1600
Chicago, IL 60604-4357
Contact: Communications Dept
312-663-3520
Fax: 312-939-8962
E-mail: ncpca@childabuse.org
Web site: http://www.childabuse.org

Nonprofit volunteer-based organization that seeks to prevent child abuse in all its forms through research, public education, programs, and advocacy. Works through a network of chapters and local affiliates.

Hotline or Toll-free Information Line
National Committee to Prevent Child Abuse Information Line: 800-55-NCPCA (800-556-2722) 24-hr automated, requests for materials.
Healthy Families America Information: 800-CHILDREN (800-244-5373) 24-hr automated line for those who wish to volunteer their services to their community.

Special Campaigns, Events, or Programs
Child Abuse Prevention Month, April, packet includes camera-ready information and resources; poster; stickers; and publications catalog, $5. Contact Public Awareness Dept, 312-663-3520.

Consumer or Patient Education Materials
Various materials available including booklets, pamphlets, posters, stickers. Please contact Communications Dept, 312-663-3520, for complete catalog.

Publications for Health Professionals
Working papers prepared by the National Center on Child Abuse Prevention, up-to-the-minute information and data.

Classes and Conferences
Healthy Families America Conference, 3 days. Contact Anna Loftus, conference coordinator, 312-663-3520 x115.

Technical Assistance
Healthy Families America initiative task force, builds partnerships, plans and provides technical assistance to local groups establishing voluntary home visitor system for all new parents in communities.

■ National Crime Prevention Council

1700 K St NW, 2nd Fl
Washington, DC 20006-3817
Contact: NCPC Fulfillment Center, 800-NCPC-911 (800-627-2911)
202-466-6272
Fax: 202-296-1356

National private nonprofit organization whose principal mission is to enable people to prevent crime and build safer, more caring communities. Coordinates the activities of the Crime Prevention Coalition, an alliance of citizens groups, government agencies, labor and law enforcement bodies, and state and national crime prevention and social service organizations.

Special Campaigns, Events, or Programs
National Citizen's Crime Prevention Campaign: 800-WE-PREVENT (800-937-7383), Stop the Violence, Start Something action guide.

Consumer or Patient Education Materials
McGruff "Take A Bite Out Of Crime" public service advertising campaign materials; books, posters. Please contact for complete catalog.

Publications for Health Professionals
Catalyst, newsletter; Making Public Service Ads Work for You, brochure, free; Partner with Media to Build Safe Communities, comprehensive guide to working effectively with the media, $19.95. Please contact for complete publications list.

Technical Assistance
Training; demonstration programs.

■ National Head Start Association

1651 Prince St
Alexandria, VA 22314
Contact: Publications Dept, 800-687-5044
703-739-0875
Fax: 703-739-0878
Web site: http://www.nhsa.org

Nonprofit organization dedicated exclusively to serving the needs of the Head Start Community. Mission includes advocating in the government, business, and private sectors; working to improve quality and expand enrollment through increased funding; and providing training and professional development for members.

Publications for Health Professionals
Healthy Families America/Head Start Partnership Guide, booklet, suggestions for linking with community-based child abuse prevention effort, $4.50.

■ National Safe Workplace Institute

2400 Crown Point Dr, Ste 100
Charlotte, NC 28227
Contact: Joseph A Kinney MPA, Executive Director
704-841-1175
Fax: 704-841-3893
E-mail: nswi@mindspring.com
Web site: http://www.nswi.com

National Safe Workplace Institute (NSWI) and its sister organization, NSWI Workplace Solutions Inc, specialize in workplace violence risk reduction. Conducts research and educational activities, and offers training and consulting services.

Publications for Health Professionals
Workplace Violence & Behavior Letter, periodical, $179/yr; Essentials of Managing Workplace Violence, set of 3 videos, $199; Violence at Work—How to Make Your Company Safer for Employees and Customers, book, $29.95. Please contact for complete publications list.

Technical Assistance
Training and consulting services available include: violence prevention; sexual harassment; diversity; hostile work environment; supervisor/work team leadership, and robbery control.

■ National School Safety Center

4165 Thousand Oaks Blvd, Ste 290
Westlake Village, CA 91362
Mailing address:
Pepperdine University
24255 Pacific Coast Hwy
Malibu, CA 90263
805-373-9977
Fax: 805-373-9277
E-mail: nsscl@pepperdine.campus.mci.net

The National School Safety Center (NSSC) is a partnership of the U.S. Departments of Justice and Education, and Pepperdine University whose mandate is to focus national attention on cooperative solutions to problems that disrupt the educational process. Special emphasis is placed on efforts to rid schools of crime, violence, and drugs, and on programs to improve student discipline, attendance, achievement, and school climate. Provides technical assistance, legal and legislative aid;

and produces publications and films. Also serves as a clearinghouse for current information about school safety issues.

Clearinghouse or Resource Center
National School Safety Center Clearinghouse: 805-373-9977; contains more than 50,000 articles, publications, and films. Current information available for research and school safety programs. Publications available upon request, $4–$65.

Publications for Health Professionals
School Safety News Service, $59/yr; School Safety, 3 times/yr newsjournal, $9–$12/issue; School Safety Update, 6 times/yr newsletter, $6–$9/issue. Please contact for complete publications list.

■ Physicians for a Violence-Free Society

PO Box 35528
Dallas, TX 75235-0528
Contact: JoAn Dwyer, Associate Executive Director
214-590-8807
Fax: 214-590-4079

National nonprofit organization of physicians, allied health care professionals, and concerned citizens who are dedicated to reducing violence in our society. Works to accomplish this goal by putting violence prevention into the practice of medicine.

Consumer or Patient Education Materials
Book and slide presentation on domestic violence targeting medical audience; Slide presentations for workplace safety and elder abuse, $11–$115.

Publications for Health Professionals
Action Notes, bimonthly, on theme focused area (domestic, elder abuse, teen, media, workplace), free with membership or $18.

Classes and Conferences
Leadership Training, 20 hours, presentation skills and media skills, $100; National Conference, 20 hours, violence prevention. Please contact for complete list and schedule.

■ Select Media

60 Warren St, 5th Fl
New York, NY 10007
Contact: Rebecca Chertok
800-707-6334
212-732-4437
Fax: 212-732-4439
E-mail: selmedbw@interport.net

For-profit distributor of educational films, videos, and CD-ROMs specializing in health and social issues.

Consumer or Patient Education Materials
No More Secrets, film, safety skills for children to protect themselves from sexual abuse, $295; A Touchy Subject, film, prevention strategies for parents, $195; Acquaintance Rape Series, 4 films with guide and study materials, depict most common form of sexual abuse among teens, $475. Please contact for complete catalog.

Publications for Health Professionals
Talking Helps, training film, to accompany No More Secrets, $49. Please contact for complete publications list.

■ Youth Development International

6365 El Apajo Rd
Rancho Sante Fe, CA 92067
Mailing Address:
PO Box 178408
San Diego, CA 92177-8408
Contact: Carie Wlege
800-HIT-HOME 800-448-4663
619-759-5683
Fax: 619-759-1450

National nonprofit organization that operates the National Youth Crisis Hotline (800-HIT-HOME). Provides crisis counseling and referral services for kids who are under 18, are a runaway struggling with drugs, physical abuse, rape, suicide, pregnancy, sexual pressure, or other crisis situations.

Hotline or Toll-free Information Line
National Youth Crisis Hotline: 800-HIT-HOME (800-448-4663) 24-hr operator assisted, crisis or emergency, referral service.

ADDITIONAL RESOURCES

■ American Humane Association Children's Division

63 Inverness Dr E
Englewood, CO 80112-5117
800-227-4645
303-792-9900
Fax: 303-792-5333
E-mail: children@amerhumane.org

■ American Medical Association

515 N State St
Chicago, IL 60610
Contact: Publications and Customer Service, 800-621-8335
312-464-5000
Web site: http://www.ama-assn.org

■ **Business & Legal Reports Inc**
39 Academy St
Madison, CT 06443-1513
800-727-5257 (Order Dept)
203-245-7448
Fax: 203-245-2559
E-mail: BLRblr@aol.com
Web site: http://www.safetyonline.net/blr

■ **Child Abuse Prevention Center**
295 Harrison Blvd, Ste 102
Ogden, UT 84409
Contact: Stacy Iverson, Program Coordinator
Shaken Baby Syndrome Information and Referral Service
801-393-3366
Fax: 801-393-7019

■ **Childhelp USA**
PO Box 630
Los Angeles, CA 90028
213-465-4016
National Child Abuse Hotline: 800-422-4453

■ **Children Now**
1212 Broadway, Ste 530
Oakland, CA 94612
510-763-2444
Fax: 510-763-1974
Web site: http://www.childnow.org

■ **Children's Safety Network National Injury and Violence Prevention Resource Center**
CSR Incorporated
1400 Eye St NW, Ste 200
Washington, DC 20005
Contact: Diane Dougherty, Director
202-842-4450
Fax: 202-842-0418
E-mail: chldsafe@erols.com

■ **Coalition for America's Children**
c/o M.B. Fund
1634 Eye St NW, 12th Fl
Washington, DC 20006
Contact: Claire Sebastian
202-638-5770
Fax: 202-638-5771
Web site: http://www.usakids.org

■ **Coalition to Stop Gun Violence**
Educational Fund to End Handgun Violence
1000 16th St NW, Ste 603
Washington, DC 20036
202-530-0340
Fax: 202-530-0331
E-mail: noguns@aol.com
Web site: http://www.gunfree.inter.net/csgv

■ **Comprehensive Health Education Foundation**
22419 Pacific Hwy S
Seattle, WA 98198
Contact: Publications, 800-323-9084
206-824-2907
Fax: 206-824-3072

■ **Crisis Prevention Institute Inc**
3315-K N 124th St
Brookfield, WI 53005
800-558-8976
414-783-5787
Fax: 414-783-5906
E-mail: cpi@execpc.com
Web site: http://www.execpc.com/~cpi

■ **ETR Associates**
PO Box 1830
Santa Cruz, CA 95061-1830
Contact: Publications, 800-321-4407
408-438-4060
Fax: 408-438-4284 (Orders)

■ **Family Resource Coalition**
200 S Michigan Ave, 16th Fl
Chicago, IL 60604
312-341-0900
Fax: 312-341-9361

■ **KidsPeace**
The National Center for Kids in Crisis
National Campaign Headquarters
575 Madison Ave, Ste 1006
New York, NY 10022
212-605-0153
Fax: 212-605-0509
Web site: http://www.kidspeace.org

■ **National Center for Assault Prevention**
606 Delsea Dr
Sewell, NJ 08080
800-258-3189
609-582-7000
Fax: 908-369-8145
Web site: http://www.ncap.org

■ **National Coalition Against Domestic Violence**
National Office
PO Box 18749
Denver, CO 80218-0749
303-839-1852
Fax: 303-831-9251

■ **National Council on Child Abuse and Family Violence**
1155 Connecticut Ave NW, Ste 400
Washington, DC 20036
202-429-6695

■ **National Domestic Violence Hotline:**
(800-799-SAFE) 800-799-7233

■ **National Exchange Club**
3050 Central Ave
Toledo, OH 43606
800-760-3413
419-535-3232
Fax: 419-535-1989
E-mail: nechq@aol.com
Web site: http://rtpnet.org/~nec/

■ **National Resource Center for Youth Mediation**
A Division of the New Mexico Center for Dispute Resolution
800 Park Ave SW
Albuquerque, NM 87102
800-24YOUTH (800-249-6884)
505-247-0571
Fax: 505-242-5966
E-mail: nmcdr@igc.apc.org

■ **SBS Prevention Plus**
National Don't Shake the Baby Campaign
649 Main St
Groveport, OH 43125
800-858-5222

■ **Workplace Violence Research Institute**
465 Forest Ave, Ste J
PO Box 4077
Laguna Beach, CA 92652-4077
Contact: Jurg W Mattman, Executive Director
714-376-3337
Fax: 714-376-3339
E-mail: tmcwvri@aol.com

■ **YWCA of the USA**
National Office
726 Broadway
New York, NY 10003
212-614-2700
Fax: 212-677-9716
Web site: http://www.ywca.org

FEDERAL AGENCIES

■ **National Center for Injury Prevention and Control (NCIPC)**
Centers for Disease Control and Prevention
4770 Buford Hwy NE, M/S K-60
Atlanta, GA 30341-3724
Div of Violence Prevention: 770-488-4362
Web site: http://www.cdc.gov/ncipc/ncipchm.htm

Lead federal agency for injury prevention working closely with other federal agencies; national, state, and local organizations; state and local health departments; and research institutions. Works to reduce morbidity, disability, mortality, and costs associated with injuries outside the workplace.

■ **National Center on Child Abuse and Neglect (NCCAN)**
Administration for Children and Families
PO Box 1182
Washington, DC 20013-1182
202-205-8586

■ **National Clearinghouse on Child Abuse and Neglect**
PO Box 1182
Washington, DC 20013-1182
800-394-3366
703-385-7565
Fax: 703-385-3206
E-mail: nccanch@calib.com
Web site: http://www.calib.com/nccanch

Serves as a major resource center for the acquisition and dissemination of child abuse and neglect materials and is the information component for the NCCAN.

■ National Criminal Justice Reference Service (NCJRS)

U.S. Department of Justice
1600 Research Blvd, 2nd Fl
Rockville, MD 20850
Mailing Address:
PO Box 6000
Rockville, MD 20849-6000
800-851-3420
301-251-5500
Fax: 301-251-5212
Electronic Bulletin Board: 301-738-8895
Web site: http://www.ncjrs.org

Centralized clearinghouse supporting all bureaus of the U.S. Department of Justice. One of the most extensive sources of information in the world; offers reference services and provides other services such as document loan, microfiche, CD-ROM, and dissemination of publications. A computerized online database contains more than 130,000 citations to documents on criminal justice issues including violence prevention, family violence and child abuse, substance abuse and treatment.

■ Safe and Drug Free Schools Program

U.S. Department of Education
1250 Maryland Ave SW, Rm 603
Washington, DC 20202
Mailing Address:
600 Independence Ave SW, PRTL Rm 604
Washington, DC 20202-6123
800-624-0100
202-260-3954
Fax: 202-260-7767
Web site: http://www.ed.gov

Responds to the continuing crisis of violence and drugs in schools by supporting comprehensive school- and community-based drug abuse and violence prevention programs; allows school districts flexibility to design their own programs. Materials are available without charge by calling 800-624-0100 or writing to the office.

Disease Management and Prevention

Asthma 151
Cancer 155
Diabetes 163
Eye Disease 167
Heart Disease and Stroke 171
Other Chronic Conditions and Diseases 177
Immunizations and Infectious Diseases 189
Sexually Transmitted Diseases, HIV Infection, and AIDS 197

Asthma

Organization	website	hotline/toll-free information line	clearinghouse/resource center	electronic information resources	database/statistical information	special campaigns/events/programs	consumer/patient education materials	publications for health professionals	classes/conferences	technical assistance	other products/services	grants/funding/awards	**Page No.**
Allergy and Asthma Network • Mothers of Asthmatics Inc	■	■					■	■	■	■			**152**
American Academy of Pediatrics	■						■						**152**
HIN Inc (The Health Information Network)							■						**152**
Medcom Inc	■						■						**152**
National Jewish Center for Immunology and Respiratory Medicine	■	■		■			■	■					**153**
Additional Resources													**153**
Federal Agencies													**153**

■ Allergy and Asthma Network • Mothers of Asthmatics Inc

3554 Chain Bridge Rd, Ste 200
Fairfax, VA 22030-2709
Contact: Jill A Braun
800-878-4403
703-385-4403
Fax: 703-352-4354
E-mail: aanma@aol.com
Web site: http://www.podi.com/health/aanma

International nonprofit patient education organization dedicated to families with asthma and allergies.

Hotline or Toll-free Information Line

Allergy and Asthma Network/Mothers of Asthmatics Inc Help Line: 800-878-4403 (M–F 9AM–3PM ET) Operator assisted, answers questions, requests for materials.

Consumer or Patient Education Materials

Consumer Update on Asthma, book, layman's version of NIH guidelines of asthma, $6.95; Asthma Organizer, booklet, personal tracking forms, $15; Many other books, videos, pamphlets, brochures, products available. Some Spanish languages available. Please contact for complete catalog.

Publications for Health Professionals

The MA Report, monthly newsletter, updates on medical research, new products, legislation, free with membership. Please contact for complete publications list.

Classes and Conferences

Asthma Educator Program, 3 days, strategies for effective patient education and enhanced patient communication, $600. Please contact for complete list and schedule.

Technical Assistance

Consulting and research activities.

■ American Academy of Pediatrics

141 Northwest Point Blvd
PO Box 927
Elk Grove Village, IL 60007-0927
Contact: Publications Dept, 800-433-9016
847-228-5005
Fax: 847-228-1281
E-mail: kidsdocs@aap.org
Web site: http://www.aap.org

Nonprofit organization of 50,000 pediatricians dedicated to the health, safety, and well-being of infants, children, adolescents, and young adults. Activities include advocacy for children and youth; public education; research; professional education; membership service and advocacy for pediatricians. More than 30 committees develop positions and programs for interest areas including nutrition; pediatric AIDS; substance abuse; child abuse and neglect; children with disabilities.

Consumer or Patient Education Materials

How To Help Your Child With Asthma, brochure, helps parents recognize asthma symptoms and directions on measuring the peak flow rate, $29.95/100; Managing Childhood Asthma: A Parent's Guide, 23-min video and guide, $39.95. Please contact for complete catalog.

■ HIN Inc (The Health Information Network)

231 Market Place, #331
San Ramon, CA 94583-9800
Contact: Lois Kamoroff
800-HIN-1121 (800-446-1121)
510-551-4800
Fax: 510-551-4808

Medical publishing company of patient education booklets in easy-to-read, understandable text and with full-color medical illustrations; authored and edited by medical experts.

Consumer or Patient Education Materials

Allergies in Childhood; Childhood Asthma, booklets, $33.75 for 25 copies, discounts available for quantity orders. Materials can be customized; Please contact for complete catalog.

■ Medcom Inc

6060 Phyllis Dr
Cypress, CA 90630
Contact: Teri Armstrong, Marketing, 714-891-1443 x225
800-541-0253
714-891-1443
Fax: 714-898-4852
Web site: http://www.medcominc.com

For-profit producer and worldwide distributor of multimedia healthcare educational products, mainly video programs and related print material, for health care professionals, their patients, and health-conscious people everywhere.

Consumer or Patient Education Materials

Videos include: Winning Against Asthma; Managing Childhood Asthma: A Parent's Guide, $39.95 ea. Please contact for complete catalog.

■ **National Jewish Center for Immunology and Respiratory Medicine**
1400 Jackson St
Denver, CO 80206
800-222-LUNG (800-222-5864)
303-388-4461
Web site: http://www.njc.org

Nonprofit, non-sectarian medical research center that provides patient care, medical education, and conducts research in the areas of respiratory, immunologic, allergic, and infectious diseases.

Hotline or Toll-free Information Line
Lung Line®: 800-222-LUNG (800-222-5864) (M–F 8AM–5PM MT) Registered trained nurses answer questions and request for information.
Electronic Information Resources
Lung Facts®: 800-552-LUNG (800-552-5864), 24-hr free automated information service on medical and non-medical topics about asthma, emphysema and other lung diseases.
Consumer or Patient Education Materials
Asthma Wizard Activity Book, teaches children ages 5–12 about managing asthma, $7; numerous booklets including Understanding Asthma, Management of Chronic Respiratory Disease, Healthy Breathing; single copy free. Contact Lung Line at 800-222-5864.
Publications for Health Professionals
Lung Line, quarterly newsletter, research and current information, call Lung Facts (800-552-5864) to receive free copy.

ADDITIONAL RESOURCES

■ **American Academy of Allergy, Asthma, and Immunology**
611 E Wells St
Milwaukee, WI 53202
414-272-6071
Fax: 414-276-3349
E-mail: info@aaaai.org
Web site: http://www.aaaai.org

■ **American Association for Respiratory Care**
11030 Ables Ln
Dallas, TX 75229-4593
214-243-2272
Fax: 214-484-2720
Web site: http://www.aarc.org

■ **American College of Allergy, Asthma and Immunology**
85 W Algonquin Rd, Ste 550
Arlington Heights, IL 60005
800-842-7777
847-427-1200
Fax: 847-427-1294
Web site: http://www.allergy.mcg.edu

■ **Asthma and Allergy Foundation of America**
1125 15th St NW, Ste 502
Washington, DC 20005
Contact: Bonnie Eiche, Public Relations
800-727-8462 800-7-ASTHMA
202-466-7643
Fax: 202-466-8940

■ **Asthma Information Center**
PO Box 790
Springhouse, PA 19477-0790
800-727-5400

FEDERAL AGENCIES

■ **National Heart, Lung, and Blood Institute (NHLBI)**
National Institutes of Health
NIH/NHLBI/OPEC, Rm 4A-03
31 Center Dr, MSC 2480
Bethesda, MD 20892-2480
301-496-4236
Web site: http://www.nhlbi.nih.gov/nhlbi/nhlbi.htm

NHLBI Information Center
PO Box 30105
Bethesda, MD 20824-0105
301-251-1222; Fax: 301-251-1223

Oversees research, demonstration, prevention, education, control, and training activities in the fields of heart, lung, and blood diseases and education concerning these diseases. The Information Center offers materials on numerous topics, including cholesterol, high blood pressure, smoking, asthma, heart disease, exercise, obesity, stroke. Treatment guidelines on high blood cholesterol, high blood pressure, and asthma; heart and lung health in the workplace and schools are available for health professionals.

Cancer

Products/Services Offered

Organization	web site	hotline/toll-free information line	clearinghouse/resource center	electronic information resources	database/statistical information	special campaigns/events/programs	consumer/patient education materials	publications for health professionals	classes/conferences	technical assistance	other products/services	grants/funding/awards	**Page No.**
American Cancer Society	■	■				■	■	■				■	**156**
American Institute for Cancer Research	■						■		■			■	**156**
American Prostate Society	■						■						**156**
Anatomical Chart Company							■						**156**
Channing L Bete Co Inc							■						**156**
The Chemotherapy Foundation							■	■	■				**157**
Customized Communications Inc							■						**157**
Exceptional Cancer Patients Inc							■		■				**157**
Health Education Services	■						■						**157**
HIN Inc (The Health Information Network)							■						**157**
Johanna's of Albany Ltd							■	■	■	■	■		**158**
Journeyworks Publishing							■						**158**
Lange Productions							■	■					**158**
Mammatech Corporation	■						■		■	■			**158**
Medcom Inc	■						■						**159**
NASCO	■						■						**159**
National Alliance of Breast Cancer Organizations (NABCO)	■	■					■	■				■	**159**
National Coalition for Cancer Survivorship	■						■		■				**159**
Select Media							■						**159**
The Wellness Community							■			■			**160**
Y-ME®	■	■					■	■	■	■			**160**

Additional Resources **160**

Federal Agencies **162**

■ American Cancer Society

1599 Clifton Rd NE
Atlanta, GA 30329
800-ACS-2345 (800-227-2345)
Fax: 404-325-2217
Web site: http://www.cancer.org

Nationwide nonprofit community-based, voluntary health organization dedicated to eliminating cancer as a major health problem by preventing cancer, saving lives, and diminishing suffering from cancer through research, education, advocacy, and service. There are 57 chartered divisions and approximately 3,400 unit organizations to provide services on the local level.

Hotline or Toll-free Information Line

American Cancer Society Cancer Response System: 800-ACS-2345 (800-227-2345) (M–F 8:30AM–4:30PM) Operator assisted, referral service, answers questions, requests for materials.

Special Campaigns, Events, or Programs

Great American Smokeout, 3rd Thursday in November, flyers, pamphlets, news releases. Contact local chapter.

Consumer or Patient Education Materials

Many fact sheets, pamphlets, and booklets, free single copy.

Publications for Health Professionals

Cancer Facts and Figures; Breast Cancer Facts and Figures; Cancer Risk Report: Prevention and Control, annual reports, free single copy.

Grants, Funding, or Awards

Research grants, post-doctoral fellowships, research professorships, clinical oncology awards. Contact 800-ACS-2345.

■ American Institute for Cancer Research

1759 R St NW
Washington, DC 20009
800-843-8114
202-328-7744
Fax: 202-328-7226
Web site: http://www.aicr.org

National nonprofit cancer charity organization focusing on cancer prevention through diet and nutrition. Also funds grants in the study of the link between diet and cancer.

Consumer or Patient Education Materials

Booklets and brochures include: Dietary Guidelines to Lower Cancer Risk; Reducing Your Risk of Prostate Cancer; Reducing Your Risk of Colon Cancer; free single copy, discounts available for quantity orders.

Classes and Conferences

Annual research conference, 2 days.

Grants, Funding, or Awards

Research grant programs for cancer prevention and cancer treatment. Contact Research Dept.

■ American Prostate Society

1340F Charwood Rd
Hanover, MD 21076
410-859-3735
Fax: 410-850-0818
E-mail: cgerard@www.ameripros.org
Web site: http://www.ameripros.org

Nonprofit volunteer-operated society whose mission is to inform and educate men about the risks of prostate disease, and their alternatives if they develop a prostate disease. Goals are to reduce death due to prostate cancer and to reduce unnecessary, or ineffective, prostate surgery.

Consumer or Patient Education Materials

Prostate Cancer Commitment, newsletter; BPH video, nature and treatment for prostate enlargement, free.

■ Anatomical Chart Company

8221 N Kimball
Skokie, IL 60076-2956
800-621-7500 (Order Dept)
847-679-4700
Fax: 847-674-0211

Mail order company catering to the professional or student in need of biological or scientific charts and models of the human anatomy.

Consumer or Patient Education Materials

The Good News About Breast Care, 16 pp booklet, breast care info, $1.50 ea; Breast Self Examination Mini-Models, models with simulated lumps, $7.25 ea.

■ Channing L Bete Co Inc

200 State Rd
S Deerfield, MA 01373-0200
800-628-7733 (Sales and Customer Service)
413-665-7611
Fax: 800-499-6464

Publisher of informational and educational booklets, videos, posters, calendars, books, and display racks. Booklets use a distinctive, condensed format—called scriptography—which combines key words and graphics to explain a variety of subjects and is appropriate for different age groups and reading levels.

Consumer or Patient Education Materials
Booklets and videos. Topics include: cancer detection and prevention, mammography, breast cancer, cervical cancer, colorectal cancer, skin cancer, and prostate cancer. Some Spanish language available. Please contact for pricing and ask for the Patient Education catalog.

■ The Chemotherapy Foundation

183 Madison Ave, Ste 403
New York, NY 10016
212-213-9292
Fax: 212-689-5164

Nonprofit foundation that supports innovative laboratory and clinical research to develop and improve drug treatment for the control and cure of cancer. Conducts a continuing education program for medical professionals and publishes free educational literature for patients and the public.

Consumer or Patient Education Materials
Chemotherapy: Your Weapon Against Cancer; The Breast Cancer Epidemic: How 15,000 More Lives Can Be Saved Each Year; What Every Woman and Her Doctor Should Discuss About Ovarian Cancer; single copy free, please contact for pricing for multiple orders.

Publications for Health Professionals
Abstracts, summary of research status regarding improved treatment and control emanating from annual 3-day symposium. Please contact Foundation office.

Classes and Conferences
Annual Symposium for Professionals (Co-Sponsored with The Page and William Black Post-Graduate School of Medicine of the Mount Sinai School of Medicine), Intense 3-day review, $75–$350. Contact Jaclyn Silverman, Conference Coordinator, 212-241-6772.

■ Customized Communications Inc

2001 E Randol Mill Rd
Arlington, TX 76011
Mailing Address:
PO Box 5566
Arlington, TX 76005
Contact: Lori O'Malley
800-476-2253
817-459-2703
Fax: 817-459-3557

For-profit company specializing in customized patient education and marketing materials; available for breast health and mammography, MRI, CT, radiology, anesthesia, surgery, ob/gyn, and well women's health.

Consumer or Patient Education Materials
Breast care booklets, brochures, shower cards, recall cards, and bookmarks. Pricing varies upon quantity ordered.

■ Exceptional Cancer Patients Inc

300 Plaza Middlesex
Middletown, CT 06457
860-343-5950
Fax: 860-343-5956

Nonprofit organization providing emotional support, education, and hope for people with chronic or life-challenging illnesses.

Consumer or Patient Education Materials
Books and tapes for self-care and wellness; coping; healing; growth; and personal development.

Classes and Conferences
Health Professional Training Programs, teaches how to start and offer similiar support groups. Please contact for complete information.

■ Health Education Services

PO Box 7126
Albany, NY 12224
518-439-7286
Fax: 518-439-7286 *51
Web site: http://www.hes.org

Nonprofit distributor of current health education, promotional publications, posters, and videos, most of which have been produced by the New York State Department of Health or the New York State Department of Environmental Conservation. (Health Education Services is a Division of Health Research Inc.)

Consumer or Patient Education Materials
Breast Self-Examination, brochure; Endometrial Cancer—A Risk for Women, pamphlet; Pap Test, pamphlet; What You Need to Know About Cervical Cancer. $12 for 100 copies.

■ HIN Inc (The Health Information Network)

231 Market Place, #331
San Ramon, CA 94583-9800
Contact: Lois Kamoroff
800-HIN-1121 (800-446-1121)
510-551-4800
Fax: 510-551-4808

Medical publishing company of patient education booklets in easy-to-read, understandable text and with full-color medical illustrations; authored and edited by medical experts.

Consumer or Patient Education Materials
Breast Awareness: Breast Lumps & Cancer; Fibroids; Benign Prostatic Hyperplasia; Prostate Cancer, booklets, $36.25 for 25 copies, discounts available for quantity orders.

■ Johanna's of Albany Ltd

199 New Scotland Ave
Albany, NY 12208
Contact: Johanna Ehman RN OCN
518-482-4178

Cancer rehabilitation nurse consultant, author, and publisher of professional and public education booklets, videos, and audiotapes developed to promote the positive image of persons with cancer and to encourage the practice of breast self-examination for early cancer detection.

Consumer or Patient Education Materials
Breast Health Diary, booklet, discusses risk for breast cancer and how to help self, $3; Maintaining a Positive Image with Cancer Therapy, booklet, step-by-step guide to keeping well with cancer, $4.50; BSE RAP, audiocassette, teaches breast self-exam through music, $8.
Publications for Health Professionals
BSE RAP, 4-min video, teaches breast self-exam, $35.
Classes and Conferences
Breast Health Awareness, 1 hr, breast cancer risk, prevention, and early detection, $250; Positive Images and Cancer, 1 hr, discusses changes in body image & self-help activities, $250; Breast Cancer Rehabilitation, 2½ hrs, issues related to breast cancer recovery, $500.
Technical Assistance
Consultation to health care professionals and oncology facilities to establish comprehensive breast cancer rehabilitation services through program development, presentations, research, and publications.
Other Products and Services
Health care policy activist works with oncology groups providing information to professionals, patients, and the public regarding pertinent legislative issues.

■ Journeyworks Publishing

736 Chestnut St
Santa Cruz, CA 95060
Mailing Address:
PO Box 8466
Santa Cruz, CA 95061-8466
800-775-1998
408-423-1400
Fax: 408-423-8102

Publisher of health promotion materials for clinics, hospitals, schools, and health departments covering a variety of topics including fitness, women's health, sexual abstinence, teen pregnancy prevention, STDs and HIV, mental wellness, tobacco use prevention, and smoking cessation.

Consumer or Patient Education Materials
Nine Ways to Lower Your Risk of Breast Cancer; 50 Great Reasons to Get a Mammogram; pamphlets, free review sample, pricing varies upon quantity ordered.

■ Lange Productions

7661 Curson Ter
Los Angeles, CA 90046
213-874-4730
213-874-0132
Fax: 213-874-3318
E-mail: langevideo@aol.com

For-profit creator, producer, and distributor of videotape and CD-ROM products on health care topics for hospitals, managed care companies, and pharmaceutical companies.

Consumer or Patient Education Materials
Be A Survivor, CD-ROM, complete treatment guide for breast cancer patients, $395; B.S.E. for Teens, 7-min video, instructional tape hosted by Jenny Garth, $225; New B.S.E., 7-min video, easy demonstration for multi-ethnic women by Mariette Hartley, available in Spanish, $225.
Publications for Health Professionals
Cancer Pain Management, 7-min video, multi-disciplinary approach, $250.

■ Mammatech Corporation

930 NW Eighth Ave
Gainesville, FL 32601
Contact: H S Pennypacker
800-626-2273
352-375-0607
Fax: 352-375-6111
E-mail: info@mammacare.com
Web site: http://www.mammacare.com

For-profit distributor of MammaCare® method of manual breast examination.

Consumer or Patient Education Materials
Professional Learning System, kit, video and breast models, $225; Personal Learning System, kit, video and one model, $69.50.

Classes and Conferences
Specialist course, 4 days, $500; CBE course, ½ day, $200.
Technical Assistance
Consulting, training in breast examination.

■ Medcom Inc
6060 Phyllis Dr
Cypress, CA 90630
Contact: Teri Armstrong, Marketing, 714-891-1443 x225
800-541-0253
714-891-1443
Fax: 714-898-4852
Web site: http://www.medcominc.com

For-profit producer and worldwide distributor of multimedia healthcare educational products, mainly video programs and related print material, for health care professionals, their patients, and health-conscious people everywhere.

Consumer or Patient Education Materials
Videos include: When Someone You Love is at Risk for Prostate Disease; Feeling Good Again: Coping with Breast Cancer; Cancer: Finding Help and Hope, $39.95 ea.

■ NASCO
901 Janesville Ave
Ft Atkinson, WI 53538-0901
Contact: Dan Christianson, Health Care Dept, 414-563-2446 x237
800-558-9595
414-563-2446
Fax: 414-563-8296
E-mail: lifeform@nascofa.com
Web site: http://www.nascofa.com

For-profit developer, producer, and distributor of health education products worldwide.

Consumer or Patient Education Materials
Breast and testicular self-exam materials include flip charts, videos, and models. $50-$229.

■ National Alliance of Breast Cancer Organizations (NABCO)
9 E 37th St, 10th Fl
New York, NY 10016
Contact: Jessica Fiorelli
800-719-9154
212-889-0606
Fax: 212-689-1213
E-mail: nabcoinfo@aol.com
Web site: http://www.nabco.org

Leading nonprofit central information resource on breast cancer and a network of more than 375 breast cancer organizations. Provides information, assistance and referral to anyone with questions about breast cancer, and acts as a voice for the interests and concerns of breast cancer survivors and women at risk.

Hotline or Toll-free Information Line
National Alliance of Breast Cancer Organizations Information Line: 800-719-9154 24-hr automated line, answers questions, requests for materials.
Consumer or Patient Education Materials
Fact sheets, pamphlets, research articles. Free.
Publications for Health Professionals
NABCO NEWS, quarterly newsletter, updates on research, activity in breast cancer field, free with membership; Breast Cancer Resource List, 60 pp booklet, resources and support groups, $3.
Grants, Funding, or Awards
Avon Breast Health Access Fund, Contact Shana Krupp.

■ National Coalition for Cancer Survivorship
1010 Wayne Ave, Ste 505
Silver Spring, MD 20910
Contact: Terry Campbell
888-650-9127
301-650-8868
Fax: 301-565-9670
Web site: http://www.access.digex.net/~mkragen/cansearch.html

Nonprofit organization that provides information and referral resources on the psychological and social impacts of cancer; advocates the needs and interests of cancer survivors before Congress and federal agencies.

Consumer or Patient Education Materials
Right to Hope, booklet, $5; other books, booklets, buttons, posters, some free to $19.
Classes and Conferences
NCCS Town Hall Meetings, length and time varies. Contact 888-650-9127 for complete information.

■ Select Media
60 Warren St, 5th Fl
New York, NY 10007
Contact: Rebecca Chertok
800-707-6334
212-732-4437
Fax: 212-732-4439
E-mail: selmedbw@interport.net

For-profit distributor of educational films, videos, and CD-ROMs specializing in health and social issues.

Consumer or Patient Education Materials
In Touch, 26-min video, breast self-examination, for inner-city teens, $149.

■ The Wellness Community
National Office
2716 Ocean Park Blvd, Ste 1040
Santa Monica, CA 90405-5207
310-314-2555
Fax: 310-314-7586

Nonprofit organization that helps cancer patients fight for their recovery by providing psychological and emotional support as an adjunct to conventional medical treatment. Ongoing support groups for cancer patients and their families are led by specially trained licensed psychotherapists; all without charge; located in 16 cities in the U.S.

Consumer or Patient Education Materials
Actions Cancer Patients Can Take in the Fight For Recovery, pamphlet, free; The Wellness Community Guide to Fighting For Recovery, book, patient active concept and action attitude for emotional support, in bookstores.
Technical Assistance
Daily support groups, workshops, physician lectures. Contact for information on programs for each city.

■ Y-ME®
212 W Van Buren St
Chicago, IL 60607-3908
Contact: Michelle Melin
800-221-2141
312-986-8338
Fax: 312-294-8597
Web site: http://www.y-me.org

National nonprofit, consumer oriented organization providing information, referrals, and emotional support to individuals concerned about or diagnosed with breast cancer. Its national toll-free hotline is staffed by trained counselors and volunteers who have experienced breast cancer. Promotes breast cancer awareness through educational workshops and its newsletter and has 19 chapters in the U.S.

Hotline or Toll-free Information Line
Y-ME® National Breast Cancer Hotline: 800-221-2141; 800-986-9505 (Spanish) 24-hr operator assisted, crisis or emergency.
Consumer or Patient Education Materials
Booklets include: A Woman's Guide to Breast Health; When the Woman You Love Has Breast Cancer; For Single Women With Breast Cancer; free single copy.
Publications for Health Professionals
Y-ME Newsletter, bimonthly, free to contributing members; Guidelines for Breast Cancer Support Programs, 150 pp, workbook; Just for Teens, educational brochure. Please contact for pricing and complete list.
Classes and Conferences
Special workshops on the psychosocial needs of breast cancer patients for health care professionals; Full-day conferences to share ideas, insights, and experiences in care and counseling.
Technical Assistance
Referral service; chapter affiliation program; educational workshop presentation to organizations and businesses; educational meetings.

ADDITIONAL RESOURCES

■ AMC Cancer Research Center
1600 Pierce St
Lakewood, CO 80214
Contact: Marketing and Public Relations Dept
800-321-1557
303-233-6501

■ American Academy of Dermatology
930 N Meacham Rd
PO Box 4014
Schaumburg, IL 60168-4014
847-330-0230
Fax: 847-330-0050
Web site: http://www.aad.org

■ American Association for Cancer Research
Public Ledger Bldg, Ste 816
150 S Independence Mall W
Philadelphia, PA 19106-3483
Contact: Joan Ritchie
215-440-9300
Fax: 215-440-9313
E-mail: aacr@aacr.org
Web site: http://www.aacr.org

■ American College of Radiology
1891 Preston White Dr
Reston, VA 22091
Contact: Publications Sales, 800-227-7762
800-227-5463
703-648-8900
Fax: 703-648-8989

American Foundation for Urologic Disease Inc
300 W Pratt St, Ste 401
Baltimore, MD 21201-2463
410-727-2908
Fax: 410-528-0550
E-mail: admin@afud.org
Web site: http://www.access.digex.net/~afud

American Health Foundation
320 E 43rd St
New York, NY 10017
212-953-1900
Fax: 212-687-2339
Web site: http://www.ahf.org

American Society of Preventive Oncology
1300 University Ave, #7C
Madison, WI 53706
Contact: Judy Bowser
608-263-6809
Fax: 608-263-4497
E-mail: jabowser@facstaff.wisc.educ

Association of Community Cancer Centers
11600 Nebel St, Ste 201
Rockville, MD 20852
301-984-9496
Fax: 301-770-1949
Web site: http://www.assoc-cancer-ctrs.org

Avon Products Foundation
9 W 57th St
New York, NY 10019
212-546-6015
Web site: http://www.avon.com/

Breast Cancer Information Clearinghouse
New York State Education and Research Network
Web site: http://www.nysernet.org/bcic

Cancer Care Inc
1180 Avenue of the Americas
New York, NY 10036
Contact: Carolyn Messner, Director, Education and Training
800-813-HOPE (800-813-4673)
212-302-2400
Fax: 212-719-0263
E-mail: info@cancercareinc.org
Web site: http://www.cancercareinc.org

The Gilda Radner Familial Ovarian Cancer Registry
Roswell Park Cancer Institute
Elm and Carlton Sts
Buffalo, NY 14263-0001
800-OVARIAN (800-682-7426)
716-845-3110
Web site: http://rpci.med.buffalo.edu/clinic/gynonc/grwp.html

Leukemia Society of America Inc
600 Third Ave
New York, NY 10016
800-955-4LSA (800-955-4572)
212-573-8484
Fax: 212-865-9686
Web site: http://www.leukemia.org

National Breast Cancer Awareness Month
PO Box 15437
Wilmington, DE 19850-5437
Contact: Lorraine Morris
302-886-3119
Fax: 302-886-5135

National Foundation for Cancer Research
7315 Wisconsin Ave, Ste 500W
Bethesda, MD 20814
Contact: Information Dept
800-321-CURE (800-321-2873)
301-654-1250
Fax: 301-654-5824

Prostate Health Council
300 W Pratt St, Ste 401
Baltimore, MD 21201
Contact: c/o American Foundation for Urologic Disease Inc
800-242-2383
410-727-2908
Fax: 410-528-0550
Web site: http://www.access.digex.net/~afud

Public Citizen
1600 20th St NW
Washington, DC 20009-1001
Contact: Health Research Group
202-588-1000
Web site: http://www.citizen.org

■ **Skin Cancer Foundation**
245 Fifth Ave, Ste 1403
New York, NY 10016
800-SKIN-490 (800-754-6490)
212-725-5176
Fax: 212-725-5752

■ **Solid Tumor Oncology Education Foundation Inc**
PO Box 1505
Secaucus, NJ 07096-1505
800-223-8978
201-271-6000
Fax: 201-865-3521

■ **Strang Cancer Prevention Center**
428 E 72nd St
New York, NY 10021
800-521-9356
212-794-4900
Fax: 212-794-0749

■ **Susan G Komen Breast Cancer Foundation**
5005 LBJ Fwy, Ste 370
Dallas, TX 75244
800-IM AWARE (800-462-9273)
972-385-5000
Fax: 972-385-5005
Web site: http://www.komen.com

■ **Women's Cancer Resource Center**
3023 Shattuck Ave
Berkeley, CA 94705
510-548-9272
Fax: 510-548-2155
TDD: 510-548-9287
E-mail: wcrc@sinewave.com

FEDERAL AGENCIES

■ **International Cancer Information Center**
National Cancer Institute (NCI)
National Institutes of Health
9030 Old Georgetown Rd
Bethesda, MD 20814
301-496-9096
Fax: 301-480-8105
Information Associates Membership Program:
800-NCI-7890 (800-624-7890)

Disseminates cancer research information useful in the prevention, diagnosis, and treatment of cancer to research scientists and clinicians around the world. Offers membership program to receive timely oncology information.

■ **Office of Cancer Communications**
National Cancer Institute (NCI)
National Institutes of Health
Bldg 31, Rm 10A-24
9000 Rockville Pike
Bethesda, MD 20892
800-4-CANCER (800-422-6237)
301-496-5583
Fax: 301-402-2594
TDD: 800-332-8615
CancerFax: 301-402-5874 (in English or Spanish)
24-hr, 7 days/wk
Web site: http://www.nci.nih.gov

The Cancer Information Service toll-free number (800-4-CANCER) provides accurate, up-to-date information on cancer to patients and their families, health professionals, and the general public. Serves as a resource for state and regional organizations; it is a nationwide network of 19 regional offices with calls automatically routed to the office serving the caller's region. Offers printed materials and technical assistance to cancer education, media campaigns, and community programs, as well as referrals to cancer-related community services.

■ **Oral Health Program, Division of Cancer Prevention and Control**
National Center for Chronic Disease Prevention & Health Promotion (NCCDPHP)
Centers for Disease Control and Prevention
4770 Buford Hwy NE, M/S F-10
Atlanta, GA 30341-3724
770-488-3038
Fax: 770-488-3065
Web site: http://www.cdc.gov/nccdphp/oh

Serves as a national resource for activities to prevent oral diseases and improve oral health; provides information on fluoridation, oral cancer, dental sealants, baby bottle tooth decay, infectious disease transmission in dentistry, and oral effects of tobacco use. Also provides consultation and technical assistance to state and local health agencies and works with health professionals on issues related to the promotion of oral health.

Diabetes

Products/Services Offered

Organization	web site	hotline/toll-free information line	clearinghouse/resource center	electronic information resources	database/statistical information	special campaigns/events/programs	consumer/patient education materials	publications for health professionals	classes/conferences	technical assistance	other products/services	grants/funding/awards	**Page No.**
American Association of Diabetes Educators	■	■		■		■	■	■	■			■	**164**
American Diabetes Association	■	■				■	■						**164**
American Dietetic Association	■						■	■					**164**
Channing L Bete Co Inc							■						**165**
Diabetes Research Institute Foundation	■						■	■					**165**
Medcom Inc	■						■						**165**
Park Nicollet HealthSource							■						**165**
Pritchett & Hull Associates Inc	■						■						**165**

Additional Resources 166

Federal Agencies 166

■ American Association of Diabetes Educators

444 N Michigan Ave, Ste 1240
Chicago, IL 60611-3901
Contact: Publications Dept
800-338-3633
312-644-2233
Fax: 312-644-4411
Web site: http://www.aadenet.org/

Nonprofit association dedicated to advancing the role of the diabetes educator and improving the quality of diabetes education and care.

Hotline or Toll-free Information Line
American Association of Diabetes Educators Self-Management Matters Line: 800-832-6874 , 24-hr operator assisted, referral service for contact names of local diabetes educators.

Electronic Information Resources
Document Fax Service: 800-338-3633, membership, publications, continuing education information. Free.

Special Campaigns, Events, or Programs
National Diabetes Education Week, 1st week in November, brochures, posters, bookmarks, videos are for sale to health professionals. Contact Mary Beach, 312-654-1710 for information; Contact AADE, 312-644-2233 for materials.

Consumer or Patient Education Materials
Self-Management Matters, brochure, 25/$3.

Publications for Health Professionals
The Diabetes Educator, journal, 6 times/yr, research in the field of diabetes education, $45/yr. Please contact for complete publications list.

Classes and Conferences
Continuing education classes; annual meeting. Please contact for complete list and schedule.

Grants, Funding, or Awards
Awards program for work done in diabetes education. Call AADE, 312-644-2233.

■ American Diabetes Association

National Center
1660 Duke St
Alexandria, VA 22314
Contact: Order Fulfillment Dept, 800-ADA-ORDER (800-232-6733), PO Box 930850, Atlanta, GA 31193-0850
800-232-3472
703-549-1500
Fax: 703-836-7439
Web site: http://www.diabetes.org

Nonprofit voluntary health organization dedicated to the prevention and cure of diabetes with affiliates and chapters in more than 800 communities in every state. Funds meritorious research, publishes the latest scientific findings, provides information and other services to people with diabetes, their families, health care professionals, and the public.

Hotline or Toll-free Information Line
American Diabetes Association Diabetes Information and Action Line: 800-DIABETES (800-342-2383) (M–F 9AM–5PM ET) Operator assisted, referral service, answers questions, requests for information.

Special Campaigns, Events, or Programs
National Diabetes Month, November, posters, buttons, brochures. Contact local chapter or National Office.

Consumer or Patient Education Materials
The Take-Charge Guide to Type 1 Diabetes, book, $13.50; Diabetes: A Positive Approach, video, $17.95; cookbooks; meal-planning guides; brochures; and pamphlets. Please contact for complete catalog.

■ American Dietetic Association

216 W Jackson Blvd, Ste 800
Chicago, IL 60606-6995
Contact: Customer Service, 312-899-0040 x5000
312-899-0040
Fax: 312-899-1757
Web site: http://www.eatright.org

Nonprofit organization of food and nutrition professionals in the U.S. whose mission is to serve the public through the promotion of optimal nutrition, health, and well-being. Members include clinical and community dietetics professionals, food service managers, educators, researchers, dietetic technicians, and students. Covers a wide range of practice areas and special interests, including diet counseling for weight control, cholesterol reduction, diabetes, renal, and other health concerns.

Consumer or Patient Education Materials
The First Step in Diabetes Meal Planning, pamphlet, $9 for 25; Exchange Lists for Meal Planning, 32 pp book, pricing varies upon quantity ordered. Please contact for complete catalog.

Publications for Health Professionals
Facilitating Lifestyle Change: A Resource Manual, book with 10 reproducible masters, Lifestyle Questionnaire and Eating Behavior Diary, $23.50; Diabetes Medical Nutrition Therapy: A Professional Guide to Management and Nutrition Education Resources, 280 pp book, comprehensive guide, $24.95; Single-Topic Diabetes Resources, book with 21 reproducible masters, $25. Please contact for complete publications list.

■ Channing L Bete Co Inc

200 State Rd
S Deerfield, MA 01373-0200
800-628-7733 (Sales and Customer Service)
413-665-7611
Fax: 800-499-6464

Publisher of informational and educational booklets, videos, posters, calendars, books, and display racks. Booklets use a distinctive, condensed format—called scriptography—which combines key words and graphics to explain a variety of subjects and is appropriate for different age groups and reading levels.

Consumer or Patient Education Materials
Booklets, videos, and 3-month diary; to help understand and control diabetes. Some Spanish language available. Please contact for pricing and ask for the Patient Education catalog.

■ Diabetes Research Institute Foundation

3440 Hollywood Blvd
Hollywood, FL 33021
Contact: Lori Weintraub or Barbara Singer
800-321-3437
954-964-4040
Fax: 954-964-7036
E-mail: lweintraub@drif.org
Web site: http://www.drif.org

Nonprofit international center whose mission is to bring together leading scientists worldwide to develop and rapidly apply promising research to treat and cure diabetes.

Consumer or Patient Education Materials
Various brochures include: What is Diabetes?, gives information on signs and symptoms, free. Please contact for complete information.

Publications for Health Professionals
DRI Update, newsletter, reports on donors, research events, with membership.

■ Medcom Inc

6060 Phyllis Dr
Cypress, CA 90630
Contact: Teri Armstrong, Marketing, 714-891-1443 x225
800-541-0253
714-891-1443
Fax: 714-898-4852
Web site: http://www.medcominc.com

For-profit producer and worldwide distributor of multimedia healthcare educational products, mainly video programs and related print material, for health care professionals, their patients, and health-conscious people everywhere.

Consumer or Patient Education Materials
Diabetes Care Series of videos include: You're in Control; Self-Monitoring: Glucose and Ketones; Diet, Exercise, and Self-Care, $39.95 ea. Please contact for complete catalog.

■ Park Nicollet HealthSource

3800 Park Nicollet Blvd
Minneapolis, MN 55416
Contact: Scott Laurent, Sales
800-372-7776
Fax: 612-993-1840

Nonprofit organization, a part of the Institute for Education and Research HealthSystem Minnesota, that develops and produces health promotion publications in self-care, health care consumerism, chronic conditions, and lifestyle education.

Consumer or Patient Education Materials
Diabetes Care Made Easy, 160 pp, written and designed for people with limited reading skills and children, available in Spanish, $9.95; Simplified Learning Series, booklets on 8 related topics, written and designed for people with limited reading skills and children, $1.95 ea; Planning and record books, $1.25–$1.95. Discounts available for quantity orders. Materials can be customized; Please contact for complete catalog.

■ Pritchett & Hull Associates Inc

3440 Oakcliff Rd NE, Ste 110
Atlanta, GA 30340-3079
800-241-4925 (Order Dept)
770-451-0602
Fax: 770-454-7130
Web site: http://www.p-h.com/

Publisher and producer of unique patient education materials that are known for clear, simple illustrations, easy reading level, humor, and "down-home" warmth and support. Materials include pamphlets, books, slides, and newsletter.

Consumer or Patient Education Materials
Flip cards, books, pamphlets covering diabetes. Materials can be customized; Please contact for complete catalog.

ADDITIONAL RESOURCES

■ Joslin Diabetes Center

1 Joslin Pl
Boston, MA 02215
Contact: Communications Dept
617-732-2415
Fax: 617-732-2562
Web site: http://www.joslin.harvard.edu

■ Juvenile Diabetes Foundation International

The Diabetes Research Foundation
120 Wall St, 19th Fl
New York, NY 10005-4001
800-JDF-CURE (800-533-2873)
212-785-9500
Fax: 212-785-9595
Web site: http://www.jdfcure.com

FEDERAL AGENCIES

■ National Diabetes Information Clearinghouse (NDIC)

One Information Way
Bethesda, MD 20892-3560
301-654-3327
Fax: 301-907-8906
E-mail: ndic@aerie.com

An information and referral service of the National Institute of Diabetes and Digestive and Kidney Disease (NIDDK); responds to written inquiries, develops and distributes publications about diabetes, and provides referrals to diabetes organizations, including support groups. Consumer materials available on diabetes management, foot care, nutrition, dental care, insulin, self-blood glucose monitoring, diabetes in older Americans, diabetes in young people, and eye care. Professional materials available about all aspects of diabetes and its management, including pregnancy, exercise, nutrition, diabetic retinopathy, and resources for patient education materials. Maintains a database of these materials from which literature searches are generated.

■ National Institute of Diabetes and Digestive and Kidney Disease (NIDDK)

National Institutes of Health
Bldg 31, Rm 9A-04
31 Center Dr, MSC 2560
Bethesda, MD 20892-2560
Information Office: 301-496-3583
Web site: http://www.niddk.nih.gov

Conducts and supports biomedical research on diabetes; endocrinology and metabolic diseases; digestive diseases and nutrition; and kidney, urologic and blood diseases. Consumer information on many of these types of disorders is collected and disseminated through NIDDK's three national information clearinghouses.

Eye Disease

Products/Services Offered

Organization	web site	hotline/toll-free information line	clearinghouse/resource center	electronic information resources	database/statistical information	special campaigns/events/programs	consumer/patient education materials	publications for health professionals	classes/conferences	technical assistance	other products/services	grants/funding/awards	**Page No.**
American Optometric Association	■					■	■	■				■	**168**
Clinical Reference Systems Ltd	■										■		**168**
The Foundation Fighting Blindness	■	■					■	■	■				**168**
The Glaucoma Foundation	■	■				■	■	■		■		■	**169**
Glaucoma Research Foundation	■						■					■	**169**
Prevent Blindness America	■	■				■	■	■		■	■	■	**169**
Federal Agencies													**170**

■ American Optometric Association

243 N Lindbergh Blvd
St Louis, MO 63141-7881
Contact: Charlotte Rancilio, 314-991-4100 x214
800-262-2210 (Order Dept)
314-991-4100
Fax: 314-991-4101
Web site: http://www.aoanet.org/aoanet

National nonprofit organization representing three-fourths of the optometrists in the U.S. Its mission is to advance the quality, availability and accessibility of eye, vision and related health care; to represent the profession of optometry; to enhance and promote the independent and ethical decision making of its members; and to assist doctors of optometry in practicing successfully in accordance with the highest standards of patient care.

Special Campaigns, Events, or Programs
Save Your Vision Week, first full week in March, suggestions for teachers, health care centers and businesses on how to celebrate. Contact Barb Fischer.

Consumer or Patient Education Materials
Family Guide To Vision Care, pamphlet, eye care information for whole family, $26.63/100 copies; A Journey Through Your Eyes, videotape, how the eye works and common vision conditions and their treatment, $57.75; For The Sake of Your Eyes, videotape, introduction to primary eye care, $57.75. Some Spanish languages available. Please contact for complete catalog.

Publications for Health Professionals
AOA News, semi-monthly newspaper, association news and news affecting optometry, $50/yr; Journal of the American Optometric Association, monthly research on eye diseases and vision conditions, $50/yr; Optometric Economics, quarterly magazine, practice management information, $30/yr.

Grants, Funding, or Awards
Apollo Award, recognizes individuals or organizations for outstanding service on behalf of the visual welfare of others. Contact Communication Center at address above.

■ Clinical Reference Systems Ltd

7100 E Belleview Ave, Ste 208
Greenwood Village, CO 80111-1635
Contact: Ellen Graves, Marketing Coordinator
800-237-8401
303-220-1661
Fax: 303-220-1685
E-mail: crs-info@cliniref.com
Web site: http://www.patienteducation.com

Publisher of patient education and clinical reference software for the international healthcare community. Committed to development of computer-based health information to enhance communication between provider and patient. More than 30,000 programs are now at work in physician offices, clinics, hospitals, medical school residency programs, occupational clinics, medical and consumer libraries.

Other Products and Services
Arthritis Advisor software program, customized patient information handouts including 70 topics adapted from Arthritis Foundation brochures; Ophthalmology Advisor software program, customized patient information handouts including preventive eye care. Please contact for pricing and complete information.

■ The Foundation Fighting Blindness

Executive Plaza 1, Ste 800
11350 McCormick Rd
Hunt Valley, MD 21031-1014
888-394-3937
410-785-1414
Fax: 410-771-9470
TDD: 800-683-5551; 410-785-9687 (local)
Web site: http://www.blindness.org

National nonprofit eye research organization dedicated to finding treatments and cures for blinding retinal degenerative diseases such as retinitis pigmentosa (RP), macular degeneration, and Usher syndrome. Serves as an information source for affected individuals, families, and eye care professionals.

Hotline or Toll-free Information Line
Foundation Fighting Blindness Information Line: 888-394-3937 (M–F 9AM–4:30PM ET) Operator assisted, referral service, requests for materials.

Consumer or Patient Education Materials
Additional materials available include: brochures, booklets, articles, resource lists, free. Some low literacy. Contact Information and Referral Line: 888-394-3937.

Publications for Health Professionals
Comprehensive information kits available for macular degeneration, retinitis pigmentosa (RP), and Usher syndrome, free; Fighting Blindness News, 3 to 4 times/yr newsletter, articles on activities and research updates, free.

Classes and Conferences
VISIONS, biennially, national conference with sessions on research and coping. Macular degeneration workshops, open to public in different cities. Please contact for schedule and registration.

■ The Glaucoma Foundation

33 Maiden Ln
New York, NY 10038
Contact: Erin Martineau
800-GLAUCOMA (800-452-8266)
212-504-1900
Fax: 212-504-1933
E-mail: glaucomafdn@interramp.com
Web site: http://www.glaucoma-foundation.org/info

International nonprofit organization dedicated to eradicating glaucoma, the leading cause of preventable blindness. Works to raise public awareness concerning the necessity of regular eye exams and to fund critical research.

Hotline or Toll-free Information Line
Glaucoma Foundation Information Line: 800-GLAUCOMA (800-452-8266) (M–F 9AM–5PM ET) Operator assisted, referral service, answers questions, requests for materials.

Special Campaigns, Events, or Programs
Glaucoma Awareness Week, in January, general information and press kit. Contact Erin Martineau.

Consumer or Patient Education Materials
Doctor, I Have a Question, 16 pp brochure, overview of disease, free.

Publications for Health Professionals
Eye to Eye, quarterly newslettter, activities and developments, free.

Technical Assistance
Referral service to specialists and support groups in local area.

Grants, Funding, or Awards
Scientific research awarded biennially. Contact Erin Martineau for application.

■ Glaucoma Research Foundation

490 Post St, Ste 830
San Francisco, CA 94102-1409
800-826-6693
415-986-3162
Fax: 415-986-3763
E-mail: info@glaucoma.org
Web site: http://www.glaucoma.org

National nonprofit organization dedicated to protecting the sight of people with glaucoma through research and education with the ultimate goal of finding a cure.

Consumer or Patient Education Materials
Gleams, quarterly newsletter, for patients, free; Understanding and Living with Glaucoma, booklet, free. Please contact for complete catalog.

Grants, Funding, or Awards
Grants available. Contact Mel Garrett: 415-986-3162.

■ Prevent Blindness America

500 E Remington Rd
Schaumburg, IL 60173-5611
Contact: Ann Horan, Manager Information Services
800-331-2020
847-843-2020
Fax: 847-843-8458
E-mail: 74777.100@compuserve.com
Web site: http://www.prevent_blindness.org

National nonprofit voluntary eye health and safety organization dedicated to fighting blindness and saving sight. Serves millions of people a year through public and professional education, patient services, community programs, and research.

Hotline or Toll-free Information Line
Prevent Blindness America Information Line: 800-331-2020 (M–F 8AM–5PM CT) Operator assisted, requests for materials.

Special Campaigns, Events, or Programs
Various campaigns throughout the year promoting eye safety and health, including: National Glaucoma Awareness Week, in January; Sight Saving Sabbath, 2 Sundays in January; Macular Degeneration Month, February; Cataract Awareness Month, March; Sports Eye Safety Month, April; National Sight-Saving Month, May; Fireworks Safety Month, June; Children's Eye Health and Safety Month, September; Diabetic Eye Disease Awareness Month, November; Safe Toys Month, December. Pamphlets available, contact Marketing Department.

Consumer or Patient Education Materials
In the Blink of An Eye, video, emphasizes importance of home and industrial eye protection, $79.95; Play It Safe with Your Eyes, video and curriculum materials, eye safety and health for children, $89.95; various pamphlets, posters, fact sheets on common eye diseases, safety and health, free single copy of pamphlets, discounts available for quantity orders. Some Spanish language available. Please contact for pricing and complete catalog.

Publications for Health Professionals
Prevent Blindness News, 3 times/yr newsletter, $10/yr; Vision Problems in the U.S., book, statistical information on blindness and vision impairment, $22. Please contact for complete publications list.

Technical Assistance
Provides vision screening instruction, fee based.

Other Products and Services
Affiliates and divisions throughout the U.S. provide vision screenings, educational and professional materials.

Grants, Funding, or Awards
Fight For Sight Program supports research funding for pilot opthalmology, vision and related sciences, Grants-In-Aid, Post-Doc Research Fellowship, Student Fellowships.

FEDERAL AGENCIES

■ National Eye Institute (NEI)

National Institutes of Health
Bldg 31, Rm 6A-32
31 Center Dr, MSC 2510
Bethesda, MD 20892-2510
301-496-4583
Fax: 301-402-1065
E-mail: 2020@b31.nei.nih.gov
Web site: http://www.nei.nih.gov

National Eye Health Education Program
2020 Vision Pl
Betheda, MD 20892-3655
Information Line: 301-496-5248
Publications Distribution Center: 800-869-2020

Supports and conducts research aimed at improving the prevention, diagnosis, treatment, and rehabilitation of diseases that affect the eye and vision. Responds to requests from both professional and lay audiences by providing information directly and providing referrals to other organizations and agencies when appropriate.

Heart Disease and Stroke

Products/Services Offered

Organization	web site	hotline/toll-free information line	clearinghouse/resource center	electronic information resources	database/statistical information	special campaigns/events/programs	consumer/patient education materials	publications for health professionals	classes/conferences	technical assistance	other products/services	grants/funding/awards	**Page No.**
American Heart Association	■	■					■	■	■		■		**172**
Channing L Bete Co Inc							■						**172**
The Coalition for Hypertension Prevention											■		**172**
Hall-Foushee Communications Inc							■			■			**172**
HIN Inc (The Health Information Network)							■						**172**
Mayo Clinic Health Information				■			■						**173**
Medcom Inc	■						■						**173**
National Hypertension Association Inc							■		■				**173**
National Stroke Association	■	■				■	■	■	■	■			**173**
Pritchett & Hull Associates Inc	■						■						**174**
Stanford Center for Research in Disease Prevention	■						■						**174**

Additional Resources **174**

Federal Agencies **174**

■ American Heart Association

7272 Greenville Ave
Dallas, TX 75231-4596
Contact: Fulfillment Center, 800-611-6083
800-AHA-USA1 (800-242-8721)
214-373-6300
Web site: http://www.amhrt.org

National nonprofit voluntary organization of 56 affiliated state and metropolitan organizations with 2,000 local offices. Funds and supports basic biomedical research, public policy advocacy, and educational programs for the public, business and industry, and health professionals.

Hotline or Toll-free Information Line
Stroke Connection: 800-553-6321 24-hr automated line, answers questions, referral service to support groups, requests for materials.

Special Campaigns, Events, or Programs
Healthy Choice American Heart Walk, October, call 214-706-1327; American Heart Month, February, call 800-242-8721.

Consumer or Patient Education Materials
Stroke Connection, 6 times/yr magazine, free. Please contact for complete catalog.

Publications for Health Professionals
Primer in Preventive Cardiology, 314 pp book, risk factor screening and treatment strategies, $10; Hypertension Primer, 370 pp book, covers all aspects of hypertension, $13; Nutrition Slide Kit, 130 slides, narrator's text, and reproducible handouts, role of nutrition in heart disease and hypertension, $33. Please contact for complete publications list.

Technical Assistance
Patient Provider Team: 214-706-1239

■ Channing L Bete Co Inc

200 State Rd
S Deerfield, MA 01373-0200
800-628-7733 (Sales and Customer Service)
413-665-7611
Fax: 800-499-6464

Publisher of informational and educational booklets, videos, posters, calendars, books, and display racks. Booklets use a distinctive, condensed format—called scriptography—which combines key words and graphics to explain a variety of subjects and is appropriate for different age groups and reading levels.

Consumer or Patient Education Materials
Booklets and videos covering common heart problems and preventive measures, high blood pressure, and cholesterol. Some Spanish language available. Please contact for pricing and ask for the Patient Education catalog.

■ The Coalition for Hypertension Prevention

PO Box 1626
Ventura, CA 93002
800-600-7111 x222
Fax: 800-600-7112

Public and private partnership formed to promote the concept of community blood pressure monitoring, augmenting regular doctor visits with self-monitoring provided outside the clinical setting.

Other Products and Services
Sit and Screen for Healthier Hearts Campaign, directs people to the nearest available public blood pressure monitoring device when calling 800-251-9910 x4057.

■ Hall-Foushee Communications Inc

1313 Fifth St SE, Ste 214B
Minneapolis, MN 55414
Contact: Nancy Hall
800-478-3829
612-379-3829
Fax: 612-379-3829
E-mail: 76633.3416@compuserve.com

For-profit company specializing in health communications planning and production of audiovisual and print materials. Focus on disease prevention and health promotion campaigns and materials.

Consumer or Patient Education Materials
The Heart Care Program, 4 videos, 4 classes, and 14 reproducible handouts, for cholesterol management, $199. Please contact for complete catalog.

Technical Assistance
Consulting services available for special projects.

■ HIN Inc (The Health Information Network)

231 Market Place, #331
San Ramon, CA 94583-9800
Contact: Lois Kamoroff
800-HIN-1121 (800-446-1121)
510-551-4800
Fax: 510-551-4808

Medical publishing company of patient education booklets in easy-to-read, understandable text and with full-color medical illustrations; authored and edited by medical experts.

Consumer or Patient Education Materials

How to Reduce Your Risk of Heart Disease, booklet, $36.25 for 25 copies, discounts available for quantity orders. Materials can be customized; Please contact for complete catalog.

■ Mayo Clinic Health Information

200 First St SW
Rochester, MN 55905
Contact: Mike Casey or Dan Newton
800-430-9699
Fax: 507-284-5410

Division of the Mayo Clinic that produces consumer health publications including newsletters, booklets, books, and CD-ROMs, providing people with timely, reliable, and easy-to-understand health, wellness, and self-care information. Materials appropriate for health promotion initiatives.

Electronic Information Resources

Mayo Health Oasis online health information web site: http://www.mayo.ivi.com/

Consumer or Patient Education Materials

Mayo Clinic Heart Book, $25; Mayo Clinic: The Total Heart CD-ROM, $34.95. Please contact for volume discounts and complete catalog.

■ Medcom Inc

6060 Phyllis Dr
Cypress, CA 90630
Contact: Teri Armstrong, Marketing, 714-891-1443 x225
800-541-0253
714-891-1443
Fax: 714-898-4852
Web site: http://www.medcominc.com

For-profit producer and worldwide distributor of multimedia health care educational products, mainly video programs and related print material, for health care professionals, their patients, and health-conscious people everywhere.

Consumer or Patient Education Materials

Heart and Stress Series of videos include: Lifestyles for a Healthy Heart; Hypertension: Managing Your Blood Pressure; After a Heart Attack: Steps Toward Recovery. Please contact for complete catalog.

■ National Hypertension Association Inc

324 E 30th St
New York, NY 10016
Contact: Francine Rowley
212-889-3557
Fax: 212-447-7032

Nonprofit organization whose central mission is to vigorously combat the chronic health problem of hypertension by developing, directing, and implementing effective programs to research the cause of essential hypertension and enhance the understanding of certain secondary types; to educate and alert the lay public to the severe, life-threatening dangers and inform physicians and medical students of the most current advances; and to detect the problem wherever it exists in the most economical and effective way and urge treatment if indicated.

Consumer or Patient Education Materials

High Blood Pressure and What You Can Do About It, pamphlet, $2.50; Lower Your Blood Pressure and Live Longer, book, $8.50; Week by Week to a Strong Heart, book, $8.50. Discounts available for quantity orders.

Classes and Conferences

Annual 1-day seminar on hypertension and hypercholesterolemia coordinated with a Medical Center and Medical School. Contact Francine Rowley.

■ National Stroke Association

96 Inverness Dr E, Ste I
Englewood, CO 80112-5112
Contact: Jennifer Converse, 303-649-9299 x925
800-STROKES (800-787-6537)
303-649-9299
Fax: 303-649-1328
E-mail: info@stroke.org
Web site: http://www.stroke.org

Nonprofit organization dedicated to reducing the incidence and impact of stroke. Focuses on stroke prevention, treatment, research, rehabilitation, and support for stroke survivors and their families.

Hotline or Toll-free Information Line

National Stroke Association Information Line: 800-STROKES (800-787-6537) (M–Th 8AM–4:30PM, F 8AM–4PM MT) Automated and operator assisted, answers questions, requests for materials.

Special Campaigns, Events, or Programs

Stroke Awareness Month, May, contact Jennifer Converse, Communications Coordinator.

Consumer or Patient Education Materials

The Brain at Risk: Understanding and Preventing Stroke, 19-min video, $25; Brochures and booklets include: Reducing Risk and Recognizing Symptoms, High Blood Pressure & Stroke, The Brain at Risk—Understanding and Preventing Stroke, first copy free. Some Spanish, French languages available. Please contact for complete catalog.

Publications for Health Professionals
Journal of Stroke and Cerebrovascular Diseases, quarterly, multidisciplinary and clinical info, $80–$115/yr; Community Stroke Prevention Screening Guide, comprehensive turnkey guide, $25; Clinical Program for Evaluating and Managing Stroke-at-Risk Patients, includes stroke risk appraisal forms, $10. Please contact for complete publications list.

Classes and Conferences
North American Stroke meeting, 3 days.

Technical Assistance
Stroke Prevent, assessment form for personal stroke risk profile. Contact Stroke Prevention Program Dept at 303-649-9299 x 905 for prices and options.

■ Pritchett & Hull Associates Inc

3440 Oakcliff Rd NE, Ste 110
Atlanta, GA 30340-3079
800-241-4925 (Order Dept)
770-451-0602
Fax: 770-454-7130
Web site: http://www.p-h.com/

Publisher and producer of unique patient education materials that are known for clear, simple illustrations, easy reading level, humor, and "down-home" warmth and support. Materials include pamphlets, books, slides, and newsletter.

Consumer or Patient Education Materials
Books including Blood Pressure Control; Wake Up Call for Your Heart; Materials can be customized; Please contact for complete catalog.

■ Stanford Center for Research in Disease Prevention

Health Promotion Resource Center
1000 Welch Rd
Palo Alto, CA 94304-1885
Contact: SCRDP Distribution Center
415-723-0003
Fax: 415-725-6906
E-mail: distribution@scrdp.stanford.edu
Web site: http://www-med.Stanford.EDU:8/MedCenter/SCRDP/

Nonprofit educational resource center that produces and disseminates print and video materials on cardiovascular disease risk factors, injury prevention, and community health promotion.

Consumer or Patient Education Materials
Staying Healthy, booklet, overview of main risk factors for heart disease, $3.50; blood pressure brochures, 3 kinds for people with different blood pressure categories, $.50 ea. Materials can be customized; Spanish languages available. Please contact for complete catalog.

ADDITIONAL RESOURCES

■ Citizens for Public Action on Blood Pressure and Cholesterol

PO Box 30374-HBP
Bethesda, MD 20824
Contact: Jerry Wilson, Executive Director
301-770-1711

■ National Heart Savers Association

9140 W Dodge Rd
Omaha, NE 68114
402-398-1993
Fax: 402-398-1994

FEDERAL AGENCIES

■ National Heart, Lung, and Blood Institute (NHLBI)

National Institutes of Health
NIH/NHLBI/OPEC, Rm 4A-03
31 Center Dr, MSC 2480
Bethesda, MD 20892-2480
301-496-4236
National High Blood Pressure Education Program: 800-575-WELL (800-575-9355)
Web site: http://www.nhlbi.nih.gov/nhlbi/nhlbi.htm

NHLBI Information Center
PO Box 30105
Bethesda, MD 20824-0105
301-251-1222
Fax: 301-251-1223

Oversees research, demonstration, prevention, education, control, and training activities in the fields of heart, lung, and blood diseases and education concerning these diseases. The Information Center offers materials on numerous topics, including cholesterol, high blood pressure, smoking, asthma, heart disease, exercise, obesity, stroke. Treatment guidelines on high blood cholesterol, high blood pressure, and asthma; heart and lung health in the workplace and schools are available for health professionals.

■ National Institute of Neurological Disease and Stroke (NINDS)
National Institutes of Health
PO Box 5801
Bethesda, MD 20824
301-496-5751
Public Information Office: 800-352-9424
Web site: http://www.ninds.nih.gov/

Conducts and supports research and research training on the causes, prevention, diagnosis, and treatment of neurological disorders and stroke. Awards grants for research projects, program projects, and center grants; provides training support to institutions and fellowships to individuals in the field of neurological disorders and stroke; conducts intramural and collaborative research; and collects and disseminates research information.

Other Chronic Conditions and Diseases

Products/Services Offered

Organization	web site	hotline/toll-free information line	clearinghouse/resource center	electronic information resources	database/statistical information	special campaigns/events/programs	consumer/patient education materials	publications for health professionals	classes/conferences	technical assistance	other products/services	grants/funding/awards	**Page No.**
Alzheimer's Association	■	■	■			■	■	■					**179**
American Academy of Ophthalmology	■	■				■							**179**
American Kidney Fund	■	■					■	■	■			■	**179**
American Liver Foundation		■				■	■	■		■		■	**180**
The CFIDS Association of America Inc	■	■	■			■	■	■				■	**180**
Channing L Bete Co Inc							■						**180**
Crohn's and Colitis Foundation of America Inc	■	■					■					■	**180**
Epilepsy Foundation of America	■	■			■	■	■	■		■	■	■	**181**
The Food Allergy Network	■	■					■	■	■				**181**
Health Professions Press								■					**182**
Huntington's Disease Society of America Inc	■	■				■	■	■				■	**182**
Lupus Foundation of America	■	■				■	■					■	**182**
Muscular Dystrophy Association	■	■					■	■			■	■	**182**
National Chronic Fatigue Syndrome and Fibromyalgia Association						■	■	■		■			**183**
National Headache Foundation	■	■				■	■	■				■	**183**
National Kidney Foundation	■	■				■	■						**183**
National Lymphedema Network	■	■					■	■	■				**183**
National Multiple Sclerosis Society	■	■	■				■		■				**184**
National Organization for Rare Disorders	■				■		■	■	■	■		■	**184**
National Osteoporosis Foundation	■	■				■	■	■	■	■		■	**185**
National Reye's Syndrome Foundation	■	■					■	■				■	**185**

Products/Services Offered

Organization	web site	hotline/toll-free information line	clearinghouse/resource center	electronic information resources	database/statistical information	special campaigns/events/programs	consumer/patient education materials	publications for health professionals	classes/conferences	technical assistance	other products/services	grants/funding/awards	Page No.
Osteoporosis and Related Bone Diseases National Resource Center	■				■		■						185
Parkinson's Disease Foundation Inc	■	■					■	■		■		■	186
Thyroid Foundation of America Inc		■					■	■					186

Additional Resources 186

Federal Agencies 187

■ Alzheimer's Association

919 N Michigan Ave, Ste 1000
Chicago, IL 60611-1676
800-272-3900
312-335-8700
Fax: 312-335-1110
TDD: 312-355-8882
E-mail: info@alz.org
Web site: http://www.alz.org

National nonprofit voluntary organization that researches the prevention, cures, and treatments of Alzheimer's disease and related disorders. Over 200 local chapters provide information and services in the community and offer support and education services for families.

Hotline or Toll-free Information Line
Alzheimer's Association: 800-272-3900 (M–F 8:30AM–5PM CT) Operator assisted, 24-hr automated line, referral service, answers questions, requests for materials.

Clearinghouse or Resource Center
Benjamin B Greenfield National Alzheimer's Library and Resource Center: 312-335-9602; Fax: 312-335-0214

Special Campaigns, Events, or Programs
Alzheimer's Association Memory Walk, October
National Alzheimer's Disease Awareness Month, November

Consumer or Patient Education Materials
Audiotapes, books, booklets, brochures, fact sheets available. Some Spanish languages available. Please contact for complete catalog.

Publications for Health Professionals
Program guides; caregiver packets and kits. Please contact for complete publications list.

■ American Academy of Ophthalmology

655 Beach St
San Francisco, CA 94109
Mailing Address:
PO Box 7424
San Francisco, CA 94120-7424
415-561-8500
Fax: 415-561-8533
E-mail: media@aao.org
Web site: http://www.eyenet.org

International nonprofit association of ophthalmologists, physicians who provide comprehensive eye care, including medical, surgical, and optical care. Provides authoritative information about eye care for the public and serves the professional need of the Academy members.

Hotline or Toll-free Information Line
American Academy of Ophthalmology Helpline: 800-222-EYES (800-222-3937) (M–F 8AM–4PM PT) Operator assisted; information about the National Eye Care Project (nationwide outreach program to provide medical eye care to disadvantaged adults 65 yrs or older); written materials on conditions affecting the eye.

Special Campaigns, Events, or Programs
National Eye Care Month, January, complete information packet. Contact Rosemary Rushka, Public Information.

■ American Kidney Fund

6110 Executive Blvd, Ste 1010
Rockville, MD 20852-9813
Contact: Public Education Dept, 800-638-8299 x125
800-638-8299
301-881-3052
Fax: 301-881-0898
Web site: http://www.arbon.com/kidney

National nonprofit voluntary health organization providing direct financial aid to needy kidney patients, transplant recipients, and donors to help cover the cost of treatment-specific expenses. Grants are available to assist patients afford medication, transportation, emergency transient dialysis, special diet needs, etc. Eligibility for financial assistance must be demonstrated by filing an application, available through the patient's nephrologist or renal social worker. In addition, it supports public and professional education, kidney donor development, and sponsors clinical scientist nephrology fellowship awards.

Hotline or Toll-free Information Line
American Kidney Fund Help Line: 800-638-8299 (M–F 8:30AM–5PM ET)

Consumer or Patient Education Materials
Brochures and booklets include: The American Kidney Fund Helps When Nobody Else Will; Kidney Disease: A Guide for Patients and Their Families, Kidneys for Kids, written especially for children. First copy free, additional copies range from $.20 to $.45 each. Some Spanish languages available. Please contact for complete catalog.

Publications for Health Professionals
Clinical Strategies Newsletter, semiannual, for health professionals, free.

Classes and Conferences
Regional conferences held throughout the country for health care professionals, $45–$50. Contact Phylis Ermann, 301-881-3052 x123 for complete list and schedule.

Grants, Funding, or Awards
Clinical Scientist in Nephrology Fellowship Award. Contact Carolyn Halal, 800-638-8299 x114.

■ American Liver Foundation

1425 Pompton Ave
Cedar Grove, NJ 07009
Contact: Ari Maravel, 800-223-0179 x228
800-223-0179
201-256-2550
Fax: 201-256-3214

National nonprofit organization dedicated to preventing, treating, and curing hepatitis and other liver and gallbladder diseases through research and education.

Hotline or Toll-free Information Line
American Liver Foundation: 800-GO-LIVER (800-463-4837) (M–F 9AM–5PM ET) Operator assisted, answers questions, requests for materials.
Special Campaigns, Events, or Programs
Liver Awareness Month, October, Packets, printed materials, and posters available. Contact Ari Maravel, 800-223-0179 x228.
Consumer or Patient Education Materials
Brochures and fact sheets. Some Spanish language available. Please contact for pricing and complete catalog.
Publications for Health Professionals
Liver Update, 3 times yearly journal; Progress, quarterly newsletter; both update on research activities for professionals; included with membership.
Technical Assistance
Doctor referrals available.
Grants, Funding, or Awards
Research grants available include: Liver Scholar Award, Post Graduate Award, and Student Award. Contact Barbara Ramsthaler, 800-223-0179 x230.

■ The CFIDS Association of America Inc

6827-A Fairview Rd
Charlotte, NC 28210
Mailing Address:
PO Box 220398
Charlotte, NC 28222-0398
Contact: Kristina Hopkins, 704-364-0016
800-442-3437
Fax: 704-365-9755
E-mail: cfids@vnet.net
Web site: http://cfids.org/cfids

Nonprofit charitable organization dedicated to conquering chronic fatigue and immune dysfunction syndrome (CFIDS) by supporting education, public policy and research programs.

Hotline or Toll-free Information Line
CFIDS Information Line: 800-442-3437 (24-hr) Automated line, leave name and address to receive information.
Clearinghouse or Resource Center
CFIDS Resource Line: 704-365-2343; books, pamphlets, audiotapes, videotapes, media articles, medical articles.
Special Campaigns, Events, or Programs
CFIDS Awareness Day, May 12, Brochures and general information. Contact Kristina Hopkins, 704-364-0016.
Consumer or Patient Education Materials
Contact the CFIDS Resource Line, 704-365-2343, for information or catalog of educational materials.
Publications for Health Professionals
The CFIDS Chronicle, quarterly newsmagazine, $35/yr. Please contact for complete publications list.
Grants, Funding, or Awards
Research grants available. Contact Allison Beam, 704-364-0016.

■ Channing L Bete Co Inc

200 State Rd
S Deerfield, MA 01373-0200
800-628-7733 (Sales and Customer Service)
413-665-7611
Fax: 800-499-6464

Publisher of informational and educational booklets, videos, posters, calendars, books, and display racks. Booklets use a distinctive, condensed format—called scriptography—which combines key words and graphics to explain a variety of subjects and is appropriate for different age groups and reading levels.

Consumer or Patient Education Materials
Booklets and videos. Topics include: asthma, allergies, arthritis, kidney disorders, multiple sclerosis, ulcers. Some Spanish language available. Please contact for pricing and ask for the Patient Education catalog.

■ Crohn's and Colitis Foundation of America Inc

386 Park Ave S
New York, NY 10016-8804
Contact: Membership Services
800-343-3637
212-685-3440
Fax: 212-779-4098
Web site: http://www.ccfa.org

Nonprofit, research-oriented voluntary health organization dedicated to finding a cure for Crohn's disease and ulcerative colitis and to improving the quality of life for those affected by these illnesses. Three-pronged mission includes research, education, and support.

Hotline or Toll-free Information Line
Crohn's and Colitis Foundation Information Line: 800-343-3637 (M–F 8AM–5PM ET) Operator assisted, requests for materials.

Consumer or Patient Education Materials
Books and brochures. Please contact for complete catalog.

Grants, Funding, or Awards
Research grants and fellowship awards.

■ Epilepsy Foundation of America

4351 Garden City Dr
Landover, MD 20785-2267
Contact: Peter Van Haverbeke or Sandy Cutts, 301-459-3700 x642
800-EFA-1000 (800-332-1000)
301-459-3700
Fax: 301-577-2684
E-mail: cuttssan@efa.org
Web site: http://www.efa.org

National nonprofit voluntary health organization that works for people affected by seizures through research, education, advocacy, and service.

Hotline or Toll-free Information Line
Epilepsy Foundation of America Information Line: 800-EFA-1000 (800-332-1000) (M–F 8:30AM–5:30PM ET) Operator assisted, referral service, answers questions, requests for information.

Database or Statistical Information
Epilepsy: Frequency, Causes & Consequences, statistical study, $69.95.

Special Campaigns, Events, or Programs
National Epilepsy Awareness Month, November, promotion kit contains posters, fact sheets, communicating guidelines, and suggested feature stories.

Consumer or Patient Education Materials
Living Well with Epilepsy, 166 pp book, $12.95; Seizures and Epilepsy in Childhood, 287 pp book, written for parents, $16.95; Does Your Child Have Epilepsy?, 201 pp book, $22. Pamphlets, videos, and other materials. Some Spanish language available. Please call 800-213-5821 or 301-459-3700 x706 for complete catalog.

Publications for Health Professionals
Students with Seizures, 131 pp manual, for use by school nurse and reviews epilepsy and seizure classifications, $24.95. Please call 800-213-5821 or 301-459-3700 x706 for complete publications list.

Technical Assistance
Women and Epilepsy Task Force, studies unique health concerns of women with seizure disorders; TAPS (Training & Assessment for Placement Success), program assisting people with epilepsy with employment issues.

Other Products and Services
National Epilepsy Library: 800-332-4050.

Grants, Funding, or Awards
Journalism Awards, encourages and recognizes significant contributions by the media to public's understanding of epilepsy. Contact Sandy Cutts, 301-459-3700 x642.

■ The Food Allergy Network

10400 Eaton Place, Ste 107
Fairfax, VA 22030-2208
800-929-4040
703-691-3179
Fax: 703-691-2713
E-mail: fan@worldweb.net
Web site: http://www.foodallergy.org

Nonprofit organization established to increase public awareness about food allergies and anaphylaxis and to help families living with food allergies. Provides education, emotional support, and coping strategies to patients, and serves as the communication link between the food industry, the government, the airline industry, and the food-allergic consumer.

Hotline or Toll-free Information Line
Food Allergy Network Information Line: 800-929-4040 (M–F 9AM–5PM ET) Operator assisted, referral service, answers questions, requests for information.

Consumer or Patient Education Materials
Food Allergy News, bimonthly newsletter, included with membership, sample copy free; How to Read a Label, laminated card, $1; books, pamphlets, cookbook, videotapes also available, $1–$20. Please contact for complete catalog.

Publications for Health Professionals
School Food Allergy Program, for school nurses to educate staff, $75. Please contact for complete publications list.

Classes and Conferences
Food Allergy Network Patient Conference, 1 day, symposium with leading food allergy experts. $35 per person. Please contact for complete list and schedule.

■ Health Professions Press

409 Washington Ave, Ste 500
Baltimore, MD 21204
Mailing Address:
PO Box 10624
Baltimore, MD 21285
410-337-9585
Fax: 410-337-8539
E-mail: hpp@pbrookes.com

Publisher of professional references and textbooks on long-term care, gerontology, and health adminstration, plus practical resources for nursing home staff, caregivers, and other service providers.

Publications for Health Professionals
Developing Support Groups for Individuals with Early-Stage Alzheimer's Disease: Planning, Implementation, and Evaluation, book, $27. Please contact for complete publications list.

■ Huntington's Disease Society of America Inc

140 W 22nd St, 6th Fl
New York, NY 10011-2420
Contact: Marilyn Wolff, National Family Services Coordinator
800-345-HDSA (800-345-4372)
212-242-1968
Fax: 212-243-2443
E-mail: curehd@hdsa.ttisms.com
Web site: http://neuro-www2.mgh.harvard.edu/hdsa/hdsamain.nclk

National nonprofit voluntary health organization that funds research and operates education, advocacy and family service programs through a nationwide network of chapters, affiliates, and support groups. Huntington's Disease is an inherited, progressively degenerative brain disease.

Hotline or Toll-free Information Line
Huntington's Disease Information Line: 800-345-HDSA (800-345-4372) Automated line, referral to local groups, requests for materials.

Special Campaigns, Events, or Programs
Huntington's Disease Awareness Month, May.

Consumer or Patient Education Materials
Various materials available. Please contact for complete catalog.

Publications for Health Professionals
Various publications available. Please contact for complete publications list.

Grants, Funding, or Awards
Funding for clinical and basic science research; and post-doctoral fellowships.

■ Lupus Foundation of America

1300 Piccard Dr, Ste 200
Rockville, MD 20850-4303
800-558-0121
301-670-9292
Fax: 301-670-9486
Web site: http://www.lupus.org/lupus

Nonprofit voluntary health foundation whose purpose is to assist local chapters in their efforts to provide supportive services to individuals living with lupus, to educate the public about lupus, and to support research into the cause and cure of lupus.

Hotline or Toll-free Information Line
Lupus Foundation of America Information Line: 800-558-0121 24-hr automated line, request for materials.

Special Campaigns, Events, or Programs
Lupus Awareness Month, October, posters, brochures, and bookmarks.

Consumer or Patient Education Materials
Books and brochures on lupus and chronic illness, $3.95–$23.95. Please contact for complete catalog.

Grants, Funding, or Awards
Research grant and fellowship programs. Contact central office.

■ Muscular Dystrophy Association

3300 E Sunrise Dr
Tucson, AZ 85718
Contact: Program Services Dept
800-572-1717
520-529-2000
Fax: 520-529-5300
E-mail: 74431,2513@compuserve.com
Web site: http://www.mdausa.org

Nonprofit voluntary health organization fighting 40 neuromuscular diseases through worldwide research; a nationwide network of clinics providing selected medical services; and far-reaching professional and public education.

Hotline or Toll-free Information Line
Muscular Dystrophy Association LifeLine: 800-572-1717 (M–F 8:30AM–5PM MT) Referral service, answers questions, requests for information.

Consumer or Patient Education Materials
Brochures, pamphlets, and videotapes, provides information about various neuromuscular diseases, free single copy. Some Spanish languages available. Please contact for complete catalog.

Publications for Health Professionals
Quest, bimonthly magazine, $12/yr; The ALS Newsletter, bimonthly newsletter, free.

Other Products and Services
Summer camping programs for youngsters ages 6–21.
Grants, Funding, or Awards
Grants available for research into neuromuscular disease. Contact MDA Research Dept, 520-529-2000.

■ National Chronic Fatigue Syndrome and Fibromyalgia Association

PO Box 18426
Kansas City, MO 64133
816-313-2000
Fax: 816-524-6782

Nonprofit organization formed to educate and inform the public about the nature and impact of Chronic Fatigue Syndrome and Fibromyalgia and to offer scientifically accurate information.

Special Campaigns, Events, or Programs
National Chronic Fatigue Syndrome Awareness Month, March, posters.
Consumer or Patient Education Materials
Brochures, bibliographies, audio and video tapes. Please contact for complete catalog.
Publications for Health Professionals
Quarterly newsletter, scientific info.
Technical Assistance
Referrals to support groups, phone contacts, physicians.

■ National Headache Foundation

428 W St James Pl, 2nd Fl
Chicago, IL 60614-2750
800-843-2256
773-388-6399
Fax: 773-525-7357
Web site: http://www.headaches.org

Nonprofit organization that works to educate the public to the fact that headaches are serious disorders and sufferers need understanding and continuity of care; to promote research into headache causes and treatments; to serve as an information resource to sufferers, their families, and the physicians who treat them.

Hotline or Toll-free Information Line
National Headache Foundation Information Line: 800-843-2256 (M–F 9AM–5PM CT) Answers questions.
Special Campaigns, Events, or Programs
National Headache Awareness Week, in June.
Consumer or Patient Education Materials
Headache—A Guide to Prevention & Treatment, brochure, free with SASE; Hormone Headache, book, $14.95; No More Headaches, video, causes and triggers of headache, $24.95. Information available with a description of headache or diagnosis, send SASE with three 1st class stamps. Please contact for complete catalog.
Publications for Health Professionals
Head Lines, quarterly newsletter, free with membership or $20/yr.
Grants, Funding, or Awards
Reseach grants and fellowship grant. Call 800-843-2256, x86394.

■ National Kidney Foundation

30 E 33rd St
New York, NY 10016
Contact: Crystal Tucker
800-622-9010
212-889-2210
Fax: 212-689-9261
Web site: http://www.kidney.org

Nonprofit major voluntary organization dedicated to the prevention, treatment, and cure of kidney and urologic diseases. Conducts programs in research, professional education, patient and community services, public education, and organ donations through 52 affiliates nationwide.

Hotline or Toll-free Information Line
National Kidney Foundation Information Line: 800-622-9010 (M–F 8:30AM–5:30PM ET) Operator assisted, requests for materials.
Special Campaigns, Events, or Programs
National Organ Tissue Donor Awareness Week, in April, Organ Donor Program brochure and organ donor cards. Contact 800-622-9010.
Consumer or Patient Education Materials
Videos, organ donor cards, and brochures including: High Blood Pressure and Your Kidneys; About Kidney Stones. Pricing varies upon quantity ordered. Some Spanish languages available. Please contact for complete catalog.

■ National Lymphedema Network

2211 Post St, Ste 404
San Francisco, CA 94115
800-541-3259
415-921-1306
Fax: 415-921-4284
E-mail: lymphnet@hooked.net
Web site: http://www.hooked.net/~lymphnet

Nonprofit organization whose mission is to provide education and support to patients, health care professionals, and the general public by disseminating information on the prevention and management of primary and secondary lymphedema. Also supports research into the causes and possible alternative treatments.

Hotline or Toll-free Information Line
National Lymphedema Network Information Line: 800-541-3259 24-hr automated, referral service, answers questions, requests for materials.
Consumer or Patient Education Materials
Videotapes on self-care, $20–$50; reprint articles from Newsletter, $1.50–$5. Low literacy; Some Spanish languages available. Please contact for complete catalog.
Publications for Health Professionals
NLN Newsletter, quarterly, contains articles and Resource Guide, free with membership.
Classes and Conferences
How to Set Up a Lymphedema Treatment Center, 2-day workshop, $250–$350; NLN Conference, biennial (even yrs), international. Please contact for complete list and schedule.

■ National Multiple Sclerosis Society

733 Third Ave
New York, NY 10017-3288
800-344-4867
212-986-3240
Fax: 212-986-7981
Web site: http://www.nmss.org

Nonprofit organization serving persons with MS, their families, health professionals, and the interested public. Provides funding for research, public and professional education, advocacy, and the design of rehabilitative and psychosocial programs. Direct services are provided through 140 local chapters and branches.

Hotline or Toll-free Information Line
National Multiple Sclerosis Society Information Line: 800-FIGHT-MS (800-344-4867) (M–F 11AM–5PM ET) Automated and operator assisted, answers questions, requests for materials, contact to local chapter.
Clearinghouse or Resource Center
National Multiple Sclerosis Society Resource Center and Library: 800-344-4867; information database; research service; publications.
Consumer or Patient Education Materials
Inside MS, periodical for members; pamphlets and flyers include: What Is MS?, A Booklet About Multiple Sclerosis for Family Members. Free, nominal charge for greater quantity. Some Spanish languages available. Please contact for complete catalog.
Classes and Conferences
Contact local chapter for schedule of classes and special programs or events.

■ National Organization for Rare Disorders

100 Rt 37, 2nd Fl
PO Box 8923
New Fairfield, CT 06812-8923
800-999-6673
203-746-6518
Fax: 203-746-6481
TDD: 203-746-6927
E-mail: orphan@nord-rdb.com
Web site: http://www.nord-rdb.com/~orphan

Unique federation of more than 140 nonprofit health organizations dedicated to helping people with rare "orphan" diseases and assisting the organizations that serve them. Committed to the identification, treatment, and cure of rare disorders through programs of education, advocacy, research, and service.

Database or Statistical Information
Access through web site: http://www.nord-rdb.com/~orphan are 3 databases: Rare Disease Database, users may read abstracts of over 1,070 disease reports or order full-text versions for $5; Organizational Database; Orphan Drug Designation Database. No charge for conducting keyword search of databases.
Consumer or Patient Education Materials
Disease Reports, $5. Please contact for complete catalog.
Publications for Health Professionals
Orphan Disease Update, 3 times/yr newsletter, reports and articles, free with membership; NORD Resource Guide, book, organizational referrals, $25; Physician Guide to Rare Diseases, book, summary of rare diseases, $97.50. Please contact for complete publications list.
Classes and Conferences
Annual patient/family conference, 3 days, workshops and networking. Contact Jean Campbell for complete information.
Technical Assistance
Technical assistance to support groups, helping to start and grow with minimal waste of resources.
Grants, Funding, or Awards
Research grant program. Contact or write to central office for application.

■ National Osteoporosis Foundation

1150 17th St NW, Ste 500
Washington, DC 20036-4603
202-223-2226
Fax: 202-223-2237
TDD: 202-466-4315
Web site: http://www.nof.org

Nonprofit voluntary health organization devoted solely to osteoporosis. Strives to reduce and ultimately to eliminate the widespread prevalence of osteoporosis through programs of public and professional education, research, patient information, and advocacy.

Hotline or Toll-free Information Line
National Osteoporosis Foundation Patient Information Center: 800-223-9994 contact to obtain free 22pp booklet, Stand Up to Osteoporosis, and other materials. Call 800-464-6700 for the location of a bone density testing center in your area.

Special Campaigns, Events, or Programs
National Osteoporosis Prevention Week, May, patient education brochures, posters, slide sets, cards. Contact Diane Shnitzler, Assistant Director of Communications.

Consumer or Patient Education Materials
Patient Education Sample Pack, educational materials, $5; numerous booklets, some available in Spanish. Please contact for complete catalog.

Publications for Health Professionals
Osteoporosis Clinical Updates, quarterly, case-based discussion of osteoporosis, free; Osteoporosis Report, quarterly newsletter, free with membership of $15/yr. Please contact for complete publications list.

Classes and Conferences
Symposia, seminars, and workshops for physicians, nurses, physical therapists. Call for complete information.

Technical Assistance
Support group contacts.

Grants, Funding, or Awards
Research grants for basic and clinical osteoporosis research. Contact Robert Recker, MD, Chair, Research Grants Subcommittee at foundation address.

■ National Reye's Syndrome Foundation

426 N Lewis
PO Box 829
Bryan, OH 43506-0829
Contact: Sandi Nelson
800-233-7393
419-636-2679
Fax: 419-636-3366
E-mail: reyessyn@bright.net
Web site: http://www.bright.net/~reyessyn

Nonprofit voluntary health organization that provides awareness information to the public and medical communities; supports research into cause, management, treatment, and prevention; gives support and guidance to individuals, families, and friends of victims.

Hotline or Toll-free Information Line
National Reye's Syndrome Foundation Information Line: 800-233-7393 (M–F 8AM–5PM ET) Operator assisted, answers questions, requests for materials.

Consumer or Patient Education Materials
Videotapes and slides; Because You Need to Know, brochure, symptoms and background information; Aspirin product list, sheet, products containing aspirin; Free single copy, nominal charge for greater quantities. Spanish, Vietnamese, Laotian, Cambodian languages available. Please contact for complete catalog.

Publications for Health Professionals
Articles available concerning treatment, research, symptoms, free. Please contact for complete publications list.

Grants, Funding, or Awards
Research grants available. Contact Sandi Nelson, 800-233-7393.

■ Osteoporosis and Related Bone Diseases National Resource Center

1150 17th St NW, Ste 500
Washington, DC 20036-4603
800-624-BONE (800-624-2663)
202-223-0344
Fax: 202-223-2237
TDD: 202-466-4315
E-mail: orbdnrc@nof.org
Web site: http://www.osteo.org

Federally funded information center operated by the National Osteoporosis Foundation in partnership with The Paget Foundation and the Osteogenesis Imperfecta Foundation. Collects information on materials, programs, and support services on metabolic bone diseases and disseminates this information widely to patients, health professionals, and the public. Its mission is to expand the awareness and enhance knowledge and understanding of the prevention, early detection, and treatment of these diseases as well as strategies for coping with them.

Database or Statistical Information
BoneData database, contains references to clinical journal articles, books, chapters, fact sheets, organizations and programs on prevention, diagnosis, treatment, and strategies for coping with metabolic bone diseases. Cumulative Index to Metabolic Bone Diseases Literature (CIMBDL), database of scientific

information containing the latest clinical research and seminal studies.

Consumer or Patient Education Materials

General public/patient information packet includes fact sheets: Fast Facts on Osteoporosis; Exercise for Your Bone Health; Calcium: Important at Every Age; and other materials; free.

■ Parkinson's Disease Foundation Inc

710 W 168th St
New York, NY 10032
Contact: Renay D Crooms
800-457-6676
212-923-4700
Fax: 212-923-4778
E-mail: pdf cpmc@aol.com
Web site: http://www.parkinsons-foundation.org

Nonprofit organization whose goal is to support research into the cause and cure of Parkinson's disease and related disorders.

Hotline or Toll-free Information Line

Parkinson's Disease Foundation Information Line: 800-457-6676 (M–F 9AM–5PM ET) Operator assisted, referral service, answers questions, requests for materials.

Consumer or Patient Education Materials

Pamphlets include: The Parkinson's Patient at Home; Exercises for the Parkinson's Patient; Progress, Promise and Hope; free single copy. Please contact for complete catalog.

Publications for Health Professionals

Parkinson's Disease Manual for the Health Care Team, $10; Quarterly newsletter. Please contact for complete publications list.

Technical Assistance

Support groups; physician referral service; counseling; advocacy.

Grants, Funding, or Awards

Research funding available. Contact Renay D Crooms.

■ Thyroid Foundation of America Inc

Ruth Sleeper Hall, RSL 350
40 Parkman St
Boston, MA 02114-2698
800-832-8321
617-726-8500
Fax: 617-726-4136

National nonprofit organization that provides information, support, and physician referrals to thyroid patients or others interested in thyroid disease.

Hotline or Toll-free Information Line

Thyroid Foundation of America Information Line: 800-832-8321 (M–F 8:30AM–4PM ET) Automated, referral service, answers questions, requests for materials.

Consumer or Patient Education Materials

Series of brochures on thyroid topics for patients, free. Please contact for information.

Publications for Health Professionals

The Bridge, quarterly newsletter, includes information for patients, $15–$25/yr.

ADDITIONAL RESOURCES

■ Allergy Research Institute

5800 E Evans Ave
Denver, CO 80222
Contact: Mike Garcia
303-756-1251
Fax: 303-757-1518
E-mail: snowfish@aol.com

■ American Lung Association

National Office
1740 Broadway
New York, NY 10019-4374
Mailing Address:
GPO Box 596
New York, NY 10016-0596
Contact: Call 800-LUNG-USA (800-586-4872) to reach a local chapter
212-315-8700
Web site: http://www.lungusa.org

■ American Thoracic Society

1740 Broadway
New York, NY 10019-4374
212-315-8778
Fax: 212-315-6498
Web site: http://www.thoracic.org

■ Arthritis Foundation

1330 W Peachtree St
Atlanta, GA 30309
Contact: Elnetta Mitchell
800-283-7800
404-872-7100
Web site: http://www.arthritis.org

■ **Digestive Disease National Coalition**
507 Capitol Ct NE, Ste 200
Washington, DC 20002
202-544-7497
Fax: 202-546-7105

■ **Sickle Cell Disease Association of America Inc**
200 Corporate Point, Ste 495
Culver City, CA 90230-7633
800-421-8453
310-216-6363
Fax: 310-215-3722

FEDERAL AGENCIES

■ **Alzheimer's Disease Education and Referral Center (ADEAR Center)**
PO Box 8520
Silver Spring, MD 20907-8250
800-438-4380
Fax: 301-495-3334
E-mail: adear@alzheimers.org
Web site: http://www.alzheimers.org/adear

A service of the National Institute on Aging (NIA) that provides information and publications on Alzheimer's disease to health and service professionals, patients and their families, caregivers, and the public. Information specialists are available M–F 8:30AM–5PM ET (the hours that the Center's reading room is open to visitors).

■ **National Center for Chronic Disease Prevention & Health Promotion (NCCDPHP)**
Centers for Disease Control and Prevention
4770 Buford Hwy NE
Atlanta, GA 30341-3724
Technical Information Services Branch: 770-488-5080
Chronic Disease Notes and Reports: 770-488-5050; Fax: 770-488-5095
Web site: http://www.cdc.gov/nccdphp/nccdhome.html

Plans, directs, and coordinates a national program for the prevention of premature mortality, morbidity, and disability due to chronic illnesses and conditions and promotes the overall health of the population.

■ **National Digestive Diseases Information Clearinghouse (NDDIC)**
Two Information Way
Bethesda, MD 20892-3570
Mailing address:
7910 Woodmont Ave, Ste 300
Bethesda, MD 20814
301-654-3810
Fax: 301-907-8906
E-mail: nddic@aerie.com

An information and referral service of National Institute of Diabetes and Digestive and Kidney Disease (NIDDK); responds to written inquiries, develops and distributes publications about digestive diseases, and provides referrals to digestive disease organizations, including support groups. Patient and professional materials available on cirrhosis, diarrhea, gallstone disease, heartburn, hiatal hernia, hepatitis B, ulcers, ulcerative colitis, irritable bowel syndrome, and Crohn's disease. Directories of professional and patient digestive disease organizations are available also.

■ **National Institute of Allergy and Infectious Diseases (NIAID)**
National Institutes of Health
Bldg 31, Rm 7A-50
31 Center Dr, MSC 2520
Bethesda, MD 20892-2520
Communications Office: 301-496-5717
E-mail: ocpostoffice@flash.niaid.nih.gov
Web site: http://www.niaid.nih.gov

Conducts and supports research on the prevention, diagnosis, and treatment of infectious, immunologic, and allergic diseases, including major responsibility for research on the immune system and on its disorders, including AIDS.

■ **National Institute of Arthritis and Musculoskeletal and Skin Diseases (NIAMS)**
National Institutes of Health
Bldg 31, Rm 4C-05
31 Center Dr, MSC 2350
Bethesda, MD 20892-2350
301-496-8188
Web site: http://www.nih.gov/niams/

NIAMS Information Clearinghouse
One AMS Circle
Bethesda, MD 20892-3675
301-495-4484; Fax: 301-587-4352
TTY: 301-565-2966

Conducts and supports basic, clinical, and epidemiologic research and research training and disseminates information on many debilitating diseases. Information available from the Clearinghouse includes bibliographies, reference sheets, and directories for professionals on such topics as arthritis, musculoskeletal diseases, rheumatic diseases, skin diseases, systemic lupus erythematosus, scleroderma, Lyme disease, gout, ankylosing spondylitis, biofeedback, nutrition, pharmaceuticals, patient education, statistics, health care personnel, physical exercise, and treatment centers.

■ National Institute of Diabetes and Digestive and Kidney Disease (NIDDK)

National Institutes of Health
Bldg 31, Rm 9A-04
31 Center Dr, MSC 2560
Bethesda, MD 20892-2560
Information Office: 301-496-3583
Web site: http://www.niddk.nih.gov

Conducts and supports biomedical research on diabetes; endocrinology and metabolic diseases; digestive diseases and nutrition; and kidney, urologic and blood diseases. Consumer information on many of these types of disorders is collected and disseminated through NIDDK's three national information clearinghouses.

■ National Institute of Neurological Disease and Stroke (NINDS)

National Institutes of Health
PO Box 5801
Bethesda, MD 20824
301-496-5751
Public Information Office: 800-352-9424
Web site: http://www.ninds.nih.gov/

Conducts and supports research and research training on the causes, prevention, diagnosis, and treatment of neurological disorders and stroke. Awards grants for research projects, program projects, and center grants; provides training support to institutions and fellowships to individuals in the field of neurological disorders and stroke; conducts intramural and collaborative research; and collects and disseminates research information.

■ National Institute on Aging (NIA)

National Institutes of Health
Bldg 31, Rm 5C-27
31 Center Dr, MSC 2292
Bethesda, MD 20892-2292
800-222-2225
Public Information Office: 301-496-1752
Fax: 301-496-1072
Web site: http://www.nih.gov/nia/

NIA Information Center
PO Box 8057
Gaithersburg, MD 20898-8057
800-222-2225; TTY: 800-222-4225

Conducts and supports biomedical, social, and behavioral research and training related to the aging process and the diseases and other special problems and needs of the aged. Materials are available on menopause, nutrition, arthritis, cancer, aging, constipation, crime, diabetes, exercise, hearing, high blood pressure, osteoporosis, medicines, flu, urinary incontinence, skin care, dental care, and other health topics from the NIA Information Center.

■ National Kidney and Urologic Diseases Information Clearinghouse (NKUDIC)

Three Information Way
Bethesda, MD 20892-3580
301-654-4415
Fax: 301-907-8906
E-mail: nkudic@aerie.com

An information and referral service of the National Institute of Diabetes and Digestive and Kidney Disease (NIDDK); responds to written inquiries, develops and distributes publications about kidney and urologic diseases, and provides referrals to digestive disease organizations, including support groups. Patient and professional materials available on various kidney and urologic conditions, including urinary tract infections, kidney stones, urinary incontinence, impotence, benign prostatic hyperplasia, and end-stage renal disease.

■ NIDCD Information Clearinghouse

One Communication Ave
Bethesda, MD 20892-3456
800-241-1044
TDD: 800-241-1055
E-mail: nidcd@aerie.com
Web site: http://www.nih.gov/nidcd/

A program of National Institute on Deafness and Other Communication Disorders (NIDCD) and serves as a national resource center for information about hearing, balance, smell, taste, voice, speech, and language for health professionals, patients, industry, and the public. Provides an information service; a database of references to journal articles, books, audiovisual materials, brochures, fact sheets, newsletter articles, manuals, and other education materials; and publications.

Immunizations and Infectious Diseases

Organization	web site	hotline/toll-free information line	clearinghouse/resource center	electronic information resources	database/statistical information	special campaigns/events/programs	consumer/patient education materials	publications for health professionals	classes/conferences	technical assistance	other products/services	grants/funding/awards	Page No.
American Academy of Pediatrics	■						■	■					**190**
American Conference of Governmental Industrial Hygienists	■							■					**190**
American Liver Foundation		■				■	■	■					**190**
American Lyme Disease Foundation Inc	■	■					■	■		■		■	**190**
Channing L Bete Co Inc							■						**191**
Every Child By Two	■							■					**191**
Healthy Mothers, Healthy Babies								■		■			**191**
Hepatitis Foundation International	■						■	■		■		■	**191**
Immunization Action Coalition	■						■	■					**192**
National Coalition for Adult Immunization	■					■	■	■		■			**192**
National Council of La Raza Center for Health Promotion	■		■				■			■			**192**
National Foundation for Infectious Diseases								■	■	■		■	**193**

Additional Resources 193

Federal Agencies 194

■ American Academy of Pediatrics

141 Northwest Point Blvd
PO Box 927
Elk Grove Village, IL 60007-0927
Contact: Publications Dept, 800-433-9016
847-228-5005
Fax: 847-228-1281
E-mail: kidsdocs@aap.org
Web site: http://www.aap.org

Nonprofit organization of 50,000 pediatricians dedicated to the health, safety, and well-being of infants, children, adolescents, and young adults. Activities include advocacy for children and youth; public education; research; professional education; membership service and advocacy for pediatricians. More than 30 committees develop positions and programs for interest areas including nutrition; pediatric AIDS; substance abuse; child abuse and neglect; children with disabilities.

Consumer or Patient Education Materials
Brochures, fact sheets and reminder sheets about vaccines, including the new chickenpox vaccine and hepatitis B, $12.95–$29.95/100. Some Spanish languages available. Please contact for complete catalog.

Publications for Health Professionals
Red Book: Report of the Committee on Infectious Diseases, manual, resource for the control of infectious diseases in children, $79.95. Please contact for complete publications list.

■ American Conference of Governmental Industrial Hygienists

1330 Kemper Meadow Dr
Cincinnati, OH 45240
513-742-2020
Fax: 513-742-3355
E-mail: acgih_pubs@pol.com
Web site: http://www.acgih.org

Nonprofit membership organization of professionals or students in the fields of occupational or environmental health that promotes excellence in environmental and occupational health; provides technical information of the highest quality; benefits the health and well-being of people worldwide; and serves the membership and continually improves the organization, including its financial and human resources.

Publications for Health Professionals
Infectious Disease Handbook, book, how to protect emergency care personnel from infectious disease; Bloodborne Pathogen, Tuberculosis Pocket Guides, booklets, quick reference for exposure prevention. Please contact for pricing and complete publications list.

■ American Liver Foundation

1425 Pompton Ave
Cedar Grove, NJ 07009
Contact: Ari Maravel, 800-223-0179 x228
800-223-0179
201-256-2550
Fax: 201-256-3214

National nonprofit organization dedicated to preventing, treating, and curing hepatitis and other liver and gallbladder diseases through research and education.

Hotline or Toll-free Information Line
American Liver Foundation: 888-4HEP-ABC (888-443-7222) (M–F 9AM–5PM ET) Operator assisted, answers questions, requests for materials.

Special Campaigns, Events, or Programs
Hepatitis Awareness Week, 3rd week in October, packets, printed materials, and posters available. Contact Ari Maravel, 800-223-0179 x228.

Consumer or Patient Education Materials
Brochures and fact sheets. Some Spanish language available. Please contact for pricing and complete catalog.

Publications for Health Professionals
Hepatitis C video, 40 minutes, for health care professionals; included with membership.

■ American Lyme Disease Foundation Inc

Mill Pond Offices
293 Rte 100
Somers, NY 10589
Contact: Anita Burrachio
800-876-LYME (800-876-5963)
914-277-6970
Fax: 914-277-6974
E-mail: aldf@computer.net
Web site: http://www.2.com/docs 2/d5/lyme.html

International nonprofit pro-active organization dedicated to the prevention, diagnosis, treatment, and control of Lyme disease and other tick-borne infections. Supports critical scientific research and plays a key role in providing reliable and scientifically accurate information to the public, medical community, and government agencies about tick-borne diseases and their potentially serious effects on our health and quality of life.

Hotline or Toll-free Information Line
American Lyme Disease Foundation Information: 800-876-LYME (800-876-5963) (M–F 9AM–5PM ET) Referral service, answers questions and requests for material.

Consumer or Patient Education Materials
Quick Guide to Lyme Disease, 11 pp booklet; Homeowner's Guide to the Ecology and Environmental Management of Lyme Disease, booklet; first copy free, additional copies varies upon quantity ordered. Please contact for complete catalog.

Publications for Health Professionals
Lyme Disease: Clinical Update for Physicians, booklet, technical information including poster, first copy $3; Proceedings of a National Clinical Conference on Lyme Disease, April 1995, reprint from the American Journal of Medicine, first copy $6.50. Please contact for complete publications list.

Technical Assistance
Physician referral system available.

Grants, Funding, or Awards
Some grants given for research.

■ Channing L Bete Co Inc

200 State Rd
S Deerfield, MA 01373-0200
800-628-7733 (Sales and Customer Service)
413-665-7611
Fax: 800-499-6464

Publisher of informational and educational booklets, videos, posters, calendars, books, and display racks. Booklets use a distinctive, condensed format—called scriptography—which combines key words and graphics to explain a variety of subjects and is appropriate for different age groups and reading levels.

Consumer or Patient Education Materials
Booklets and videos on hepatitis and tuberculosis. Some Spanish language available. Please contact for pricing and ask for the Patient Education catalog.

■ Every Child By Two

600 Maryland Ave SW
Washington, DC 20024-2571
Contact: Janis Lambert
800-215-3727
202-651-7226
Fax: 202-651-7001
E-mail: aarbuckle@ana.org
Web site: http://www.ecbt.org

Nonprofit Carter/Bumpers campaign for early immunization and a program of the American Nurses Foundation. Goals are to raise awareness of the critical need for timely immunization and foster putting in place a systematic way to immunize our nation's children by the age of two.

Publications for Health Professionals
Immunization Kit contains complete Leadership Kit with set of Every Child By Two immunization posters; Immunization Partners Conference Booklet, Every Child By Two posters. Call 800-637-0323 for pricing and to order these materials; ECBT newsletter, 3 times/yr, activities and immunization news, free.

■ Healthy Mothers, Healthy Babies

409 12th St SW, Rm 309
Washington, DC 20024-2188
Contact: Leslie Dunne
202-863-2458
Fax: 202-554-4346

National nonprofit coalition of health care providers and administrators concerned about the health of pregnant women, children, and families. Helps develop networks for sharing information among groups and assists in the establishment of additional Healthy Mothers, Healthy Babies coalitions in states and communities.

Publications for Health Professionals
Immunization Education and Action Committee News, quarterly newsletter, free; IEAC Directory of Immunization Coalitions, $5. Contact Dena Wichansky, IEAC, 202-863-4993

Technical Assistance
Immunization Education and Action Committee, an issue committee whose mission is to promote the vaccination of preschool age children.

■ Hepatitis Foundation International

30 Sunrise Ter
Cedar Grove, NJ 07009
Contact: Thelma King Thiel
800-891-0707
201-239-1035
Fax: 201-857-5044
E-mail: hfi@intac.com
Web site: http://www.hepfi.org

Nonprofit organization dedicated to reducing the suffering of individuals with viral hepatitis worldwide. Supports preventive education, patient advocacy, and increased research for treatment and cures.

Consumer or Patient Education Materials
Primer for Parents, pamphlet for parents about vaccinations; Liv and Lucky workbook, coloring book for children; information sheets on hepatitis A, B, or C;

poster and brochures. Low literacy; Some Spanish languages available. Please contact for complete catalog.

Publications for Health Professionals

Hepatitis Alert, quarterly newsletter; Primer for Teachers, guide for teaching children. Please contact for complete publications list.

Technical Assistance

Patient Advocacy/Information Telecommunications System (PATS) support group by phone; physician referrals.

Grants, Funding, or Awards

Career Development Award. Contact for more information.

■ Immunization Action Coalition

1573 Selby Ave, Ste 229
St Paul, MN 55104-6328
612-647-9009
Fax: 612-647-9131
E-mail: editor@immunize.org
Web site: http://www.immunize.org/

National nonprofit coalition working to boost immunization rates by promoting physician, community, and family awareness of and responsibility for appropriate immunization of people of all ages against all vaccine-preventable diseases.

Consumer or Patient Education Materials

Faces of vaccine-preventable diseases, slide set and simple script, 30 slides of people who are now routinely vaccinated, $23; Questions Frequently Asked about Hepatitis B, brochure, $1; When to Immunize, When to Wait, 22-min video with accompanying materials that can be used for CME credit, $10. Low literacy; Spanish, Russian, Hmong, Vietnamese, Laotian, Cambodian, Chinese languages available. Please contact for complete catalog.

Publications for Health Professionals

Needle Tips and the Hepatitis B Coalition News, semiannual periodical, updates for providers and individuals, free with membership or $25 donation.

■ National Coalition for Adult Immunization

4733 Bethesda Ave., Ste 750
Bethesda, MD 20814-5228
Contact: Alison D Roth
301-656-0003
Fax: 301-907-0878
E-mail: adultimm@aol.com
Web site: http://www.medscape.com/ncai

Nonprofit organization composed of more than 85 professional medical and health care associations, advocacy groups, voluntary organizations, vaccine manufacturers, and government health agencies. Common goal is improving the immunization status of adults to levels specified by the U.S. Public Health Service.

Special Campaigns, Events, or Programs

National Adult Immunization Awareness Week, in October, campaign kit includes: fact sheets on 20 vaccine-preventable diseases, adult immunization schedule, poster, camera-ready ads, brochures, media guide, radio PSAs. Contact Alison D Roth.

Consumer or Patient Education Materials

Fact sheets, poster, and camera-ready ads, for 10 adult vaccine-preventable diseases, free. Spanish languages available. Please contact for complete catalog.

Publications for Health Professionals

Coalition News, quarterly newsletter, updates on members' work; Resource Guide for Adult Immunization, yearly, lists of materials; Standards for Adult Immunization Practice. All free. Please contact for complete publications list.

Technical Assistance

List of adult immunization and adult health care coalitions located throughout the U.S. and assistance in how to establish local coalitions.

■ National Council of La Raza Center for Health Promotion

1111 19th St NW, Ste 1000
Washington, DC 20036
Contact: Lupe Lemus, 202-785-1670
202-785-1670
Fax: 202-776-1792
E-mail: hpacheco@nclr.org
Web site: http://www.nclr.org

Private, nonprofit, nonpartisan organization that serves as an advocate for Hispanic Americans on health and other public policy issues. The NCLR's Center for Health Promotion works to increase the access of Hispanics to health care and to provide public health materials and capacity-building assistance to Hispanic community-based organizations. The Center has three major programs: Maternal and Child Health Program; HST Prevention Project, and Hispanic Health Liaison Project.

Clearinghouse or Resource Center

NCLR Distribution Center: 301-604-7983; PO Box 291, Annapolis Junction, MD 20701; Health, immigration, poverty, and general public information available. Cost of materials $5 to $15.

Consumer or Patient Education Materials
Center for Maternal and Child Health, fact sheet, provides information on issues related to health of Hispanic children. Please contact for complete catalog.
Technical Assistance
Maternal and Child Health Program, focuses primarily on combating high rates of vaccine-preventable diseases among Latinos; technical assistance, trainings, educational information to community-based organizations.

■ National Foundation for Infectious Diseases
4733 Bethesda Ave, Ste 750
Bethesda, MD 20814-5228
Contact: Marlene L Maroulis
301-656-0003
Fax: 301-907-0878
E-mail: nfid@aol.com

Nonprofit public organization dedicated to supporting research that will lead to a better understanding of the causes, cures, and prevention of infectious diseases; to encouraging and sponsoring public and professional educational programs; and aiding in the prevention of infectious diseases.

Publications for Health Professionals
Clinical Updates in Infectious Diseases, quarterly, for practicing physicians, free; The Double Helix, bimonthly newsletter, free; Nursing Home Book, text, dealing with infections in nursing homes, $6. Please contact for complete publications list.
Classes and Conferences
Educational seminars.
Technical Assistance
Awareness campaigns.
Grants, Funding, or Awards
Grants and fellowships for research. Contact for application.

ADDITIONAL RESOURCES

■ All Kids Count—National Program Office
c/o The Task Force for Child Survival & Development
One Copenhill
Atlanta, GA 30307
Contact: Carol Gilligan, Administrative Assistant
404-687-5615
Fax: 404-371-1087
Web site: http://www.allkidscount.org

■ American College of Physicians
Sixth St at Race
Philadelphia, PA 19106-1572
800-523-1546
215-351-2653
Fax: 215-351-2799
Web site: http://www.acponline.org

■ American Pharmaceutical Association
2215 Constitution Ave NW
Washington, DC 20037
800-237-APHA (800-237-2742)
202-628-4410
Fax: 202-783-2351

■ The Carter Center
453 Freedom Pkwy
Atlanta, GA 30307
Contact: Office of Public Information, 404-331-3900
404-420-5165
E-mail: carterweb@emory.edu
Web site: http://www.emory.edu/CARTER_CENTER

■ Children's Defense Fund
25 E St NW
Washington, DC 20001
Contact: Publications Dept, 202-662-3652
202-628-8339
Fax: 202-628-8333
E-mail: cdfinfo@childrensdefense.org
Web site: http://www.childrensdefense.org

■ Children's Health Fund
317 E 64th St
New York, NY 10021
212-535-9400
Fax: 212-535-7488

■ Connaught Laboratories Inc
PO Box 187, Route 611
Swiftwater, PA 18370
Contact: Chuck Gottlieb, Associate Product Manager
717-839-7187
717-839-4446
Fax: 717- 839-7235

■ Hope for Kids
190 New York Ave
Brooklyn, NY 11216
Contact: Marie Alexander, Project Director
718-771-4435
Fax: 718-771-3011

■ **Infectious Diseases Society of America**
99 Canal Center Plaza, Ste 210
Alexandria, VA 22314
703-299-0200
Fax: 703-299-0204
E-mail: info@idsociety.org
Web site: http://www.idsociety.org

■ **Kiwanis International**
3636 Woodview Trace
Indianapolis, IN 46268-3196
800-549-2647
317-875-8755
Fax: 317-879-0204
E-mail: kiwanismail@kiwanis.org
Web site: http://www.kiwanis.org

■ **Lyme Disease Foundation Inc**
One Financial Plaza
Hartford, CT 06103-2610
Contact: Catherine Beldren, PR Counsel
800-886-LYME (800-886-5963)
860-525-2000
Fax: 860-525-8425
E-mail: lymefnd@aol.com

■ **Merck Vaccine Division**
One Merck Dr
PO Box 100
Whitehouse Station, NJ 08889-0100
Contact: Isabelle Claxton, Public Relations, 908-423-4374
908-423-1000
Fax: 908-735-1232
Web site: http://www.merck.com

■ **National Governors' Association**
444 N Capitol St NW, Ste 267
Washington, DC 20001
Contact: Nancy Sartor, Public Relations Dept, 202-624-5371
202-624-5300
Fax: 202-624-5313
Web site: http://www.nga.org

■ **Rotary International**
One Rotary Center
1560 Sherman Ave
Evanston, IL 60201
Contact: Order Desk, 847-866-3149
847-866-3000
Fax: 847-328-8554
Web site: http://www.rotary.org

■ **Save the Children Federation**
54 Wilton Rd
Westport, CT 06881
Contact: Lee Mullane, Director of Public Information
203-221-4000
Fax: 203-454-3914

■ **SmithKline Beecham Corporation**
PO Box 7929
Philadelphia, PA 19101
Contact: Product Information Dept, 215-751-5231
800-VACCNET (800-822-2638)
800-366-8900
Web site: http://www.sb.com

■ **Visiting Nurse Associations of America**
3801 E Florida Ave, Ste 900
Denver, CO 80210
888-866-8773
303-753-0218
Fax: 303-753-0258

FEDERAL AGENCIES

■ **Center for Biologics Evaluation and Research (CBER)**
U.S. Food and Drug Administration
1401 Rockville Pike, HFM-46
Rockville, MD 20852
800-835-4709
301-827-1800
Web site: http://www.fda.gov/cber/cberftp.html

Responsible for regulating blood and blood products, vaccines, and biological therapeutics; also inspects facilities where biological products are manufactured to ensure regulatory standards are met.

■ **National Center for HIV, STD & TB Prevention (NCHSTP)**
Centers for Disease Control and Prevention
1600 Clifton Rd NE, M/S E-06
Atlanta, GA 30333
Communications Dept: 404-639-8063
NCHSTP Voice Information System: 404-639-1819
TB Voice Information System: 404-330-1231
HIV/AIDS and TB Fax Information Service: 404-332-4565
Web site: http://www.cdd.gov/nchstp/od/nchstp.html

Responsible for public health surveillance and programs to prevent and control human immunodeficiency virus (HIV) infection and acquired immunodeficiency (AIDS), other sexually transmitted diseases (STDs), and tuberculosis (TB). Works closely with its partners in state and local health agencies, national and community-based organizations, business, and academia to design and test prevention programs that work.

■ National Center for Infectious Diseases (NCID)

Centers for Disease Control and Prevention
1600 Clifton Rd NE, M/S C-12
Atlanta, GA 30333
404-639-3286
CDC Parasitic Diseases Information Line:
404-330-1242
Web site: http://www.cdc.gov/ncidod/ncid.htm

Supports surveillance, research, prevention efforts, and training in the area of traditional, new, and reemerging diseases in the U.S. and around the world.

■ National Immunization Program (NIP)

Centers for Disease Control and Prevention
1600 Clifton Rd NE, M/S E-52
Atlanta, GA 30333
404-639-8204
National Immunization Information Hotline:
800-232-2522
National Hispanic Immunization Hotline:
800-232-0233
CDC Immunization Information: 800-232-7468
International Travelers' Information: 404-332-4559
Web site: http://www.cdc.gov/nip.home.htm

Provides national leadership for the planning, coordination, and conduct of immunization activities nationwide.

■ National Institute of Allergy and Infectious Diseases (NIAID)

National Institutes of Health
Bldg 31, Rm 7A-50
31 Center Dr, MSC 2520
Bethesda, MD 20892-2520
Communications Office: 301-496-5717
E-mail: ocpostoffice@flash.niaid.nih.gov
Web site: http://www.niaid.nih.gov

Conducts and supports research on the prevention, diagnosis, and treatment of infectious, immunologic, and allergic diseases, including major responsibility for research on the immune system and on its disorders, including AIDS.

Sexually Transmitted Diseases, HIV Infection, and AIDS

Products/Services Offered

Organization	web site	hotline/toll-free information line	clearinghouse/resource center	electronic information resources	database/statistical information	special campaigns/events/programs	consumer/patient education materials	publications for health professionals	classes/conferences	technical assistance	other products/services	grants/funding/awards	**Page No.**
Advocates for Youth								■		■			**199**
The AIDS Treatment Data Network (The Network)	■	■					■	■		■	■		**199**
American Academy of Pediatrics	■						■						**199**
American Public Health Association	■			■				■					**199**
American Social Health Association	■	■	■	■			■	■					**200**
Anatomical Chart Company							■						**200**
CD Publications								■					**200**
Channing L Bete Co Inc							■						**200**
Health Education Services	■						■						**201**
Health Information Network									■	■			**201**
Impact AIDS							■			■			**201**
Journeyworks Publishing							■						**201**
NASCO	■						■						**202**
National Center for Health Education	■							■		■			**202**
National Council of La Raza Center for Health Promotion	■		■				■	■		■			**202**
National Minority AIDS Council								■	■	■			**202**
National Native American AIDS Prevention Center		■		■			■	■	■	■			**203**
Project Inform	■	■					■	■					**203**
San Francisco AIDS Foundation	■	■		■				■	■	■			**203**

Products/Services Offered

Organization	web site	hotline/toll-free information line	clearinghouse/resource center	electronic information resources	database/statistical information	special campaigns/events/programs	consumer/patient education materials	publications for health professionals	classes/conferences	technical assistance	other products/services	grants/funding/awards	Page No.
Select Media							■						**204**
Sexuality Information and Education Council of the United States (SIECUS)	■						■	■					**204**
Women's AIDS Network (WAN)							■						**204**

Additional Resources **204**

Federal Agencies **206**

■ Advocates for Youth

1025 Vermont Ave NW, Ste 200
Washington, DC 20005
Contact: Robin Hatziyannis
202-347-5700
Fax: 202-347-2263

Nonprofit organization works to increase the opportunities for and abilities of youth to make healthy decisions about sexuality. Provides information, education, and advocacy to youth-serving agencies and professionals, policy makers, and the media at the international, national, state, and local levels.

Publications for Health Professionals

Reaching High Risk Youth Through Model HIV/AIDS Education Programs, 21 pp monograph, overview and evaluation of Advocates' High Risk Youth Demonstration Project, $2. Please contact for complete publications list.

Technical Assistance

Teens for AIDS Prevention, peer education program.

■ The AIDS Treatment Data Network (The Network)

611 Broadway, Ste 613
New York, NY 10012
Contact: Ken Fornataro, Executive Director
800-734-7104
212-260-8868
Fax: 212-260-8869
E-mail: atdn@aidsnyc.com
Web site: http://www.aidsnyc.org/network

National nonprofit community-based organization providing treatment education and counseling, case management support, and user friendly educational materials in English and Spanish.

Hotline or Toll-free Information Line

The Network: 800-734-7104 (M–F 10AM–6PM ET) Operator assisted, emergency, referral service, answers questions, requests for materials. Counselors assist health care professionals, educators, and clients in English and Spanish.

Consumer or Patient Education Materials

The Experimental Treatment Guide, directory, clinical trials, description, contact info and glossary; simple one-page Fact Sheets, on drugs, conditions, symptoms; Should I Enter a Trial?, booklets, patient guide to deciding about clinical trial options. Free (annual contribution suggested, but not required). Spanish languages available.

Publications for Health Professionals

Treatment Review, 8 times/yr, review of approved experimental treatments and studies for AIDS, $16.

Technical Assistance

Workshops-forums on AIDS/HIV treatment; information management; consumer education and other topics for on-site presentations available; Internet training (work with community groups in New York to set up Internet access as a joint project with The New York Academy of Medicine).

Other Products and Services

The Access Project, information and assistance accessing entitlement insurance and other treatment assistance programs (Medicaid, ADAP, etc), call 800-734-7104.

■ American Academy of Pediatrics

141 Northwest Point Blvd
PO Box 927
Elk Grove Village, IL 60007-0927
Contact: Publications Dept, 800-433-9016
847-228-5005
Fax: 847-228-1281
E-mail: kidsdocs@aap.org
Web site: http://www.aap.org

Nonprofit organization of 50,000 pediatricians dedicated to the health, safety, and well-being of infants, children, adolescents, and young adults. Activities include advocacy for children and youth; public education; research; professional education; membership service and advocacy for pediatricians. More than 30 committees develop positions and programs for interest areas including nutrition; pediatric AIDS; substance abuse; child abuse and neglect; children with disabilities.

Consumer or Patient Education Materials

Know The Facts About HIV and AIDS, brochure, suggestions for teaching young children and teens, $29.95/100. Please contact for complete catalog.

■ American Public Health Association

1015 15th St NW
Washington, DC 20005
Contact: Publication Sales, 301-893-1894, PO Box 753, Waldorf, MD 20604-0753
202-789-5600
TDD: 202-789-6573
Web site: http://www.apha.org

National nonprofit multi-disciplinary association of professionals in public health and related fields that works to protect and promote personal and environmental health. Develops standards, promulgates recommended rules, and publishes pamphlets, books, model codes, and educational materials.

Electronic Information Resources
Fax-on-Demand: 202-274-4577

Publications for Health Professionals
AIDS Prevention in the Community: Lessons from the First Decade, book, $48. Please contact for complete publications list.

■ American Social Health Association

100 Capitola Dr
Durham, NC 27713
Mailing Address:
PO Box 13827
Research Triangle Park, NC 27709-3827
Contact: Customer Service, 919-361-8422 or 800-783-9877
ASHA HealthLine: 800-972-8500
919-361-8400
Fax: 919-361-8425
Web site: http://sunsite.unc.edu/asha/

Nonprofit advocacy organization whose mission is to stop the spread of STDs through educational materials, information and referrals to the public and health care providers. Operates the National AIDS Hotline, National STD Hotline, National Herpes Hotline; and the First Step Hotline and Health Check Hotlines in North Carolina.

Hotline or Toll-free Information Line
National STD Hotline: 800-227-8922 (M–F 8AM–11PM ET) Confidential and anonymous information on all sexually transmitted diseases and referral for health care.
National Herpes Hotline: 919-361-8488 (M–F 9AM–7PM ET) Confidential and anonymous information and counseling on herpes.
National AIDS Hotline: 800-342-AIDS (800-342-2437) (7 days/wk, 24 hrs/day); Spanish: 800-344-7432 (7 days/wk, 8AM–2AM ET); TTY: 800-243-7889 (M–F 10AM–10PM ET) Confidential and anonymous information on HIV and AIDS and referral for health care and support groups.

Electronic Information Resources
STD Info and Referral Center: 800-357-3675, Fax-on-Demand and hotline connections available.
Herpes Resource Center Order Line: 800-230-6039; Herpes and HPV materials including books, booklets, pamphlets, posters. Please contact for pricing and complete catalog.

Consumer or Patient Education Materials
Books, pamphlets, booklets, brochures, posters. Some Spanish language available. Please contact for pricing and complete catalog.

Publications for Health Professionals
STD Counseling and Treatment Guide, book, includes CDC guidelines, counseling info, sample personal health history form, $14.95. Please contact for complete publications list.

■ Anatomical Chart Company

8221 N Kimball
Skokie, IL 60076-2956
800-621-7500 (Order Dept)
847-679-4700
Fax: 847-674-0211

Mail order company catering to the professional or student in need of biological or scientific charts and models of the human anatomy.

Consumer or Patient Education Materials
AIDS Flip Chart, 6 panels, illustrates the ways the disease is transmitted and can be avoided, $55; AIDS Folding Display, explains how AIDS affects the immune system and other parts of the body, includes minitexts with test questions, $89; AIDS—What You Don't Know Can Kill You, booklet, $1.50 ea; Please contact for complete catalog.

■ CD Publications

8204 Fenton St
Silver Spring, MD 20910-4571
800-666-6380
301-588-6380
Fax: 301-588-6385
E-mail: cdpubs@clark.net

Publisher of newsletters, reports, and resource guides that identify funding sources, provide fundraising advice, and keep readers updated on budget proposals affecting public policy in health, education, and social services.

Publications for Health Professionals
AIDS/STD News Report, semi-monthly newsletter, funding and news for agencies and hospitals, $269/yr. Please contact for complete publications list.

■ Channing L Bete Co Inc

200 State Rd
S Deerfield, MA 01373-0200
800-628-7733 (Sales and Customer Service)
413-665-7611
Fax: 800-499-6464

Publisher of informational and educational booklets, videos, posters, calendars, books, and display racks. Booklets use a distinctive, condensed format—called scriptography—which combines key words and graphics to explain a variety of subjects and is appropriate for different age groups and reading levels.

Consumer or Patient Education Materials
Booklets and videos about STDs (chlamydia, genital warts, gonorrhea, herpes, syphilis); HIV, and AIDS prevention. Some Spanish language available. Please contact for pricing and ask for the Patient Education catalog.

■ Health Education Services

PO Box 7126
Albany, NY 12224
518-439-7286
Fax: 518-439-7286 *51
Web site: http://www.hes.org

Nonprofit distributor of current health education, promotional publications, posters, and videos, most of which have been produced by the New York State Department of Health or the New York State Department of Environmental Conservation. (Health Education Services is a Division of Health Research Inc.)

Consumer or Patient Education Materials
Booklets, comic books, posters, bookmarks, videos; covering Syphilis, Gonorrhea, Pelvic Inflammatory Disease (PID), HIV, and AIDS; many targeted at teens. $.75–$25. Some Spanish languages available. Please contact for complete catalog.

■ Health Information Network

PO Box 30762
Seattle, WA 98103
Contact: Kathi Knowles
206-784-5655

Nonprofit organization providing health education and community resource information and referral, focusing on the STD and HIV/AIDS areas. Also provides telephone access to other health related resources, and on occasion printed materials for other diseases.

Classes and Conferences
HIV Licensing Course, 7 hrs, fulfills Washington state requirements for licensing, $40.

Technical Assistance
Consulting provided on project, fee for service basis (e.g., exposure control manuals, educational plans).

■ Impact AIDS

440 Cerrillos Rd, Ste F
Sante Fe, NM 87501
Contact: Jeff Steeno
415-861-3397
Fax: 505-995-0252

For-profit producer and distributor of AIDS-related educational materials for people at risk, people with HIV, and their caregivers. Also produces materials related to death and dying.

Consumer or Patient Education Materials
Brochures, booklets, videos, manuals, books, posters, and cards available covering: Teens and HIV, women and HIV, people with HIV, safe sex; Alcohol, drugs and needle use; AIDS in the workplace. Materials can be customized; Low literacy; Spanish languages available. Please contact for complete catalog.

Technical Assistance
Consultation on the development of patient education materials available.

■ Journeyworks Publishing

736 Chestnut St
Santa Cruz, CA 95060
Mailing Address:
PO Box 8466
Santa Cruz, CA 95061-8466
800-775-1998
408-423-1400
Fax: 408-423-8102

Publisher of health promotion materials for clinics, hospitals, schools, and health departments covering a variety of topics including fitness, women's health, sexual abstinence, teen pregnancy prevention, STDs and HIV, mental wellness, tobacco use prevention, and smoking cessation.

Consumer or Patient Education Materials
Ten Ways to Protect Yourself from STDs & HIV; A Teen's Guide to HIV and AIDS; STDs: When Should I Worry?; pamphlets, free review sample, pricing varies upon quantity ordered. Materials can be customized; Please contact for complete catalog.

■ NASCO

901 Janesville Ave
Ft Atkinson, WI 53538-0901
Contact: Dan Christianson, Health Care Dept, 414-563-2446 x237
800-558-9595
414-563-2446
Fax: 414-563-8296
E-mail: lifeform@nascofa.com
Web site: http://www.nascofa.com

For-profit developer, producer, and distributor of health education products worldwide.

Consumer or Patient Education Materials
Posters, laminated charts, folding displays, videotapes, computer programs covering STDs, HIV, and AIDS. $25–$125. Discounts available for quantity orders. Please contact for complete catalog.

■ National Center for Health Education

72 Spring St, Ste 208
New York, NY 10012-4019
Contact: Urvi R Dalal, 212-334-9470 x25
212-334-9470
Fax: 212-334-9845
Web site: http://www.nche.org

Nonprofit organization dedicated to leading the nation in the implementation of life-long comprehensive health education. Designs and disseminates Growing Healthy®, a comprehensive school health education curriculum for students in grades K–6, which teaches students skills that will enable them to adopt healthy attitudes and behaviors. Call WRS Group Inc at 800-551-3488 for Growing Healthy and National Health Education Week materials.

Publications for Health Professionals
Adolescent Health Issues Guidebook, manual, for health educators discussing HIV/AIDS, sexuality, birth control, $40. Please contact for complete publications list.

Technical Assistance
Technical assistance available for comprehensive school health education, and teacher training.

■ National Council of La Raza Center for Health Promotion

1111 19th St NW, Ste 1000
Washington, DC 20036
Contact: Lupe Lemus, 202-785-1670
202-785-1670
Fax: 202-776-1792
E-mail: hpacheco@nclr.org
Web site: http://www.nclr.org

Private, nonprofit, nonpartisan organization that serves as an advocate for Hispanic Americans on health and other public policy issues. The NCLR's Center for Health Promotion works to increase the access of Hispanics to health care and to provide public health materials and capacity-building assistance to Hispanic community-based organizations. The Center has three major programs: Maternal and Child Health Program; HST Prevention Project, and Hispanic Health Liaison Project.

Clearinghouse or Resource Center
NCLR Distribution Center: 301-604-7983; PO Box 291, Annapolis Junction, MD 20701; Health, immigration, poverty, and general public information available. Cost of materials $5 to $15.

Consumer or Patient Education Materials
NCLR AIDS Center, fact sheet, provides Hispanic data on HIV/STD/TB topics, free. Please contact for complete catalog.

Publications for Health Professionals
Do's and Don'ts for . . . , guide, HIV Prevention Community Planning Program, $10. Please contact for complete publications list.

Technical Assistance
HST Prevention Project works to reduce the spread of HIV, STDs and tuberculosis; technical assistance, trainings, educational information to community-based organizations.

■ National Minority AIDS Council

1931 13th St NW
Washington, DC 20009-4432
Contact: Chris Morrison, 202-483-6622 x335
202-483-6622
Fax: 202-483-1135
E-mail: nmac2@aol.com

Nonprofit organization whose purpose is to develop leadership with communities of color to address issues of HIV/AIDS infection. Accomplishes this by providing conferences; public policy, research and treatment advocacy; technical assistance; special events; newsletters and publications.

Publications for Health Professionals
How-to training manuals include: HIV Treatment; Strategic Planning; Board Development, $15–$25. Please contact for complete publications list.

Classes and Conferences
National Skills Building Conference, 4 days, management training, $300–$450; Prevention Summit, 3 days, HIV community planning, $120; Minority Executive Directors Conference, 3 days, Executive Directors retreat, $95. Contact Vince

Rodriguez, 202-483-1124 x315 for complete information.

Technical Assistance

Technical assistance consultants provide skills for minority community-based organization; public speakers available for professional events.

■ National Native American AIDS Prevention Center

2100 Lake Shore Ave, Ste A
Oakland, CA 94606
Contact: Sally Ramon
800-283-2437
510-444-2051
Fax: 510-444-1593
E-mail: nnaapc@aol.com

Nonprofit organization whose mission is to stop the spread of HIV and related diseases among American Indians, Alaska Natives, and Native Hawaiians and to improve the quality of life for members of our communities infected and affected by HIV/AIDS.

Hotline or Toll-free Information Line

Indian AIDS Information Line: 800-283-2437 (M–F 8:30AM–1PM, 2PM–5PM PT) Operator assisted and automated line, emergency, referral service, answers questions, requests for materials.

Electronic Information Resources

Fax Back Service: 800-283-6880, Agency information; statistics; alcohol and drug mortality rates; 1990 census of Native population by state; state hotlines. Free.

Consumer or Patient Education Materials

Living with HIV Infection; Women and HIV; free. Please contact for complete catalog.

Publications for Health Professionals

Seasons, quarterly newsmagazine, free; HIV Prevention in Native American Communities: A Manual for Native American Health and Human Service Workers, $20; HIV Prevention with Native American Youth: A Program Planning Manual, $20. Please contact for complete publications list.

Classes and Conferences

Regional skills building workshops. Contact Sally Ramon for complete information.

Technical Assistance

Targeted, individualized technical assistance to help Native Americans develop successful HIV programs. Consultation of needs assessment, program development, leadership development, and other capacity-building activities.

■ Project Inform

1965 Market St, Ste 220
San Francisco, CA 94103
800-822-7422
415-558-8669
Fax: 415-558-0684
E-mail: pinform@hooked.net
Web site: http://www.projinf.org

National nonprofit community-based HIV/AIDS treatment information and advocacy organization that serves HIV-infected individuals, their caregivers, and their healthcare and service providers through its national, toll-free treatment hotline, information publications, educational Town Meetings, on-line services and research and drug access advocacy programs.

Hotline or Toll-free Information Line

Project Inform National HIV/AIDS Treatment Hotline: 800-822-7422 or 415-558-9051 (M–F 9AM–5PM, Sat 10AM–4PM PT) Operator assisted, referral service, answers questions, requests for materials. HIV treatment info and data on various therapies.

Consumer or Patient Education Materials

Fact sheets; discussion papers available.

Publications for Health Professionals

PI Perspective, semi-annual journal, in-depth analysis of the state of the art in AIDS treatment/research and issues affecting lives of people with HIV.

■ San Francisco AIDS Foundation

10 United Nations Plaza
San Francisco, CA 94102-4910
Mailing address:
PO Box 426182
San Francisco, CA 94142-6182
800-FOR-AIDS (Northern California) (in-state)
415-487-3000
Fax: 415-487-3009
TDD: 415-864-6606
Web site: http://www.sfaf.org

Nonprofit organization whose purpose is to hasten the end of the HIV epidemic and to mitigate its impact on society. Educates the public to: prevent the transmission of HIV; help individuals make informed choices about HIV-related concerns; and assure the protection of the human rights of all those affected by HIV disease. Also provides and supports designated client services for those in San Francisco affected by HIV disease; provides leadership to create innovative non-duplicative educational programs, directs services, and public policy initiatives in cooperation with other agencies; and initiates and supports public policies that further these goals.

Hotline or Toll-free Information Line
Northern California HIV/AIDS Hotline: 800-FOR-AIDS (800-367-2437) (M–F 9AM–9PM, Sat–Sun 11AM–5PM PT) Offers help and referral on AIDS prevention, education, and other support services, volunteer operators speak English, Spanish, and Filipino, as well as TDD.

Electronic Information Resources
SFAF John P Maguire HIV/AIDS Referral Database, http://www.sfaf.org
Online AIDs agency referral database canvassing Northern California.

Publications for Health Professionals
Bulletin of Experimental Treatments on AIDS (BETA), quarterly updates.

Classes and Conferences
Hotline Training, 2-week intensive, for volunteers who staff hotline.

Technical Assistance
Ongoing prevention campaigns for distribution in the community.

■ Select Media

60 Warren St, 5th Fl
New York, NY 10007
Contact: Rebecca Chertok
800-707-6334
212-732-4437
Fax: 212-732-4439
E-mail: selmedbw@interport.net

For-profit distributor of educational films, videos, and CD-ROMs specializing in health and social issues.

Consumer or Patient Education Materials
Be Proud! Be Responsible!, video and curriculum, strategies to empower youth to reduce their risk of AIDS, $95; Eagle Scout, video, story of Henry Nicols, 17, with AIDS, $149; Sex, Drugs, & HIV, video with guide, critical prevention information & strategies, $295. Spanish languages available. Please contact for complete catalog.

■ Sexuality Information and Education Council of the United States (SIECUS)

130 W 42nd St, Ste 350
New York, NY 10036-7802
Contact: Publications Dept, 212-819-9770 x303
212-819-9770
Fax: 212-819-9776
E-mail: siecus@siecus.org
Web site: http://www.siecus.org/

International nonprofit organization that develops, collects, and disseminates information, promotes comprehensive education about sexuality, and advocates the right of individuals to make responsible sexual choices.

Consumer or Patient Education Materials
How to Talk to Your Children about AIDS, 16 pp booklet, available in Spanish, free single copy with #10 SASE, discounts available for quantity orders. Please contact for complete catalog.

Publications for Health Professionals
Winning the Battle: Developing Support for Sexuality and HIV/AIDS Education, 64 pp booklet, $10; HIV/AIDS SIECUS Reprint Series, selection of articles, $2; HIV/AIDS: A SIECUS Annotated Bibliography of available print material, $2. Please contact for complete publications list.

■ Women's AIDS Network (WAN)

3543 18th St, Ste 11
San Francisco, CA 94110
415-621-4160
Fax: 415-575-1181

Nonprofit organization, also the oldest known women and HIV organization in the world, whose mission is to advocate and provide for the development and improvement of public policies, education, and services for the diverse population of women affected by HIV disease.

Consumer or Patient Education Materials
Women and HIV resource packet; Lesbians and HIV resource packet; other miscellaneous resources available. Please contact by mail or phone for complete information.

ADDITIONAL RESOURCES

■ Academy for Educational Development

1875 Connecticut Ave NW, Ste 900
Washington, DC 20009
202-884-8000
Fax: 202-884-8400
Web site: http://www.aed.org

■ American College Health Association

PO Box 28937
Baltimore, MD 21240-8937
410-859-1500
Fax: 410-859-1510
E-mail: ACHA@access.digex.net
Web site: http://www.clbalt.com/acha.org/

■ **American Foundation for AIDS Research (AmFAR)**
733 Third Ave, 12th Fl
New York, NY 10017-3204
800-39-AMFAR (800-392-6327)
212-682-7440
Fax: 212-682-9812

■ **American Red Cross**
Web site: http://www.redcross.org
Contact: Contact your local chapter for information on workplace HIV/AIDS prevention and other safety programs.

■ **ETR Associates**
PO Box 1830
Santa Cruz, CA 95061-1830
Contact: Publications, 800-321-4407
408-438-4060
Fax: 408-438-4284 (orders)

■ **International Association of Physicians in AIDS Care**
225 W Washington, Ste 2200
Chicago, IL 60606
312-419-7295
Fax: 312-418-7160
E-mail: iapac@iapac.org
Web site: http://www.iapac.org

■ **National AIDS Fund**
1400 I St NW, Ste 1220
Washington, DC 20005
Contact: Melina Eller, Program Associate
202-408-4848
Fax: 202-408-1818

■ **National Association of People with AIDS**
1413 K St NW, 7th Fl
Washington, DC 20005
202-898-0414
Fax: 202-898-0435
Web site: http://www.thecure.org

■ **National Conference of State Legislatures**
1560 Broadway, Ste 700
Denver, CO 80202-5140
Contact: Michelle Solis, Marketing Dept
303-830-2200
Fax: 303-863-8003
Web site: http://www.ncsl.org

■ **National Hemophilia Foundation**
The Sotto Bldg
110 Greene St, Ste 303
New York, NY 10012
800-42-HANDI (800-424-2634)
212-219-8180
Fax: 212-966-9247
Web site: http://www.infonhf.org/

■ **National Indian AIDS Hotline**
2100 Lake Shore Ave, Ste A
Oakland, CA 94606
800-283-2437
510-444-2051
Fax: 510-444-1593

■ **National Leadership Coalition on AIDS**
1400 I St NW, Ste 1220
Washington, DC 20005
202-408-4848
Fax: 202-408-1818

■ **National Pediatric and Family HIV Resource Center**
15 S Ninth St
Newark, NJ 07107
800-362-0071
201-268-8251
Fax: 201-485-2752
E-mail: nphrc@daiid.umdnj.edu

■ **National Resource Center on Women and AIDS**
Center for Women Policy Studies
1211 Connecticut Ave NW, Ste 312
Washington, DC 20036
202-872-1770
Fax: 202-296-8962

■ **Young Adult Institute**
460 W 34th St, 11th Fl
New York, NY 10001
Contact: Professional Information
212-563-7474
Fax: 212-563-4836
TDD: 212-290-2787
E-mail: staff@yai.org
Web site: http://www.yai.org

FEDERAL AGENCIES

■ AIDS Clinical Trials Information Service

PO Box 6421
Rockville, MD 20849-6421
800-TRIALS-A (800-874-2574)
301-217-0023 (International number)
Fax: 301-738-6616
TDD: 800-243-7012
E-mail: actis@cdcnac.aspensys.com
Web site: http://www.actis.org

Provides current information on federally and privately sponsored clinical trials for persons with AIDS and HIV infection and maintains two online databases available through the National Library of Medicine, one on trial protocols (AIDSTRIALS) and one on drugs (AIDS DRUGS). A Public Health Service project sponsored by the Centers for Disease Control and Prevention, National Institute of Allergy and Infectious Diseases, Food and Drug Administration, and National Library of Medicine.

■ Bureau of Primary Health Care (BPHC)

Health Resources and Services Administration
4350 East West Hwy
Bethesda, MD 20814
Program for Special Populations Division:
301-594-4420

Mission is to increase access to comprehensive primary and preventive health care and to improve the health status of underserved and vulnerable populations, such as the homeless and people with or at risk for HIV infection. Materials are available from the National Clearinghouse for Primary Care Information: 800-400-2742.

■ CDC National AIDS Clearinghouse

Centers for Disease Control and Prevention
PO Box 6003
Rockville, MD 20849-6003
800-458-5231
Fax: 301-738-6616
TDD: 800-243-7012
Web site: http://www.cdcnac.org

Provides information about HIV/AIDS prevention and education materials, programs and services, funding, CDC surveillance activities, guidelines and statements, and HIV-related upcoming events to AIDS program managers and health professionals. It distributes single and bulk copies of CDC educational brochures, posters, reports, and videotapes.

■ HIV/AIDS Treatment Information Service

PO Box 6303
Rockville, MD 20849-6303
800-HIV-0440 (800-448-0440)
301-217-0023 (International number)
Fax: 301-738-6616
TDD: 800-243-7012
E-mail: atis@cdcnac.aspensys.com
Web site: http://www.hivatis.org

Provides information about federally approved treatment guidelines for HIV and AIDS. Staffed by bilingual (English and Spanish) health information specialists who answer questions on HIV treatment options using HSTAT, the National Library of Medicine database of HIV/AIDS treatment information, and other federal resources. Can also refer callers to an extensive network of federal information services and national and community-based organizations for treatment-related information. A Public Health Service coordinated project sponsored by the Centers for Disease Control and Prevention, Agency for Health Care Policy and Research, Health Resources and Services Administration, Indian Health Service, National Institute of Allergy and Infectious Diseases, National Library of Medicine, and Substance Abuse and Mental Health Services Administration.

■ National Center for HIV, STD & TB Prevention (NCHSTP)

Centers for Disease Control and Prevention
1600 Clifton Rd NE, M/S E-06
Atlanta, GA 30333
Communications Dept: 404-639-8063
CDC National AIDS Hotline: 800-342-AIDS (800-342-2437) English; 800-344-2437 (Spanish); 800-243-7889 (TTY)
CDC National STD Hotline: 800-227-8922
HIV/AIDS and TB Fax Information Service: 404-332-4565
Web site: http://www.cdd.gov/nchstp/od/nchstp.html

Responsible for public health surveillance and programs to prevent and control human immunodeficiency virus (HIV) infection and acquired immunodeficiency (AIDS), other sexually transmitted diseases (STDs), and tuberculosis (TB). Works closely with its partners in state and local health agencies, national and community-based organizations, business, and academia to design and test prevention programs that work.

■ National HIV-AIDS Telephone Consulting Service
800-933-3413

Established for clinical consultation telephone service for physicians and other health care professionals who have questions about providing care to people with HIV infection or AIDS. Staffed by experienced physician, nurse practitioner, and pharmacist M–F, 7:30AM–5PM PST; other times can leave message for a return call. Funded by the Health Resources and Services Administration of the Public Health Service and operates out of San Francisco General Hospital.

■ National Institute of Allergy and Infectious Diseases (NIAID)
National Institutes of Health
Bldg 31, Rm 7A-50
31 Center Dr, MSC 2520
Bethesda, MD 20892-2520
Communications Office: 301-496-5717
E-mail: ocpostoffice@flash.niaid.nih.gov
Web site: http://www.niaid.nih.gov

Conducts and supports research on the prevention, diagnosis, and treatment of infectious, immunologic, and allergic diseases, including major responsibility for research on the immune system and on its disorders, including AIDS.

■ Office of AIDS/HIV Policy
Office of Public Health and Science
U.S. Dept of Health & Human Services
Humphrey Bldg, Rm 736-E
200 Independence Ave SW
Washington, DC 20201
202-690-5560

Advises the Assistant Secretary for Health and senior HHS officials on the appropriate and timely development of HIV/AIDS policy, establishment of priorities and implementation of HIV/AIDS programs, activities, and initiatives across the Department's health agencies.

Special Needs and Populations

Family Planning and Sex Education 211
Maternal/Child and Women's Health 217
Older Adults 235
People with Disabilities 241

Family Planning and Sex Education

Products/Services Offered

Organization	web site	hotline/toll-free information line	clearinghouse/resource center	electronic information resources	database/statistical information	special campaigns/events/programs	consumer/patient education materials	publications for health professionals	classes/conferences	technical assistance	other products/services	grants/funding/awards	Page No.
Advocates for Youth			■				■	■		■		■	**212**
American Academy of Natural Family Planning									■		■		**212**
American Society for Reproductive Medicine	■						■	■	■		■	■	**212**
Association of Reproductive Health Professionals	■						■	■	■				**213**
Channing L Bete Co Inc							■						**213**
Family Health International	■							■					**213**
Health Education Services	■						■						**213**
Intermedia	■						■						**213**
Journeyworks Publishing							■						**214**
NASCO	■						■						**214**
National Abortion Federation		■					■	■	■				**214**
Population Information Program	■		■		■		■	■					**214**
Select Media							■						**215**
Sexuality Information and Education Council of the United States (SIECUS)	■		■				■	■		■			**215**

Additional Resources 215

Federal Agencies 216

Advocates for Youth

1025 Vermont Ave NW, Ste 200
Washington, DC 20005
Contact: Robin Hatziyannis
202-347-5700
Fax: 202-347-2263

Nonprofit organization works to increase the opportunities for and abilities of youth to make healthy decisions about sexuality. Provides information, education, and advocacy to youth-serving agencies and professionals, policy makers, and the media at the international, national, state, and local levels.

Clearinghouse or Resource Center
Mary Lee Tatum Resource Center: 202-347-5700; has thousands of publications and other materials on adolescent health. Support Center for School-Based Health Care: 202-347-5700; Assists school health centers in their offering of on-site reproductive and sexual health care.
National School Condom Availability Clearinghouse: 202-347-5700; Monitors and reports on programs that make condoms available to students as part of a comprehensive, community-wide reponse to unintended pregnancy and HIV/AIDS.

Consumer or Patient Education Materials
It's No Secret, 16 pp pamphlet, overview of contraception, $1 ea (1–40 copies), $.90 ea (41–500 copies); other materials include condom roses, condom key chains, posters, brochures, pamphlets. Some Spanish, French languages available. Please contact for complete catalog.

Publications for Health Professionals
Life Planning Education, 400 pp loose-leaf binder, exercises, handouts, guide, $44.95; Condom Availability in Schools, 250 pp, case studies, resources, worksheets, guide, $39.95; Transitions, quarterly newsletter, updates on current issues, $15/yr, $25/2 yrs. Please contact for complete publications list.

Technical Assistance
Advocates for Youth Media Project, 3733 Motor Ave, Ste 204, Los Angeles, CA 90034, 310-559-5700, Fax: 310-559-5784; offers information, research findings and free script consultation to writers and producers.

Grants, Funding, or Awards
Nancy Susan Reynolds Awards, honors television programs, music videos, and theatrical films that address sexuality issues in a creative, sensitive, and factual manner. Contact: Advocates for Youth Media Project, 310-559-5700.

American Academy of Natural Family Planning

615 S New Ballas Rd
St Louis, MO 63141
314-991-5766

National nonprofit organization of natural family planning professionals and supporters whose purpose is to foster, advance, and promote quality natural family planning through service, education, leadership, and research.

Classes and Conferences
Annual meeting, 3½ days, continuing education through research and development, $350. Please contact for complete list and schedule.

Other Products and Services
Accreditation of Natural Family Planning Education Programs.

American Society for Reproductive Medicine

1209 Montgomery Hwy
Birmingham, AL 35216-2809
Contact: Judy Rogers
205-978-5000
Fax: 205-978-5005
E-mail: asrm@asrm.com
Web site: http://www.asrm.com

Nonprofit organization devoted to advancing knowledge and expertise in reproductive medicine. Nationally and internationally recognized as the foremost organization promoting the study of reproduction and reproductive disorders.

Consumer or Patient Education Materials
Booklets cover several aspects of infertility, $1; Flyers provide overview of some conditions, free. Some Spanish languages available.

Publications for Health Professionals
Guidelines for Practice, pamphlet, guidelines for health professionals to aid in practice decision making, $1; Fertility and Sterility, monthly journal, juried articles, $135/yr; Menopausal Medicine, semi-annual newsletter, for physicians who treat the older female patient, free.

Classes and Conferences
Annual meeting, 6 days, postgraduate courses, seminars, $300 avg; Regional Postgraduate Courses, 3 days, $500 avg; Government workshop, 2 days, meet with legislators on reproductive medicine, free.

Other Products and Services
Patient Information Line, 205-978-5000 (M–F 8:30AM–5PM CT) accepts requests for materials.

Grants, Funding, or Awards
Research grants. Contact Jo Kirkpatrick, 205-978-5000.

■ Association of Reproductive Health Professionals

2401 Pennsylvania Ave NW, Ste 350
Washington, DC 20037-1718
Contact: Elizabeth Callihan
202-466-3825
Fax: 202-466-3826
E-mail: arhp@aol.com
Web site: http://www.arhp.org

Nonprofit interdisciplinary medical professional association whose mission is to educate health care professionals and the public on family planning, contraception, and other reproductive health issues including STDs, HIV, urogenital disorders, abortion, menopause, cancer prevention/detection, sexual health, and infertility.

Consumer or Patient Education Materials
Pamphlets include: Better Choices, Better Health; Choosing a Birth Control Method; Perimenopause; some videotapes available, Spanish languages available. Please contact for complete catalog.

Publications for Health Professionals
Clinical proceedings, 1 to 2 times/yr, topics vary, free; Health and Sexuality, quarterly journal, for clinical audience, free.

Classes and Conferences
Annual meeting, clinical conference rotates between women's health in the perimenopause and adolescent reproductive health. Contact Amy McCormick.

■ Channing L Bete Co Inc

200 State Rd
S Deerfield, MA 01373-0200
800-628-7733 (Sales and Customer Service)
413-665-7611
Fax: 800-499-6464

Publisher of informational and educational booklets, videos, posters, calendars, books, and display racks. Booklets use a distinctive, condensed format—called scriptography—which combines key words and graphics to explain a variety of subjects and is appropriate for different age groups and reading levels.

Consumer or Patient Education Materials
Booklets and videos. Topics include: abstinence, natural family planning, talking to adolescents about sex. Some Spanish language available. Please contact for pricing and ask for the Patient Education catalog.

■ Family Health International

PO Box 13950
Research Triangle Park, NC 27709
919-544-7040
Fax: 919-544-7261
Web site: http://www.fhi.org

Nonprofit research and technical assistance organization that works to improve reproductive health around the world, with an emphasis on developing countries. Is committed to helping women and men have access to safe, effective, acceptable, and affordable family planning methods to ensure that they achieve their desired number and spacing of children; preventing the spread of AIDS and other STDs; and improving the health of women and children.

Publications for Health Professionals
Network, quarterly, bulletin on family planning and reproductive health, free to developing countries; Contraceptive Technology Update Series®, slides, narrative and handouts, presentations on contraceptive technology for use in seminars, workshops, and training of health professionals, available in Spanish and French. Contact Carol Smith for pricing and complete information.

■ Health Education Services

PO Box 7126
Albany, NY 12224
518-439-7286
Fax: 518-439-7286 *51
Web site: http://www.hes.org

Nonprofit distributor of current health education, promotional publications, posters, and videos, most of which have been produced by the New York State Department of Health or the New York State Department of Environmental Conservation. (Health Education Services is a Division of Health Research Inc.)

Consumer or Patient Education Materials
Birth control method pamphlets for: condoms, creams, etc; diaphragm, IUD, natural family planning, norplant, pill, tubal ligation, vasectomy, $12/100 copies.

■ Intermedia

1300 Dexter Ave N
Seattle, WA 98109
Contact: Susan Hoffman
800-553-8336
206-284-2995
800-553-1655 (toll-free fax)
Fax: 206-283-0778
E-mail: shoffman@intermedia-inc.com
Web site: http://www.intermedia-inc.com

Publisher and distributor of video products for education and training needs on topics of social interest to customers in the U.S. and Canada.

Consumer or Patient Education Materials
Teen Contraception, video. Please contact for complete catalog.

■ Journeyworks Publishing

736 Chestnut St
Santa Cruz, CA 95060
Mailing address:
PO Box 8466
Santa Cruz, CA 95061-8466
800-775-1998
408-423-1400
Fax: 408-423-8102

Publisher of health promotion materials for clinics, hospitals, schools, and health departments covering a variety of topics including fitness, women's health, sexual abstinence, teen pregnancy prevention, STDs and HIV, mental wellness, tobacco use prevention, and smoking cessation.

Consumer or Patient Education Materials
Booklets and pamphlets. Topics include: abstinence, sexual pressure, birth control, teen pregnancy prevention, male responsibility. Free review sample, pricing varies upon quantity ordered. Materials can be customized; Some Spanish languages available. Please contact for complete catalog.

■ NASCO

901 Janesville Ave
Ft Atkinson, WI 53538-0901
Contact: Dan Christianson, Health Care Dept, 414-563-2446 x237
800-558-9595
414-563-2446
Fax: 414-563-8296
E-mail: lifeform@nascofa.com
Web site: http://www.nascofa.com

For-profit developer, producer, and distributor of health education products worldwide.

Consumer or Patient Education Materials
Laminated chart and cards, posters, folding displays, videotapes, video discs, computer programs covering responsible sexual behavior and birth control. $16–$389. Discounts available for quantity orders. Please contact for complete catalog.

■ National Abortion Federation

1436 U St NW, Ste 103
Washington , DC 20009
Contact: Susan Dudley PhD
202-667-5881
Fax: 202-667-5890

Nonprofit professional association of abortion providers that works to ensure quality care is provided.

Hotline or Toll-free Information Line
National Abortion Federation Hotline: 800-772-9100 (M–F 9:30AM–5:30PM ET) Operator assisted, crisis or emergency, referral service, answers questions.

Consumer or Patient Education Materials
Various brochures addressing female patients seeking an abortion. Please contact for complete catalog.

Publications for Health Professionals
Various brochures for physicians providing facts and assistance about abortion. Please contact for complete publications list.

Classes and Conferences
Annual Conference and Risk Management Conference. Please contact for complete list and schedule.

■ Population Information Program

Johns Hopkins Center for Communication Programs
111 Market Pl, Ste 310
Baltimore, MD 21202-4024
410-659-6300
Fax: 410-659-6266
E-mail: ccp@charm.net
Web site: http://www.charm.net/~ccp/pip.html

Nonprofit organization whose purpose is to strengthen family planning and related health programs in developing countries through a variety of information services.

Clearinghouse or Resource Center
Media/Materials Clearinghouse: 410-659-6300; 111 Market Pl, Ste 310, Baltimore, MD 21202-4024; Health communication materials that promote family planning, reproductive health, and related issues include: videos, audiotapes, pamphlets, posters, flipcharts; free to developing countries, at cost to developed countries.

Database or Statistical Information
POPLINE, the world's largest bibliographic population database providing citations and abstracts of the worldwide literature on population, family planning, and related health issues. Free to developing countries. Available online at the National Library of Medicine.

Consumer or Patient Education Materials

Various materials available through the Media/Materials Clearinghouse. Contact for complete information.

Publications for Health Professionals

Population Reports, quarterly journal, overview of important developments, $2 ea; What's New, semi-annual newsletter, annotated, illustrated listing of health communication materials on a specific topic, $1; Papers, occasionally, exploration of topics in health and family planning communication, $5.

■ Select Media

60 Warren St, 5th Fl
New York, NY 10007
Contact: Rebecca Chertok
800-707-6334
212-732-4437
Fax: 212-732-4439
E-mail: selmedbw@interport.net

For-profit distributor of educational films, videos, and CD-ROMs specializing in health and social issues.

Consumer or Patient Education Materials

Making Choices, interactive videodisc, sexual decision-making for teens, $495; In Due Time, video, strategies for postponing parenthood, $275; No Time Soon, video, increasing male responsibility, $275. Please contact for complete catalog.

■ Sexuality Information and Education Council of the United States (SIECUS)

130 W 42nd St, Ste 350
New York, NY 10036-7802
Contact: Publications Dept, 212-819-9770 x303
212-819-9770
Fax: 212-819-9776
E-mail: siecus@siecus.org
Web site: http://www.siecus.org/

International nonprofit organization that develops, collects, and disseminates information, promotes comprehensive education about sexuality, and advocates the right of individuals to make responsible sexual choices.

Clearinghouse or Resource Center

Mary S Calderone Library: 212-819-9770 x304; 130 W 42nd St, Ste 350, New York, NY 10036-7802; books, articles, education curricula, journals, newsletters and extensive vertical reference files; books and journals indexed in SIECUS database, searches free to members, $10 for nonmembers.

Consumer or Patient Education Materials

Various booklets, bibliographies, fact sheets, reports. Pricing varies upon quantity ordered. Some Spanish languages available. Please contact for complete catalog.

Publications for Health Professionals

SIECUS Report, bimonthly journal, free to members or $67.50/yr; Sexuality Education for the 21st Century, 16-min video, explains and makes case for comprehensive sexuality education, $12.95; Community Action Kit: An Information Pack to Support Comprehensive Sexuality Education, updated 1995, $19.95. Please contact for complete publications list.

Technical Assistance

Library information services for professionals, media, and general public; workshops for educators; technical assistance to communities.

ADDITIONAL RESOURCES

■ Alan Guttmacher Institute

120 Wall St, 21st Fl
New York, NY 10005
212-248-1111
Fax: 212-248-1951
E-mail: info@agi-usa.org
Web site: http://www.agi-usa.org

■ Best Friends Foundation

4455 Connecticut Ave, Ste 310
Washington, DC 20008
202-237-8156
Fax: 202-822-9276

■ Child Trends Inc

4301 Connecticut Ave NW, Ste 100
Washington, DC 20008
202-362-5580
Fax: 202-362-5533
Web site: http://www.childtrends.org

■ Coalition on Addiction, Pregnancy and Parenting

349 Broadway, 2nd Fl
Cambridge, MA 02139
617-661-3991
Fax: 617-661-7277

■ **ETR Associates**
PO Box 1830
Santa Cruz, CA 95061-1830
Contact: Publications, 800-321-4407
408-438-4060
Fax: 408-438-4284 (Orders)

■ **The National Campaign To Prevent Teen Pregnancy**
2100 M St NW, Ste 500
Washington, DC 20037
202-857-8655
Fax: 202-331-7735

■ **National Family Planning and Reproductive Health Association**
122 C St NW, Ste 380
Washington, DC 20001
202-628-3535
Fax: 202-737-2690

■ **National Organization on Adolescent Pregnancy, Parenting, and Prevention**
1319 F St NW, Ste 401
Washington, DC 20004
888-766-2777
202-783-5770
Fax: 202-783-5775

■ **Natural Family Planning Center of Washington, DC**
8514 Bradmoor Dr
Bethesda, MD 20817-3810
301-897-9323
Fax: 301-571-5267
E-mail: hklaus@act.net

■ **Planned Parenthood Federation of America**
810 Seventh Ave
New York, NY 10019-5882
Contact: Marketing Dept, 800-669-0156
800-230-PLAN (800-230-7526)
212-541-7800
Fax: 212-261-4352

FEDERAL AGENCIES

■ **National Institute of Child Health and Human Development (NICHD)**
National Institutes of Health
Bldg 31, Rm 2A-32
31 Center Dr, MSC 2425
Bethesda, MD 20892-2425
Communications Branch: 301-496-5133
Fax: 301-496-7101
Web site: http://www.nih.gov/nichd

Conducts and supports basic research and supports laboratory, clinical, and epidemiologic research on the reproductive, neurobiologic, developmental, social and behavioral processes that determine and maintain the health of children, adults, families, and populations. Professional materials available on sudden infant death syndrome, developmental disabilities, pregnancy, and genetics; consumer materials available on cesarean childbirth, Down syndrome, oral contraception, and vasectomy.

■ **Office of Population Affairs (OPA)**
Office of Public Health and Science
U.S. Dept of Health & Human Services
4330 East West Hwy
Bethesda, MD 20814
301-594-4000

OPA Clearinghouse
PO Box 30686
Bethesda, MD 20824-0686
301-654-6190
Fax: 301-907-9655

Assists in making comprehensive voluntary family planning services readily available to all persons desiring such services and coordinates domestic population and family planning research with the present and future needs of family planning programs.

Maternal/Child and Women's Health

Products/Services Offered

Organization	web site	hotline/toll-free information line	clearinghouse/resource center	electronic information resources	database/statistical information	special campaigns/events/programs	consumer/patient education materials	publications for health professionals	classes/conferences	technical assistance	other products/services	grants/funding/awards	Page No.
American Academy of Pediatrics	■					■	■	■					219
American College of Obstetricians and Gynecologists	■		■				■	■	■				219
American Social Health Association	■	■											219
American Sudden Infant Death Syndrome (SIDS) Institute	■	■			■		■	■	■	■		■	220
The Arc	■						■	■					220
ASPO/Lamaze (American Society for Psychoprophylaxis in Obstetrics)	■	■	■				■	■	■				220
Association of SIDS and Infant Mortality Programs										■			221
Association of Women's Health, Obstetric, and Neonatal Nurses				■			■	■	■	■		■	221
Best Start Inc							■			■			221
Child Health Foundation							■	■				■	222
Clinical Reference Systems Ltd	■										■		222
Customized Communications Inc							■						222
DES Action	■						■						222
Endometriosis Association		■				■	■	■					223
FastMark Inc							■						223
Group B Strep Association	■						■	■					223
Healthy Mothers, Healthy Babies								■	■	■			223
March of Dimes Birth Defects Foundation	■	■					■	■		■			224
Maternity Center Association							■	■				■	224
Mayo Clinic Health Information				■			■						224
Medcom Inc	■						■						224

Products/Services Offered

Organization	web site	hotline/toll-free information line	clearinghouse/resource center	electronic information resources	database/statistical information	special campaigns/events/programs	consumer/patient education materials	publications for health professionals	classes/conferences	technical assistance	other products/services	grants/funding/awards	Page No.
Motherwell Maternity Health and Fitness	■						■		■	■			**225**
National Asian Women's Health Organization							■	■	■				**225**
National Association of Childbearing Centers					■		■	■	■	■			**225**
National Association of Nurse Practitioners in Reproductive Health	■						■			■			**225**
National Association of Pediatric Nurse Associates and Practitioners							■	■	■	■		■	**226**
National Association of Women's Health Professionals								■	■	■	■		**226**
National Center for Children in Poverty	■							■					**226**
National Center for Education in Maternal and Child Health (NCEMCH)	■				■		■	■					**227**
National Council of La Raza Center for Health Promotion	■		■				■			■			**227**
National Council on Alcoholism and Drug Dependence Inc (NCADD)	■					■	■						**227**
National Women's Health Resource Center							■	■		■			**228**
Public Health Foundation	■							■	■	■			**228**
Reproductive Toxicology Center					■								**228**
Vida Health Communications Inc							■						**228**
Wellstart International							■	■	■	■			**229**
The Willapa Bay Company	■						■						**229**
Zero to Three: National Center for Infants, Toddlers and Families	■						■	■		■			**229**
Additional Resources													**230**
Federal Agencies													**231**

American Academy of Pediatrics

141 Northwest Point Blvd
PO Box 927
Elk Grove Village, IL 60007-0927
Contact: Publications Dept, 800-433-9016
847-228-5005
Fax: 847-228-1281
E-mail: kidsdocs@aap.org
Web site: http://www.aap.org

Nonprofit organization of 50,000 pediatricians dedicated to the health, safety, and well-being of infants, children, adolescents, and young adults. Activities include advocacy for children and youth; public education; research; professional education; membership service and advocacy for pediatricians. More than 30 committees develop positions and programs for interest areas including nutrition; pediatric AIDS; substance abuse; child abuse and neglect; children with disabilities.

Special Campaigns, Events, or Programs

Child Health Month, October, packet includes fact sheets, camera-ready information, brochures, posters, and product catalog. Contact Division of Member Communications.

Consumer or Patient Education Materials

Child Health Guide, 40 pp booklet, gives parents basic information about preventive services and personal record tracker; Child Health Record, 24 pp booklet, forms for tracking and recording health info; Short Medical Record, compact medical record keeper; many other books, booklets, videos. Some Spanish languages available. Please contact for complete catalog.

Publications for Health Professionals

Clinician's Handbook of Preventive Services, handbook, to create a protocol of preventive care and concise reference source, $20; Guidelines for Perinatal Care, manual, multidisciplinary approach to perinatal care, $55; Pediatric Nutrition Handbook, manual, nutritional requirements and impact on health, $69.95. Please contact for complete publications list.

American College of Obstetricians and Gynecologists

409 12th St SW
Washington, DC 20024
Mailing Address:
PO Box 96920
Washington, DC 20090-6920
Contact: Distribution Center (Orders), 800-762-2264
202-638-5577
Fax: 202-484-5107
TDD: 202-488-1426
E-mail: pvanhine@acog.com
Web site: http://www.acog.com

Nonprofit professional organization of more than 33,000 physicians specializing in obstetric-gynecologic care. Serves as a strong advocate for quality health care for women; maintains highest standards of clinical practice and continuing education; promotes patient education, understanding of, and involvement in medical care; and increases awareness of changing issues facing women's health care.

Clearinghouse or Resource Center

ACOG Resource Center: 202-863-2518; library of information; also samples of many ACOG materials.

Consumer or Patient Education Materials

Pamphlets and booklets, series of over 100 titles, covering full range of health care topics for women of all ages, including: Staying Healthy, 32 pp guide to reducing risk factors; Menopause Packet includes preventing osteoporosis. Some Spanish language available. Please contact for pricing and complete catalog.

Publications for Health Professionals

Guidelines for Women's Health Care, 256 pp book, synopsis of policy and management issues, $50; Guidelines for Perinatal Care, 320 pp, multidisciplinary approach directed toward improving the outcome of pregnancy, $40. Please contact for complete publications list.

Classes and Conferences

Annual meeting, 1 week; Regional meetings, 3 days. Please contact for complete list and schedule.

American Social Health Association

100 Capitola Dr
Durham, NC 27713
Mailing Address:
PO Box 13827
Research Triangle Park, NC 27709-3827
Contact: Customer Service, 919-361-8422 or 800-783-9877
ASHA HealthLine: 800-972-8500
919-361-8400
Fax: 919-361-8425
Web site: http://sunsite.unc.edu/asha/

Nonprofit advocacy organization whose mission is to stop the spread of STDs through educational materials, information, and referrals to the public and health care providers. Operates the National AIDS Hotline, National STD Hotline, National Herpes Hotline; and the First Step Hotline and Health Check Hotlines in North Carolina.

Hotline or Toll-free Information Line

FIRST STEP Hotline: 800-FOR-BABY (800-367-2229) and Health Check Hotline 800-474-900 (M–F 9AM–7PM ET); both only in North Carolina. Answers questions and provides technical assistance.

■ American Sudden Infant Death Syndrome (SIDS) Institute

6065 Roswell Rd, Ste 876
Atlanta, GA 30328
Contact: Heather Murray, LMSW
800-232-SIDS (800-232-7437)
800-847-SIDS (800-847-7437) (in-state)
404-843-1030
Fax: 404-843-0577
E-mail: prevent@sids.org
Web site: http://www.sids.org

National nonprofit organization dedicated to the prevention of SIDS and the promotion of infant health through the provision of state-of-the-art clinical services and empathetic family support. Mission is to eliminate SIDS in the near future through an aggressive comprehensive national program of research, education, and health care.

Hotline or Toll-free Information Line

American SIDS Institute: 800-232-SIDS (800-232-7437); (in GA): 800-847-SIDS (800-847-7437) (M–F 8AM–5PM ET) Operator assisted, crisis or emergency, answers questions, requests for information.

Database or Statistical Information

Some statistical information on SIDS available. Contact Donna Ramaswamy, Epidemiologist, 404-843-1030.

Consumer or Patient Education Materials

Toward An Understanding and Prevention and Improved Infant Health; Grief and Bereavement; Raising Funds to Fight SIDS; all brochures, free. Spanish languages available. Please contact for complete catalog.

Publications for Health Professionals

Research articles available. Please contact for complete publications list.

Classes and Conferences

Please contact for complete list and schedule.

Technical Assistance

Can respond to questions regarding the use of home monitoring equipment, phone modems, and telemedicine related to SIDS and program services. Social worker and nurses also available to respond to questions. Please contact April Levine, Director of Development, for information on special programs.

Grants, Funding, or Awards

Please contact April Levine, Director of Development, for information.

■ The Arc

500 E Border St, Ste 300
Arlington, TX 76010
Contact: Ann Balson
800-433-5255
817-261-6003
Fax: 817-277-3491
TDD: 817-277-0553
E-mail: thearc@metronet.com
Web site: http://thearc.org/welcome.html

Nonprofit volunteer organization solely devoted to improving the lives of all children and adults with mental retardation and their families. Fosters research and education regarding the prevention of mental retardation in infants and young children.

Consumer or Patient Education Materials

Brochures: Think Before You Drink; take care of yourself; free with SASE; You and Your Baby, booklet, covers prevention measures for planning healthy pregnancy, $3.50 ea, discounts available for quantity orders. Please contact for complete catalog.

Publications for Health Professionals

Preventing Fetal Alcohol Syndrome and Other Alcohol-Related Birth Defects: Teacher's Manual, curriculum, $10; 10 Projects for Preventing Fetal Alcohol Syndrome and Other Alcohol-Related Birth Defects, manual, for student involvement in community prevention activities, $5; FAS action kits, for community awareness and education activities, $3.50. Please contact for complete publications list.

■ ASPO/Lamaze (American Society for Psychoprophylaxis in Obstetrics)

1200 19th St NW, Ste 300
Washington, DC 20036-2422
Contact: Membership Services
800-368-4404
202-857-1128
Fax: 202-223-4579
E-mail: aspo@sba.com
Web site: http://www.lamaze_childbirth.com/

International nonprofit society whose purpose is to develop and promote standards for prenatal education, Lamaze childbirth education, early parenting education, and family-centered maternity care through education, advocacy, and reform.

Hotline or Toll-free Information Line
ASPO/Lamaze Information Line: 800-368-4404 (M–F 9AM–5PM ET) Referral service, answers questions, and requests for materials.

Clearinghouse or Resource Center
Lamaze Media Center: 800-368-4404; 1200 19th St NW, Ste 300, Washington, DC 20036; Books, videotapes and audiotapes pertaining to pregnancy, labor, birth, breastfeeding, and early parenting; ASPO/Lamaze specialty items. Costs range: free to $60. Catalog available.

Consumer or Patient Education Materials
Lamaze Parents Magazine, pregnancy, labor & delivery concerns, free; Lamaze Baby Magazine, early parents' concerns, free; You and Your Baby, video, early parenting tips, free. Some Spanish languages available. Please contact for complete catalog.

Publications for Health Professionals
Journal of Perinatal Education, quarterly, for childbirth educators or others interested in perinatal education, $39/issue; $140/yr.

Classes and Conferences
Three Advanced Skill workshops: Breastfeeding Support Specialist, Labor Support Specialist, and Teen Specialist Program; 2 days, $250 each. Annual conference, 3 days, educational sessions, paper/poster presentations, commercial exhibits, varied costs. Please contact for complete list and schedule.

■ Association of SIDS and Infant Mortality Programs

Center for Infant and Child Loss
630 W Fayette St, Rm 5-684
Baltimore, MD 21201-1585
Contact: Jodi Shaefer RN, PhD, President
410-706-5062
Fax: 410-706-0146

National nonprofit association of health and human service providers building programs of counseling, education, advocacy, and research to ensure a supportive community response for those affected by infant and child death and to reduce the risk of death for future children.

Technical Assistance
Consultation and technical assistance to organizations working with infant mortality.

■ Association of Women's Health, Obstetric, and Neonatal Nurses

700 14th St NW, Ste 600
Washington, DC 20005-2006
800-673-8499
202-662-1600
800-245-0231 (Canada)
Fax: 202-737-0575

Nonprofit professional association of nearly 22,000 members promoting excellence in nursing practice to improve the health of women and newborns throughout the U.S., Canada, and abroad.

Electronic Information Resources
Fax-on-Demand: 800-395-7373, many documents available including position statements, Ask the Experts reprints from Voice newsletter, clinical commentary, research grants, and other programs. Free.

Consumer or Patient Education Materials
Various materials available. Please contact for complete catalog.

Publications for Health Professionals
AWHONN Voice, monthly newsletter, critical and current news, free with membership or $35–$69. Please contact for complete publications list.

Classes and Conferences
Intrapartum Nursing Summit, 2 days, $225–$275; Perinatal Home Care, 2 days, $259–$279; Primary Care for Women, 2 days, $299–$319. Please contact for complete list and schedule.

Technical Assistance
Practice Line to assist members with clinical practice issues: 202-662-1638; Reference literature searches for members, $25 each search, contact Kathie DeGeorges, 202-662-1621.

Grants, Funding, or Awards
Research Grants and Research Utilization Program. Contact Corinne Haslett, 202-662-1613.

■ Best Start Inc

3500 E Fletcher Ave, Ste 519
Tampa, FL 33613
Contact: James H Lindenberger
800-277-4975
813-971-2119
Fax: 813-971-2280
E-mail: best@holonet.net

Nonprofit social marketing agency serving public health, education, and social service organizations. Develops and publishes training, educational, outreach, advertising materials, and the professional journal, Social Marketing Quarterly.

Consumer or Patient Education Materials
Your New Life Magazine, 20 pp, information guide to breastfeeding for teens and teen mothers, $1.95; Pamphlets on breastfeeding, pricing varies upon

quantity ordered; Low literacy; Spanish languages available. Please contact for complete catalog.

Technical Assistance

Social marketing research, strategy formation, campaign development and implementation, and technical assistance services.

■ Child Health Foundation

Century Plaza
10630 Little Patuxent Pkwy, Ste 325
Columbia, MD 21044
Contact: Charlene D Riikonen
301-596-4514
Fax: 410-992-5641
E-mail: chf@clark.net

Nonprofit organization that works through a unique network of health professionals and organizations committed to improving health policies and practices. Mission is to save the greatest number of children's lives at the lowest possible cost.

Consumer or Patient Education Materials

When Your Baby Has Diarrhea, flyer, specific instructions for treatment, free; Prevent Diarrhea, information card (also in Spanish and Portuguese), free.

Publications for Health Professionals

CHF News, quarterly newsletter, organization news and recent health findings, free single copy, $20/yr; Training Manual for Treatment and Prevention of Childhood Diarrhea, 81 pp manual, ORT, proper nutrition, and hygiene, $29.95; ORS Fact Sheet, flyer, specific facts about formula, free.

Grants, Funding, or Awards

Annual small grants proposal campaign for interested health workers, investigators, and community organizations in the U.S. and abroad. Submit written request to Small Grants Program for information and application.

■ Clinical Reference Systems Ltd

7100 E Belleview Ave, Ste 208
Greenwood Village, CO 80111-1635
Contact: Ellen Graves, Marketing Coordinator
800-237-8401
303-220-1661
Fax: 303-220-1685
E-mail: crs-info@cliniref.com
Web site: http://www.patienteducation.com

Publisher of patient education and clinical reference software for the international healthcare community. Committed to development of computer-based health information to enhance communication between provider and patient. More than 30,000 programs are now at work in physician offices, clinics, hospitals, medical school residency programs, occupational clinics, medical and consumer libraries.

Other Products and Services

Software programs that produce customized patient information handouts (some available in Spanish). Women's Health Advisor, over 500 handouts, including information on birth control, STDs and new baby care; Pediatric Advisor, over 800 handouts; ACOG Patient Advisior, patient education pamphlets of the American College of Obstetrics and Gynecology. Please contact for complete catalog and topic index.

■ Customized Communications Inc

2001 E Randol Mill Rd
Arlington, TX 76011
Mailing Address:
PO Box 5566
Arlington, TX 76005
Contact: Lori O'Malley
800-476-2253
817-459-2703
Fax: 817-459-3557

For-profit company specializing in customized patient education and marketing materials; available for breast health and mammography, MRI, CT, radiology, anesthesia, surgery, ob/gyn, and well women's health.

Consumer or Patient Education Materials

Prenatal, labor and delivery, postpartum care guides. Pricing varies upon quantity ordered; Materials can be customized; Spanish languages available. Please contact for complete catalog.

■ DES Action

1615 Broadway, #510
Oakland, CA 94612
Contact: Pat Cody
800-DES-9288 (800-337-9288)
510-465-4011
Fax: 510-465-4815
E-mail: desact@well.com
Web site: http://www.desaction.org

Nonprofit consumer group for those exposed in utero to synthetic estrogen diethylstilbestrol. Provides medical information and referrals.

Consumer or Patient Education Materials

Fertility and Pregnancy Guide for DES Daughters and Sons, $6; booklets on DES exposure and DES Daughters, both free. Please contact for complete catalog.

■ Endometriosis Association

8585 N 76th Pl
Milwaukee, WI 53223
Contact: Mary Lou Ballweg
800-992-3636
414-355-2200
Fax: 414-355-6065

International nonprofit self-help organization of women with endometriosis and others interested in exchanging information about endometriosis, offering mutual support and help to those affected by endometriosis, educating the public and medical community about the disease, and promoting research related to it.

Hotline or Toll-free Information Line
Endometriosis Association Information Line: 800-992-3636 24-hr automated line, requests for materials.

Special Campaigns, Events, or Programs
Endometriosis Awareness Week, in March, brochures. Contact Chapter or Support Group Coordinator.

Consumer or Patient Education Materials
Audiotapes and videotapes; The Endometriosis Sourcebook, 500 pp comprehensive resource, $15; Diagnostic Kit, $3.75; Informational brochure, available in 14 languages including one for teens, free. Please contact for complete catalog.

Publications for Health Professionals
Newsletter, bimonthly, treatment, coping, research info, free with membership. Please contact for complete publications list.

■ FastMark Inc

125 University Ave, Ste 250
Palo Alto, CA 94301
Contact: Leah Jacobs, Marketing Manager
800-406-2035
415-327-7760
Fax: 415-327-7734
E-mail: fastmark.com

Publisher of first aid and wellness reference guides using a patented laminated format that allows thickly laminated products to lie flat when folded. Health topics include: women's health, children's health, seniors' health, allergies/asthma, diabetes, heart disease, fitness, nutrition, and stress management.

Consumer or Patient Education Materials
5-panel folded laminated brochures, covers self-care and prevention: FastCare for Women, topics include anemia, breast issues, osteoporosis; FastCare for Children, covers 7 topics. Pricing varies upon quantity ordered; Materials can be customized; Please contact for complete catalog.

■ Group B Strep Association

PO Box 16515
Chapel Hill, NC 27516
Contact: Gina Burns
919-932-5344
Fax: 919-932-5344
Web site: http://www.groupbstrep.org

Nonprofit organization that is dedicated to the prevention of GBS infection. Seeks to educate the public about GBS disease, to promote screening of mothers during pregnancy, and the development of a vaccine.

Consumer or Patient Education Materials
Awareness of Group B Streptococcus Infection during Pregnancy, pamphlet, $.30 each, in multiple quantities of 25, additional discounts for quantities over 100.

Publications for Health Professionals
GBSA Newsletter, $20/yr; GBSA Visionaries, documentary video, $50.

■ Healthy Mothers, Healthy Babies

409 12th St SW, rm 309
Washington, DC 20024-2188
Contact: Leslie Dunne
202-863-2458
Fax: 202-554-4346

National nonprofit coalition of health care providers and administrators concerned about the health of pregnant women, children, and families. Helps develop networks for sharing information among groups and assists in the establishment of additional Healthy Mothers, Healthy Babies coalitions in states and communities.

Publications for Health Professionals
Quarterly newsletters include: Healthy Mothers, Healthy Babies News, for maternal and child health professionals; Immunization Education and Action Committee News, for immunization professionals; POWER News, for outreach workers; all free. Please contact for complete publications list.

Classes and Conferences
National Conference, 3 days, biennially, health education conference, $300.

Technical Assistance
Coalition building, cultural competence, and partnerships.

■ March of Dimes Birth Defects Foundation

National Office
1275 Mamaroneck Ave
White Plains, NY 10605
Contact: Fulfillment Center, 800-367-6630, PO Box 1657, Wilkes-Barre, PA 18703-1657
888-MO-DIMES (888-663-4637)
914-428-7100
E-mail: resourcecenter@modimes.org
Web site: http://www.modimes.org/

National voluntary health organization whose mission is to improve the health of babies by preventing birth defects and infant mortality with 101 chapters nationwide. Supports programs of research, community services, education, and advocacy.

Hotline or Toll-free Information Line
March of Dimes Birth Defects Foundation Information Line: 888-MO-DIMES (888-663-4637) 24-hr operator assisted, answers questions.

Consumer or Patient Education Materials
Numerous booklets, pamphlets, information sheets, videos on topics including alcohol, drugs, and smoking during pregnancy; genetics; nutrition and folic acid; preconception and prenatal care. Some Spanish languages available. Please contact for complete catalog.

Publications for Health Professionals
Healthy Babies, Healthy Business, An Employer's Guidebook on Improving Maternal and Infant Health, guidebook and worksheets, $95 (diskette, $110) Please contact for complete publications list.

Technical Assistance
Babies and You, worksite prenatal health promotion program, please call your local March of Dimes chapter or the National Office's Worksite Programs Division at 914-997-4441.

■ Maternity Center Association

281 Park Ave S, 5th Fl
New York, NY 10010
Contact: Josie Galarza, 212-777-5000 x32
212-777-5000
Fax: 212-777-9320

Nonprofit health organization that promotes family centered maternity care through education, advocacy, and demonstration projects.

Consumer or Patient Education Materials
Brochures include: Comfort during Pregnancy; Relaxation and Breathing, $.50 ea. Spanish languages available. Please contact for complete catalog.

Publications for Health Professionals
Birth Atlas, charts, for childbirth educators, $53; Growing Uterus Charts, charts, for childbirth educators, $42.95; Prelude to Action II Reforming Maternity Care, book, for health care professionals, $16.95.

Grants, Funding, or Awards
Hazel Corbin Scholarship Fund, for graduate nurse-midwifery students. Write for information.

■ Mayo Clinic Health Information

200 First St SW
Rochester, MN 55905
Contact: Mike Casey or Dan Newton
800-430-9699
Fax: 507-284-5410

Division of the Mayo Clinic that produces consumer health publications including newsletters, booklets, books, and CD-ROMs, providing people with timely, reliable, and easy-to-understand health, wellness, and self-care information. Materials appropriate for health promotion initiatives.

Electronic Information Resources
Mayo Health Oasis online health information web site: http://www.mayo.ivi.com

Consumer or Patient Education Materials
Mayo Clinic Complete Book of Pregnancy & Baby's First Year, 768 pp book, comprehensive guide, $30. Please contact for volume discounts and complete catalog.

■ Medcom Inc

6060 Phyllis Dr
Cypress, CA 90630
Contact: Teri Armstrong, Marketing, 714-891-1443 x225
800-541-0253
714-891-1443
Fax: 714-898-4852
Web site: http://www.medcominc.com

For-profit producer and worldwide distributor of multimedia healthcare educational products, mainly video programs and related print material, for health care professionals, their patients, and health-conscious people everywhere.

Consumer or Patient Education Materials
Ob/Gyn Having Your Baby Series of videos include: Prenatal Care, $39.95; Making A Difference: A Mother's Guide to Prenatal Care, $99. Please contact for complete catalog.

Motherwell Maternity Health and Fitness

1106 Stratford Dr
Carlisle, PA 17013
Contact: Bonnie Berk RN
800-MOM-WELL (800-666-9355)
717-258-4641
Fax: 717-258-1241
E-mail: momwell@epix.net
Web site: http://www.epix.net/~momwell

For-profit provider of medically-proven health promotion programs for pregnant women and new mothers. Available to health care facilities, fitness facilities, corporations, and private practitioners for their patients, community, and employees.

Consumer or Patient Education Materials

Motherwell, 90-min video, home exercises including relaxation, $34.95. Please contact for complete catalog.

Classes and Conferences

Motherwell Land Instructor Certification, 3 days, train-the-trainer workshop, $600; Motherwell Water Fitness Instructor Certification, 2 days, train-the-trainer workshop, $300. Please contact for complete list and schedule.

Technical Assistance

Speaker, author, and consultant addressing special health and fitness needs of pregnant women and new mothers.

National Asian Women's Health Organization

250 Montgomery St, Ste 410
San Francisco, CA 94104
415-989-9747
Fax: 415-989-9758

Nonprofit, community based health advocacy organization committed to improving the overall health status of Asian women and girls. Develops and implements a broad agenda for Asian women's health.

Consumer or Patient Education Materials

Pathways to Wellness: A California Statewide Resource Handbook for Asian Women and Girls, handbook, articles on how to take better care of your health, $13.

Publications for Health Professionals

Coming Together: Proceedings of the First National Asian Women's Health Conference, 100 pp book, $15; Perceptions of Risk: The Factors Influencing Use of Reproductive and Sexual Health Services by Asian American Women, report on Asian women's attitudes on health care services, $10. Please contact for complete publications list.

Classes and Conferences

Annual conference, 2 days, educational materials on different health topics.

National Association of Childbearing Centers

3123 Gottschall Rd
Perkiomenville, PA 18074
Contact: Kate Bauer, Executive Director
215-234-8068
Fax: 215-234-8829
E-mail: birthctrs@midwives.org

Nonprofit membership organization dedicated to developing quality, holistic services for childbearing families that promote self-reliance and confidence in birth and parenting. Most comprehensive resource on birth centers; works on public and policy levels in government, industry, and the health professions; collects and disseminates information on birth centers; sets national standards for birth center operation; promotes state regulation for licensure; and national accreditation.

Database or Statistical Information

NACC Uniform Data Set, database program based on Epi6 for birth center practices to collect outcome data. Please contact for cost.

Consumer or Patient Education Materials

The Birth Center, brochure, generic educational brochure, $1; Parent Information Service, for consumers looking for birth center, please send written request and $1 donation.

Publications for Health Professionals

Quality Improvement Manual, manual, foundation and forms for implementation, $150; Sample Birth Center Policies and Procedures, loose leaf manual and diskette, $300.

Classes and Conferences

How to Start a Birth Center, 2-day workshop, $350. Please contact for complete list and schedule.

Technical Assistance

NACC Consulting Network, services include: on-site, telephone, birth center practicum.

National Association of Nurse Practitioners in Reproductive Health

1090 Vermont Ave NW, Ste 800
Washington, DC 20005
Contact: Alison Heron
202-408-7025
Fax: 202-408-0902
E-mail: nanprh@aol.com
Web site: http://www.nurse.org/nanprh

Nonprofit association representing nurse practitioners who practice in obstetrics, gynecology, contraception, reproductive endocrinology, and infertility. Purpose is to assure quality reproductive health services by nurse practitioners. Is the national accrediting body of woman's health (OB/GYN) nurse practitioner programs and is recognized by the U.S. Department of Education.

Consumer or Patient Education Materials
A Nurse Practitioner for My Reproductive Health?, in English and Spanish.
Technical Assistance
Experts available for a wide variety of reproductive health topics.

■ National Association of Pediatric Nurse Associates and Practitioners

1101 Kings Hwy N, #206
Cherry Hill, NJ 08034-1912
Contact: Joe Casey
609-667-1773
Fax: 609-667-7187
E-mail: 74224.51@compuserve.com or napnapi@aol.com

Nonprofit interdisciplinary membership association for professionals who influence health care for women. Promotes excellence and provides leadership, resources, and collegial support to professionals who influence and champion quality health care for women and their communities.

Consumer or Patient Education Materials
Baby's First Cold; Mommy, Daddy, What's AIDS?; Starting Solids; brochures for parents, $31–$35 for 100 copies.
Publications for Health Professionals
Scope of Practice, brochure, $31 for 100; Risk Management Guide, booklet, $12 for 100. Please contact for complete publications list.
Classes and Conferences
Annual conference, 4 days, $360. Please contact for complete list and schedule.
Technical Assistance
Special interest groups on: childcare, immunization, and school-based health clinics.
Grants, Funding, or Awards
Several research grant opportunities for members.

■ National Association of Women's Health Professionals

175 W Jackson Blvd, Ste A-1711
Chicago, IL 60604-9674
Contact: C Coglianese
312-786-1468
Fax: 312-786-0376

Nonprofit interdisciplinary membership association for professionals who influence health care for women. Promotes excellence and provides leadership, resources, and collegial support to professionals who influence and champion quality health care for women and their communities.

Publications for Health Professionals
Business of Women's Health, one-time compilation of articles on management, strategic planning, marketing for women's health services, $45; Focus, quarterly newsletter, provides information specific to needs of those responsible for women's health programs, included with membership; audiotapes, covers range of women's health topics, $10–$12. Please contact for complete publications list.
Classes and Conferences
Annual Women's Health Conference, 3–4 days, addresses both clinical and business aspects of women's health, $415–$595. Please contact for complete list and schedule.
Technical Assistance
Members can access women's health experts who share information, offer site visits, and provide resources in outcomes measurement, managed care contracting, strategic planning, clinical issues, educational programming, and more.
Other Products and Services
Peer mentor program, faxed briefings on women's health.

■ National Center for Children in Poverty

Columbia School of Public Health
154 Haven Ave
New York, NY 10032
Contact: Carole Oshinsky, 212-304-7130
212-304-7100
Fax: 212-544-4200
E-mail: cjo1@columbia.edu
Web site: http://cpmcnet.columbia.edu/dept/nccp/

Nonprofit organization whose mission is to identify and promote strategies that reduce the number of young children living in poverty in the U.S., and that improve the life chances of the millions of children under six who are growing up poor.

Publications for Health Professionals
News and Issues, 3 issues annually, free; Map and Track: State Initiatives for Young Children and Families, 171 pp, $19.95; Alive and Well? A Research and Policy Review of Health Programs for Poor Young Children, 132 pp, $11.95. Please contact for complete publications list.

■ National Center for Education in Maternal and Child Health (NCEMCH)

2000 15th St N, Ste 701
Arlington, VA 22201-2617
Contact: Olivia Kredel Pickett, Director of Information Services
703-524-7802
Fax: 703-524-9335
Web site: http://www.ncemch.georgetown.edu

Federally funded resource center. Provides information services, technical assistance, and educational materials to organizations, agencies, and individuals with an interest in maternal and child health (MCH). Maintains a reference collection of policy papers, agency reports, conference proceedings, annuals, guidelines, sample consumer education materials, curricula, and materials on the history of MCH services. Some staff speak Spanish and French and also utilize services of Georgetown University School of Linguistics to assist in responding to foreign language mail requests. NCEMCH's library is publicly accessible by appointment. Publications are disseminated through NCEMCH's sister organization, the National Maternal and Child Health Clearinghouse, 2070 Chain Bridge Rd, Ste 450, Vienna, VA 22182-2536; 703-821-8955; (fax) 703-821-2098.

Database or Statistical Information
Maintains database of maternal and child health organizations and publications. A thesaurus is available. Also maintains files on conferences, and on projects funded by or administered by the Maternal and Child Health Bureau, particularly Special Projects of Regional and National Significance (SPRANS) and Community Integrated Service Systems (CISS). Beginning in 1992, materials in the reference collection are listed in the Combined Health Information Database (CHID), which is available through the online vendor, OVID Technologies.

Consumer or Patient Education Materials
Materials available on topics such as prenatal care, nutrition, infant care, breastfeeding, child health, dental care, and the sickle cell trait. Please contact for complete catalog.

Publications for Health Professionals
Professional resources include directories, proceedings, reports, and resource guides on subjects such as prenatal care; infant, child, and adolescent health; nutrition; breastfeeding; lead poisoning; disabilities; MCH legislation; and social work. Please contact for complete publications list.

■ National Council of La Raza Center for Health Promotion

1111 19th St NW, Ste 1000
Washington, DC 20036
Contact: Lupe Lemus, 202-785-1670
202-785-1670
Fax: 202-776-1792
E-mail: hpacheco@nclr.org
Web site: http://www.nclr.org

Private, nonprofit, nonpartisan organization that serves as an advocate for Hispanic Americans on health and other public policy issues. The NCLR's Center for Health Promotion works to increase the access of Hispanics to health care and to provide public health materials and capacity-building assistance to Hispanic community-based organizations. The Center has three major programs: Maternal and Child Health Program; HST Prevention Project, and Hispanic Health Liaison Project.

Clearinghouse or Resource Center
NCLR Distribution Center: 301-604-7983; PO Box 291, Annapolis Junction, MD 20701; Health, immigration, poverty, and general public information available. Cost of materials $5 to $15.

Consumer or Patient Education Materials
Center for Maternal and Child Health, fact sheet, provides information on issues related to health of Hispanic children. Please contact for complete catalog.

Technical Assistance
Maternal and Child Health Program, focuses primarily on combating high rates of vaccine preventable diseases among Latinos; technical assistance, trainings, educational information to community-based organizations.

■ National Council on Alcoholism and Drug Dependence Inc (NCADD)

12 W 21st St
New York, NY 10010
Contact: Public Information Dept
212-206-6770
Fax: 212-645-1690
E-mail: national@ncadd.org
Web site: http://www.ncadd.org

Nonprofit voluntary health organization with more than 128 affiliates in the U.S. providing education, information, help and hope in the fight against the chronic, often fatal disease of alcoholism and other drug addictions. Advocate for prevention, intervention, research, and treatment programs.

Special Campaigns, Events, or Programs
Alcohol & Other Drug-Related Birth Defects Awareness Week, May, awareness kit. Contact Public Information Dept, 212-206-6770.

Consumer or Patient Education Materials
Alcohol-Related Birth Defects fact sheet, $.20

■ National Women's Health Resource Center

2425 L St NW, 3rd Fl
Washington, DC 20037
202-293-6045
Fax: 202-778-6306
E-mail: nwhrc.02.erol.com

Nonprofit organization that is the national clearinghouse for women's health information. Dedicated to providing women with comprehensive, objective information to help them make informed decisions about health-related issues.

Consumer or Patient Education Materials
Health Information Packets with comprehensive medical information, resource lists, suggested readings, on more than 20 topics including breast cancer, osteoporosis, hysterectomy, infertility, $15. Please contact for complete catalog.

Publications for Health Professionals
National Women's Health Report, bimonthly newsletter, $25/yr, $5 single copy.

Technical Assistance
Personalized health information research; referrals to women's health centers nationwide that are contained in a database.

■ Public Health Foundation

1220 L St NW, Ste 350
Washington, DC 20005
Contact: Rita Kelliher, Sarah Pfau, Mike Barry, 202-898-5600 x3015
202-898-5600
Fax: 202-898-5609
Web site: http://www.phf.org

National nonprofit organization whose mission is to assist the Association of State and Territorial Health Officers and the National Association of County and City Health Officials in supporting official state and local public health agencies' efforts to achieve healthy people and healthy communities within their jurisdictions. Develops and maintains partnerships with the academic community and other public and private organizations engaged in public health related activities.

Publications for Health Professionals
Child Health USA, handbook and slides, national and state data on health status and health services utilization of children, free.

Classes and Conferences
Maternal Child Health Data Speak Audioconferences, series of four annually, contact Sarah Pfau or Rita Kelliher at 202-842-2000 for program topics and informational packet.

Technical Assistance
National graduate student internship program placing qualified interns to assist state and local MCH programs with data and analytic activities, needs assessments, and policy initiatives for a 90-day period.

■ Reproductive Toxicology Center

Columbia Hospital for Women Medical Center
2440 M St NW, Ste 217
Washington, DC 20037-1404
Contact: G Kay Padgett
202-293-5137
Fax: 202-778-6199

Nonprofit organization gathers and disseminates information about the effects of the chemical and physical environment on human fertility, pregnancy, and fetal development. Access is available on an annual subscription basis through the consultative format of the Clinical Inquiry Program or by direct access to the REPROTOX database.

Database or Statistical Information
REPROTOX database provides information summary on over 4,000 agents. Available online, written and/or on diskette. Annual subscription cost for various levels range $215–$910.

■ Vida Health Communications Inc

6 Bigelow St
Cambridge, MA 02139
Contact: Rita Rebidue
617-864-4334
Fax: 617-864-7862
E-mail: vidahealth@aol.com

National for-profit company that specializes in the production and distribution of award-winning educational video programs addressing maternal and child health care.

Consumer or Patient Education Materials

Hello Baby!, 3 video segments covering preparation for labor and delivery, $395; Home Before You Know It, 30-min video, practical advice on postpartum care for mom and baby, also available in Spanish, $245; Just in Case . . . , video, covers cesarean childbirth and recovery, $245. Please contact for complete catalog.

■ Wellstart International

4062 First Ave
San Diego, CA 92103-2045
Contact: Monica J L King, 619-574-8162
619-295-5192
Fax: 619-294-7787
E-mail: inquiry@wellstart.org

Private, nonprofit organization, and a World Health Organization Collaborating Center on Breastfeeding Promotion and Protection, working to expand and support the expertises necessary for establishing and maintaining optimal infant feeding practices. Offers education and technical assistance primarily to medical professionals from health organizations and government institutions in developing countries, but also provides services and collaboration on a variety of related activities within the U.S.

Consumer or Patient Education Materials

Breastfeeding is Remarkable, booklet, overview with description of what can be done to increase optimal infant feeding, free; Investing in the Future: Women, Work, & Breastfeeding, video, encourages employers to offer time, space, support necessary for mothers to sustain breastfeeding while working, $14.50. Some Spanish, French, Russian languages available. Please contact for complete catalog.

Publications for Health Professionals

Community-based Breastfeeding Support Trilogy, 3 manuals: Planning Manual, Training Manual, and A Guide for Trainers and Supervisors, designed to complement each other as support for breastfeeding in the community unfolds, $40/set or $15–$20 ea. Please contact for complete publications list.

Classes and Conferences

Customized courses, workshops are available on request.

Technical Assistance

Consulting services provided in areas of technical expertise, including the science of lactation, clinical management, education and training, curriculum development, communication and social marketing, program planning and development.

■ The Willapa Bay Company

5223 NE 187th St
Lake Forest Park, WA 98155
Contact: Chung Ho Lee
800-403-1424
206-364-5696
Fax: 206-364-5992
E-mail: willapa@nwlink.com
Web site: http://www.twbc.com

Publishing company that specializes in low-literacy materials that are easy-to-use, inclusive, and accessible to people of all backgrounds and abilities with primary focus on pregnancy and newborn care.

Consumer or Patient Education Materials

Baby and Me, The Essential Guide to Pregnancy, book, prenatal health care; Baby Talk, The Essential Videoguide to New Parents, video, newborn care; Pricing varies upon quantity ordered; Materials can be customized; Low literacy; Spanish languages available. Please contact for complete catalog.

■ Zero to Three: National Center for Infants, Toddlers and Families

734 15th St NW, Ste 1000
Washington, DC 20005-1013
Contact: Publications Dept, 800-899-4301 or 202-638-0840, PO Box 25494, Richmond, VA 23260-5494
202-638-1144
Fax: 202-638-0851
E-mail: 0-3@zerotothree.org
Web site: http://www.zerotothree.org

National nonprofit leading resource on the first three years of life whose mission is to advance the healthy development of America's babies and young children.

Consumer or Patient Education Materials

Wall charts and posters, $4. Please contact for complete catalog.

Publications for Health Professionals

Zero to Three, bimonthly bulletin, multidisciplinary approach to a single topic, $37/yr; New Visions for the Developmental Assessment of Infants and Young Children, book, 400 pp, $35; Please contact for complete publications list.

Technical Assistance

Provides training and technical assistance to professionals and direct service providers; is one of six collaborating organizations in a technical assistance network, National Early Childhood Technical Assistance System (NEC*TAS).

ADDITIONAL RESOURCES

■ **Alliance of Genetic Support Groups**
35 Wisconsin Cir, Ste 440
Chevy Chase, MD 20815
800-336-GENE (800-336-4363)
301-652-5553
Fax: 301-654-0171
E-mail: alliance@capaccess.org
Web site: http://medhelp.org/www/agsg.htm

■ **American College of Nurse-Midwives**
818 Connecticut Ave NW, #900
Washington, DC 20006
Contact: Publications Dept, 202-728-9879
202-728-9860
Fax: 202-728-9897
E-mail: info@acnm.org
Web site: http://www.midwife.org

■ **Association of Maternal and Child Health Programs**
1350 Connecticut Ave NW, Ste 803
Washington, DC 20036
202-775-0436
Fax: 202-775-0061

■ **Back-to-Sleep Campaign**
NICHD/Back to Sleep
31 Center Dr, Rm 2A32
Bethesda, MD 20892-2425
800-505-CRIB (800-505-2742)
Fax: 301-496-7101

■ **Black Women's Health Council**
PO Box 31089
Capitol Heights, MD 20731
301-808-0786
Fax: 301-808-0963

■ **Board on Children, Youth, and Families**
Institute of Medicine, National Research Council
2101 Constitution Ave NW, HA 156
Washington, DC 20418
Contact: Publications, 202-334-3965
202-334-1935
Fax: 202-334-3829
Web site: http://www.nas.edu

■ **Center for Women Policy Studies**
1211 Connecticut Ave NW, Ste 312
Washington, DC 20036
202-872-1770
Fax: 202-296-8962
E-mail: HN4066@Handsnet.org

■ **Childbirth Graphics**
A Division of WRS Group Inc
PO Box 21207
Waco, TX 76702-1207
800-299-3366 x287
817-776-6461
Fax: 817-751-0221
E-mail: sales@wrsgroup.com
Web site: http://www.wrsgroup.com

■ **Family Service America Inc**
11700 W Lake Park Dr
Milwaukee, WI 53224
Contact: Publications, 800-852-1944
414-359-1040
Fax: 414-359-1074

■ **Fetal Alcohol Education Program**
Boston University School of Medicine
1975 Main St
Concord, MA 01742
Contact: Fetal Alcohol Education Program
617-739-1424

■ **International Medical Services for Health (INMED)**
45449 Severn Way, Ste 161
Sterling, VA 20166-8918
Contact: Kim McAndrews, Communications Asst
703-444-4477
Fax: 703-444-4471

■ **Jacobs Institute of Women's Health**
409 12th St SW
Washington, DC 20024-2188
202-863-4990
Fax: 202-488-4229
E-mail: JacobsInst@aol.com

■ **National Association of Child Advocates**
1522 K St NW, Ste 600
Washington, DC 20005
Contact: Publications Dept
202-289-0777
Fax: 202-289-0776

■ **National Association of Children's Hospitals & Related Institutions**
401 Wythe St
Alexandria, VA 22314
703-684-1355
Fax: 703-684-1589

■ **National Black Child Development Institute**
1023 15 St NW, Ste 600
Washington, DC 20005
202-387-1281
Fax: 202-234-1738
E-mail: moreinfo@nbcdi.org
Web site: http://www.nbcdi.org

■ **National Black Women's Health Project**
1211 Connecticut Ave NW, Ste 310
Washington, DC 20036
202-835-0117
Fax: 202-833-8790
E-mail: nbwhpdc@aol.com

■ **National Council of Catholic Women**
1275 K St NW, Ste 975
Washington, DC 20005
800-506-9407 (Order Dept)
202-682-0334
Fax: 202-682-0338
E-mail: nccw@usa.net
Web site: http://ourworld.compuserve.com/homepages.nccw

■ **National Early Childhood Technical Assistance System (NEC*TAS)**
500 NationsBank Plaza
137 E Franklin St
Chapel Hill, NC 27514
Contact: Coordinating Office
919-962-2001
Fax: 919-966-7463
TDD: 919-966-4041
E-mail: nectasta.nectas@mhs.unc.edu
Web site: http://www.nectas.unc.edu

■ **National Foundation for Jewish Genetic Diseases**
250 Park Ave, Ste 1000
New York, NY 10017
Contact: George Crohn
212-371-1030
Fax: 212-319-5808

■ **National Organization on Fetal Alcohol Syndrome**
1819 H St NW, Ste 750
Washington, DC 20006
800-666-6327
202-785-4585
Fax: 202-466-6456
E-mail: nofas@erols.com
Web site: http://www.nofas.org

■ **National Perinatal Association**
3500 E Fletcher Ave, Ste 209
Tampa, FL 33613-4712
813-971-1008
Fax: 813-971-9306

■ **National Perinatal Information Center**
1 State St, Ste 102
Providence, RI 02908-5035
Contact: David Gagnon, Executive Director
401-274-0650
Fax: 401-455-0377

■ **National Women's Health Network**
514 10th St NW, Ste 400
Washington, DC 20004
Contact: Information Clearinghouse, 202-628-7814
202-347-1140
Fax: 202-347-1168

■ **Sudden Infant Death Syndrome Alliance**
1314 Bedford Ave, Ste 210
Baltimore, MD 21208
800-638-SIDS (800-638-7437)
410-653-8226
Fax: 410-653-8709
E-mail: sidshq@charm.net

FEDERAL AGENCIES

■ **Administration for Children and Families (ACF)**
U.S. Dept of Health & Human Services
370 L'Enfant Promenade SW
Washington, DC 20447
Public Affairs: 202-401-9215
Head Start Bureau: 202-205-8572; Fax: 202-260-9336
Developmental Disabilities: 202-690-6590
Family & Youth Services Bureau: 202-205-8054

Federal health agency that brings together in one organization the broad range of federal programs that address the needs of children and families.

■ Food and Consumer Services (FCS)

U.S. Department of Agriculture
3101 Park Center Dr
Alexandria, VA 22302-1594
Public Inquiries: 703-305-2286
Fax: 703-305-1117
Nutrition and Technical Services: 703-305-2556
Web site: http://www.usda.gov/fcs/fcsinfo.htm

Administers federal food assistance programs.

■ Maternal and Child Health Bureau (MCHB)

Health Resources and Services Administration
Parklawn Bldg, Rm 18-20
5600 Fishers Ln
Rockville, MD 20857
301-443-0205
Fax: 301-443-1797
Healthy Start Division: 301-443-0543
Maternal, Infant, Child, and Adolescent Health Division: 301-443-2250
Web site: http://www.os.dhhs.gov/hrsa/mchb

Provides leadership to both the public and private sector to build the infrastructure for delivery of health care services to all mothers and children. Administers block grant funds and a wide range of activities and projects. Healthy Start is an initiative to reduce infant mortality. Materials are available from the National Maternal and Child Health Clearinghouse: 703-821-8955.

■ National Center for Environmental Health (NCEH)

Centers for Disease Control and Prevention
4770 Buford Hwy NE, M/S F-29
Atlanta, GA 30341-3724
770-488-7030
Division of Birth Defects & Developmental Disabilities: 404-488-7160
E-mail: ncehinfo@cehodl.em.cdc.gov
Web site: http://www.cdc.gov/nceh/ncehhome.htm

NCEH's mission is to provide national leadership, through science and service, to promote health and quality of life by preventing and controlling disease, birth defects, disability, and death resulting from interactions between people and their environment. The Division of Birth Defects & Developmental Disabilities works to prevent birth defects, genetic diseases, and developmental disabilities.

■ National Institute of Child Health and Human Development (NICHD)

National Institutes of Health
Bldg 31, Rm 2A-32
31 Center Dr, MSC 2425
Bethesda, MD 20892-2425
Communication Branch: 301-496-5133
Fax: 301-496-7101
Web site: http://www.nih.gov/nichd

Conducts and supports basic research and supports laboratory, clinical and epidemiologic research on the reproductive, neurobiologic, developmental, social and behavioral processes that determine and maintain the health of children, adults, families, and populations. Professional materials available on sudden infant death syndrome, developmental disabilities, pregnancy, and genetics; consumer materials available on cesarean childbirth, Down syndrome, oral contraception, and vasectomy.

■ National Maternal and Child Health Clearinghouse

2070 Chain Bridge Rd, Ste 450
Vienna, VA 22182-2536
703-821-8955

Clearinghouse that provides information services and distributes publications focusing on maternal and child health. Large inventory of publications and selected consumer education titles available in Spanish, Haitian Creole and nine Asian languages. Distributes directories of federal programs and other organizations and topical resource guides; provides referrals to additional information agencies. Sponsored by the Maternal and Child Health Bureau, Health Resources and Services Administration.

■ National Sudden Infant Death Syndrome Resource Center

2070 Chain Bridge Rd, Ste 450
Vienna, VA 22182-2536
703-821-8955

Clearinghouse that provides information and educational materials on sudden infant death syndrome (SIDS), apnea, and other related issues. Responds to information requests from professionals and the public.

Maintains a library of standard reference materials on topics related to SIDS; Maintains and updates mailing lists of state programs, groups, and individuals concerned with SIDS. Also develops fact sheets, catalogs, and bibliographies on areas of special interest to the community. Conducts customized searches of database on SIDS and SIDS-related materials. Sponsored by the Maternal and Child Health Bureau, Health Resources and Services Administration.

■ Office of Women's Health

Office of Public Health and Science
U.S. Dept of Health & Human Services
Humphrey Bldg, Rm 718-E
200 Independence Ave SW
Washington, DC 20201
202-690-7650

Serves as the focal point for women's health activities within HHS and works to improve the health of women across their lifespan by stimulating and coordinating crosscutting activities in women's health research, health care service delivery, and public and health professional education and training within the HHS; and with other government agencies, public and private organizations, and consumer and health care professional groups.

Older Adults

Products/Services Offered

Organization	web site	hotline/toll-free information line	clearinghouse/resource center	electronic information resources	database/statistical information	special campaigns/events/programs	consumer/patient education materials	publications for health professionals	classes/conferences	technical assistance	other products/services	grants/funding/awards	Page No.
American Association for Geriatric Psychiatry	■							■					**236**
American Geriatrics Society								■					**236**
Channing L Bete Co Inc							■						**236**
Clinical Reference Systems Ltd	■										■		**236**
FastMark Inc							■						**236**
Geriatric Psychiatry Alliance	■	■					■	■		■			**237**
Geriatric Video Productions	■							■					**237**
The Gerontological Society of America	■							■	■	■		■	**237**
Health Professions Press								■					**237**
National Asian Pacific Center on Aging				■			■	■					**237**
National Association of State Units on Aging		■	■	■				■	■	■			**238**
National Policy and Resource Center on Women and Aging	■						■						**238**

Additional Resources **238**

Federal Agencies **239**

■ American Association for Geriatric Psychiatry

7910 Woodmont Ave, Ste 1350
Bethesda, MD 20814
Contact: Clea English
301-654-7850
Fax: 301-654-4137
E-mail: aagpgpa@aol.com
Web site: http://www.aagpgpa.org

Nonprofit association dedicated to promoting the mental health and well-being of older people and improving the care of those with late-life mental disorders. Mission is to enhance the knowledge base and standard of practice in geriatric psychiatry through education and research and to advocate for meeting the mental health needs of older Americans.

Publications for Health Professionals

American Journal of Geriatric Psychiatry, quarterly, peer-reviewed scientific articles; Essentials of Geriatric Psychiatry: A Guide for the Health Professional, reference book, $29.95.

■ American Geriatrics Society

770 Lexington Ave, Ste 300
New York, NY 10021
212-308-1414
Fax: 212-832-8646
E-mail: agsnyc@mem.po.com

Nonprofit professional medical society dedicated to improving the health and well-being of all older adults.

Publications for Health Professionals

Journal of the American Geriatrics Society, monthly, articles relevant in broadest terms to the clinical care of older persons, $19/issue; AGS Newsletter, bimonthly, free.

■ Channing L Bete Co Inc

200 State Rd
S Deerfield, MA 01373-0200
800-628-7733 (Sales and Customer Service)
413-665-7611
Fax: 800-499-6464

Publisher of informational and educational booklets, videos, posters, calendars, books, and display racks. Booklets use a distinctive, condensed format–called scriptography–which combines key words and graphics to explain a variety of subjects and is appropriate for different age groups and reading levels.

Consumer or Patient Education Materials

Booklets on topics specific to older adults include: accident prevention, fire safety, elder abuse. Please contact for pricing and ask for the Patient Education catalog.

■ Clinical Reference Systems Ltd

7100 E Belleview Ave, Ste 208
Greenwood Village, CO 80111-1635
Contact: Ellen Graves, Marketing Coordinator
800-237-8401
303-220-1661
Fax: 303-220-1685
E-mail: crs-info@cliniref.com
Web site: http://www.patienteducation.com

Publisher of patient education and clinical reference software for the international health care community. Committed to development of computer-based health information to enhance communication between provider and patient. More than 30,000 programs are now at work in physician offices, clinics, hospitals, medical school residency programs, occupational clinics, medical and consumer libraries.

Other Products and Services

Senior Health Advisor software program, customized patient information handouts covering a broad range of geriatric health topics. Please contact for pricing and complete information.

■ FastMark Inc

125 University Ave, Ste 250
Palo Alto, CA 94301
Contact: Leah Jacobs, Marketing Manager
800-406-2035
415-327-7760
Fax: 415-327-7734
E-mail: fastmark.com

Publisher of first aid and wellness reference guides using a patented laminated format that allows thickly laminated products to lie flat when folded. Health topics include: women's health, children's health, seniors' health, allergies/asthma, diabetes, heart disease, fitness, nutrition, and stress management.

Consumer or Patient Education Materials

FastCare for Seniors, 5-panel folded laminated brochure, self-care and prevention topics include 17 conditions from arteriosclerosis to prostate problems. Pricing varies upon quantity ordered; Materials can be customized; Please contact for complete catalog.

■ Geriatric Psychiatry Alliance

1201 Connecticut Ave, # 300
Washington, DC 20036
888-463-6472
301-654-7850
Fax: 202-835-8891
E-mail: aagpgpa@aol.com
Web site: http://www.aagpgpa.org

Nonprofit educational program of the American Association of Geriatric Psychiatry whose mission is to raise awareness of psychiatric disorders affecting the elderly by educating primary care physicians, other providers of health care services, policy makers, and consumers.

Hotline or Toll-free Information Line
Geriatric Psychiatry Alliance Information Line: 888-INFO-GPA (888-463-6472) (M–F 8AM–10PM ET) Operator assisted, referral service, requests for information.

Consumer or Patient Education Materials
Growing Older & Wiser, 230 pp book, coping with changes in later years, $11; Depression in Late Life: Not a Natural Part of Aging, brochure, comprehensive consumer education information, free. Please contact for complete catalog.

Publications for Health Professionals
Diagnosis and Treatment of Late-Life Depression: Making a Difference, 23 pp monograph, designed primarily for primary care physicians, free. Please contact for complete publications list.

Technical Assistance
Speakers bureau.

■ Geriatric Video Productions

2989 Bald Mountain Rd
Wilkes-Barre, PA 18702
Mailing Address:
PO Box 1757
Shavertown, PA 18708
Contact: Joanne Bennett, 317-579-0400
800-621-0402
717-829-1095
Fax: 717-829-1095
E-mail: geriat@ptd.net
Web site: http://www.geriatricvideo.com

For-profit producer and distributor of award-winning video products to enhance geriatric care skills and improve patient outcomes.

Publications for Health Professionals
Educational videos to improve geriatric nursing skills, written guides, 15–30 mins long. Topics include: preventing falls, preventing undernutrition, wandering, agitation and restlessness, depression. $199–$285. Please contact for complete publications list.

■ The Gerontological Society of America

1275 K St NW, Ste 350
Washington, DC 20005-4006
202-842-1275
Fax: 202-842-1150
E-mail: geron@geron.org
Web site: http://www.geron.org

Nonprofit organization that promotes the scientific study of aging and fosters growth and diffusion of knowledge relating to problems of aging.

Publications for Health Professionals
The Gerontologist, bimonthly, for practitioners, $112/yr; Journal of Gerontology, bimonthly, research info, $195/yr; Gerontology News, monthly newsletter, $50/yr.

Classes and Conferences
Annual scientific meeting.

Technical Assistance
Referral services to experts and resources in aging.

Grants, Funding, or Awards
Awards available. Contact Stephanie Gordon.

■ Health Professions Press

409 Washington Ave, Ste 500
Baltimore, MD 21204
Mailing Address:
PO Box 10624
Baltimore, MD 21285
410-337-9585
Fax: 410-337-8539
E-mail: hpp@pbrookes.com

Publisher of professional references and textbooks on long-term care, gerontology, and health adminstration, plus practical resources for nursing home staff, caregivers, and other service providers.

Publications for Health Professionals
Abuse, Neglect and Exploitation of Older Persons, book, assessment and intervention strategies, $27.50. Please contact for complete publications list.

■ National Asian Pacific Center on Aging

1511 Third Ave, Ste 914
Seattle, WA 98101-1626
Contact: Valerie Gungap
206-624-1221
Fax: 206-624-1023

Nonprofit leading advocacy organization committed to the well-being of elderly Asians and Pacific Islanders in America. Develops and administers programs to enhance the dignity and quality of life of its constituents.

Electronic Information Resources
Fax-it: 206-624-0185, over 300 documents in 15 Asian/Pacific languages covering health, wellness, social services, employment and related matters available at no cost; order catalog of available information first.

Consumer or Patient Education Materials
Guide to Supplemental Security Income for Asian/ Pacific Elderly, $2.

Publications for Health Professionals
Pacific/Asian Elderly Bibliography, covers approximately 750 gerontology technical references, $3; Demographic and Socio-Economic Characteristics of Elderly Asian and Pacific Island Americans, 50 pp, $5. Please contact for complete publications list.

■ National Association of State Units on Aging

1225 I St NW, Ste 725
Washington, DC 20005
Contact: Cindy Wellons
202-898-2578
Fax: 202-898-2583
E-mail: staff@nasua.org

Nonprofit public interest organization that provides information, technical assistance, and professional development support to its members—the 57 state and territorial government agencies on aging. Works to promote social policy at the federal and state levels responsive to the needs of older Americans.

Hotline or Toll-free Information Line
Eldercare Locator: 800-677-1116 (M–F 9AM–11PM ET) Operator assisted, referral service, answers questions. Designed to help older persons and caregivers link to local aging services.

Clearinghouse or Resource Center
National Long Term Care Ombudsman Resource Center: 202-898-2578; 1225 I St NW, Ste 725, Washington, DC 20005; Publications, studies, and technical assistance materials aimed at enhancing operations of the long-term care ombudsman advocacy services to older persons residing in nursing homes and other care settings. (Operated in collaboration with National Citizen's Coalition for Nursing Home Reform)

Electronic Information Resources
AGE-NET: 202-898-4794, Computer bulletin board service designed specifically to meet the information and support needs of professionals in the aging network.

Publications for Health Professionals
Linking Elderly Patients to Community Services, $75; A Guide for Hospital Discharge Planners, $5. Please contact for complete publications list.

Classes and Conferences
Annual membership meeting; Orientation and training for state aging directors and staff. Please contact for complete list and schedule.

Technical Assistance
Training and technical assistance available.

■ National Policy and Resource Center on Women and Aging

Heller Graduate School, Brandeis University
415 South St
Waltham, MA 02254-9110
Contact: Phyllis H Mutschler, PhD, Director
800-929-1995
617-736-3866
Fax: 617-736-3881
E-mail: natwomctr@binah.cc.brandeis.edu
Web site: http://www.brandeis.edu/heller/national/national.html

National nonprofit research organization whose goal is to improve the quality of older women's lives and to provide women with the information they need to make good decisions about their health, their safety, their living conditions, their financial security, and the care they provide for others. The Center's activities—community education, research, and policy analysis—seek to address the inequities that affect midlife and older women.

Consumer or Patient Education Materials
The Women & Aging Letter, bimonthly newsletter, $5; Estrogen Replacement: Is It Right for You?, booklet, $3; Estrogen Replacement: Interpreting Media Reports about New Research, booklet, $3.

ADDITIONAL RESOURCES

■ The Alliance for Aging Research

2021 K St NW, Ste 305
Washington, DC 20006
800-639-2421
202-293-2856
Fax: 202-785-8574
E-mail: agecom@aol.com

■ **American Association of Retired Persons**
601 E St NW
Washington, DC 20049
Contact: Health Advocacy Services/Health Promotion, 202-434-2240
202-434-2277
Fax: 202-434-2588
Web site: http://www.aarp.org/

■ **American Society on Aging**
833 Market St, Ste 511
San Francisco, CA 94103-1824
Contact: Publications, 800-537-9728
415-974-9600
Fax: 415-974-0300
Web site: http://www.housecall.com/oac/asa

■ **Fanlight Productions**
47 Halifax St
Boston, MA 02130
Contact: Jennifer Norris
800-937-4113
617-524-0980
Fax: 617-524-8838
E-mail: fanlight@tiac.net
Web site: http://www.fanlight.com

National distributor of educational videos focusing on health care, mental health, aging, and disability issues.

■ **National Association for Human Development**
1424 16th St NW, Ste 102
Washington, DC 20036
202-328-2191
Fax: 202-265-6682

■ **National Association for the Hispanic Elderly**
3325 Wilshire Blvd, Ste 800
Los Angeles, CA 90010
213-487-1922
Fax: 213-385-3014

■ **National Association of Area Agencies on Aging**
1112 16th St NW, Ste 100
Washington, DC 20036
202-296-8130
Fax: 202-296-8134

■ **National Caucus and Center on Black Aged**
1424 K St NW, Ste 500
Washington, DC 20005
202-637-8400
Fax: 202-347-0895

■ **National Council on the Aging**
409 Third St SW, 2nd Fl
Washington, DC 20024
Contact: Health Promotion
800-424-9046
202-479-6678
202-479-1200
Fax: 202-479-0735
E-mail: info@ncoa.org
Web site: http://www.ncoa.org

■ **National Hispanic Council on Aging**
2713 Ontario Rd NW
Washington, DC 20009
202-265-1288
Fax: 202-745-2522

■ **National Indian Council on Aging**
10501 Montgomery Blvd NE, Ste 210
Albuquerque, NM 87111
Contact: Dave Baldridge or Eva Gardipe
505-292-2001
Fax: 505-292-1922

■ **Shepherd's Centers of America**
6700 Troost Ave
Kansas City, MO 64131
Contact: Charles Huyett or Lois Stock
800-547-7073
816-523-1080
Fax: 816-523-5790
E-mail: shepherd@qni.com

FEDERAL AGENCIES

■ **Administration on Aging**
U.S. Dept of Health & Human Services
330 Independence Ave SW
Washington, DC 20201
Public Inquiries: 202-619-0724
Publications: 202-619-1006
Web site: http://www.aoa.dhhs.gov
National Aging Information Center: 301-907-6743
E-mail: info@ageinfo.org
Web site: http://www.ageinfo.org

Federal agency devoted exclusively to providing services and opportunities for older Americans. Help is provided through programs administered by AOA, together with its 10 regional offices and 57 state and territorial units on aging, approximately 670 area agencies on aging, and Indian tribes.

■ Alzheimer's Disease Education and Referral Center (ADEAR Center)

PO Box 8520
Silver Spring, MD 20907-8250
800-438-4380
Fax: 301-495-3334
E-mail: adear@alzheimers.org
Web site: http://www.alzheimers.org/adear

A service of the National Institute on Aging (NIA) that provides information and publications on Alzheimer's disease to health and service professionals, patients and their families, caregivers, and the public. Information specialists are available M–F 8:30AM–5PM ET (the hours that the Center's reading room is open to visitors).

■ National Institute on Aging (NIA)

National Institutes of Health
Bldg 31, Rm 5C-27
31 Center Dr, MSC 2292
Bethesda, MD 20892-2292
800-222-2225
Public Information Office: 301-496-1752
Fax: 301-496-1072
Web site: http://www.nih.gov/nia/

NIA Information Center
PO Box 8057
Gaithersburg, MD 20898-8057
800-222-2225; TTY: 800-222-4225

Conducts and supports biomedical, social, and behavioral research and training related to the aging process and the diseases and other special problems and needs of the aged. Materials are available on menopause, nutrition, arthritis, cancer, aging, constipation, crime, diabetes, exercise, hearing, high blood pressure, osteoporosis, medicines, flu, urinary incontinence, skin care, dental care, and other health topics from the NIA Information Center.

People with Disabilities

Organization	web site	hotline/toll-free information line	clearinghouse/resource center	electronic information resources	database/statistical information	special campaigns/events/programs	consumer/patient education materials	publications for health professionals	classes/conferences	technical assistance	other products/services	grants/funding/awards	Page No.
American Spinal Injury Association								■	■			■	242
The Arc	■						■						242
Better Hearing Institute		■					■						242
CD Publications								■					242
Channing L Bete Co Inc							■						242
Dial A Hearing Screening Test							■				■		243
Disabled Sports USA	■								■				243
International Hearing Society		■					■						243
National Center for Youth with Disabilities	■			■				■		■			243
National Down Syndrome Society	■	■				■	■	■				■	244
National Rehabilitation Information Center (NARIC)	■	■			■			■					244
National Spinal Cord Injury Association	■	■	■				■	■					244
National Stroke Association	■						■	■					245
Research Grant Guides Inc								■					245
Spina Bifida Association of America	■	■						■	■				245

Additional Resources 245

Federal Agencies 246

■ American Spinal Injury Association

345 E Superior St, Rm 1436
Chicago, IL 60611
Contact: Lesley M Hudson, 404-355-9772, 2020 Peachtree Rd NW, Atlanta, GA 30309
312-908-6207
Fax: 312-503-0869
E-mail: mars@merle.acns.nww.edu

National multidisciplinary organization of health care professionals devoted to the care of individuals who have sustained a spinal cord injury.

Publications for Health Professionals
International Standards for Neurological Classification, teaching package, $185. Please contact for complete publications list.

Classes and Conferences
Annual scientific meeting, 3 days, paper/poster presentations, instructional courses, commercial/ scientific exhibits, $300 avg fee. Please contact for complete list and schedule.

Grants, Funding, or Awards
G Heiner Sell Research and Educational Fund, funds small (up to $5,000) educational projects annually. Contact Central Office, 312-908-6207.

■ The Arc

500 E Border St, Ste 300
Arlington, TX 76010
Contact: Ann Balson
800-433-5255
817-261-6003
Fax: 817-277-3491
TDD: 817-277-0553
E-mail: thearc@metronet.com
Web site: http://thearc.org/welcome.html

Nonprofit volunteer organization solely devoted to improving the lives of all children and adults with mental retardation and their families. Fosters research and education regarding the prevention of mental retardation in infants and young children.

Consumer or Patient Education Materials
The Arc Today, quarterly newsletter, free to members, $15/yr; Learning about the Americans with Disabilities Act and title II: Opening up government services and activities for people with disabilities, book, easy-to-read guide geared toward self-advocates, $15. Please contact for complete catalog.

■ Better Hearing Institute

5021B Backlick Rd
Annandale, VA 22003
Mailing Address:
PO Box 1840
Washington, DC 20013
800-EAR-WELL (800-327-9355)
703-642-0580
Fax: 703-750-9302
TDD: 800-327-9355

Nonprofit educational organization that implements national public information programs on hearing loss and available medical, surgical, hearing aid, and rehabilitation assistance for people with uncorrected hearing problems. Maintains a toll-free "hearing helpline" telephone service that provides information on hearing loss and hearing help to callers in the U.S. and Canada.

Hotline or Toll-free Information Line
Better Hearing Institute Helpline: 800-EAR-WELL (800-327-9355) (M–F 9AM–5PM ET) Operator assisted, answers questions, request for materials.

Consumer or Patient Education Materials
Brochures include: Your Guide to Better Hearing and A Guide to Your Child's Hearing, free. Some Spanish languages available. Please contact for complete catalog.

■ CD Publications

8204 Fenton St
Silver Spring, MD 20910-4571
800-666-6380
301-588-6380
Fax: 301-588-6385
E-mail: cdpubs@clark.net

Publisher of newsletters, reports, and resource guides that identify funding sources, provide fundraising advice, and keep readers updated on budget proposals affecting public policy in health, education, and social services.

Publications for Health Professionals
Disability Funding News, semi-monthly newsletter, funding and news for agencies and hospitals, $269/yr. Please contact for complete publications list.

■ Channing L Bete Co Inc

200 State Rd
S Deerfield, MA 01373-0200
800-628-7733 (Sales and Customer Service)
413-665-7611
Fax: 800-499-6464

Publisher of informational and educational booklets, videos, posters, calendars, books, and display racks. Booklets use a distinctive, condensed format—called scriptography—which combines key words and graphics to explain a variety of subjects and is appropriate for different age groups and reading levels.

Consumer or Patient Education Materials
Booklets include: Children with Special Needs; Mental Retardation; People with Disabilities. Some Spanish language available. Please contact for pricing and ask for the Patient Education catalog.

■ Dial A Hearing Screening Test

300 S Chester Rd
Swarthmore, PA 19081
Mailing Address:
PO Box 1880
Media, PA 19063
Contact: George Biddle, Executive Director
800-222-EARS (800-222-3277)
610-544-7700
Fax: 610-543-2802
E-mail: dabiddle@aol.com

For-profit company offering telephone hearing screening test system allowing people to identify hearing loss quickly, conveniently, and confidentially.

Consumer or Patient Education Materials
Hearing Loss: Your Doctor Can Help, booklet; Facts About Hearing Aids, flyer; The Truth About Buying Hearing Aids, booklet. Free.

Other Products and Services
Provides referral service to local telephone hearing screening tests, health care providers and specialists.

■ Disabled Sports USA

451 Hungerford Dr, Ste 100
Rockville, MD 20850
Contact: Neal A Lichter, Public Information, 301-217-0960 x6
301-217-0960
Fax: 301-217-0968
TDD: 301-217-0963
E-mail: dsusa@dsusa.org
Web site: http://www.dsusa.org/~dsusa/dsusa.html

National nonprofit organization providing athletic, recreational, and physical educational opportunities for individuals with disabilities.

Classes and Conferences
"Learn to" programs in variety of summer and winter recreation and sports activities; family-training workshops. Please contact for complete information.

■ International Hearing Society

20361 Middlebelt Rd
Livonia, MI 48152-2095
800-521-5247
810-478-2610
Fax: 810-478-5420

Nonprofit professional association of specialists who test hearing and select, fit, and dispense hearing aids. Conducts programs of competence qualifications, education, and training, and promotes specialty-level accreditation. Consumer information is provided through helpline.

Hotline or Toll-free Information Line
Hearing Aid Helpline: 800-521-5247 (M–F 10AM–4PM ET) Operator assisted, referral service, answers questions, requests for materials.

Consumer or Patient Education Materials
World of Sound, booklet, covers hearing loss and hearing aids, free.

■ National Center for Youth with Disabilities

University of Minnesota, Box 721
420 Delaware St SE
Minneapolis, MN 55455-0392
Contact: Shari Morrison or Elizabeth Latts
612-626-2825
Fax: 612-626-2134
TDD: 612-624-3939
E-mail: ncyd@gold.tc.umn.edu
Web site: http://www.peds.umn.edu/centers/ncyd

Nonprofit information, policy, and resource center focusing on adolescents with chronic illnesses and disabilities, and the issues surrounding their transition to adult life.

Electronic Information Resources
National Resource Library, offers a comprehensive source of information related to adolescents, chronic illness, disability, and transition; assists researchers, planners, service providers. Access is via an information specialist. Charge based on material received.

Publications for Health Professionals
Children's and Youth's Health Issues, 3 times/yr newsletter; Cydline Reviews, topical annotated bibliographic series; FYI Bulletins and Special Reports. Nominal cost. Please contact for complete publications list.

Technical Assistance
Technical Assistance Center services include: review and comment on policy materials, books, chapters, and articles; consultation; planning and co-sponsoring

conferences and workshops; presentations and lectures.

■ National Down Syndrome Society

666 Broadway, 8th Fl
New York, NY 10023-2317
212-460-9330
Fax: 212-979-2873
Web site: http://www.ndss.org

Nonprofit organization that works to ensure that all people with Down syndrome are provided the opportunity to achieve their full potential in community life and does this through education, research, and advocacy.

Hotline or Toll-free Information Line
National Down Syndrome Society Information Line: 800-221-4602 (M–F 9AM–5PM ET) Operator assisted, referral service, answers questions. Information packet available to new parents.

Special Campaigns, Events, or Programs
National Down Syndrome Awareness Month, October, events to raise awareness include Buddy Walk. Contact 800-221-4602 for complete information.

Consumer or Patient Education Materials
General Information Pack, free. Materials can be customized; Please contact for complete catalog.

Publications for Health Professionals
Clinical Care booklets, first copy free; Teaching Partnership Posters, first copy free. Please contact for complete publications list.

Grants, Funding, or Awards
NDSS Science Scholar Award Program, 2-year research grant. Call 212-460-9330 for information and application.

■ National Rehabilitation Information Center (NARIC)

8455 Colesville Rd, Ste 935
Silver Spring, MD 20910
Contact: Information Specialist
800-346-2742
301-588-9284
Fax: 301-587-1967
TDD: 301-495-5626
Web site: http://www.naric.com/naric

The National Rehabilitation Information Center (NARIC) is a library and information center on disability and rehabilitation. Funded by the National Institute on Disability and Rehabilitation Research (NIDRR), Department of Education, it collects and disseminates the results of federally funded research projects. Collection of over 47,000 items and growing, also includes commercially produced books, journal articles, and audiovisuals.

Hotline or Toll-free Information Line
National Rehabilitation Information Center: 800-346-2742 (M–F 8AM–6PM ET) Referral service, requests for materials, information searches available, most free but extensive searches, $5 or more, and $5 minimum for copying and delivery fee.

Database or Statistical Information
REHABDATA, bibliographic literature database, contains abstracts of products in the NARIC collection, nominal fee for some searches, nominal charge for copying and shipping. ABLEDATA, database of assistive devices.

Publications for Health Professionals
NIDRR Program Directory, annual, lists all projects funded by NIDRR during the fiscal year, $5; Directory of National Information Sources on Disabilities, bi-annual, $15, Guide to Disability and Rehabilitation Periodicals, bi-annual, $15. Please contact for complete publications list.

■ National Spinal Cord Injury Association

8300 Colesville Rd, Ste 551
Silver Spring, MD 20910
Contact: Bernadette Mauro, Resource Center Coordinator
800-962-9629
301-588-6959
Fax: 301-588-9414
E-mail: nscia2@aol.com
Web site: http://www.spinalcord.org

Nonprofit membership organization with more than 60 chapters and support groups nationally for people with disabilities, their family and friends, and the professionals involved in their care. Maintains a comprehensive approach to managing spinal cord injury by focusing on prevention, services, and research programs.

Hotline or Toll-free Information Line
National Spinal Cord Injury Association Member Hotline: 800-962-9629 (M–F 8:30AM–4PM ET and 24-hr voice mail) Referral service, answers questions, requests for materials.

Clearinghouse or Resource Center
National Spinal Cord Injury Association Resource Center: 800-962-9629; responds to any question pertaining to SCI or paralysis.

Consumer or Patient Education Materials
Books, abstracts, audiotape lectures, fact sheets available. Please contact for complete catalog.

Publications for Health Professionals
SCI Life, quarterly magazine, free with membership. Please contact for complete publications list.

■ National Stroke Association

96 Inverness Dr E, Ste I
Englewood, CO 80112-5112
Contact: Jennifer Converse, 303-649-9299 x925
800-STROKES (800-787-6537)
303-649-9299
Fax: 303-649-1328
E-mail: info@stroke.org
Web site: http://www.stroke.org

Nonprofit organization dedicated to reducing the incidence and impact of stroke. Focuses on stroke prevention, treatment, research, rehabilitation, and support for stroke survivors and their families.

Consumer or Patient Education Materials
Adaptive Resources Guide, annual listing of products and manufacturers, $1.00; Be Stroke Smart Series, fact sheets, full packet contains most-frequently asked questions, $5. Please contact for complete catalog.
Publications for Health Professionals
Stroke: Putting the Pieces Back Together, training program designed for LTC facilities, $195.

■ Research Grant Guides Inc

PO Box 1214
Loxahatchee, FL 33470-1214
407-795-6129
Fax: 407-795-7794 (Orders)

Publisher of directory guides listing foundation profiles and information on grant funding.

Publications for Health Professionals
Directory of Grants for Organizations Serving People with Disabilities, Ninth Edition, 847 foundation profiles with 2,700 grant entries, $55.50. Order must be mailed or faxed.

■ Spina Bifida Association of America

4590 MacArthur Blvd NW, Ste 250
Washington, DC 20007-4226
Contact: Information and Referral Dept
800-621-3141
202-944-3285
Fax: 202-944-3295
E-mail: spinabifida@aol.com
Web site: http://www.infohiway.com/spinabifida

National nonprofit organization that addresses the specific needs of the spina bifida community with over 70 chapters in the U.S. Mission is to promote the prevention of spina bifida and to enhance the lives of all affected.

Hotline or Toll-free Information Line
Spina Bifida Association of America Request Line: 800-621-3141 (M–F 9AM–5PM ET) Automated, requests for materials.
Publications for Health Professionals
Insights, bimonthly newsletter, free; Parent/teacher packet, set of educational materials, $12; Healthcare Guidelines, guidelines for health care services, $16.50. Please contact for complete publications list.
Classes and Conferences
Annual conference, 3 days, educational, medical, and research meeting. Costs vary. Please contact for complete list and schedule.

ADDITIONAL RESOURCES

■ American Association on Mental Retardation

444 N Capitol St NW, Ste 846
Washington, DC 20001-1512
Mailing Address:
PO Box 1202
Washington, DC 20013-1202
Contact: Publications, 301-604-1340
800-424-3688
202-387-1968
Fax: 202-387-2193
E-mail: aamr@access.digex.net
Web site: http://www.aamr.org

■ American Speech-Language-Hearing Association

10801 Rockville Pike
Rockville, MD 20852
800-638-8255
301-897-5700
Fax: 301-571-0457
Web site: http://www2.asha.org/asha/

■ National Association of State Boards of Education

1012 Cameron St
Alexandria, VA 22314
703-684-4000
Fax: 703-836-2313
Web site: http://www.nasbe.org

■ **National Council on Disability**
1331 F St NW, Ste 1050
Washington, DC 20004-1107
202-272-2004
Fax: 202-272-2022
TDD: 202-272-2074
Web site: http://www.ncd.gov

■ **National Easter Seal Society**
230 W Monroe St, Ste 1800
Chicago, IL 60606-4802
800-221-6827
312-726-6200
Fax: 312-726-1494
TDD: 312-726-4258
Web site: http://www.seals.com

■ **National Information Center for Children and Youth with Disabilities (NICHCY)**
PO Box 1492
Washington, DC 20013-1492
800-695-0285
202-884-8200
Fax: 202-884-8441
E-mail: nichcy@aed.org
Web site: http://www.aed.org/nichcy

■ **Twin Peaks Press**
PO Box 129
Vancouver, WA 98666-0129
360-694-2462
Fax: 360-696-3210
E-mail: 73743.2634@compuserve.com
Web site: http://www.netm.com/mall/infoprod/twinpeak/helen.htm

FEDERAL AGENCIES

■ **National Institute on Disability and Rehabilitation Research (NIDRR)**
U.S. Department of Education
400 Maryland Ave SW, Rm 3060
Washington, DC 20202-2646
202-205-8134
Fax: 202-205-8515
Web site: http://www.ed.gov/offices/OSERS/NIDRR

Provides leadership and support for rehabilitation research and also disseminates information concerning developments in rehabilitation procedures, methods, and devices that can improve the lives of people of all ages with physical and mental disabilities, especially those who are severely disabled. Provides statistical data on disabilities, as well as information on research funding, which is available from the National Rehabilitation Information Center at 800-346-2742.

■ **NIDCD Information Clearinghouse**
One Communication Ave
Bethesda, MD 20892-3456
800-241-1044
TDD: 800-241-1055
E-mail: nidcd@aerie.com
Web site: http://www.nih.gov/nidcd/

A program of the National Institute on Deafness and Other Communication Disorders (NIDCD) and serves as a national resource center for information about hearing, balance, smell, taste, voice, speech, and language for health professionals, patients, industry, and the public. Provides an information service; a database of references to journal articles, books, audiovisual materials, brochures, fact sheets, newsletter articles, manuals, and other education materials; and publications.

Federal Agencies and Offices

■ **Administration for Children and Families (ACF)**
U.S. Dept of Health & Human Services
370 L'Enfant Promenade SW
Washington, DC 20447
Public Affairs: 202-401-9215

■ **Administration on Aging (AOA)**
U.S. Dept of Health & Human Services
330 Independence Ave SW
Washington, DC 20201
Public Inquiries: 202-619-0724
Publications: 202-619-1006
Web site: http://www.aoa.dhhs.gov

■ **Agency for Health Care Policy and Research (AHCPR)**
Office of Public Health and Science
U.S. Dept of Health & Human Services
2101 E Jefferson St
Rockville, MD 20852
301-594-1433
AHCPR Publications Clearinghouse: 800-358-9295
Web site: http://www.ahcpr.gov/

■ **Agency for Toxic Substances and Disease Registry (ASTDR)**
Office of Public Health and Science
U.S. Dept of Health & Human Services
1600 Clifton Rd NE, MSC E-29
Atlanta, GA 30333
Information Center: 404-639-6357
Web site: http://atsdr1.atsdr.cdc.gov:8080/astdrhome.html

■ **Bureau of Health Professions (BHPr)**
Health Resources and Services Administration
Parklawn Bldg, Rm 8-05
5600 Fishers Ln
Rockville, MD 20857
301-443-1590

■ **Bureau of Primary Health Care (BPHC)**
Health Resources and Services Administration
4350 East West Hwy
Bethesda, MD 20814
Program for Special Populations Division: 301-594-4420
Office of Minority and Women's Health: 301-594-4490
National Clearinghouse for Primary Care Information: 800-400-2742

■ **Center for Biologics Evaluation and Research (CBER)**
U.S. Food and Drug Administration
1401 Rockville Pike, HFM-46
Rockville, MD 20852
800-835-4709
Web site: http://www.fda.gov/cber/cberftp.html

■ **Center for Devices & Radiological Health (CDRH)**
U.S. Food and Drug Administration
9200 Corporate Blvd, MSC HFZ-1
Rockville, MD 20850
301-443-4690
Consumer Information Service: 301-443-4190
Fax: 301-443-9535
Fax-on-Demand: 800-899-0381
Web site: http://www.fda.gov/cdrh

■ **Center for Drug Evaluation and Research (CDER)**
U.S. Food and Drug Administration
5600 Fishers Ln, HFD-700
Rockville, MD 20857
301-827-4573
Fax-on-Demand and Inquiries: 800-342-2722
Web site: http://www.fda.gov/cder

■ **Center for Food Safety and Applied Nutrition (CFSAN)**
U.S. Food and Drug Administration
200 C St SW, M/S HFS-55
Washington, DC 20204
Consumer Education Staff: 202-205-5004
General Inquiries and Seafood Hotline: 800-FDA-4010 (800-332-4010)
Office of Food Labeling (Division of Technical Evaluation): 202-205-5483
Web site: http://vm.cfsan.fda.gov/list.html

■ **Center for Mental Health Services (CMHS)**
Substance Abuse and Mental Health Services Administration

Parklawn Bldg, Rm 13-103
5600 Fishers Ln
Rockville, MD 20857
External Liaison Office: 301-443-2792
Web site: http://www.samhsa.gov/cmhs/cmhs.htm

■ Center for Substance Abuse Prevention (CSAP)

Substance Abuse and Mental Health Services Administration
Rockwall 2 Bldg, Rm 9D-10
5600 Fishers Ln
Rockville, MD 20857
301-443-0365
Division of State Prevention Systems Programs: 301-443-7942
Web site: http://www.samhsa.gov/csap/csap.htm

■ Center for Substance Abuse Treatment (CSAT)

Substance Abuse and Mental Health Services Administration
Rockwall 2 Bldg, Ste 840
5600 Fishers Ln
Rockville, MD 20857
Communications Office: 301-443-5052
Web site: http://www.samhsa.gov/csat/csat.htm

■ Centers for Disease Control and Prevention (CDC)

Office of Public Health and Science
U.S. Dept of Health & Human Services
1600 Clifton Rd NE, M/S D-25
Atlanta, GA 30333
Public Inquiries: 404-639-3286
Fax: 404-639-1537
Publications: 404-639-3534
CDC Voice Information System: 404-332-4555 (M–F 8AM–4:30PM ET)
CDC Wonder web site: http://wonder.cdc.gov/ (to locate reports, guidelines, or data)
CDC National AIDS Clearinghouse: 800-458-5231
Public Health Practice Program Office: 404-639-1938
Morbidity and Mortality Weekly Report (MMWR): 404-639-2104
Web site: http://www.cdc.gov

■ Consumer Information Center (CIC)

18th and F Streets NW, Rm G142
Washington, DC 20405
202-501-1794

■ Food and Consumer Services (FCS)

U.S. Department of Agriculture
3101 Park Center Dr
Alexandria, VA 22302-1594
Public Inquiries: 703-305-2286
Fax: 703-305-1117
Nutrition and Technical Services: 703-305-2556
Web site: http://www.usda.gov/fcs/fcsinfo.htm

■ Food and Nutrition Information Center (FNIC)

National Agricultural Library
Argricultural Research Service, U.S. Department of Agriculture
10301 Baltimore Blvd, Rm 304
Beltsville, MD 20705-2351
301-504-5719
E-mail: fnic@nal.usda.gov
Web site: http://www.nal.usda.gov/fnic/

■ Food Safety and Inspection Service (FSIS)

U.S. Department of Agriculture
1400 Independence Ave SW, Rm 1175-South
Washington, DC 20250
202-720-7943
USDA Meat and Poultry Hotline: 800-535-4555 and 202-720-3333
Web site: http://www.usda.gov/agency.fsis/homepage.htm

■ Health Care Financing Administration (HCFA)

U.S. Dept of Health & Human Services
Baltimore, MD 21244
General Information: 410-786-3000
Bureau of Data Management and Strategy: 410-786-1800
Office of National Health Statistics: 410-786-7933
Medicare Statistical Hotline: 410-786-3689
Web site: http://www.hcfa.gov

■ Health Resources and Services Administration (HRSA)

Office of Public Health and Science
U.S. Dept of Health & Human Services
5600 Fishers Ln, Rm 14-45
Rockville, MD 20857
Communications Office: 301-443-3376
Web site: http://www.hrsa.dhhs.gov/

■ **Indian Health Service (IHS)**
Office of Public Health and Science
U.S. Dept of Health & Human Services
Parklawn Bldg, Rm 6-35
5600 Fishers Ln
Rockville, MD 20857
Communications Office: 301-443-3376
Web site: http://www.tucson.ihs.gov

■ **Maternal and Child Health Bureau (MCHB)**
Health Resources and Services Administration
Parklawn Bldg, Rm 18-20
5600 Fishers Ln
Rockville, MD 20857
301-443-0205
Healthy Start Division: 301-443-0543
Maternal, Infant, Child, and Adolescent Health Division: 301-443-2250
National Maternal and Child Health Clearinghouse: 703-821-8955
Web site: http://www.os.dhhs.gov/hrsa/mchb

■ **National Cancer Institute (NCI)**
National Institutes of Health
Bldg 31, Rm 10A-24
9000 Rockville Pike
Bethesda, MD 20892
Cancer Information Service: 800-4-CANCER (800-422-6237)
CancerFax: 301-402-5874 (in English or Spanish) 24-hr, 7 days/wk
International Cancer Information Center: 301-496-9096
Web site: http://www.nci.nih.gov

■ **National Center for Chronic Disease Prevention & Health Promotion (NCCDPHP)**
Centers for Disease Control and Prevention
4770 Buford Hwy NE
Atlanta, GA 30341-3724
Technical Information Services Branch: 770-488-5080
Chronic Disease Notes and Reports: 770-488-5050; Fax: 770-488-5095
Division of Nutrition and Physical Activity: 770-488-4721
Office on Smoking and Health: 770-488-5705
Oral Health Program: 770-488-3038
Web site: http://www.cdc.gov/nccdphp/nccdhome.html

■ **National Center for Environmental Health (NCEH)**
Centers for Disease Control and Prevention
4770 Buford Hwy NE, M/S F-29
Atlanta, GA 30341-3724
E-mail: ncehinfo@cehodl.em.cdc.gov
Web site: http://www.cdc.gov/nceh/ncehhome.htm

■ **National Center for Health Statistics (NCHS)**
Centers for Disease Control and Prevention
6525 Belcrest Rd, Rm 1064
Hyattsville, MD 20782
301-436-8500
E-mail: nchsquery@nch20a.em.cdc.gov
Web site: http://www.cdc.gov/nchswww/nchshome.htm

■ **National Center for HIV, STD & TB Prevention (NCHSTP)**
Centers for Disease Control and Prevention
1600 Clifton Rd NE, M/S E-06
Atlanta, GA 30333
Communications Dept: 404-639-8063
NCHSTP Voice Information System: 404-639-1819
TB Voice Information System: 404-330-1231
HIV/AIDS and TB Fax Information Service: 404-332-4565
Web site: http://www.cdd.gov/nchstp/od/nchstp.html

■ **National Center for Infectious Diseases (NCID)**
Centers for Disease Control and Prevention
1600 Clifton Rd NE, M/S C-12
Atlanta, GA 30333
404-639-3286
CDC Parasitic Diseases Information Line: 404-330-1242
Web site: http://www.cdc.gov/ncidod/ncid.htm

■ **National Center for Injury Prevention and Control (NCIPC)**
Centers for Disease Control and Prevention
4770 Buford Hwy NE, M/S K-63
Atlanta, GA 30341
NCIPC Automated Information Line: 770-488-4677
Division of Violence Prevention: 770-488-4362
Web site: http://www.cdc.gov/ncipc/ncipchm.htm

■ National Center on Child Abuse and Neglect (NCCAN)
Administration for Children and Families
PO Box 1182
Washington, DC 20013-1182
202-205-8586
National Clearinghouse on Child Abuse and Neglect: 800-394-3366

■ National Criminal Justice Reference Service (NCJRS)
U.S. Department of Justice
1600 Research Blvd, 2nd Fl
Rockville, MD 20850
Mailing Address:
PO Box 6000
Rockville, MD 20849-6000
800-851-3420
Electronic Bulletin Board: 301-738-8895
Web site: http://www.ncjrs.org

■ National Eye Institute (NEI)
National Institutes of Health
Bldg 31, Rm 6A-32
31 Center Dr, MSC 2510
Bethesda, MD 20892-2510
301-496-4583
National Eye Health Education Program Information Line: 301-496-5248
Publications Distribution Center: 800-869-2020
E-mail: 2020@b31.nei.nih.gov
Web site: http://www.nei.nih.gov

■ National Health Information Center (NHIC)
Office of Disease Prevention and Health Promotion (ODPHP)
Office of Public Health and Science (OPHS)
PO Box 1133
Washington, DC 20013-1133
800-336-4797
E-mail: nhicinfo@health.org
Web site: http://nhic-nt.health.org

■ National Heart, Lung, and Blood Institute (NHLBI)
National Institutes of Health
NIH/NHLBI/OPEC, Rm 4A-03
31 Center Dr, MSC 2480
Bethesda, MD 20892-2480
800-336-4797
National High Blood Pressure Education Program: 800-575-WELL (800-575-9355)
NHLBI Information Center: 301-251-1222
Web site: http://www.nhlbi.nih.gov/nhlbi/nhlbi.htm

■ National Highway Traffic Safety Administration (NHTSA)
U.S. Department of Transportation
400 Seventh St SW
Washington, DC 20590
Public Inquiries: 202-366-9550
Auto Safety Hotline: 800-424-9393 (202-366-0123 in DC)
Web site: http://www.nhtsa.dot.gov

■ National Immunization Program (NIP)
Centers for Disease Control and Prevention
1600 Clifton Rd NE, M/S E-52
Atlanta, GA 30333
404-639-8204
CDC Immunization Information: 800-232-7468
Web site: http://www.cdc.gov/nip.home.htm

■ National Institute for Occupational Safety and Health (NIOSH)
Centers for Disease Control and Prevention
4676 Columbia Pkwy
Cincinnati, OH 45226-1998
513-533-8328
800-35-NIOSH (800-356-4674)
Web site: http://www.cdc.gov/niosh/homepage.html

■ National Institute of Allergy and Infectious Diseases (NIAID)
National Institutes of Health
Bldg 31, Rm 7A-50
31 Center Dr, MSC 2520
Bethesda, MD 20892-2520
Communications Office: 301-496-5717
E-mail: ocpostoffice@flash.niaid.nih.gov
Web site: http://www.niaid.nih.gov

■ National Institute of Arthritis and Musculoskeletal and Skin Diseases (NIAMS)
National Institutes of Health
Bldg 31, Rm 4C-05
31 Center Dr, MSC 2350
Bethesda, MD 20892-2350
301-496-8188
NIAMS Information Clearinghouse: 301-495-4484
Web site: http://www.nih.gov/niams/

■ National Institute of Child Health and Human Development (NICHD)
National Institutes of Health
Bldg 31, Rm 2A-32
31 Center Dr, MSC 2425
Bethesda, MD 20892-2425
Communicaitions Branch: 301-496-5133
Web site: http://www.nih.gov/nichd

■ **National Institute of Dental Research (NIDR)**
National Institutes of Health
Bldg 31, Rm 2C-35
31 Center Dr, MSC 2290
Bethesda, MD 20892-2290
Public Inquiries: 301-496-4261
National Oral Health Information Clearinghouse (NOHIC): 301-402-7364
E-mail: nidr@aerie.com
Web site: http://www.nidr.nih.gov

■ **National Institute of Diabetes and Digestive and Kidney Disease (NIDDK)**
National Institutes of Health
Bldg 31, Rm 9A-04
31 Center Dr, MSC 2560
Bethesda, MD 20892-2560
Information Office: 301-496-3583
National Diabetes Information Clearinghouse: 301-654-3327
National Digestive Diseases Information Clearinghouse: 301-654-3810
National Kidney and Urologic Diseases Information Clearinghouse: 301-654-4415
Weight Control Information Network: 800-946-8098
Web site: http://www.niddk.nih.gov

■ **National Institute of Environmental Health Sciences (NIEHS)**
National Institutes of Health
PO Box 12233
Research Triangle Park, NC 27709
Communications Office: 919-541-3665
National Toxicology Program: 919-541-3419
Environmental Health Clearinghouse: 800-NIEHS-94 (800-643-4794)
Web site: http://www.niehs.nih.gov

■ **National Institute of Mental Health (NIMH)**
National Institutes of Health
5600 Fishers Ln, Rm 7C-02
Rockville, MD 20857
Information Branch: 301-443-4513
E-mail: nimhinfo@nih.gov
Web site: http://www.nimh.nih.gov

■ **National Institute of Neurological Disease and Stroke (NINDS)**
National Institutes of Health
PO Box 5801
Bethesda, MD 20824
Public Information Office: 800-352-9424
Web site: http://www.ninds.nih.gov/

■ **National Institute on Aging (NIA)**
National Institutes of Health
Bldg 31, Rm 5C-27
31 Center Dr, MSC 2292
Bethesda, MD 20892-2292
800-222-2225
Public Information Office: 301-496-1752
Alzheimer's Disease Education and Referral Center: 800-438-4380
NIA Information Center: 800-222-2225
Web site: http://www.nih.gov/nia/

■ **National Institute on Alcohol Abuse and Alcoholism (NIAAA)**
National Institutes of Health
6000 Executive Blvd, Ste 409
Bethesda, MD 20892-7003
Public Information Office: 301-443-3860
Web site: http://www.niaaa.nih.gov

■ **National Institute on Disability and Rehabilitation Research (NIDRR)**
U.S. Department of Education
400 Maryland Ave SW, Rm 3060
Washington, DC 20202-2646
202-205-8134
Web site: http://www.ed.gov/offices/OSERS/NIDRR

■ **National Institute on Drug Abuse (NIDA)**
National Institutes of Health
5600 Fishers Ln, Rm 10A-39
Rockville, MD 20857
Public Information Office: 301-443-1124
Web site: http://www.nida.nih.gov/

■ **National Institutes of Health (NIH)**
Office of Public Health and Science
U.S. Dept of Health & Human Services
Bldg 1, Rm 344
9000 Rockville Pike
Bethesda, MD 20892
Public Information Division: 301-496-5787
Web site: http://www.nih.gov

■ **National Library of Medicine (NLM)**
National Institutes of Health
Bldg 38, Rm 2S10
8600 Rockville Pike
Bethesda, MD 20894
800-272-4787
301-496-6308
NLM Reference Desk: 301-496-6095 (medical questions)

MEDLARS management service desk: 800-638-8480 or 301-496-6193
Web site: http://www.nlm.nih.gov

■ National Technical Information Service (NTIS)

5285 Port Royal Rd
Springfield, VA 22161
703-487-4650
Fax Direct® Product Information Service: 703-487-4140
NTIS Product Announcements Fax: 800-758-5804 ext. 104707
FedWorld® Help Desk: 703-487-4223
E-mail: orders@ntis.fedworld.gov
Web site: http://www.prnewswire.com

■ Occupational Safety and Health Administration (OSHA)

U.S. Department of Labor
200 Constitution Ave NW, Rm N-3647
Washington, DC 20210
Public Affairs: 202-219-8151
OSHA Publications Office: 202-219-4667
Web site: http://www.osha.gov

■ Office of AIDS/HIV Policy

Office of Public Health and Science
U.S. Dept of Health & Human Services
Humphrey Bldg, Rm 736-E
200 Independence Ave SW
Washington, DC 20201
202-690-5560
AIDS Clinical Trials Information Service: 800-TRIALS-A (800-874-2574)
HIV/AIDS Treatment Information Service: 800-HIV-0440 (800-448-0440)

■ Office of Disease Prevention and Health Promotion (ODPHP)

Office of Public Health and Science
U.S. Dept of Health & Human Services
200 Independence Ave SW, Rm 738G
Washington, DC 20201
202-401-6295
Health Communications Dept: 202-205-5968
Healthy People 2000 Management Team: 202-205-8583
National Coordinating Committee on Worksite Health Promotion: 202-205-9007
Web site: http://odphp.oash.dhhs.gov/

■ Office of Minority Health Resource Center

Office of Public Health and Science
U.S. Dept of Health & Human Services
8455 Colesville Rd, Ste 910
Silver Spring, MD 20910
Mailing Address:
PO Box 37337
Washington, DC 20013-7337
800-444-6472
Web site: http://www.omhrc.gov

■ Office of National Drug Control Policy (ONDCP)

750 17th St NW
Washington, DC 20006
202-395-6618

■ Office of Population Affairs (OPA)

Office of Public Health and Science
U.S. Dept of Health & Human Services
4330 East West Hwy
Bethesda, MD 20814
301-594-4000
OPA Clearinghouse: 301-654-6190

■ Office of Safety, Health, and Working Conditions

Bureau of Labor Statistics (BLS), U.S. Department of Labor
2 Massachusetts Ave NE, Rm 3180
Washington, DC 20212
202-606-6179
Publications: 202-606-7828
Fax-on-Demand: 202-606-6325
Web site: http://stats.bls.gov/oshhome.htm

■ Office of Women's Health

Office of Public Health and Science
U.S. Dept of Health & Human Services
Humphrey Bldg, Rm 718-E
200 Independence Ave SW
Washington, DC 20201
202-690-7650

■ Substance Abuse and Mental Health Services Administration (SAMHSA)

Office of Public Health and Science
U.S. Dept of Health & Human Services
Parklawn Bldg, Rm 13C-05
5600 Fishers Ln
Rockville, MD 20857
Public Affairs: 301-443-8956

Information Line: 301-443-3783
Funding opportunites: Bulletin Board Service: 800-424-2294 (9600,N,8,1)
Web site: http://www.samhsa.gov

U.S. Consumer Product Safety Commission (CPSC)

Washington, DC 20207
301-504-0580
CPSC Hotline: 800-638-CPSC (800-638-2772)
National Injury Information Clearinghouse: 301-504-0424
E-mail: info@cpsc.gov
Web site: http://www.cpsc.gov

U.S. Environmental Protection Agency (EPA)

Public Information Center
401 M St SW, Rm 3404
Washington, DC 20013-7133
202-260-2080
EPA Safe Drinking Water Hotline: 800-426-4791 (M–F 9AM–5PM ET)
Office of Water Resource Center: 202-260-7786
Indoor Air Quality Information Clearinghouse: 800-438-4318
Web site: http://www.epa.gov

U.S. Food and Drug Administration (FDA)

Office of Public Health and Science
U.S. Dept of Health & Human Services
5600 Fisher Ln, HFE-88
Rockville, MD 20857
Office of Consumer Affairs Inquiries Information Line: 800-532-4440; 301-827-4420
Web site: http://www.fda.gov/

U.S. Government Printing Office (GPO)

Washington, DC 20402-9325
202-512-1800
Fax: 202-512-2250
Web site: http://www.access.gpo.gov
Superintendents of Documents
PO Box 371954
Pittsburgh, PA 15250-7954
Web site: http://www.access.gpo.gov/su_docs/

State Health Promotion and Prevention Offices

Alabama
Health Promotion & Information Bureau
434 Monroe St
Montgomery, AL 36130-3017
334-613-5300
For other information, contact:
Public Health Dept: 334-613-5300

Alaska
Community Health & Emergency Medical Services
Alaska Office Bldg
PO Box 110610
Juneau, AK 99811-0610
907-465-3027
For other information, contact:
Public Health Division: 907-465-3090
Health & Social Services Dept: 907-465-3030

Arizona
Center for Prevention & Health Promotion
1400 W Washington
Phoenix, AZ 85015
602-542-7200
For other information, contact:
Health Services Dept: 602-542-1000

Arkansas
Preventive Health Services
4815 Markham
Little Rock, AR 72205-3867
501-661-2227
For other information, contact:
Public Health Programs Bureau: 501-661-2243
Health Dept: 501-661-2000

California
Prevention Services Dept
714/744 P St
PO Box 942732
Sacramento, CA 94234-7320
916-657-1493
For other information, contact:
Health Services Dept: 916-445-4171
Health & Welfare Agency: 916-654-3454

Colorado
Family & Community Health Services Division
4300 Cherry Creek Dr S
Denver, CO 80222
303-692-2310
For other information, contact:
Health Office: 303-692-2301
Public Health & Environment Dept: 303-692-2000

Connecticut
Community Health Bureau
410 Capitol Ave
PO Box 340308
Hartford, CT 06134-0308
860-509-7655
For other information, contact:
Public Health Dept: 860-509-8000

Delaware
Public Health Division
PO Box 637
Dover, DE 19903
302-739-4700
For other information, contact:
Health & Social Services Dept: 800-464-4357

District of Columbia
Preventive Health Dept
800 Ninth St SW, 2nd Fl
Washington, DC 20024
202-645-5550
For other information, contact:
Dept of Health: 202-645-5556

Florida
Health Communication & Promotion
1317 Winewood Blvd, Bldg 6, Rm 308
Tallahassee, FL 32399-0700
904-487-3220
For other information, contact:
Dept of Health: 904-487-2945

Georgia
Chronic Disease, Prevention & Health Promotion Branch
Two Peachtree St NW
Atlanta, GA 30303
404-657-2550
For other information, contact:
Public Health Division: 404-657-2700
Human Resources Dept: 404-656-5680

Hawaii
Health Promotion & Education Branch
1250 Punchbowl St
Honolulu, HI 96813
808-586-4661
For other information, contact:
Family Health Services Division: 808-586-4745
Health Dept: 808-586-3840

Idaho
Health Promotion Bureau
450 W State St
PO Box 83720
Boise, ID 83720-0036
208-334-5927
For other information, contact:
Health Division: 208-334-5945
Health & Welfare Dept: 208-334-5500

Illinois
Health Promotion Center
535 W Jefferson St
Springfield, IL 62761
217-785-2060
For other information, contact:
Community Health Office: 217-782-5945
Public Health Dept: 217-782-6187

Indiana
Health Promotion Center
2 N Meridian St
Indianapolis, IN 46204
317-233-7256
For other information, contact:
Public Health Services: 317-233-7122
Health Dept: 317-233-1325

Iowa
Family and Community Health Division
Lucas State Office Bldg
321 E Twelfth St
Des Moines, IA 50319-0075
515-281-3931
For other information, contact:
Public Health Dept: 515-281-5787

Kansas
Chronic Disease & Health Promotion
Landon State Office Bldg
900 SW Jackson St
Topeka, KS 66612-1290
913-296-1207
For other information, contact:
Health Division: 913-296-1086
Health & Environment Dept: 913-296-1500

Kentucky
Environmental Health & Community Safety Division
275 E Main St, 2nd Fl West
Frankfort, KY 40621
502-564-7398
For other information, contact:
Dept of Public Health: 502-564-3970
Health Services Cabinet: 502-564-4856

Louisiana
Health Protection & Promotion Division
325 Loyola Ave
PO Box 60630
New Orleans, LA 70160
504-568-7210
For other information, contact:
Public Health Office: 504-568-5051
Health & Hospitals Dept: 504-342-9500

Maine
Health Promotion & Education
11 State House Station
Augusta, ME 04333
207-287-5180
For other information, contact:
Health Bureau: 207-287-3201
Human Services Dept: 207-287-3707

Maryland
Community Health Surveillance Administration
201 W Preston St
5th Fl
Baltimore, MD 21201
410-767-6100
For other information, contact:
Public Health Services: 410-767-6510
Health & Mental Hygiene Dept: 410-767-6860

Massachusetts
Prevention Division
250 Washington St
Boston, MA 02108-4619
617-624-5070
For other information, contact:
Public Health Dept: 617-624-6000

Michigan
Health Promotion & Chronic Disease Prevention Center
Martin Luther King Jr Blvd
PO Box 30195
Lansing, MI 48909
517-335-8368
For other information, contact:
Community Public Health Agency: 517-335-8000
Community Health Dept: 517-373-3740

Minnesota
Community Health Services Division
717 Delaware St SE
PO Box 9441
Minneapolis, MN 55440-9441
612-296-9720
For other information, contact:
Health Dept: 612-623-5000

Mississippi
Health Promotion
PO Box 1700
Jackson, MS 39215-1700
601-960-7781
For other information, contact:
Community Health Services Office: 601-960-7725
Health Dept: 601-960-7400

Missouri
Chronic Disease Prevention & Health Promotion Division
101 Park DeVille Dr, Ste A
Columbia, MO 65203
573-876-3200
For other information, contact:
Health Dept: 573-751-6400

Montana
Chronic Disease & Health Promotion Section
PO Box 202951
Helena, MT 59620-2951
406-444-9020
For other information, contact:
Health Policy & Services: 406-444-4540
Public Health & Human Services Dept: 406-444-5622

Nebraska
Health Promotion & Education Section
301 Centennial Mall South
PO Box 95044
Lincoln, NE 68509-5044
402-471-2101
For other information, contact:
Health Promotion & Disease Prevention Division:
402-471-3711

Nevada
Bureau of Community Health Services
3656 Research Way, Ste 32
Carson City, NV 89706
702-687-6944
For other information, contact:
Health Dept: 702-687-3786
Human Resources Dept: 702-687-4400

New Hampshire
Health Promotion Bureau
Six Hazen Dr
Concord, NH 03301
603-271-4551
For other information, contact:
Office of Health Managment: 603-271-4501
Health & Human Services Dept: 603-271-4685

New Jersey
Community Health Services
50 E State St, CN 364
Trenton, NJ 08625-0364
609-984-1384
For other information, contact:
Family Health Services Division: 609-292-4043
Health & Senior Services Dept: 609-292-7837

New Mexico
Health Promotion Bureau
1190 St Francis Dr
PO Box 26110
Santa Fe, NM 87502-6110
505-827-2380
For other information, contact:
Public Health Division: 505-827-2389
Health Dept: 505-827-2562

New York
Community Health Center
Mayor Erastus Corning II Tower
Empire State Plaza
Albany, NY 12237-0001
518-474-5073
For other information, contact:
Health Dept: 518-474-7354

North Carolina
Health Promotion
PO Box 29605
Raleigh, NC 27626-0605
919-733-7081
For other information, contact:
Environment, Health & Natural Resources Dept:
919-733-4984

North Dakota
Health Promotion & Education Division
600 E Boulevard Ave, Rm 204
Bismarck, ND 58505-0200
701-328-2367
For other information, contact:
Preventive Health Section: 701-328-2493
Health Dept: 701-328-2372

Ohio
Bureau of Health Promotion & Risk Reduction
246 N High St
PO Box 118
Columbus, OH 43266-0118
614-466-2144
For other information, contact:
Prevention Division: 614-466-0302
Health Dept: 614-466-3543

Oklahoma
Health Education & Information Services
1000 NE Tenth St
Oklahoma City, OK 73117-1299
405-271-5601
For other information, contact:
Administrative Services: 405-271-5600
Health Dept: 405-271-5600

Oregon
Risk Management Division
155 Cottage St, NE
Salem, OR 97310
503-373-7233
For other information, contact:
Administrative Services Dept: 503-378-3106

Pennsylvania
Preventive Health Programs Bureau
Health and Welfare Bldg
PO Box 90
Harrisburg, PA 17108
717-787-6214
For other information, contact:
Health Promotion, Disease & Substance Abuse Prevention: 717-787-9857
Health Dept: 717-787-5901

Rhode Island
Health Promotion & Chronic Diseases
Three Capitol Hill
Providence, RI 02908-5097
401-277-1171
For other information, contact:
Health Dept: 401-277-2231

South Carolina
Preventive Health Services Bureau
PO Drawer 101106
Columbia, SC 29211
803-737-4040
For other information, contact:
Health Promotion Center: 803-737-4121
Health & Environmental Control Dept: 803-734-5000

South Dakota
Office of Disease Prevention
445 E Capitol Ave
Pierre, SD 57501-3185
605-773-3737
For other information, contact:
Health, Medical & Laboratory Services: 605-773-3361
Health Dept: 605-773-3361

Tennessee
Health Promotion & Disease Control
Cordell Hull Bldg
426 Fifth Ave, North
Nashville, TN 37247
615-741-7366
For other information, contact:
Health Services Bureau: 615-741-3380
Health Dept: 615-741-3111

Texas
Disease Control & Prevention
1100 W 49th St
Austin, TX 78756
512-458-7729
For other information, contact:
Health Dept: 512-458-7111

Utah
Health Promotion & Risk Reduction
288 N 1460 West
Salt Lake City, UT 84116-0700
801-538-6267
For other information, contact:
Community & Family Health Services: 801-538-6161
Health Dept: 801-538-6101

Vermont
Health Promotion
PO Box 70
Burlington, VT 05402
802-863-7330
For other information, contact:
Health Dept: 802-863-7200
Human Services Agency: 802-241-2220

Virginia
Health, Promotion & Chronic Disease Prevention Office
Main Street Station
PO Box 2448
Richmond, VA 23218
804-786-3551
For other information, contact:
Public Health Programs Office: 804-786-3563
Health Dept: 804-786-3561

Washington
Community & Family Health
PO Box 47890
Olympia, WA 98504-7890
360-753-7021
For other information, contact:
Health Dept: 360-586-5846

West Virginia
Epidemiology & Health Promotion Office
1411 Virginia St, East
Charleston, WV 25301
304-558-9100
For other information, contact:
Public Health Bureau: 304-558-2971
Health & Human Resources Dept: 304-558-0684

Wisconsin
Bureau of Public Health
1414 E Washington Ave
Madison, WI 53703
608-266-1251
For other information, contact:
Division of Health: 608-266-1511
Health & Family Services Dept: 608-266-1865

Wyoming
Behavioral Health-Community Programs Division
447 Hathaway Bldg
Cheyenne, WY 82002
307-777-7094
For other information, contact:
Health Dept: 307-777-7656

Hotlines and Toll-free Information Lines

Aerobics and Fitness Association of America (AFAA) Fitness Triage Team Consumer Line: 800-YOUR-BODY (800-968-7263)
(M–F 7:30AM–5:30PM PT) Operator assisted, referral service, answers questions, requests for materials.

AIDS Clinical Trials Information Service: 800-TRIALS-A (800-874-2574)

Al-Anon Meeting Information Line: 800-344-2666 (M–F 9AM–5PM ET); General Information: 800-356-9996 (M–F 9AM–5PM ET)

Allergy and Asthma Network/Mothers of Asthmatics Inc Help Line: 800-878-4403
(M–F 9AM–3PM ET) Operator assisted, answers questions, requests for materials.

Alzheimer's Association: 800-272-3900
(M–F 8:30AM–5PM CT) Operator assisted, 24-hr automated line, referral service, answers questions, requests for materials.

Alzheimer's Disease Education and Referral Center (ADEAR Center): 800-438-4380

American Academy of Ophthalmology Helpline: 800-222-EYES (800-222-3937)
(M–F 8AM–4PM PT) Operator assisted; information about the National Eye Care Project (nationwide outreach program to provide medical eye care to disadvantaged adults 65 yrs or older); written materials on conditions affecting the eye.

American Association of Diabetes Educators Self-Management Matters Line: 800-832-6874 24-hr operator assisted, referral service for contact names of local diabetes educators.

American Cancer Society Cancer Response System: 800-ACS-2345 (800-227-2345)
(M–F 8:30AM–4:30PM) Operator assisted, referral service, answers questions, requests for materials.

American Council on Alcoholism Information Line: 800-527-5344
(M–F 9AM–5PM ET) Referral service, answers questions, request for materials.

American Diabetes Association Diabetes Information and Action Line: 800-DIABETES (800-342-2383)
(M–F 9AM–5PM ET) Operator assisted, referral service, answers questions, requests for information.

American Institute for Cancer Research (AICR) Nutrition Hotline: 800-843-8114
(M–F 9AM–5PM ET); answers questions and requests for materials. Registered dietitians will research questions and return calls; no charge for service.

American Kidney Fund Help Line: 800-638-8299
(M–F 8:30AM–5PM ET)

American Liver Foundation: 800-GO-LIVER (800-463-4837)
(M–F 9AM–5PM ET) Operator assisted, answers questions, requests for materials.

American Liver Foundation: 888-4HEP-ABC (888-443-7222)
(M–F 9AM–5PM ET) Operator assisted, answers questions, requests for materials.

American Lung Association: 800-LUNG-USA (800-586-4872)

American Lyme Disease Foundation Information: 800-876-LYME (800-876-5963)
(M–F 9AM–5PM ET) Referral service, answers questions, requests for material.

American SIDS Institute Information Line: 800-232-SIDS (800-232-7437); (in GA): 800-847-SIDS (800-847-7437)
(M–F 8AM–5PM ET) Operator assisted, crisis or emergency, answers questions, requests for information.

American Suicide Foundation Information Line: 800-ASF-4042 (800-273-4042)
(M–F 9AM–5PM ET) Operator assisted, referral service, requests for materials.

American Trauma Society Information Line: 800-556-7890
(M–F 8:30AM–4:30PM ET) Operator assisted, answers questions, request for materials.

ASPO/Lamaze Information Line: 800-368-4404
(M–F 9AM–5PM ET) Referral service, answers questions, requests for materials.

Back-to-Sleep Campaign: 800-505-CRIB (800-505-2742)

Better Hearing Institute Helpline: 800-EAR-WELL (800-327-9355)
(M–F 9AM–5PM ET) Operator assisted, answers questions, request for materials.

Boat/U.S. Foundation for Boating Safety CourseLine: 800-336-2628

Campaign for Tobacco-Free Kids Request Line: 800-284-KIDS (800-284-5437) 24-hr automated, to request Action Kit.

Cancer Information Service: 800-4-CANCER (800-422-6237)

CDC Immunization Information Line: 800-232-7468

CDC National AIDS Clearinghouse: 800-458-5231

CDC Nutrition and Physical Activity Information Line: 888-232-4674

CDC Smoking, Tobacco, and Health Information Line: 800-232-1311

CFIDS Information Line: 800-442-3437 (24-hr) Automated line, leave name and address to receive information.

Child Find of America: 800-I-AM-LOST (800-426-5678) (to locate missing children); 800-A-WAY-OUT (800-292-9688) (parental abduction mediation) (M–F 9AM–5PM ET)

Coast Guard Customer Information Line: 800-368-5647

Committee for Children Information Line: 800-634-4449
(M–F 8AM–5PM PT) Answers questions and requests for materials.

Consumer Nutrition Hotline: 800-366-1655
(M–F 8AM–8PM CT) Automated line, referral service, answers questions.

Consumer Product Safety Commission Hotline: 800-638-CPSC (800-638-2772)

Crohn's and Colitis Foundation Information Line: 800-343-3637
(M–F 8AM–5PM ET) Operator assisted, requests for materials.

D/ART (Depression Awareness, Recognition & Treatment) Education Program: 800-421-4211

Eldercare Locator: 800-677-1116
(M–F 9AM–11PM ET) Operator assisted, referral service, answers questions. Designed to help older persons and caregivers link to local aging services.

Endometriosis Association Information Line: 800-992-3636
24-hr automated line, requests for materials.

Environmental Health Clearinghouse: 800-NIEHS-94 (800-643-4794)

EPA Safe Drinking Water Hotline: 800-426-4791

Epilepsy Foundation of America Information Line: 800-EFA-1000 (800-332-1000)
(M–F 8:30AM–5:30PM ET) Operator assisted, referral service, answers questions, requests for information.

FDA Office of Consumer Affairs Inquiries Information Line: 800-532-4440; 301-827-4420

FDA Seafood Hotline: 800-FDA-4010 (800-332-4010)

Food Allergy Network Information Line: 800-929-4040
(M–F 9AM–5PM ET) Operator assisted, referral service, answers questions, requests for information.

Foundation Fighting Blindness Information Line: 888-394-3937
(M–F 9AM–4:30PM ET) Operator assisted, referral service, requests for materials.

Geriatric Psychiatry Alliance Information Line: 888-INFO-GPA (888-463-6472)
(M–F 8AM–10PM ET) Operator assisted, referral service, requests for information.

Glaucoma Foundation Information Line: 800-GLAUCOMA (800-452-8266)
(M–F 9AM–5PM ET) Operator assisted, referral service, answers questions, requests for materials.

Health Resource Center on Domestic Violence Information Line: 888-Rx-ABUSE (888-792-2873)
(M–F 9AM–5PM PT) Automated line, referral service, answers questions, request materials.

Healthy Families America Information: 800-CHILDREN (800-244-5373) 24-hr automated line for those who wish to volunteer their services to their community.

Hearing Aid Helpline: 800-521-5247
(M–F 10AM–4PM ET) Operator assisted, referral service, answers questions, requests for materials.

HIV/AIDS Treatment Information Service: 800-HIV-0440 (800-448-0440)

HUD User: 800-245-2691

Huntington's Disease Information Line: 800-345-HDSA (800-345-4372) Automated line, referral to local groups, requests for materials.

Indian AIDS Information Line: 800-283-2437
(M–F 8:30AM–1PM, 2PM–5PM PT) Operator assisted and automated line, emergency, referral service, answers questions, requests for materials.

Juvenile Diabetes Foundation International Information Line: 800-JDF-CURE (800-533-2873)

Lung Line®: 800-222-LUNG (800-222-5864)
(M–F 8AM–5PM MT) Registered trained nurses answer questions and request for information.

Lupus Foundation of America Information Line: 800-558-0121
24-hr automated line, request for materials.

March of Dimes Birth Defects Foundation Information Line: 888-MO-DIMES (888-663-4637)
24-hr operator assisted, answers questions.

Muscular Dystrophy Association LifeLine: 800-572-1717
(M–F 8:30AM–5PM MT) Referral service, answers questions, requests for information.

National Abortion Federation Hotline: 800-772-9100
(M–F 9:30AM–5:30PM ET) Operator assisted, crisis or emergency, referral service, answers questions.

National AIDS Hotline: 800-342-AIDS (800-342-2437) (7 days/wk, 24hrs/day); Spanish: 800-344-7432 (7 days/wk, 8AM–2AM ET); TTY: 800-243-7889
(M–F 10AM–10PM ET) Confidential and anonymous information on HIV and AIDS and referral for health care and support groups.

National Alliance of Breast Cancer Organizations Information Line: 800-719-9154
24-hr automated line, answers questions, requests for materials.

National Clearinghouse for Alcohol and Drug Information Line: 800-729-6686
24-hr automated line; information specialists available M–F 8AM–7PM ET; answers questions, referral service, requests for materials.

National Clearinghouse for Primary Care Information: 800-400-2742

National Clearinghouse on Child Abuse and Neglect: 800-394-3366

National Cocaine Hotline: 800-COCAINE (800-262-2463)

National Committee to Prevent Child Abuse Information Line: 800-55-NCPCA (800-556-2722)
24-hr automated, requests for materials.

National Council on Alcoholism and Drug Dependence Hope Line: 800-NCA-CALL (800-622-2255) 24-hr automated, referral service, requests for materials.

National Domestic Violence Hotline: (800-799-SAFE) 800-799-7233

National Down Syndrome Society Information Line: 800-221-4602
(M–F 9AM–5PM ET) Operator assisted, referral service, answers questions. Information packet available to new parents.

National Drug and Alcohol Treatment Routing Service: 800-662-HELP (800-662-4357)

National Foundation for Depressive Illness Information Line: 800-248-4344
24-hr automated, pre-recorded information.

National Headache Foundation Information Line: 800-843-2256
(M–F 9AM–5PM CT) Answers questions.

National Health Information Center (NHIC): 800-336-4797

National Herpes Hotline: 919-361-8488
(M–F 9AM–7PM ET) Confidential and anonymous information and counseling on herpes.

National High Blood Pressure Education Program: 800-575-WELL (800-575-9355)

National Hispanic Immunization Hotline: 800-232-0233

National HIV-AIDS Telephone Consulting Service: 800-933-3413

National Immunization Information Hotline: 800-232-2522

National Indian AIDS Hotline: 800-283-2437

National Information Center for Children and Youth with Disabilities (NICHCY): 800-695-0285

National Institute for Occupational Safety and Health technical information: 800-35-NIOSH (800-356-4674)

National Institute on Deafness and Other Communication Disorders Information Clearinghouse: 800-241-1044

National Kidney Foundation Information Line: 800-622-9010
(M–F 8:30AM–5:30PM ET) Operator assisted, requests for materials.

National Lead Information Center Hotline: 800-LEAD-FYI (800-532-3394)
24-hr automated line, request for information packet

National Lymphedema Network Information Line: 800-541-3259
24-hr automated, referral service, answers questions, requests for materials.

National Mental Health Consumers' Self-Help Clearinghouse Information Line: 800-553-4539
(M–F 9AM–5PM ET) Automated, referral service, answers questions, requests for materials.

National Mental Health Information Center Inquiry Line: 800-969-NMHA (800-969-6642)
24-hr operator assisted, referral service, answers questions, requests for materials.

National Mental Health Services Knowledge Exchange Network Telephone Service: 800-789-2647
(8:30AM–5PM ET) Operator assisted, referral service, answers questions, requests for materials.

National Multiple Sclerosis Society Information Line: 800-FIGHT-MS (800-344-4867)
(M–F 11AM–5PM ET) Automated and operator assisted, answers questions, requests for materials, contact to local chapter.

National Osteoporosis Foundation Patient Information Center: 800-223-9994 contact to obtain free 22 pp booklet, Stand Up to Osteoporosis, and other materials. Call 800-464-6700 for the location of a bone density testing center in your area.

National Rehabilitation Information Center: 800-346-2742
(M–F 8AM–6PM ET) Referral service, requests for materials, information searches available, most free but extensive searches, $5 or more, and $5 minimum for copying and delivery fee.

National Reye's Syndrome Foundation Information Line: 800-233-7393
(M–F 8AM–5PM ET) Operator assisted, answers questions, requests for materials.

National Spinal Cord Injury Association Member Hotline: 800-962-9629
(M–F 8:30AM–4PM ET and 24-hr voice mail) Referral service, answers questions, requests for materials.

National STD Hotline: 800-227-8922
(M–F 8AM–11PM ET) Confidential and anonymous information on all sexually transmitted diseases and referral for health care.

National Stroke Association Information Line: 800-STROKES (800-787-6537)
(M–Th 8AM–4:30PM, F 8AM–4PM MT) Automated and operator assisted, answers questions, requests for materials.

National Workplace Helpline: 800-843-4971

National Youth Crisis Hotline: 800-HIT-HOME (800-448-4663) 24-hr operator assisted, crisis or emergency, referral service.

NIH Weight Control Information Network (WIN): 800-946-8098

Northern California HIV/AIDS Hotline: 800-FOR-AIDS (800-367-2437)
(M–F 9AM–9PM, Sat–Sun 11AM–5PM PT) Offers help and referral on AIDS prevention, education, and other support services, volunteer operators speak English, Spanish, and Filipino, as well as TDD.

NTSA Auto Safety Hotline: 800-424-9393 (202-366-0123 in D.C.)

Osteoporosis and Related Bone Diseases National Resource Center: 800-624-BONE (800-624-2663)

Panic and Other Anxiety Disorders Education Program: 800-64-PANIC (800-647-2642) (Spanish-speaking operators available) and 888-8-ANXIETY (888-826-9438)

Parkinson's Disease Foundation Information Line: 800-457-6676
(M–F 9AM–5PM ET) Operator assisted, referral service, answers questions, requests for materials.

Prevent Blindness America Information Line: 800-331-2020
(M–F 8AM–5PM CT) Operator assisted, requests for materials.

Project Inform National HIV/AIDS Treatment Hotline: 800-822-7422 or 415-558-9051
(M–F 9AM–5PM, Sat 10AM–4PM PT) Operator assisted, referral service, answers questions, requests for materials. HIV treatment info and data on various therapies.

Radon Hotline: 800-SOS-RADON (800-767-7236)
24-hr automated line, request for information packet, answers questions

Research!America Information Line: 800-FON-CURE (800-366-2873)
(M–F 9AM–5:30PM ET) Operator assisted, referral service, requests for materials.

Spina Bifida Association of America Request Line: 800-621-3141
(M–F 9AM–5PM ET) Automated, requests for materials.

Stroke Connection: 800-553-6321
24-hr automated line, answers questions, referral service to support groups, requests for materials.

The AIDS Treatment Data Network: 800-734-7104
(M–F 10AM–6PM ET) Operator assisted, emergency, referral service, answers questions, requests for materials. Counselors assist health care professionals, educators, and clients in English and Spanish.

Thyroid Foundation of America Information Line: 800-832-8321
(M–F 8:30AM–4PM ET) Automated, referral service, answers questions, requests for materials.

USDA Meat and Poultry Hotline: 800-535-4555 and 202-720-3333

Women's Sports Foundation Sports Infoline: 800-227-3988
(M–F 9AM–5PM ET) Operator assisted, referral service, answers questions, requests for materials.

Y-ME® National Breast Cancer Hotline: 800-221-2141; 800-986-9505 (Spanish) 24-hr operator assisted, crisis or emergency.

Resources for Racial and Ethnic Populations

Asian and Pacific Islanders American Health Forum Inc
116 New Montgomery St, Ste 531
San Francisco, CA 94105
415-541-0866
Fax: 415-512-3881

Asian Health Project
The Clinic
3860 W Martin Luther King Blvd
Los Angeles, CA 90008
213-295-6571
Fax: 213-295-6577

Association of Asian Pacific Community Health Organizations
1440 Broadway, Ste 510
Oakland, CA 94612
510-272-9536
Fax: 510-272-0817

Black Womens' Health Council
PO Box 31089
Capitol Heights, MD 20731
301-808-0786
Fax: 301-808-0963

Bureau of Primary Health Care (BPHC)
Health Resources and Services Administration
4350 East West Hwy
Bethesda, MD 20814
Program for Special Populations Division: 301-594-4420
Office of Minority and Women's Health: 301-594-4490

Indian Health Service (IHS)
Office of Public Health and Science
U.S. Dept of Health & Human Services
Parklawn Bldg, Rm 6-35
5600 Fishers Ln
Rockville, MD 20857
Communications Office: 301-443-3593
Fax: 301-443-0507
Web site: http://www.tucson.ihs.gov

Korean Health Education, Information and Referral Center
545 S Gramercy Pl
Los Angeles, CA 90020
213-427-4000
Fax: 213-427-4008

National Asian Pacific American Families Against Substance Abuse
1887 Maplegate St
Monterey Park, CA 91755-6536
Contact: Frances Kuramoto
213-278-0031
Fax: 213-278-9078
E-mail: napafasn@igc.apc.org
Web site: http://www.emory.edu/NFIA/

National Asian Pacific Center on Aging
1511 Third Ave, Ste 914
Seattle, WA 98101-1626
Contact: Valerie Gungap
206-624-1221
Fax: 206-624-1023

National Asian Women's Health Organization
250 Montgomery St, Ste 410
San Francisco, CA 94104
415-989-9747
Fax: 415-989-9758

National Association for Native American Children of Alcoholics
1402 Third Ave, Ste 1110
Seattle, WA 98101
Contact: Annette Squetimkin-Anquoe
206-467-7686
Fax: 206-467-7689
E-mail: nanacoa@aol.com

National Association for the Hispanic Elderly
3325 Wilshire Blvd, Ste 800
Los Angeles, CA 90010
213-487-1922
Fax: 213-385-3014

Please check individual organization listings for resources available in languages appropriate for racial and ethnic populations.

National Association of Community Health Centers Inc
1330 New Hampshire Ave NW, Ste 122
Washington, DC 20036
202-659-8008
Fax: 202-659-8519

National Black Child Development Institute
1023 15 St NW, Ste 600
Washington, DC 20005
202-387-1281
Fax: 202-234-1738
E-mail: moreinfo@nbcdi.org
Web site: http://www.nbcdi.org

National Black Women's Health Project
1211 Connecticut Ave NW, Ste 310
Washington, DC 20036
202-835-0117
Fax: 202-833-8790
E-mail: nbwhpdc@aol.com

National Caucus and Center on Black Aged
1424 K St NW, Ste 500
Washington, DC 20005
202-637-8400
Fax: 202-347-0895

National Coalition of Hispanic Health and Human Services Organization
1501 16th St NW
Washington, DC 20036
202-387-5000
Fax: 202-797-4353
Web site: http:www.cossmho.org/

National Council of La Raza Center for Health Promotion
1111 19th St NW, Ste 1000
Washington, DC 20036
Contact: Lupe Lemus, 202-785-1670
202-785-1670
Fax: 202-776-1792
E-mail: hpacheco@nclr.org
Web site: http://www.nclr.org

National Foundation for Jewish Genetic Diseases
250 Park Ave, Ste 1000
New York, NY 10017
Contact: George Crohn
212-371-1030
Fax: 212-319-5808

National Hispanic Council on Aging
2713 Ontario Rd NW
Washington, DC 20009
202-265-1288
Fax: 202-745-2522

National Indian Council on Aging
10501 Montgomery Blvd NE, Ste 210
Albuquerque, NM 87111
Contact: Dave Baldridge or Eva Gardipe
505-292-2001
Fax: 505-292-1922

National Native American AIDS Prevention Center
2100 Lake Shore Ave, Ste A
Oakland, CA 94606
Contact: Sally Ramon
800-283-2437
510-444-2051
Fax: 510-444-1593
E-mail: nnaapc@aol.com

Novela Health Education
1001 Broadway, Ste 100
Seattle, WA 98122
800-677-4799
Fax: 206-720-4382
E-mail: novela@u.washington.edu
Web site: http://weber.u.washington.edu/~novela

Office of Minority Health Resource Center
Office of Public Health and Science
U.S. Dept. of Health & Human Services
8455 Colesville Rd, Ste 910
Silver Spring, MD 20910
Mailing address:
PO Box 37337
Washington, DC 20013-7337
800-444-6472
Fax: 301-589-0884
Web site: http://www.omhrc.gov

Zuni Wellness Center
PO Box 308
Zuni, NM 87327
505-782-2665
Fax: 505-782-4388

Organization Index

A

AAA Foundation for Traffic Safety, 134
ACA Council on Sports Injuries and Physical Fitness, 64
Academy for Educational Development, 204
Access Health Inc, 8
Action on Smoking and Health (ASH), 84
Administration for Children and Families (ACF), 231, 247
Administration on Aging (AOA), 239, 247
Advertising Council Inc, The, 5
Advocates for Youth, 199, 212
Aerobics and Fitness Association of America, 64
Agency for Health Care Policy and Research (AHCPR), 19, 247
Agency for Toxic Substances and Disease Registry (ASTDR), 108, 247
AIDS Clinical Trials Information Service, 206, 252
AIDS Treatment Data Network (The Network), The, 199
Alabama Health Promotion & Information Bureau, 255
Alan Guttmacher Institute, 215
Al-Anon Family Groups Headquarters Inc, 80
Alaska Community Health & Emergency Medical Services, 255
Alcoholics Anonymous, 80
Alexander & Alexander Consulting Group, 14
All Kids Count—National Program Office, 193
Allergy and Asthma Network • Mothers of Asthmatics Inc, 152
Allergy Research Institute, 186
Alliance for Aging Research, The, 238
Alliance of Genetic Support Groups, 230
Alliance To End Childhood Lead Poisoning, 104
Alzheimer's Association, 179
Alzheimer's Disease Education and Referral Center (ADEAR Center), 187, 240, 251
AMC Cancer Research Center, 160
American Academy of Allergy, Asthma, and Immunologyy, 153
American Academy of Dermatology, 160
American Academy of Family Physicians, 91
American Academy of Natural Family Planning, 212
American Academy of Ophthalmology, 179
American Academy of Pediatrics, 75, 130, 139, 152, 190, 199, 219
American Alliance for Health, Physical Education, Recreation, and Dance (AAHPERD), 69
American Anorexia/Bulimia Association, 54
American Association for Cancer Research, 160
American Association for Geriatric Psychiatry, 236
American Association for Health Education, 91
American Association for Health Plans, 14
American Association for Respiratory Care, 85, 153
American Association of Diabetes Educators, 164
American Association of Occupational Health Nurses Inc, 118
American Association of Poison Control Centers, 134
American Association of Public Health Dentistry, 126
American Association of Retired Persons, 239
American Association of School Administrators, 14
American Association of Suicidology, 45
American Association on Mental Retardation, 245
American Automobile Association (AAA) Traffic Safety Department, 134
American Business Publishing, 91
American Cancer Society, 156
American Chiropractic Association, 97
American Coalition for Traffic Safety Inc, 134
American College Health Association, 85, 97, 204
American College of Allergy, Asthma and Immunology, 153
American College of Epidemiology, 14, 97
American College of Nurse Practitioner, 97
American College of Nurse-Midwives, 230
American College of Obstetricians and Gynecologists, 219
American College of Occupational and Environmental Medicine, 118
American College of Physicians, 193
American College of Preventive Medicine, 91
American College of Radiology, 160
American College of Sports Medicine, 64
American Conference of Governmental Industrial Hygienists, 104, 118, 190
American Council on Alcoholism Inc, 81
American Council on Exercise, 69
American Council on Science and Health, 112
American Dental Association, 126
American Dental Hygienists' Association, 126
American Diabetes Association, 164
American Dietetic Association, 58, 112, 164
American Foundation for AIDS Research (AmFAR), 205
American Foundation for Urologic Disease Inc, 161
American Geriatrics Society, 236
American Health Foundation, 161
American Health Planning Association, 14
American Heart Association, 9, 172
American Hospital Association, 5, 35

American Humane Association Children's Division, 144
American Industrial Hygiene Association, 122
American Institute for Cancer Research, 58, 156
American Institute for Preventive Medicine, 9, 25, 45, 51, 58, 82
American Institute of Stress, The, 52
American Journal of Health Promotion, 91
American Kidney Fund, 179
American Liver Foundation, 180, 190
American Lung Association, 85, 107, 186
American Lyme Disease Foundation Inc, 190
American Medical Association, 97, 144
American Medical Athletic Association, 64
American Mental Health Counselors Association, 45
American Optometric Association, 168
American Osteopathic Association, 97
American Outreach Association, 75
American Pharmaceutical Association, 193
American Physical Therapy Association, 69
American Prostate Society, 156
American Psychiatric Association, 54
American Psychological Association, 54
American Public Health Association, 5, 92, 199
American Red Cross, 205
American Running and Fitness Association, 65
American School Food Service Association, 61
American School Health Association, 15
American Self-Help Clearinghouse, 46
American Social Health Association, 200, 219
American Society for Reproductive Medicine, 212
American Society of Dentistry for Children, 126
American Society of Preventive Oncology, 161
American Society on Aging, 239
American Speech-Language-Hearing Association, 245
American Spinal Injury Association, 242
American Sudden Infant Death Syndrome (SIDS) Institute, 220
American Suicide Foundation, 46
American Thoracic Society, 186
American Trauma Society, 130
American Water Works Association Research Foundation, 107
American Water Works Association, 107
Americans for Nonsmokers' Rights, 83, 104
Anatomical Chart Company, 58, 83, 156, 200
Anorexia Nervosa and Related Eating Disorders Inc, 50
Arc, The, 220, 242
Arizona Center for Prevention & Health Promotion, 255
Arkansas Preventive Health Services, 255
Arthritis Foundation, 186
Ashby*Montrose & Company, 9
Asian and Pacific Islanders American Health Forum Inc, 15, 267
Asian Health Project, 267
Aspen Publishers Inc, 5
ASPO/Lamaze (American Society for Psychoprophylaxis in Obstetrics), 220
Association for Applied Psychophysiology and Biofeedback, 52
Association for the Advancement of Automotive Medicine, 130
Association for Worksite Health Promotion, 92
Association of Women's Health, Obstetric, and Neonatal Nurses, 221
Association of Asian Pacific Community Health Organizations, 15, 267
Association of Community Cancer Centers, 161
Association of Hospital Health and Fitness, 69, 97
Association of Maternal and Child Health Programs, 230
Association of Reproductive Health Professionals, 213
Association of Schools of Public Health, 97
Association of SIDS and Infant Mortality Programs, 221
Association of State and Territorial Health Officials (ASTHO), 92
Association of Teachers of Preventive Medicine, 93
Asthma and Allergy Foundation of America, 153
Asthma Information Center, 153
Audio Vision, 52
Avery Publishing Group, 31
Avon Products Foundation, 161
Award-Winning Presentations, 52

B

BACCHUS and GAMMA Peer Education Network, The, 75
Back School of Atlanta, 118
Back-to-Sleep Campaign, 230
Balboa Publishing, 59
Benfield Group, The, 69
Best Friends Foundation, 215
Best Start Inc, 221
Better Hearing Institute, 242
Bicycle Helmet Safety Institute, 130
BioFitness Systems Inc, 65
Black Women's Health Council, 230, 267
Board on Children, Youth, and Families; Institute of Medicine, 230
Brain Injury Association Inc, 134
Breast Cancer Information Clearinghouse, New York State Education and Research Network, 161
Bureau For At-Risk Youth, The, 75
Bureau of Health Professions (BHPr), 99, 247
Bureau of Labor Statistics, see Office of Safety, Health, and Working Conditions
Bureau of Primary Health Care (BPHC), 19, 206, 247, 267
Business & Legal Reports Inc, 122, 145

C

California Prevention Services Dept, 255
Cancer Care Inc, 161
CAR SAFE Inc, Community Auto Restraint Safety and Family Education, 134
Carter Center, The, 54, 193
Catholic Health Association, 15
CD Publications, 5, 200, 242
CDC National AIDS Clearinghouse, 206, 252
Center for Biologics Evaluation and Research (CBER), 194, 247
Center for Devices & Radiological Health (CDRH), 114, 247
Center for Drug Evaluation and Research (CDER), 114, 247
Center for Food Safety and Applied Nutrition (CFSAN), 62, 114, 247
Center for Health Promotion, 85
Center for Medical Consumers, 25
Center for Mental Health Services (CMHS), 55, 247
Center for Science in the Public Interest, 112
Center for Studying Health System Change, 15
Center for Substance Abuse Prevention (CSAP), 86, 248
Center for Substance Abuse Treatment (CSAT), 86, 248
Center for the Advancement of Health, 15
Center for Training in Mind/Body Medicine, 93
Center for Women Policy Studies, 205, 230
Center to Prevent Handgun Violence, 139
Center to Protect Workers' Rights, The, 119
Centers for Disease Control and Prevention (CDC), 20, 248
CFIDS Association of America Inc, The, 180
Channing L Bete Co Inc, 25, 46, 53, 59, 76, 126, 131, 139, 156, 165, 172, 180, 190, 200, 213, 236, 243
Check Up Centers of America, 35
Chemical Injury Information Network, 104
Chemotherapy Foundation, The, 157
Child Abuse Prevention Center, 145
Child Find of America Inc, 139
Child Health Foundation, 222
Child Trends Inc, 215
Child Welfare League of America, 140
Childbirth Graphics, A Division of WRS Group Inc, 230
Childhelp USA, 145
Children Now, 145
Children's Defense Fund, 193
Children's Environmental Health Network, 107
Children's Health Fund, 193
Children's Safety Network National Injury and Violence Prevention Resource Center, 134, 145
Chiltern Hills Wellness, 31
Choice Diets Inc, 59
Circle Solutions Inc, 15
Citizens Against Drug Impaired Drivers, 134
Citizens for Public Action on Blood Pressure and Cholesterol, 174
Clinical Reference Systems Ltd, 25, 46, 168, 222, 236
Coalition for America's Children, 145
Coalition for Hypertension Prevention, The, 172
Coalition on Addiction, Pregnancy and Parenting, 215
Coalition on Smoking or Health, 85
Coalition to Stop Gun Violence, 145
Coffey Communications Inc, 26
Colorado Family & Community Health Services Division, 255
Committee for Children, 140
Commonwealth Fund, The, 6
Community Anti-Drug Coalitions of America, 85
Community Health Improvement, The, 19
Comprehensive Health Education Foundation, 145
Computerized Health Systems Inc, 35
Conference Board Inc, The, 15
Connaught Laboratories Inc, 193
Connecticut Community Health Bureau, 255
Consumer Information Center (CIC), 32, 248
Cooper Aerobics Center, The, 69
Cooper Institute for Aerobics Research, The, 69
Corporate Fitness Midwest Inc, 9, 65
Corporate Fitness Works, 15
Council of State and Territorial Epidemiologists, 15
Council on Education for Public Health, 97
Council on Family Health, 112
Council on Foundations, 15
Courier Communications, 31
Crisis Prevention Institute Inc, 145
Crohn's and Colitis Foundation of America Inc, 180
Customized Communications Inc, 157, 222
CWE Inc, 134

D

Dairy Management Inc, 61
Delaware Public Health Division, 255
Dental Health Foundation, 126
Depression After Delivery Inc (D.A.D.), 47
DES Action, 222
Diabetes Research Foundation, The, 166
Diabetes Research Institute Foundation, 165
Dial A Hearing Screening Test, 243
Digestive Disease National Coalition, 187
DINE Systems Inc, 59
Disabled Sports USA, 243
District of Columbia Preventive Health Dept, 255
Division of Nutrition and Physical Activity, NCCDPHP, 62, 70
Dreyfuss Hunt Inc, 26
Drug Prevention Resources Inc, 81
Dump Your Plump, 61
DuPont Company, 122, 135

E

Eating Disorders Awareness and Prevention (EDAP), 50
Education Development Center Inc, 15
Education Programs Associates, 31
Educational Fund to End Handgun Violence, The, 140, 145
EMC2 (Employee Managed Care Corporation), 10, 35
Employee Assistance Program Association, 15
Employee Assistance Society of North America, 97
Endometriosis Association, 223
Environmental Action Foundation, 107
Environmental Defense Fund, 107
Environmental Health Center, 105
Environmental Health Clearinghouse, 108, 251
Epidemiology Program Office (EPO), 20
Epilepsy Foundation of America, 181
Eris Survey Systems Inc, 40
ETR Associates, 145, 205, 216
Every Child By Two, 191
Exceptional Cancer Patients Inc, 157

F

Family Health International, 213
Family Resource Coalition, 145
Family Service America Inc, 230
Family Violence Prevention Fund, 140
Fanlight Productions, 239
FastMark Inc, 131, 223, 236
Feistritzer Publications, 93
Felix, Burdine and Associates Inc, 6, 35
Fetal Alcohol Education Program, Boston University School of Medicine, 230
Films for the Humanities & Sciences, 26
Fire and Injury Prevention Association, 135
First Marketing Company, 31
Fitcorp, 10, 65
Fitness Finders Inc, 66
Fitness Products Council, 69
Fitness Systems, 15
Florida Health Communication & Promotion, 255
Food Allergy Network, The, 181
Food and Consumer Services (FCS), 232, 248
Food and Nutrition Board, Institute of Medicine, 61
Food and Nutrition Information Center (FNIC), 62, 248
Food Safety and Inspection Service (FSIS), 115
Foundation Center, The, 15
Foundation Fighting Blindness, The, 168

G

Genium Publishing Corporation, 119
Georgia Chronic Disease, Prevention & Health Promotion Branch, 256
Geriatric Psychiatry Alliance, 47, 237
Geriatric Video Productions, 237
Gerontological Society of America, The, 237
Gilda Radner Familial Ovarian Cancer Registry , The, 161
Glaucoma Foundation, The, 169
Glaucoma Research Foundation, 169
Government Institutes, 107
Grafeeties and Company, 76
Grantsmanship Center, The, 16
Greater Talent Network Inc, 16
Greenstone Healthcare Solutions, 10, 36
Group B Strep Association, 223
Group Health Cooperative of Puget Sound, 85
Gürze Books, 50

H

Hall-Foushee Communications Inc, 26, 172
Hancock, Dr. Trevor, 6
Harvard Injury Control Center, 131, 141
Harvard Medical School Health Publications Group, 26
Hawaii Health Promotion & Education Branch, 256
Hazelden, 85
HCIA–Response, 40
Health Awareness Inc, 16
Health Care Financing Administration (HCFA), 20, 248
Health Connection, The, 85
Health Decisions International LLC, 10
Health Edco, A Division of WRS Group Inc, 31
Health Education Foundation, 16
Health Education Services, 6, 60, 66, 105, 131, 157, 201, 213
Health Enhancement Systems Inc, 16
Health Evaluation Systems Inc, 11, 36
Health Examinetics Inc, 36, 119
Health First Consulting Corporation, 11, 36
Health Information Network, 201
Health Information Resource Center, 27
Health Insurance Association of America, 16
Health Letter Associates, 27
Health Management Corporation, 16
Health Management Research Center, University of Michigan, 40
Health Management Resources, 40
Health Professions Press, 47, 182, 237
Health Project, The, 16
Health Promotion Resource Center, 8
Health Resource Center on Domestic Violence, 140
Health Resources and Services Administration (HRSA), 20, 248
Health Resources Publishing, 16, 97
Healthcare Forum, The, 93
HealthDesk Corporation, 16
Healthier People Network Inc, 36

Healthier People Software, 11, 36
HealthMatters, 16
HealthStyle, 11, 66
Healthwise Incorporated, 27
Healthwork, 54
Healthworks, 69
Healthy Achievers, 11, 66, 119
Healthy Mothers, Healthy Babies, 191, 223
Healthy People 2000 Management Team, 22, 252
Hepatitis Foundation International, 191
Higher Education Center for Alcohol and Other Drug Prevention, 85
HIN Inc (The Health Information Network), 120, 132, 152, 157, 172
HIV/AIDS Treatment Information Service, 206, 252
Homeopathic Educational Services, 27
Hope for Kids, 193
Hope Publications, 27
HUD User, 108
Human Dynamics Inc, 53
Human Kinetics Publishers, 66
Human Resources Institute Inc, 11, 37
Huntington's Disease Society of America Inc, 182

I

IAQ Publications, 105, 120
Idaho Health Promotion Bureau, 256
IDEA: International Association of Fitness Professionals, 69
Illinois Health Promotion Center, 256
Immunization Action Coalition, 192
Impact AIDS, 201
Indian Health Service (IHS), 136, 249, 267
Indiana Health Promotion Center, 256
Indoor Air Quality Information Clearinghouse, 109, 253
Industrial Health Foundation Inc, 105, 120
Infectious Diseases Society of America, 194
Info Vision, 28
Infoline, 97
Information Transfer Systems Inc, 40
Informed Access Systems Inc, 12
Institute for Alternative Futures, 16, 40
Institute for Educational Leadership, The, 16
Institute for Healthcare Improvement, 98
Institute for Mental Health Initiative, 54
Institute of Medicine, National Academy of Sciences, 16, 61, 230
Insurance Institute for Highway Safety, 135
Intermedia, 141, 213
International Association of Physicians in AIDS Cars, 205
International Cancer Information Center, 162, 249
International Commission for the Prevention of Alcoholism and Drug Dependency, 76
International Hearing Society, 243
International Medical Services for Health (INMED), 230
International Parish Nurse Resource Center, 12
International Quality and Productivity Center, 98
Iowa Family and Community Health Division, 256

J

Jacobs Institute of Women's Health, 230
Johanna's of Albany Ltd, 158
Johns Hopkins Center for Communication Programs, Population Information Program, 214
Johnson and Johnson Health Care Systems Inc, 17, 40
Johnson Institute, 37, 76
Join Together: A National Resource for Communities Fighting Substance Abuse, 77
Joint Commission on Accreditaton of Healthcare Organizations, 17
Joslin Diabetes Center, 166
Journeyworks Publishing, 47, 67, 83, 158, 201, 214
Joyce Institute, The, 120
Just Say No International, 85
Juvenile Diabetes Foundation International, 166
Juvenile Products Manufacturers Association, 132

K

Kansas Chronic Disease & Health Promotion, 256
Kempe National Center for the Prevention and Treatment of Child Abuse and Neglect, 141
Kentucky Environmental Health & Community Safety Division, 256
KidsPeace, The National Center for Kids in Crisis, 54, 145
Kiwanis International, 194
Korean Health Education, Information and Referral Center, 267
Krames Communications, 31, 122

L

Lange Productions, 28, 158
Learn Not To Burn Foundation, 135
Learning Partnership, The, 85
Leukemia Society of America Inc, 161
Lewin Group, The, 17
Longe Life Libraries, 28
Louisiana Health Protection & Promotion Division, 256
Lowfat Lifeline, 60
LRP Publications, 122
Lupus Foundation of America, 182
Lyme Disease Foundation Inc, 194

M

Maine Health Promotion & Education, 256
Mammatech Corporation, 158
Management Intervention Services, 77

March of Dimes Birth Defects Foundation, 224
Maryland Community Health Surveillance Administration, 256
Massachusetts Prevention Division, 256
Maternal and Child Health Bureau (MCHB), 232, 249
Maternity Center Association, 224
Mayo Clinic Health Information, 28, 60, 173, 224
Medcom Inc, 152, 159, 165, 173, 224
Medical Data Source, 29
Melpomene Institute for Women's Health Research, 67
Mental Health Materials Center, 47
Merck Vaccine Division, 194
Michigan Health Promotion & Chronic Disease Prevention Center, 257
MicroFit, 37
Milner-Fenwick Inc, 31
Mind/Body Medical Institute, 93
Minnesota Community Health Services Division, 257
Mississippi Health Promotion, 257
Missouri Chronic Disease Prevention & Health Promotion Division, 257
Montana Chronic Disease & Health Promotion Section, 257
Mosby Consumer Health Division, 31
Mothers Against Drunk Driving (MADD), 135
Motherwell Maternity Health and Fitness, 225
Muscular Dystrophy Association, 182

N

NASCO, 60, 77, 159, 202, 214
National Abortion Federation, 214
National Academy for State Health Policy, 98
National Academy Press, 17
National Agricultural Library, see Food and Nutrition Information Center
National AIDS Funds, 205
National Alliance for the Mentally Ill, 54
National Alliance of Breast Cancer Organizations (NABCO), 159
National Asian Pacific American Families Against Substance Abuse, 77
National Asian Pacific Center on Aging, 237, 267
National Asian Women's Health Organization, 225, 267
National Assembly of National Voluntary Health and Social Welfare Organizations, 17, 85
National Association for Families and Addictions and Research and Education, 85
National Association for Healthcare Quality, 93
National Association for Human Development, 239
National Association for Native American Children of Alcoholics, 81, 267
National Association for the Hispanic Elderly, 239, 267
National Association of Alcoholism and Drug Abuse Counselors, 78
National Association of Anorexia Nervosa and Associated Disorders, 54
National Association of Area Agencies on Aging, 239
National Association of Chain Drug Stores, 114
National Association of Child Advocates, 230
National Association of Childbearing Centers, 225
National Association of Children's Hospitals & Related Institutions, 231
National Association of Community Action Agencies, 17
National Association of Community Health Centers Inc, 17, 268
National Association of County & City Health Officials (NACHO), 17, 98
National Association of Governor's Councils on Physical Fitness and Sports, 67
National Association of Nurse Practitioners in Reproductive Health, 225
National Association of Pediatric Nurse Associates and Practitioners, 226
National Association of People with AIDs, 205
National Association of School Nurses, 37
National Association of State Boards of Education, 17, 98, 245
National Association of State Units on Aging, 60, 141, 238
National Association of Women's Health Professionals, 94, 226
National Association on Drug Abuse Problems, 85
National Black Child Development Institute, 231, 268
National Black Women's Health Project, 231, 268
National Breast Cancer Awareness Month, 161
National Business Coalition on Health, The, 98
National Campaign for Healthcare Worker Safety, 120
National Campaign To Prevent Teen Pregnancy, The, 216
National Cancer Institute (NCI), 162, 249
National Cattlemen's Beef Association, 70
National Caucus and Center on Black Aged, 239, 268
National Center for Assault Prevention, 146
National Center for Children in Poverty, 226
National Center for Chronic Disease Prevention & Health Promotion (NCCDPHP), 20, 187, 249
National Center for Education in Maternal and Child Health (NCEMCH), 227
National Center for Environmental Health (NCEH), 109, 232, 249
National Center for Environmental Health Strategies Inc, 107
National Center for Health Education, 6, 81, 142, 202
National Center for Health Promotion, The, 17, 54, 61
National Center for Health Statistics (NCHS), 41, 249
National Center for HIV, STD & TB Prevention (NCHSTP), 194, 206, 249
National Center for Infectious Diseases (NCID), 195, 249
National Center for Injury Prevention and Control (NCIPC), 136, 146, 249

National Center for Lead-Safe Housing, 107
National Center for Overcoming Overeating, 50
National Center for Tobacco-Free Kids, 83
National Center for Youth with Disabilities, 243
National Center on Child Abuse and Neglect (NCCAN), 146, 250
National Chronic Fatigue Syndrome and Fibromyalgia Association, 183
National Civic League, 17
National Clearinghouse for Alcohol and Drug Information (NCADI), 78
National Clearinghouse for Primary Care Information, 20, 247
National Clearinghouse on Child Abuse and Neglect, 146, 250
National Coalition Against Domestic Violence, 146
National Coalition for Adult Immunization, 192
National Coalition for Cancer Survivorship, 159
National Coalition for Promoting Physical Activity, 70
National Coalition of Hispanic Health and Human Services Organization, 268
National Coalition on Ergonomics, 122
National Commission Against Drunk Driving, 135
National Committee for Quality Assurance, 17
National Committee for the Prevention of Elder Abuse, 142
National Committee to Prevent Child Abuse, 142
National Community Mental Healthcare Council, 48
National Community Pharmacists Association, 114
National Conference of State Legislatures, 205
National Consumers League, 112, 132
National Coordinating Committee on Worksite Health Promotion, 22, 252
National Council of Catholic Women, 231
National Council of La Raza Center for Health Promotion, 7, 192, 202, 227, 268
National Council on Alcoholism and Drug Dependence Inc (NCADD), 79, 227
National Council on Child Abuse and Family Violence, 146
National Council on Disability, 246
National Council on Patient Information and Education, 113
National Council on the Aging, 239
National Crime Prevention Council, 143
National Criminal Justice Reference Service (NCJRS), 147, 250
National Depressive and Manic-Depressive Association, 48
National Diabetes Information Clearinghouse (NDIC), 62, 166, 251
National Digestive Diseases Information Clearinghouse (NDDIC), 187, 251
National Domestic Violence Hotline, 146
National Down Syndrome Society, 244
National Early Childhood Technical Assistance System (NEC*TAS), 231
National Easter Seal Society, 246
National Eating Disorders Organization, 51
National Environmental Health Association, 105
National Exchange Club, 146
National Eye Institute (NEI), 170, 250
National Families in Action, 79
National Family Partnership, 79
National Family Planning and Reproductive Health Association, 216
National Federation of State High School Associations, 86
National Fire Protection Association, 135
National Foundation for Cancer Research, 161
National Foundation for Depressive Illness, 48
National Foundation for Infectious Diseases, 193
National Foundation for Jewish Genetic Diseases, 231, 268
National Governors' Association, 194
National Head Start Association, 94, 143
National Headache Foundation, 183
National Health Council, 98
National Health Enhancement Systems, 32
National Health Information Center (NHIC), 20, 250
National Health Video Inc, 53
National Heart Savers Association, 174
National Heart, Lung, and Blood Institute (NHLBI), 70, 86, 153, 174, 250
National Hemophilia Foundation, 205
National Highway Traffic Safety Administration (NHTSA), 87, 136, 250
National Hispanic Council on Aging, 239, 268
National HIV-AIDS Telephone Consulting Service, 207
National Hypertension Association Inc, 173
National Immunization Program (NIP), 195, 250
National Indian AIDS Hotline, 205
National Indian Council on Aging, 239, 268
National Information Center for Children and Youth with Disabilities (NICHCY), 246
National Injury Information Clearinghouse, 136, 253
National Institute for Health Care Management, 18
National Institute for Healthcare Research, 32
National Institute for Occupational Safety and Health (NIOSH), 123, 250
National Institute of Allergy and Infectious Diseases (NIAID), 187, 195, 207, 250
National Institute of Arthritis and Musculoskeletal and Skin Diseases (NIAMS), 71, 187, 250
National Institute of Child Health and Human Development (NICHD), 216, 232, 250
National Institute of Dental Research (NIDR), 127, 251
National Institute of Diabetes and Digestive and Kidney Disease (NIDDK), 166, 188, 251
National Institute of Environmental Health Sciences (NIEHS), 109, 251
National Institute of Mental Health (NIMH), 55, 251
National Institute of Neurological Disease and Stroke (NINDS), 175, 188, 251

National Institute on Aging (NIA), 188, 240, 251
National Institute on Alcohol Abuse and Alcoholism (NIAAA), 87, 251
National Institute on Deafness and Other Communication Disorders (NIDCD), 188, 246
National Institute on Disability and Rehabilitation Research (NIDRR), 246, 251
National Institute on Drug Abuse (NIDA), 87, 251
National Institutes of Health (NIH), 21, 251
National Jewish Center for Immunology and Respiratory Medicine, 153
National Kidney and Urologic Diseases Information Clearinghouse (NKUDIC), 188, 251
National Kidney Foundation, 183
National Leadership Coalition on AIDS, 205
National League of Cities, 18
National Library of Medicine (NLM), 21, 251
National Lymphedema Network, 183
National Managed Health Care Congress, The, 94
National Maternal and Child Health Clearinghouse, 232, 249
National Mental Health Association, 48
National Mental Health Consumers' Self-Help Clearinghouse, 49
National Mental Health Services Knowledge Exchange Network, 49
National Mental Illness Screening Project, 55
National Minority AIDS Council, 202
National Multiple Sclerosis Society, 184
National Native American AIDS Prevention Center, 203, 268
National Oral Health Information Clearinghouse (NOHIC), 127, 251
National Organization for Rare Disorders, 184
National Organization on Adolescent Pregnancy, Parenting, and Prevention, 216
National Organization on Fetal Alcohol Syndrome, 231
National Osteoporosis Foundation, 185
National Parents' Resource Institute for Drug Education Inc (PRIDE), 79
National Pediatric and Family HIV Resource Center
National Pediculosis Association, 106
National Perinatal Association, 231
National Perinatal Information Center, 231
National Pesticide Telecommunications Network, 108
National Policy and Resource Center on Women and Aging, 238
National Prevention Network / National Association of State Alcohol and Drug Abuse Directors, 80
National Program for Playground Safety, The, 135
National PTA, The, 18
National Public Health and Hospital Institute, The, 18
National Recreation and Park Association, 70
National Rehabilitation Information Center (NARIC), 244
National Resource Center for Youth Mediation: a Division of the New Mexico Center for Dispute Resolution, 146
National Resource Center on Homelessness and Mental Illness, 55
National Resource Center on Women and AIDS, 205
National Reye's Syndrome Foundation, 185
National Rural Health Association, 18, 98
National SAFE KIDS Campaign, 135
National Safe Workplace Institute, 143
National Safety Belt Coalition, 135
National Safety Council, 121, 132
National Sanitation Foundation, 108
National School Safety Center, 143
National Spinal Cord Injury Association, 244
National Stroke Association, 173, 245
National Sudden Infant Death Syndrome Resource Center, 232
National Technical Information Service (NTIS), 21, 252
National Urban League, 18
National Wellness Information Resource Center, Fisher Institute for Wellness, Ball State University, 95
National Wellness Institute Inc, 38, 95
National Wellness Speakers Bureau, 18
National Women's Health Network, 231
National Women's Health Resource Center, 228
National Women's Resource Center, 86
National Youth Sports Safety Foundation Inc, 67, 132
Natural Family Planning Center of Washington D.C., 216
Natural Resources Defense Council, 108
Nebraska Health Promotion & Education Section, 257
Network Health Systems™, 38
Nevada Bureau of Community Health Services, 257
New Hampshire Health Promotion Bureau, 257
New Jersey Community Health Services, 257
New Mexico Health Promotion Bureau, 257
New York Business Group on Health Inc, 18
New York Community Health Center, 257
NIDCD Information Clearinghouse, 188, 246
Nidus Information Services, 32
Nonprescription Drug Manufacturers Association, 114
North Carolina Health Promotion, 257
North Dakota Health Promotion & Education Division, 258
NOVA HealthCare Group, 18
Novela Health Education, 7, 268
NSF International, 108
Nutrition Screening Initiative, 61

O

Oak Ridge National Laboratory, 109
Occupational Health Strategies Inc, 106, 121
Occupational Safety and Health Administration (OSHA), 123, 252
Office of AIDS/HIV Policy, 207, 252
Office of Alternative Medicine (OAM), 32

Office of Boating Safety, U.S. Coast Guard, 136
Office of Cancer Communications, National Cancer Institute, 162
Office of Disease Prevention and Health Promotion (ODPHP), 21, 252
Office of Minority Health Resource Center, 252, 268
Office of National Drug Control Policy (ONDCP), 87, 252
Office of Population Affairs (OPA), 216, 252
Office of Safety, Health, and Working Conditions, 123, 252
Office of Women's Health, Dept of Health and Human Services, 233, 252
Office on Smoking and Health, 87
Ohio Bureau of Health Promotion & Risk Reduction, 258
Oklahoma Health Education & Information Services, 258
Oral Health America, 126
Oral Health Program, 87, 127, 162
Oregon Risk Management Division, 258
Organizational Designs in Communication Inc, 53
Osteoporosis and Related Bone Diseases National Resource Center, 185
Overeaters Anonymous, 51
OVID Technologies Inc, 95

P

Park Nicollet HealthSource, 29, 68, 121, 165
Parkinson's Disease Foundation Inc, 186
Parlay International, 32
Partnership for a Drug-Free America, 86
Partnership for Prevention, 98
PATH Associates, 53
Pennsylvania Preventive Health Programs Bureau, 258
Performance Resource Press Inc, 29
Physicians for a Violence-Free Society, 144
Planetree Health Library, 29
Planned Parenthood Federation of America, 216
PNG Publications, 95
Points of Light Foundation, 18
Poison Prevention Week Council, 133
Population Information Program, Johns Hopkins Center for Communication Programs, 214
Positive Promotions, 32
Premier, 40
President's Council on Physical Fitness and Sports, 68
Prevent Blindness America, 169
Prevention Plus Inc, 121
Preventive Medicine Research Institute, 98
Price-Pottenger Nutrition Foundation, 61
Princeton Health Systems Inc, 29, 38
Pritchett & Hull Associates Inc, 30, 165, 174
Produce for Better Health Foundation, 61
Professional Psychology Services, 54
Progressive Farmer Magazine, 133
Project ALERT, 86
Project Inform, 203
Prospectiye Medicine Center, 40
Prostate Health Council, 161
Public Citizen, 114, 161
Public Health Foundation, 7, 228
Public Health Practice Program Office (PHPPO), 99
Public Relations Society of America, 18
Public Voice for Food and Health Policy, 114

Q

QuitSmart Stop Smoking Resources, 84

R

Rachel Carson Council Inc, 106
Rational Recovery Systems Inc, 82
Reproductive Toxicology Center, Columbia Hospital for Women Medical Center, 228
Research Grant Guides Inc, 8, 245
Research!America, 95
Rhode Island Health Promotion & Chronic Diseases, 258
Robert Wood Johnson Foundation, 18
Rotary International, 194
Rutherford Publishing Inc, 30

S

Safe and Drug Free Schools Program, Dept of Education, 88, 147
Safe Ride News Publications Inc, 133
Safety By Design Ltd, 133
Safety Shorts Production Inc, 123, 135
San Francisco AIDS Foundation, 203
SAVANT Audiovisuals Inc, 122
Save the Children Federation, 194
SBS Prevention Plus: National Don't Shake the Baby Campaign, 146
Scott Publishing Inc (Personal Best), 30
Select Media, 80, 144, 159, 204, 215
Sexuality Information and Education Council of the United States (SIECUS), 204, 215
Shepherd's Centers of America, 239
Sickle Cell Disease Association of America Inc, 187
Skin Cancer Foundation, 162
SmithKline Beecham Corporation, 194
Smokenders Inc, 84
Society for Healthcare Strategy and Market Development, 38
Society for Nutrition Education, 61
Society for Occupational and Environmental Health, 123
Society for Public Health Education Inc, 98
Solid Tumor Oncology Education Foundation Inc, 162

South Carolina Preventive Health Services Bureau, 258
South Dakota Office of Disease Prevention, 258
Spina Bifida Association of America, 245
Spine Education Center Inc, 122
Sports Club Company, The, 70
Stanford Center for Research in Disease Prevention, Health Promotion Resource Center, 8, 68, 174
Stasica Associates, 12
STAT (Stop Teenage Addiction to Tobacco), 84
StayWell Health Management Systems Inc, 12, 38
STOP—Safe Tables Our Priority, 113
Strang Cancer Prevention Center, 162
Strategic Marketing Group Inc, 13, 39
Students Against Driving Drunk (SADD), 135
Substance Abuse and Mental Health Services Administration (SAMHSA), 55, 88, 252
Sudden Infant Death Syndrome Alliance, 231
Summex Corporation, 13, 39
Superintendent of Documents, 22, 253
Susan G Komen Breast Cancer Foundation, 162

T

Taft Group, The, 19
Tel-A-Train Inc, 123
Tennessee Health Promotion & Disease Control, 258
Texas Disease Control & Prevention, 258
Think First Foundation, 133
Thyroid Foundation of America Inc, 186
TMI North America Inc, 55
Toxicology Information Response Center, 109
TriHealth Preventive Health Systems, 13, 39
Twin Peaks Press, 246
Tyler Norris Associates, 8, 39

U

U.S. Conference of Local Health Officers, 40, 98
U.S. Consumer Product Safety Commission (CPSC), 136, 253
U.S. Environmental Protection Agency (EPA), 109, 253
U.S. Food and Drug Administration (FDA), 115, 253
U.S. Government Printing Office (GPO), 22, 253
U.S. Pharmacopeia, 113
United Way of America, The, 19
University of North Carolina Injury Prevention Research Center, 134
Utah Health Promotion & Risk Reduction, 258

V

Vermont Health Promotion, 258
VHA Inc, The, 19, 40
Vida Health Communications Inc, 228
Virginia Health, Promotion & Chronic Disease Prevention Office, 259
Visiting Nurse Associations of America, 194
Vitality Inc, 30

W

W K Kellogg Foundation, The, 19
Walking Magazine, 70
Washington Business Group on Health, The, 19
Washington Community & Family Health, 259
Water Environment Federation, 108
Water Quality Association, 108
Weight Control Information Network (WIN), 62, 251
Weight Watchers International, 61
Wellness Associates, 32
Wellness Community, The, 160
Wellness Councils of America (WELCOA), 13, 96
Wellness Quest, 14
Wellsource Inc, 14, 39, 96
Wellstart International, 229
WellTech International, 96
West Virginia Epidemiology & Health Promotion Office, 259
Wheat Foods Council, 62
Whole Person Associates, 32
Willapa Bay Company, The, 229
Wisconsin Bureau of Public Health, 259
Women for Sobriety Inc, 82
Women's AIDS Network (WAN), 204
Women's Cancer Resource Center, 162
Women's Sports Foundation, 68
Workplace Violence Research Institute, 146
World Federation for Mental Health, 55
World Service Office of Narcotics Anonymous, 82
Wyoming Behavioral Health-Community Programs Division, 259

Y

YMCA of the USA, 70
Y-ME®, 160
Young Adult Institute, 205
Your HealthStyle, 31
Youth Development International, 144
YWCA of the USA, 70, 146

Z

Zero to Three: National Center for Infants, Toddlers and Families, 229
Zuni Wellness Center, 268

Subject Index

A

abortion, 211–216
abstinence, 211–216
adolescence sex education, 211–216
aging, 235–240
AIDS, 197–207
air quality, 103–109
alcoholism, 73–88
allergies, 151–153, 181–188
alternative medicine, 23–32
Alzheimer's disease, 177–188
anorexia nervosa, 50–55
arthritis, 177–188
asthma, 151–153

B

baby bottle disease, 125–127
back injury and pain, 117–123
birth control, 211–216
birth defects, 217–233
breast cancer, 155–162
breast feeding, 217–233
breast self-examination, 155–162
bulimia, 50–55

C

cancer, 155–162
cervical cancer, 155–162
chemical hazards, 117–123
child abuse, 137–147
child health, 217–233
child safety seats, 129–136
childhood diarrhea prevention, 217–233
childhood injuries, 129–136
cholesterol, 57–62, 171–175
Chronic Fatigue Syndrome, 177–188
cocaine, 73–88
colitis, 177–188
colorectal cancer, 155–162
community health assessments, 33–41
community health status improvement, 5–8, 14–22
contraception, 211–216
corporate fitness programs, 8–22
crime prevention, 137–147
Crohn's disease, 177–188
cumulative trauma disorders, 117–123
customized wellness publications, 23–32

D

demand management, 8–22
dental health, 125–127
depression, 43–55
DES exposure, 217–233
diabetes, 163–166
digestive diseases, 177–188
disease management, 8–22
domestic violence, 137–147
Down syndrome, 241–246
drowning, 129–136
drug abuse, 73–88
drug labeling, 111–115
drug safety, 111–115
drunk driving, 129–136

E

eating disorders, 50–55
elder abuse, 137–147
employee assistance programs, 8–22
endometriosis, 217–233
environmental health, 103–109
epilepsy, 177–188
ergonomics, 117–123
exercise, 63–71
eye disease, 167–170
eye safety, 167–170

F

family planning, 211–216
farm safety, 129–136
fetal alcohol syndrome, 217–233
fire safety, 129–136
firearm safety, 137–147
first aid, 129–136
fitness centers, 8–22, 63–71
food allergies, 181–188
food labels, 57–62
food pyramid, 57–62
food safety, 111–115

G

gallbladder diseases, 177–188
genetic diseases/research/testing, 217–233
geriatric, 235–240
glaucoma, 167–170
Group B strep infection, 217–233
gun violence, 137–147

H

head injuries, 129–136
headaches, 177–188
health fairs, 8–22, 33–41
health futurism, 5–8, 14–22
health risk appraisals, 33–41
health screenings, 8–22, 33–41
healthy communities, 5–8, 14–22
hearing screening/loss, 241–246
heart disease, 171–175
helmet safety, 129–136
hepatitis, 189–195, 177–188
herpes, 197–207
HIV infection, 197–207
homeopathic medicine, 23–32
Huntington's disease, 177–188
hypertension, 171–175

I

immunizations, 189–195
impaired driving, 129–136
incentive programs, 8–22, 63–71
infant care, 217–233
infectious diseases, 189–195
influenza, 189–195
inhalants, 73–88
injury prevention, 117–123, 129–136

K

kidney disease, 177–188

L

lead poisoning, 103–109
libraries-consumer health, 23–32
liver disease, 177–188
lupus, 177–188
Lyme disease, 189–195
lymphedema, 177–188

M

mammograms, 155–162
marijuana, 73–88
maternal health, 217–233
meat-poultry hotline, 115
medications, 111–115
menopause, 235–240, 217–233
mental health/mental illness, 43–55
mental retardation, 241–246
motor vehicle safety, 129–136
multiple sclerosis, 177–188

N

natural family planning, 211–216
neonatal care, 217–233
neuromuscular diseases, 177–188
nurse advice lines, 8–22
nutrition, 57–62

O

obesity, 57–62
occupational health, 117–123
older adults, 235–240
oral health, 125–127
organizations for wellness and health professionals, 89–99
osteoporosis, 177–188, 217–233
outreach programs, 5–8, 14–22
overeating, 50–55

P

Parkinson's disease, 177–188
pediculosis (head lice), 103–109
people with disabilities, 241–246
periodontal disease, 125–127
pesticides, 103–109
physical fitness, 63–71
poison prevention, 129–136
population studies, 211–216
pregnancy, 217–233
prenatal care, 217–233
program funding, 5–8, 14–22
program planning, 3–22
prostate disease, 155–162
public service announcements, 5–8, 14–22

R

radon, 103–109
rare disorders, 177–188
rehabilitation, 241–246
reproductive health, 211–233
respiratory diseases, 151–153
responsible sexual behavior, 197–207, 211–216
Reye's syndrome, 177–188
runaway children, 137–147

S

safe sex, 197–207
safety belts, 129–136
school safety, 137–147
seafood hotline, 114
secondhand smoke, 73–88
self-care promotion, 8–22, 23–32
sex education, 211–216
sexual abuse, 137–147
sexually transmitted diseases, 197–207
sickle cell disease, 177–188
SIDS, 217–233
smoking cessation, 73–88
spina bifida, 241–246
spine injuries, 129–136, 241–246
sports programs, 63–71
STDs, 197–207
steroids, 73–88
stress management, 51–55
stroke, 171–175, 241–246
substance abuse, 73–88
sudden infant death syndrome, 217–233
suicide, 43–55

T

teen pregnancy, 211–216
thyroid disorders, 177–188
tobacco, 73–88
toxic agents, 103–109, 217–233
toy safety, 129–136
traffic safety, 129–136
trauma, 129–136
tuberculosis, 189–195

U

unintentional injuries, 129–136
urologic diseases, 177–188

V

vaccines, 189–195
violence-related injuries, 129–136

W

water quality, 103–109
weight control/weight lost, 57–62
wellness promotion materials, 23–32
women's health, 217–233
workplace violence, 137–147
worksite health promotion, 8–14

Y

youth violence, 137–147